THE REAL ESTATE LAW LIBRARY FROM WILEY LAW PUBLICATIONS

COMMERCIAL PREMISES LIABILITY
John A. Tarantino

COMMERCIAL REAL ESTATE LEASES: FORMS (SECOND EDITION)
Mark A. Senn

COMMERCIAL REAL ESTATE LEASES: PREPARATION AND NEGOTIATION (SECOND EDITION)
Mark A. Senn

DEVELOPING RETIREMENT FACILITIES
Paul A. Gordon

ENVIRONMENTAL LIABILITY AND REAL PROPERTY TRANSACTIONS: LAW AND PRACTICE
Joel S. Moskowitz

REAL ESTATE DEVELOPMENT: STRATEGIES FOR CHANGING MARKETS
Stuart M. Saft

INSTITUTIONAL AND PENSION FUND REAL ESTATE INVESTMENT
Stephen P. Jarchow

MANAGING AND LEASING COMMERCIAL PROPERTIES
Alan A. Alexander

NEGOTIATING REAL ESTATE TRANSACTIONS
Mark A. Senn

PREMISES SECURITY LAW AND PRACTICE
John A. Tarantino

REAL ESTATE FINANCE AND TAXATION: STRUCTURING COMPLEX TRANSACTIONS
Robert L. Nessen

REAL ESTATE INVESTMENT TRUSTS: TAX, SECURITIES, AND BUSINESS ASPECTS
Stephen P. Jarchow

REAL ESTATE SYNDICATION: SECURITIZATION AFTER TAX REFORM (SECOND EDITION)
Stephen P. Jarchow

REHABILITATING OLDER AND HISTORIC BUILDINGS
Stephen L. Kass

STRUCTURING COMPLEX REAL ESTATE TRANSACTIONS: LAW, PROCEDURE, FORMS
James L. Lipscomb

COMMERCIAL REAL
ESTATE LEASES:
FORMS
Second Edition

COMMERCIAL REAL ESTATE LEASES
FORMS
Second Edition

MARK A. SENN

**Member of the Bars
of the States of
California and Colorado**

Wiley Law Publications
JOHN WILEY & SONS
New York • Chichester • Brisbane • Toronto • Singapore

This publication is designed to provide accurate and
authoritative information in regard to the subject
matter covered. It is sold with the understanding that
the publisher is not engaged in rendering legal, accounting,
or other professional services. If legal advice or other
expert assistance is required, the services of a competent
professional person should be sought.

*From a Declaration of Principles jointly adopted by a
Committee of the American Bar Association and a
Committee of Publishers.*

Library of Congress Cataloging-in-Publication Data

Senn, Mark A.
    Commercial real estate leases—forms / Mark A. Senn. — 2nd ed.
      p.   cm. — (Real estate law library)
    Includes bibliographical references.
    ISBN 0-471-51500-0
    1. Commercial leases—United States—Forms. I. Title.
  II. Series.
  KF593.C6S39   1990
  346.7304'3462'0269—dc20
  [347.306434620269   90-12778
                                      CIP

Printed in the United States of America

10 9 8 7 6 5 4

For Barbara, Eli, and Anna

PREFACE

This volume is comprised entirely of forms commonly used in commercial real estate leases. The forms include complete leases for office buildings, shopping centers, and single tenant properties. There are also complete forms of many ancillary documents, such as assignments, subleases, estoppel certificates, and guaranties. Finally, there are innumerable form provisions that are keyed to the corresponding discussions of the companion volume, *Commercial Real Estate Leases: Preparation and Negotiation* (Second Edition). Except for Chapters 1 and 2, each form number is the same as the corresponding section in *Commercial Real Estate Leases* that discusses the clause.

When appropriate, the real estate professional will have a complete form at his or her disposal or a form that can be adapted for the pertinent situation. All of the forms—both complete forms and form provisions—can be "cannibalized" for their relevant parts. With these forms, the real estate professional can propose new or substitute provisions and promptly prepare complete leases or complete ancillary documents.

No book of forms does a service unless it reminds the user that each form must be read carefully in order to be certain that it is appropriate for the transaction at hand. The lease or other document is the servant of the transaction; the transaction is not at the mercy of the available form. Although it is quite possible that the forms in this book will be perfectly sufficient for most transactions that present themselves to the real estate professional, once again, their fitness for the transaction must be confirmed before they are used.

Denver, Colorado   MARK A. SENN
June 1990

USING THESE FORMS

These forms illustrate that there is more than one way to express a provision in a lease. These forms should be used after reading the text which accompanies the comparable provisions in the second edition of *Commercial Real Estate Leases: Preparation and Negotiation.* Many of these provisions are unique for the document for which they were prepared. The office building and shopping center lease forms in this book do not include any exhibits. However, this book does contain forms of rules and regulations for both office building leases and shopping center leases—and a workletter form for office building leases.

The office building lease is used by a major national real estate developer. Although it is an extensive and thorough lease, this developer wanted to present an image of fairness in its documentation. As a result this lease is certainly slanted toward the landlord but is not oppressive and unfair. The office building lease is the type commonly known as a full-service lease. These leases are discussed more fully in §§ **6.10** and **6.11** of the second edition of *Commercial Real Estate Leases: Preparation and Negotiation.*

The shopping center lease has been used for shopping centers having between 50,000 and 100,000 square feet of leasable area. It is not appropriate for an enclosed mall. All operating expenses are passed through to the tenants. This lease has one economic provision that is unusual in retail leases: there is no percentage rent. The reason for eschewing percentage rent and requiring instead cost of living increases grew out of the landlord's conviction that it would waste too much time verifying the tenants' reports of gross sales. The many ways in which tenants can cheat at percentage rent—some of which are discussed in § **6.23** of the second edition of *Commercial Real Estate Leases: Preparation and Negotiation*—are leading more and more landlords to require a simple cost of living adjustment. To convert this lease to one that requires percentage rent, the real estate professional should consider not only a percentage rent paragraph such as that set forth in §§ **6.17** and **6.20** through **6.22** of the second edition of *Commercial Real Estate Leases: Preparation and Negotiation;* he or she should also consider a continuous occupancy provision, a radius provision, and an appropriate modification to the default provision, all as discussed in the book. A shopping center lease without percentage rent may be easier for a trustee in bankruptcy to assign than a lease which requires percentage rent; this idea is explained in § **10.15** of the second edition of *Commercial Real Estate Leases: Preparation and Negotiation.*

Finally, the single tenant building lease is typical of what might be used for an industrial warehouse. It has fixed rent with a renewal option at fair market value. This lease is a "net" lease in which the tenant pays all occupancy costs. In substantially this form, this lease was used in a transaction between an owner/landlord and his wholly-owned company/tenant. As a result it is somewhat even-handed. This lease is somewhat unusual in that the landlord's lender insisted on the tenant's obligation to rebuild the premises in case of damage or destruction. In more typical transactions this obligation might be shared by the landlord and tenant. Finally, the condemnation provision contemplates the possibility that tenant will have made some substantial improvements to the premises. Many warehouse leases have landlord's lien provisions; although this lease does not, the book discusses the landlord's liens and appropriate form provisions.

To reiterate a persistent theme of the book, these forms should not be used without the user's absolute certainty that they have been changed in order to reflect the agreement of the landlord and tenant. Thoughtless use of these forms will lead to an agreement which governs the transaction rather than a transaction which governs the agreement. At all cost that outcome must be avoided.

Denver, Colorado   MARK A. SENN
June 1990

ABOUT THE AUTHOR

Mark A. Senn was graduated with honors from Stanford University in 1969, and received his J.D. from the University of California at Berkeley (Boalt Hall) in 1972. He is the founding partner of Senn Lewis Hoth & Strahle, P.C., Denver, Colorado. After practicing in a major San Francisco law firm, Mr. Senn moved to Denver, where his practice emphasizes real estate, particularly commercial real estate leases. In addition to acting as a receiver of many properties and lecturing on receivership, he has also participated in Colorado's committee on opinion letters in real estate loan transactions. He has spoken throughout the country for such groups as the Northwest Center for Professional Education, the International Council of Shopping Centers, the National Mall Monitor, and many continuing legal education programs. Mr. Senn is editor of *Negotiating Real Estate Transactions* (John Wiley & Sons 1988) and has published articles on topics such as escrows, self-help for commercial landlords, and drafting expansion options and "free-rent" provisions.

SUMMARY CONTENTS

PART I	**COMPLETE FORMS**	
Chapter 1	Lease Forms	3
Chapter 2	Additional Agreements	171
PART II	**THE ESSENTIAL LEASE PROVISIONS**	
Chapter 3	Introductory Provisions	223
Chapter 4	The Premises	227
Chapter 5	The Term	243
Chapter 6	Rent	251
PART III	**ADDITIONAL EXPENSES FOR THE TENANT**	
Chapter 7	Taxes and Assessments	271
Chapter 8	Utilities	279
Chapter 9	Insurance	283
PART IV	**CONTROLLING THE TENANT'S CONDUCT**	
Chapter 10	Use	293
Chapter 11	Compliance with Laws	299
Chapter 12	Assignments and Subleases	307
Chapter 13	Signs	319
Chapter 14	Rules and Regulations	323
Chapter 15	Merchants' Associations, Promotion Funds, and Advertising Funds	325
PART V	**GIVING THE TENANT RIGHTS**	
Chapter 16	Landlord's Services	331
Chapter 17	Common Areas	335
PART VI	**PRESERVING THE PREMISES**	
Chapter 18	Repairs and Maintenance	345
Chapter 19	Alterations	349
Chapter 20	Mechanics' Liens	353
Chapter 21	Surrender	355
Chapter 22	Damage and Destruction	357
Chapter 23	Condemnation	363

PART VII   PROTECTING THE LANDLORD

Chapter 24   Subordination   373
Chapter 25   Landlord's Access   375
Chapter 26   Indemnification, Waiver, and Release   377
Chapter 27   Security Deposits   379
Chapter 28   Covenant of Quiet Enjoyment   383
Chapter 29   Limitation on Tenant's Recourse; Sale of Premises   385

PART VIII   DEFAULT AND ARBITRATION

Chapter 30   Default   389
Chapter 31   Arbitration   399

PART IX   MISCELLANEOUS PROVISIONS

Chapter 32   Miscellaneous   403

Table of Forms   415

DETAILED CONTENTS

PART I   **COMPLETE FORMS**

Chapter 1   **Lease Forms**

§ 1.1   Office Lease
§ 1.2   Shopping Center Lease
§ 1.3   Single Tenant Lease
§ 1.4   Office Lease (A Tenant's Response to Landlord's Form)
§ 1.5   Office Lease (Space Users Network Office Building Lease)

Chapter 2   **Additional Agreements**

§ 2.1   Guaranty of Lease
§ 2.2   Lease for Use of Storage Space
§ 2.3   Workletter
§ 2.4   Assignment—Form
§ 2.5   Sublease—Form
§ 2.6   Sublease (Another Form)
§ 2.7   Rules and Regulations for a Shopping Center
§ 2.8   Rules and Regulations for an Office Building
§ 2.9   Subordination—Nondisturbance, Attornment, Estoppel, and Subordination Agreement
§ 2.10 Estoppel, Subordination, Nondisturbance, and Attornment Agreement
§ 2.11 Estoppel Certificate Form
§ 2.12 Tenant Estoppel Certificate
§ 2.13 Memorandum of Lease
§ 2.14 Short Form Lease
§ 2.15 Commencement Date Certificate
§ 2.16 Lease Commencement Memorandum
§ 2.17 Basic Lease Information—Office Building
§ 2.18 Basic Lease Information—Shopping Center
§ 2.19 Basic Lease Information—Single Tenant Building
§ 2.20 Amendment to Office Lease
§ 2.21 Lease Summary

PART II   **THE ESSENTIAL LEASE PROVISIONS**

Chapter 3   **Introductory Provisions**

§ 3.1   Presenting Basic Lease Information (Reserved)
§ 3.2   Identifying the Lease
§ 3.3   Date of the Lease (Reserved)
§ 3.4   Tradenames and Service Marks (Reserved)
§ 3.5   Individuals
§ 3.6   Co-Owners and Co-Tenants (Reserved)
§ 3.7   Corporations
§ 3.8   Partnerships
§ 3.9   Agents, Representatives, and Guardians
§ 3.10   Charitable Associations, Campaign Committees, and Government Entities (Reserved)
§ 3.11   Tax-Exempt Organizations (Reserved)
§ 3.12   Tenants with Sovereign Immunity (Reserved)
§ 3.13   Franchisors and Franchisees (Reserved)
§ 3.14   Guarantors (Reserved)
§ 3.15   Guaranty of Lease (Reserved)
§ 3.16   Contesting Guaranties (Reserved)
§ 3.17   "and/or Assigns" (Reserved)
§ 3.18   Grant or Agreement of Lease

Chapter 4   **The Premises**

§ 4.1   An Approach to Description of Premises (Reserved)
§ 4.2   Description of Single Tenant Building
§ 4.3   Description of Shopping Center Premises
§ 4.4   Measurement of Shopping Center Premises
§ 4.5   Appurtenances in a Shopping Center (Reserved)
§ 4.6   Designating Certain Areas (Reserved)
§ 4.7   Preserving Flexibility in Shopping Center Development (Reserved)
§ 4.8   Description of Office Building Premises
§ 4.9   An Approach to Measurement of Office Building Premises (Reserved)
§ 4.10   Introduction to BOMA Measurement (Reserved)
§ 4.11   Usable Area (Reserved)
§ 4.12   Rentable Area (Reserved)
§ 4.13   Importance of Measurement (Reserved)
§ 4.14   An Illustration of Office Building Measurement (Reserved)
§ 4.15   Appurtenances in an Office Building (Reserved)

§ 4.16 Personal Property (Reserved)

§ 4.17 Storage Space (Reserved)

§ 4.18 Lenders' Concerns about Premises (Reserved)

§ 4.19 Options (Reserved)

§ 4.20 Options to Expand Premises

§ 4.21 "Build-Out" Expansion Option

§ 4.22 Right of First Refusal to Lease Additional Space

§ 4.23 Options to Purchase

§ 4.24 Lenders' Concerns about Options to Purchase (Reserved)

§ 4.25 Right of First Refusal to Purchase Premises

§ 4.26 Lenders' Concerns about Right of First Refusal to Purchase Premises (Reserved)

§ 4.27 Landlord's Right to Relocate Premises

Chapter 5 The Term

§ 5.1 Defining the Term (Reserved)

§ 5.2 Landlord's Failure to Deliver Possession

§ 5.3 Existing Premises

§ 5.4 Completion of New Office Premises

§ 5.5 Workletters (Reserved)

§ 5.6 —Checklist for Reviewing Workletters (Reserved)

§ 5.7 Building Standard Specifications (Reserved)

§ 5.8 Completion and Acceptance of New Shopping Center Premises

§ 5.9 Requiring Completion of Other Parts of the Shopping Center and Occupancy by Other Tenants (Reserved)

§ 5.10 Allowing Early Occupancy

§ 5.11 Implied Warranty of Fitness (Reserved)

§ 5.12 Lenders' Concerns about Term (Reserved)

§ 5.13 Option to Extend or Renew a Lease

§ 5.14 —Notice (Reserved)

§ 5.15 —Terms of Renewal

§ 5.16 Tenant's Option to Terminate Lease

Chapter 6 Rent

§ 6.1 Fixed Rent

§ 6.2 "Free Rent" Arrangements (Reserved)

§ 6.3 Stepped Up Rent

§ 6.4 An Approach to Cost of Living Adjustments (Reserved)

§ 6.5 Preparing the Cost of Living Adjustment Provision

§ 6.6 Refining the Cost of Living Adjustment

§ 6.7 Common Mistakes in Cost of Living Adjustments (Reserved)

§ 6.8   Porters' Wage Escalations (Reserved)
§ 6.9   Operating Expense Escalations (Reserved)
§ 6.10   Operating Costs in Office Building Leases (Reserved)
§ 6.11   Preparing an Office Building Operating Expenses Provision
§ 6.12   "Grossing Up" Operating Expenses
§ 6.13   Comparing Several Office Leases (Reserved)
§ 6.14   Operating Expenses in Shopping Centers (Reserved)
§ 6.15   Operating Expenses in Single Tenant Leases
§ 6.16   An Approach to Percentage Rent (Reserved)
§ 6.17   Definition of Gross Sales
§ 6.18   Deductions and Exclusions from Gross Sales (Reserved)
§ 6.19   How to Choose an Appropriate Percentage Rate (Reserved)
§ 6.20   Computation and Payment Period
§ 6.21   Recordkeeping
§ 6.22   Verification
§ 6.23   Controlling Percentage Rent (Reserved)
§ 6.24   Lenders' Concerns about Rent (Reserved)

PART III   ADDITIONAL EXPENSES FOR THE TENANT

Chapter 7   Taxes and Assessments

§ 7.1   Introduction (Reserved)
§ 7.2   Definition of Taxes
§ 7.3   Taxes and the Single Tenant Building
§ 7.4   Net Tax Provision in a Multitenant Development
§ 7.5   Base Amount Tax Provision in a Multitenant Development
§ 7.6   Base Year Tax Provision in a Multitenant Development

Chapter 8   Utilities

§ 8.1   Utilities in Single Tenant Building Lease
§ 8.2   Utilities in Shopping Center Lease
§ 8.3   Utilities in Office Building Lease
§ 8.4   Direct Metering, Submetering, and Electric Rent Inclusion
          (Reserved)

Chapter 9   Insurance

§ 9.1   A Method of Management (Reserved)
§ 9.2   Finding Risk Management Provisions (Reserved)
§ 9.3   The Law and Basic Terms (Reserved)
§ 9.4   Liability Insurance (Reserved)
§ 9.5   Property Insurance (Reserved)

§ 9.6   Actual Cash Value and Replacement Cost (Reserved)

§ 9.7   Co-Insurance (Reserved)

§ 9.8   Contributing Policies (Reserved)

§ 9.9   Insuring the Rent Stream (Reserved)

§ 9.10   Tenant's Insurance (Reserved)

§ 9.11   Waiver of Subrogation

§ 9.12   Blanket Insurance, Excess Insurance, Umbrella Coverage, and Self-Insurance

§ 9.13   Insurance Provision for Office Building Leases

§ 9.14   Insurance Provision for Shopping Center Leases

§ 9.15   Insurance Provision for Single Tenant Building Leases

§ 9.16   Conclusion (Reserved)

PART IV   CONTROLLING THE TENANT'S CONDUCT

Chapter 10   Use

§ 10.1   The Law

§ 10.2   Use Provisions in Leases of Office Buildings and Single Tenant Buildings

§ 10.3   Lenders' Concerns about General Use Provisions (Reserved)

§ 10.4   Use Provisions in Shopping Center Leases

§ 10.5   Drafting an Exclusive Use Provision (Reserved)

§ 10.6   Tenant's Remedies (Reserved)

§ 10.7   Antitrust Implications of Exclusive Uses (Reserved)

§ 10.8   Federal Trade Commission's Response to Exclusive Uses (Reserved)

§ 10.9   Lenders' Concerns about Exclusive Uses (Reserved)

§ 10.10   Express Covenant of Continuous Operation

§ 10.11   Implied Covenant of Continuous Operation (Reserved)

§ 10.12   Manner of Conducting Business

§ 10.13   Radius Restriction

§ 10.14   Use Provisions in a Bankruptcy Not Involving a Shopping Center Lease (Reserved)

§ 10.15   Use Provisions in a Shopping Center Bankruptcy (Reserved)

Chapter 11   Compliance with Laws

§ 11.1   General Compliance Provisions

§ 11.2   Right to Contest

§ 11.3   Landlord's Warranty of Compliance

§ 11.4   Compliance with Environmental Laws

§ 11.5   Negotiating the Environmental Compliance Provisions

Chapter 12   Assignments and Subleases

§ 12.1   An Approach to Provisions for Assignments and Subleases (Reserved)

§ 12.2   Assignment and Sublease Defined (Reserved)

§ 12.3   Privity (Reserved)

§ 12.4   Promises Running with the Land (Reserved)

§ 12.5   An Absolute Prohibition

§ 12.6   Requirement of Landlord's Consent

§ 12.7   Requirement of Consent Not to Be Unreasonably Withheld (Reserved)

§ 12.8   Limiting the Tenant's Remedies (Reserved)

§ 12.9   Redefining the Assignment and Sublease

§ 12.10   Imposing Further Conditions to Consent (Reserved)

§ 12.11   Relationship of Prohibitions of Assignment and Sublease to Default Provisions (Reserved)

§ 12.12   Recapture and Profit Sharing (Reserved)

§ 12.13   Lenders' Concerns about Assignments and Subleases

§ 12.14   Preparing a Form of Assignment (Reserved)

§ 12.15   Preparing a Form of Sublease

Chapter 13   Signs

§ 13.1   Introduction (Reserved)

§ 13.2   Signs in Single Tenant Leases

§ 13.3   Signs in Office Building Leases

§ 13.4   Signs in Shopping Center Leases

Chapter 14   Rules and Regulations

§ 14.1   Introduction

§ 14.2   Rules and Regulations for Shopping Centers (Reserved)

§ 14.3   Rules and Regulations for Office Buildings (Reserved)

§ 14.4   Rules and Regulations for Single Tenant Buildings (Reserved)

Chapter 15   Merchants' Associations, Promotion Funds, and Advertising Funds

§ 15.1   Introduction to Merchants' Associations (Reserved)

§ 15.2   Purposes of Merchants' Associations (Reserved)

§ 15.3   Requirements of Merchants' Associations (Reserved)

§ 15.4   Payments to Merchants' Associations (Reserved)

§ 15.5   Voting in Merchants' Associations (Reserved)

§ 15.6   Concluding Thoughts about Merchants' Associations

§ 15.7   Promotion Funds and Advertising Funds (Reserved)

PART V   **GIVING THE TENANT RIGHTS**

Chapter 16   **Landlord's Services**

§ 16.1   Introduction (Reserved)
§ 16.2   Short Provision for Landlord's Services
§ 16.3   Long Provision for Landlord's Services

Chapter 17   **Common Areas**

§ 17.1   Introduction (Reserved)
§ 17.2   Common Areas in Office Buildings
§ 17.3   Common Areas in Shopping Centers—Grant
§ 17.4   —Definition (Reserved)
§ 17.5   —Landlord's Reserved Rights
§ 17.6   —Expenses (Reserved)
§ 17.7   —Allocation of Expenses (Reserved)
§ 17.8   —Payment of Expenses (Reserved)
§ 17.9   —Landlord's Obligations

PART VI   **PRESERVING THE PREMISES**

Chapter 18   **Repairs and Maintenance**

§ 18.1   Common Law Rules (Reserved)
§ 18.2   Practical Overview (Reserved)
§ 18.3   Repairs Provisions in Shopping Center Leases
§ 18.4   Repairs Provisions in Office Building Leases
§ 18.5   Comments on the Typical Multitenant Provision (Reserved)
§ 18.6   Repairs Provisions in Single Tenant Leases

Chapter 19   **Alterations**

§ 19.1   The Law (Reserved)
§ 19.2   Further Considerations (Reserved)
§ 19.3   Alterations Provisions in Office Building Leases
§ 19.4   Alterations Provisions in Shopping Center Leases
§ 19.5   Alterations Provisions in Single Tenant Leases
§ 19.6   Lenders' Concerns about Alterations (Reserved)

Chapter 20   **Mechanics' Liens**

§ 20.1   Introduction (Reserved)
§ 20.2   Mechanics' Lien Provision

Chapter 21   Surrender

§ 21.1   Early Termination of Lease (Reserved)
§ 21.2   Redelivery at End of Term
§ 21.3   Fixtures (Reserved)

Chapter 22   Damage and Destruction

§ 22.1   The Law (Reserved)
§ 22.2   Landlord's and Tenant's Concerns (Reserved)
§ 22.3   —Is the Lease Affected? (Reserved)
§ 22.4   —Is the Rent Affected? (Reserved)
§ 22.5   —How Are the Premises Affected? (Reserved)
§ 22.6   —How Is the Lease Affected? (Reserved)
§ 22.7   Damage and Destruction in Office Building Premises
§ 22.8   Damage and Destruction in Shopping Center Premises
§ 22.9   Damage and Destruction in Single Tenant Premises
§ 22.10   Lenders' Concerns about Damage and Destruction (Reserved)

Chapter 23   Condemnation

§ 23.1   Condemnation and Eminent Domain (Reserved)
§ 23.2   Total Taking (Reserved)
§ 23.3   Partial Taking (Reserved)
§ 23.4   Temporary Taking (Reserved)
§ 23.5   Condemnation of Office Buildings
§ 23.6   Condemnation of Shopping Centers
§ 23.7   Condemnation of Areas of a Shopping Center Other than Premises (Reserved)
§ 23.8   Consequences of Condemnation (Reserved)
§ 23.9   Landlord's Restoration of Premises (Reserved)
§ 23.10   Allocation of Condemnation Award (Reserved)
§ 23.11   Condemnation of Single Tenant Premises
§ 23.12   Lenders' Concerns about Condemnation (Reserved)
§ 23.13   Deceptive Role of Some Mortgages (Reserved)

PART VII   PROTECTING THE LANDLORD

Chapter 24   Subordination

§ 24.1   Introduction and General Rules (Reserved)
§ 24.2   Significance to Lender
§ 24.3   Significance to Tenant (Reserved)

Chapter 25   Landlord's Access

§ 25.1   General Access Provisions
§ 25.2   Considerations for Shopping Center Tenants (Reserved)

Chapter 26   Indemnification, Waiver, and Release

§ 26.1   Introduction (Reserved)
§ 26.2   Indemnification
§ 26.3   Waiver and Release

Chapter 27   Security Deposits

§ 27.1   Preparing and Reviewing a Security Deposit Provision
§ 27.2   Lender's Obligation to Return Security Deposits (Reserved)
§ 27.3   Lenders' Other Concerns about Security Deposits (Reserved)

Chapter 28   Covenant of Quiet Enjoyment

§ 28.1   General Rules
§ 28.2   Limitations of Covenant (Reserved)
§ 28.3   Inappropriate Uses (Reserved)

Chapter 29   Limitation on Tenant's Recourse; Sale of Premises

§ 29.1   Introduction (Reserved)
§ 29.2   Limitation on Tenant's Recourse
§ 29.3   Sale of Premises

PART VIII   DEFAULT AND ARBITRATION

Chapter 30   Default

§ 30.1   Landlord's Default
§ 30.2   Lenders' Concerns about Tenant's Cure Rights (Reserved)
§ 30.3   Introduction to Tenant's Default (Reserved)
§ 30.4   Tenant's Default and Other Parts of the Lease
§ 30.5   Landlord's Right to Cure
§ 30.6   Events of Default
§ 30.7   Remedies
§ 30.8   —Termination (Reserved)
§ 30.9   —Maintaining the Lease (Reserved)
§ 30.10   —Reentry (Reserved)
§ 30.11   —Rent Acceleration (Reserved)
§ 30.12   —Retained Jurisdiction (Reserved)
§ 30.13   —Form (Reserved)

§ 30.14   Special Bankruptcy Provisions (Reserved)

§ 30.15   Duty to Mitigate (Reserved)

§ 30.16   Landlord's Lien

Chapter 31   Arbitration

§ 31.1   Introduction (Reserved)

§ 31.2   Possible Arbitration Provisions

PART IX   MISCELLANEOUS PROVISIONS

Chapter 32   Miscellaneous

§ 32.1   Submission of the Lease

§ 32.2   Brokers

§ 32.3   No Recordation

§ 32.4   Notice, Possession, and Recordation (Reserved)

§ 32.5   Importance of Recordation (Reserved)

§ 32.6   Memorandum of Lease and Short-Form Lease (Reserved)

§ 32.7   Leasehold Title Insurance (Reserved)

§ 32.8   Holding Over

§ 32.9   Time of the Essence

§ 32.10   No Light, Air, and View Easements

§ 32.11   No Partnership

§ 32.12   No Merger

§ 32.13   Modification and Financing Conditions

§ 32.14   Consents and Approvals

§ 32.15   Estoppel Certificates

§ 32.16   No Waiver

§ 32.17   Joint and Several Liability

§ 32.18   Authority

§ 32.19   Captions, Exhibits, Gender, and Number

§ 32.20   Entire Agreement

§ 32.21   Amendments

§ 32.22   Severability

§ 32.23   No Construction Against Preparer of Lease

§ 32.24   Notices

§ 32.25   Attorneys' Fees

§ 32.26   Waiver of Jury Trial

§ 32.27   Governing Law and Venue

§ 32.28   Binding Effect

Table of Forms

PART I

COMPLETE FORMS

CHAPTER 1

LEASE FORMS

§ 1.1   Office Lease

§ 1.2   Shopping Center Lease

§ 1.3   Single Tenant Lease

§ 1.4   Office Lease (A Tenant's Response to Landlord's Form)

§ 1.5   Office Lease (Space Users Network Office Building Lease)

§ 1.1   Office Lease

Office Lease

between

[tenant]

and

[landlord]

Date [date], 19 [00]

Office Lease

Table of Contents

Article 1 Basic Lease Information
      1.1 Basic Lease Information
      1.2 Definitions
      1.3 Exhibits
Article 2 Agreement
Article 3 Term, Delivery, and Acceptance of Premises
      3.1 Delivery of Possession
      3.2 Early Entry
Article 4 Monthly Rent
Article 5 Operating Expenses
      5.1 General
      5.2 Estimated Payments
      5.3 Annual Settlement

5.4 Final Proration
5.5 Other Taxes
5.6 Additional Rent
Article 6 Insurance
6.1 Landlord's Insurance
6.2 Tenant's Insurance
6.3 Forms of Policies
6.4 Waiver of Subrogation
6.5 Adequacy of Coverage
Article 7 Use
Article 8 Requirements of Law; Fire Insurance
8.1 General
8.2 Hazardous Materials
8.3 Certain Insurance Risks
Article 9 Assignment and Subletting
9.1 General
9.2 Submission of Information
9.3 Payments to Landlord
9.4 Prohibited Transfers
9.5 Permitted Transfer
9.6 Remedies
Article 10 Rules and Regulations
Article 11 Common Areas
Article 12 Landlord's Services
12.1 Landlord's Repair and Maintenance
12.2 Landlord's Other Services
12.3 Tenant's Costs
12.4 Limitation on Liability
Article 13 Tenant's Care of the Premises
Article 14 Alterations
14.1 General
14.2 Free-Standing Partitions
14.3 Removal
Article 15 Mechanics' Liens
Article 16 End of Term
Article 17 Eminent Domain
Article 18 Damage and Destruction
Article 19 Subordination
19.1 General
19.2 Attornment and Nondisturbance
Article 20 Entry by Landlord
Article 21 Indemnification, Waiver, and Release
21.1 Indemnification
21.2 Waiver and Release
Article 22 Security Deposit
Article 23 Quiet Enjoyment
Article 24 Effect of Sale

Article 25 Default
      25.1 Events of Default
      25.2 Landlord's Remedies
      25.3 Certain Damages
      25.4 Continuing Liability After Termination
      25.5 Cumulative Remedies
      25.6 Waiver of Redemption
Article 26 Parking
Article 27 Miscellaneous
      27.1 No Offer
      27.2 Joint and Several Liability
      27.3 No Construction Against Drafting Party
      27.4 Time of the Essence
      27.5 No Recordation
      27.6 No Waiver
      27.7 Limitation on Recourse
      27.8 Estoppel Certificates
      27.9 Waiver of Jury Trial
      27.10 No Merger
      27.11 Holding Over
      27.12 Notices
      27.13 Severability
      27.14 Written Amendment Required
      27.15 Entire Agreement
      27.16 Captions
      27.17 Notice of Landlord's Default
      27.18 Authority
      27.19 Brokers
      27.20 Governing Law
      27.21 Late Payments
      27.22 No Easements for Air or Light
      27.23 Tax Credits
      27.24 Relocation of the Premises
      27.25 Financial Reports
      27.26 Landlord's Fees
      27.27 Binding Effect
Exhibit A: The Premises
Exhibit B: Legal Description of the Land
Exhibit C: Workletter
Exhibit D: Rules and Regulations
Exhibit E: Commencement Date Certificate

OFFICE LEASE

THIS OFFICE LEASE is entered into by landlord and tenant as described in the following basic lease information on the date that is set forth for reference only in the following basic lease information. Landlord and tenant agree:

ARTICLE 1   BASIC LEASE INFORMATION

1.1   Basic Lease Information. In addition to the terms that are defined elsewhere in this lease, these terms are used in this lease:

(a)   LEASE DATE: [date]

(b)   LANDLORD: [name]

(c)   LANDLORD'S ADDRESS: with a copy at the same time to:
[address]   [* * *]

(d)   TENANT: [name]

(e)   TENANT'S ADDRESS: with a copy at the same time to:
[address]   [* * *]

(f)   BUILDING ADDRESS: [address]

(g)   PREMISES: The premises shown on Exhibit A to this lease, known as Suite [number].

(h)   RENTABLE AREA OF THE PREMISES: [number] square feet.

(i)   RENTABLE AREA OF THE BUILDING: [number] square feet.

(j)   TERM: [number] months, beginning on the commencement date and expiring on the expiration date.

(k)   COMMENCEMENT DATE: [date], or as extended pursuant to the work letter.

(l)   EXPIRATION DATE: [date], or as extended pursuant to the workletter.

(m)   SECURITY DEPOSIT: $[amount]

(n)   MONTHLY RENT: $[amount] per month commencing [date] and ending [date]; $[amount] per month commencing [date] and ending [date]; and $[amount] per month commencing [date] and ending [date]. The monthly rent includes the product of $1/12$th of the operating expenses base times the rentable area of the premises.

(o)   OPERATING EXPENSES BASE: $[amount] per rentable square foot of the premises per annum.

(p)   TENANT'S SHARE: [percent] % (determined by dividing the rentable area of the premises by the rentable area of the building, multiplying the resulting quotient by 100, and rounding to the 3rd decimal place).

(q)   PARKING SPACES: [number] spaces according to Article 26.

(r)   PARKING CHARGE: $[amount] per parking space per month, subject to adjustments specified in Article 26.

(s)   BROKER: [name]

1.2   Definitions:

(a)   ADDITIONAL RENT: Any amounts that this lease requires tenant to pay in addition to monthly rent.

(b)   BUILDING: The building located on the land and of which the premises are a part.

(c)   LAND: The land on which the project is located and which is described on Exhibit B.

(d)   PRIME RATE: The rate of interest from time to time announced by [* * *] ("[* * *]"), or any successor to it, as its prime rate. If [* * *] or any successor to it ceases to announce its prime rate, the prime rate will be a comparable interest rate designated by landlord to replace the prime rate.

(e)   PROJECT: The development consisting of the land and all improvements built on the land, including without limitation the building, parking lot, parking structure, if any, walkways, driveways, fences, and landscaping.

(f)   RENT: The monthly rent and additional rent.

(g)   WORKLETTER: The workletter attached to this lease as Exhibit C (if any).

If any other provision of this lease contradicts any definition of this Article, the other provision will prevail.

1.3   Exhibits. The following addendum and exhibits are attached to this lease and are made part of this lease:

ADDENDUM [* * *]
EXHIBIT A—The Premises
EXHIBIT B—Legal Description of the Land
EXHIBIT C—Workletter
EXHIBIT D—Rules and Regulations
EXHIBIT E—Commencement Date Certificate

ARTICLE 2   AGREEMENT

Landlord leases the premises to tenant, and tenant leases the premises from landlord, according to this lease. The duration of this lease will be the term.

The term will commence on the commencement date and will expire on the expiration date.

ARTICLE 3   DELIVERY OF PREMISES

3.1   Delivery of Possession. Landlord will be deemed to have delivered possession of the premises to tenant on the commencement date, as it may be adjusted pursuant to the workletter. Landlord will construct or install in the premises the improvements to be constructed or installed by landlord according to the workletter. If no workletter is attached to this lease, it will be deemed that landlord delivered to tenant possession of the premises as is in its present condition on the commencement date. Tenant acknowledges that neither landlord nor its agents or employees have made any representations or warranties as to the suitability or fitness of the premises for the conduct of tenant's business or for any other purpose, nor has landlord or its agents or employees agreed to undertake any alterations or construct any tenant improvements to the premises except as expressly provided in this lease and the workletter. If for any reason landlord cannot deliver possession of the premises to tenant on the commencement date, this lease will not be void or voidable, and landlord will not be liable to tenant for any resultant loss or damage. Tenant will execute the commencement date certificate attached to this lease as Exhibit E within 15 days of landlord's request.

3.2   Early Entry. If tenant is permitted entry to the premises prior to the commencement date for the purpose of installing fixtures or any other purpose permitted by landlord, the early entry will be at tenant's sole risk and subject to all the terms and provisions of this lease as though the commencement date had occurred, except for the payment of rent, which will commence on the commencement date. Tenant, its agents, or employees will not interfere with or delay landlord's completion of construction of the improvements. All rights of tenant under this Section 3.2 will be subject to the requirements of all applicable building codes, zoning requirements, and federal, state, and local laws, rules, and regulations, so as not to interfere with landlord's compliance with all laws, including the obtaining of a certificate of occupancy for the premises. Landlord has the right to impose additional conditions on tenant's early entry that landlord, in its reasonable discretion, deems appropriate, including without limitation an indemnification of landlord and proof of insurance, and will further have the right to require that tenant execute an early entry agreement containing those conditions prior to tenant's early entry.

ARTICLE 4   MONTHLY RENT

Throughout the term of this lease, tenant will pay monthly rent to landlord as rent for the premises. Monthly rent will be paid in advance on or before the first day of each calendar month of the term. If the term commences on a day other than the first day of a calendar month or ends on a day other than the last day of a calendar month, then monthly rent will be appropriately prorated by landlord based on the actual number of calendar days in such month. If the term commences on a day other than the first day of a calendar month, then the prorated monthly rent for such month will be paid on or before the first day of the term. Monthly rent will be paid to landlord, without written notice or demand, and without deduction or offset, in lawful money of the United States of America at landlord's address, or to such other address as landlord may from time to time designate in writing.

ARTICLE 5   OPERATING EXPENSES

5.1   General.

(a)   In addition to monthly rent, beginning on the commencement date tenant will pay tenant's share of the amount by which the operating expenses paid, payable, or incurred by landlord in each calendar year or partial calendar year during the term exceeds the product of the operating expenses base times the rentable area of the building. If operating expenses are calculated for a partial calendar year, the operating expenses base will be appropriately prorated.

(b)   As used in this lease, the term "operating expenses" means:

(1)   All reasonable costs of management, operation, and maintenance of the project, including without limitation real and personal property taxes and assessments (and any tax levied in whole or in part in lieu of or in addition to real property taxes); wages, salaries, and compensation of employees; consulting, accounting, legal, janitorial, maintenance, guard, and other services; management fees and costs (charged by landlord, any affiliate of landlord, or any other entity managing the project and determined at a rate consistent with prevailing market rates for comparable services and projects); reasonable reserves for operating expenses; that part of office rent or rental value of space in the project used or furnished by landlord to enhance, manage, operate, and maintain the project; power, water, waste disposal, and other utilities; materials and supplies; maintenance and repairs; insurance obtained with respect to the project; depreciation on personal property and equipment, except as set forth in (c) below or which is or should be capitalized on the books of landlord; and any other costs, charges, and expenses that under generally accepted accounting principles would be regarded as management, maintenance, and operating expenses; and

(2)   The cost (amortized over such period as landlord will reasonably determine) together with interest at the greater of the prime rate prevailing plus 2% or landlord's borrowing rate for such capital improvements plus 2% on the unamortized balance of any capital improvements that are made to the project by landlord (i) for the purpose of reducing operating expenses, or (ii) after the lease date and by requirement of any governmental law or regulation that was not applicable to the project at the time it was constructed and not as a result of special requirements for any tenant's use of the building.

(c)   The operating expenses will not include:

(1)   depreciation on the project (other than depreciation on personal property, equipment, window coverings on exterior windows provided by landlord and carpeting in public corridors and common areas);

(2)   costs of alterations of space or other improvements made for tenants of the project;

(3)   finders' fees and real estate brokers' commissions;

(4)   ground lease payments, mortgage principal, or interest;

(5)   capital items other than those referred to in clause (b)(2) above;

(6)   costs of replacements to personal property and equipment for which depreciation costs are included as an operating expense;

(7)   costs of excess or additional services provided to any tenant in the building that are directly billed to such tenants;

(8)   the cost of repairs due to casualty or condemnation that are reimbursed by third parties;

(9)   any cost due to landlord's breach of this lease;

(10)   any income, estate, inheritance, or other transfer tax and any excess profit, franchise, or similar taxes on landlord's business;

(11)   all costs, including legal fees, relating to activities for the solicitation and execution of leases of space in the building; and

(12)   any legal fees incurred by landlord in enforcing its rights under other leases for premises in the building.

(d) The operating expenses that vary with occupancy and that are attributable to any part of the term in which less than 95% of the rentable area of the building is occupied by tenants will be adjusted by landlord to the amount that landlord reasonably believes they would have been if 95% of the rentable area of the building had been so occupied.

(e) Tenant acknowledges that landlord has not made any representation or given tenant any assurances that the operating expenses base will equal or approximate the actual operating expenses per square foot of rentable area of the premises for any calendar year during the term.

5.2 Estimated Payments. During each calendar year or partial calendar year in the term, in addition to monthly rent, tenant will pay to landlord on the first day of each month an amount equal to $1/12$ of the product of tenant's share multiplied by the "estimated operating expenses" (defined below) for such calendar year. "Estimated operating expenses" for any calendar year means landlord's reasonable estimate of operating expenses for such calendar year, less the product of the operating expenses base, multiplied by the rentable area of the building and will be subject to revision according to the further provisions of this Section 5.2 and Section 5.3. During any partial calendar year during the term, estimated operating expenses will be estimated on a full-year basis. During each December during the term, or as soon after each December as practicable, landlord will give tenant written notice of estimated operating expenses for the ensuing calendar year. On or before the first day of each month during the ensuing calendar year (or each month of the term, if a partial calendar year), tenant will pay to landlord $1/12$ of the product of tenant's share multiplied by the estimated operating expenses for such calendar year; however, if such written notice is not given in December, tenant will continue to make monthly payments on the basis of the prior

year's estimated operating expenses until the month after such written notice is given, at which time tenant will commence making monthly payments
based upon the revised estimated operating expenses. In the month tenant
first makes a payment based upon the revised estimated operating expenses,
tenant will pay to landlord for each month which has elapsed since December the difference between the amount payable based upon the revised estimated operating expenses and the amount payable based upon the prior
year's estimated operating expenses. If at any time or times it reasonably appears to landlord that the actual operating expenses for any calendar year
will vary from the estimated operating expenses for such calendar year, landlord may, by written notice to tenant, revise the estimated operating expenses for such calendar year, and subsequent payments by tenant in such
calendar year will be based upon such revised estimated operating expenses.

5.3   Annual Settlement. Within 120 days after the end of each calendar
year or as soon after such 120-day period as practicable, landlord will deliver
to tenant a statement of amounts payable under Section 5.1 for such calendar
year prepared and certified by landlord. Such certified statement will be final
and binding upon landlord and tenant unless tenant objects to it in writing to
landlord within 30 days after it is given to tenant. If such statement shows an
amount owing by tenant that is less than the estimated payments previously
made by tenant for such calendar year, the excess will be held by landlord
and credited against the next payment of rent; however, if the term has ended
and tenant was not in default at its end, landlord will refund the excess to
tenant. If such statement shows an amount owing by tenant that is more than
the estimated payments previously made by tenant for such calendar year,
tenant will pay the deficiency to landlord within 30 days after the delivery of
such statement. Tenant may review landlord's records of the operating expenses, at tenant's sole cost and expense, at the place landlord normally main-
tains such records during landlord's normal business hours upon reasonable
advance written notice.

5.4   Final Proration. If this lease ends on a day other than the last day of a
calendar year, the amount of increase (if any) in the operating expenses
payable by tenant applicable to the calendar year in which this lease ends will
be calculated on the basis of the number of days of the term falling within
such calendar year, and tenant's obligation to pay any increase or landlord's
obligation to refund any overage will survive the expiration or other termination of this lease.

5.5   Other Taxes.

(a)   Tenant will reimburse landlord upon demand for any and all taxes
payable by landlord (other than as set forth in subparagraph (b) below), whether
or not now customary or within the contemplation of landlord and tenant:

(1)   upon or measured by rent, including without limitation, any gross
revenue tax, excise tax, or value added tax levied by the federal government
or any other governmental body with respect to the receipt of rent; and

(2)   upon this transaction or any document to which tenant is a party
creating or transferring an interest or an estate in the premises.

(b)   Tenant will not be obligated to pay any inheritance tax, gift tax, transfer tax, franchise tax, income tax (based on net income), profit tax, or capital levy imposed upon landlord.

(c)   Tenant will pay promptly when due all personal property taxes on tenant's personal property in the premises and any other taxes payable by tenant that if not paid might give rise to a lien on the premises or tenant's interest in the premises.

5.6   Additional Rent. Amounts payable by tenant according to this Article 5 will be payable as rent, without deduction or offset. If tenant fails to pay any amounts due according to this Article 5, landlord will have all the rights and remedies available to it on account of tenant's failure to pay rent.

ARTICLE 6   INSURANCE

6.1   Landlord's Insurance. At all times during the term, landlord will carry and maintain:

(a)   Fire and extended coverage insurance covering the project, its equipment, common area furnishings, and leasehold improvements in the premises to the extent of the tenant finish allowance (as that term is defined in the workletter);

(b)   Bodily injury and property damage insurance; and

(c)   Such other insurance as landlord reasonably determines from time to time.

The insurance coverages and amounts in this Section 6.1 will be reasonably determined by landlord, based on coverages carried by prudent owners of comparable buildings in the vicinity of the project.

6.2   Tenant's Insurance. At all times during the term, tenant will carry and maintain, at tenant's expense, the following insurance, in the amounts specified below or such other amounts as landlord may from time to time reasonably request, with insurance companies and on forms satisfactory to landlord:

(a)   Bodily injury and property damage liability insurance, with a combined single occurrence limit of not less than $3,000,000. All such insurance will be equivalent to coverage offered by a commercial general liability form, including without limitation personal injury and contractual liability coverage for the performance by tenant of the indemnity agreements set forth in Article 21 of this lease;

(b)   Insurance covering all of tenant's furniture and fixtures, machinery, equipment, stock, and any other personal property owned and used in tenant's business and found in, on, or about the project, and any leasehold improvements to the premises in excess of the allowance, if any, provided pursuant to the workletter in an amount not less than the full replacement cost. Property forms will provide coverage on a broad form basis insuring against "all risks of direct physical loss." All policy proceeds will be used for the repair or replacement of the property damaged or destroyed; however, if this lease ceases under the provisions of Article 18, tenant will be entitled to any proceeds resulting from damage to tenant's furniture and fixtures, machinery, equipment, stock, and any other personal property;

(c)   Worker's compensation insurance insuring against and satisfying tenant's obligations and liabilities under the worker's compensation laws of the state in which the premises are located, including employer's liability insurance in the limits required by the laws of the state in which the project is located; and

(d)   If tenant operates owned, hired, or nonowned vehicles on the project, comprehensive automobile liability at a limit of liability not less than $500,000 combined bodily injury and property damage.

6.3   Forms of Policies. Certificates of insurance, together with copies of the endorsements, when applicable, naming landlord and any others specified by landlord as additional insureds, will be delivered to landlord prior to tenant's occupancy of the premises and from time to time at least 10 days prior to the expiration of the term of each such policy. All commercial general liability or comparable policies maintained by tenant will name landlord and such other persons or firms as landlord specifies from time to time as additional insureds, entitling them to recover under such policies for any loss sustained by them, their agents, and employees as a result of the negligent acts or omissions of tenant. All such policies maintained by tenant will provide that they may not be terminated nor may coverage be reduced except after 30 days' prior written notice to landlord. All commercial general liability and property policies maintained by tenant will be written as primary policies, not contributing with and not supplemental to the coverage that landlord may carry.

6.4   Waiver of Subrogation. Landlord and tenant each waive any and all rights to recover against the other or against any other tenant or occupant of the project, or against the officers, directors, shareholders, partners, joint venturers, employees, agents, customers, invitees, or business visitors of such other party or of such other tenant or occupant of the project, for any loss or damage to such waiving party arising from any cause covered by any property insurance required to be carried by such party pursuant to this Article 6 or any other property insurance actually carried by such party to the extent of the limits of such policy. Landlord and tenant from time to time will cause their respective insurers to issue appropriate waiver of subrogation rights endorsements to all property insurance policies carried in connection with the project or the premises or the contents of the project or the premises. Tenant agrees to cause all other occupants of the premises claiming by, under, or through tenant to execute and deliver to landlord such a waiver of claims and to obtain such waiver of subrogation rights endorsements.

6.5   Adequacy of Coverage. Landlord, its agents, and employees make no representation that the limits of liability specified to be carried by tenant pursuant to this Article 6 are adequate to protect tenant. If tenant believes that any of such insurance coverage is inadequate, tenant will obtain such additional insurance coverage as tenant deems adequate, at tenant's sole expense.

ARTICLE 7   USE

The premises will be used only for general business office purposes and purposes incidental to that use, and for no other purpose. Tenant will use the premises in a careful, safe, and proper manner. Tenant will not use or permit the premises to be used or occupied for any purpose or in any manner prohibited by any applicable laws. Tenant will not commit waste or suffer or permit waste to be committed in, on, or about the premises. Tenant will conduct its business and control its employees, agents, and invitees in such a manner as not to create any nuisance or interfere with, annoy, or disturb any other tenant or occupant of the project or landlord in its operation of the project.

ARTICLE 8   REQUIREMENTS OF LAW; FIRE INSURANCE

8.1   General. At its sole cost and expense, tenant will promptly comply with all laws, statutes, ordinances, and governmental rules, regulations, or requirements now in force or in force after the lease date, with the requirements of any board of fire underwriters or other similar body constituted now or after the date, with any direction or occupancy certificate issued pursuant to any law by any public officer or officers, as well as with the provisions of all recorded documents affecting the premises, insofar as they relate to the condition, use, or occupancy of the premises, excluding requirements of structural changes to the premises or the building, unless required by the unique nature of tenant's use or occupancy of the premises.

8.2   Hazardous Materials.

(a)   For purposes of this lease, "hazardous materials" means any explosives, radioactive materials, hazardous wastes, or hazardous substances, including without limitation substances defined as "hazardous substances" in the Comprehensive Environmental Response, Compensation and Liability Act of 1980, as amended, 42 U.S.C. §§ 9601–9657; the Hazardous Materials Transportation Act of 1975, 49 U.S.C. §§ 1801–1812; the Resource Conservation and Recovery Act of 1976, 42 U.S.C. §§ 6901–6987; or any other federal, state, or local statute, law, ordinance, code, rule, regulation, order, or decree regulating, relating to, or imposing liability or standards of conduct concerning hazardous materials, waste, or substances now or at any time hereafter in effect (collectively, "hazardous materials laws").

(b)   Tenant will not cause or permit the storage, use, generation, or disposition of any hazardous materials in, on, or about the premises or the project by tenant, its agents, employees, or contractors. Tenant will not permit the premises to be used or operated in a manner that may cause the premises or the project to be contaminated by any hazardous materials in violation of any hazardous materials laws. Tenant will immediately advise landlord in writing of (1) any and all enforcement, cleanup, remedial, removal, or other governmental or regulatory actions instituted, completed, or threatened pursuant to any hazardous materials laws relating to any hazardous materials affecting the premises;

and (2) all claims made or threatened by any third party against tenant, landlord, or the premises relating to damage, contribution, cost recovery, compensation, loss, or injury resulting from any hazardous materials on or about the premises. Without landlord's prior written consent, tenant will not take any remedial action or enter into any agreements or settlements in response to the presence of any hazardous materials in, on, or about the premises.

(c) Tenant will be solely responsible for and will defend, indemnify and hold landlord, its agents, and employees harmless from and against all claims, costs, and liabilities, including attorneys' fees and costs, arising out of or in connection with tenant's breach of its obligations in this Article 8. Tenant will be solely responsible for and will defend, indemnify, and hold landlord, its agents, and employees harmless from and against any and all claims, costs, and liabilities, including attorneys' fees and costs, arising out of or in connection with the removal, cleanup, and restoration work and materials necessary to return the premises and any other property of whatever nature located on the project to their condition existing prior to the appearance of tenant's hazardous materials on the premises. Tenant's obligations under this Article 8 will survive the expiration or other termination of this lease.

8.3 Certain Insurance Risks. Tenant will not do or permit to be done any act or thing upon the premises or the project which would (a) jeopardize or be in conflict with fire insurance policies covering the project and fixtures and property in the project; (b) increase the rate of fire insurance applicable to the project to an amount higher than it otherwise would be for general office use of the project; or (c) subject landlord to any liability or responsibility for injury to any person or persons or to property by reason of any business or operation being carried on upon the premises.

ARTICLE 9   ASSIGNMENT AND SUBLETTING

9.1 General. Tenant, for itself, its heirs, distributees, executors, administrators, legal representatives, successors, and assigns, covenants that it will not assign, mortgage, or encumber this lease, nor sublease, nor permit the premises or any part of the premises to be used or occupied by others, without the prior written consent of landlord in each instance, which consent will not be unreasonably withheld or delayed. Any assignment or sublease in violation of this Article 9 will be void. If this lease is assigned, or if the premises or any part of the premises are subleased or occupied by anyone other than tenant, landlord may, after default by tenant, collect rent from the assignee, subtenant, or occupant, and apply the net amount collected to rent. No assignment, sublease, occupancy, or collection will be deemed (a) a waiver of the provisions of this Section 9.1; (b) the acceptance of the assignee, subtenant, or occupant as tenant; or (c) a release of tenant from the further performance by tenant of covenants on the part of tenant contained in this lease. The consent by landlord to an assignment or sublease will not be construed to relieve tenant from obtaining landlord's prior written consent in writing to any further assignment or sublease. No permitted subtenant may assign or encumber its sublease or further sublease all or any portion of its subleased space, or otherwise permit the subleased space or any part of its subleased space to be used or occupied by others, without landlord's prior written consent in each instance.

9.2   Submission of Information. If tenant requests landlord's consent to a specific assignment or subletting, tenant will submit in writing to landlord (a) the name and address of the proposed assignee or subtenant; (b) the business terms of the proposed assignment or sublease; (c) reasonably satisfactory information as to the nature and character of the business of the proposed assignee or subtenant, and as to the nature of its proposed use of the space; (d) banking, financial, or other credit information reasonably sufficient to enable landlord to determine the financial responsibility and character of the proposed assignee or subtenant; and (e) the proposed form of assignment or sublease for landlord's reasonable approval.

9.3   Payments to Landlord. If landlord consents to a proposed assignment or sublease, then landlord will have the right to require tenant to pay to landlord a sum equal to (a) any rent or other consideration paid to tenant by any proposed transferee that (after deducting the costs of tenant, if any, in effecting the assignment or sublease, including reasonable alterations costs, commissions and legal fees) is in excess of the rent allocable to the transferred space then being paid by tenant to landlord pursuant to this lease; (b) any other profit or gain (after deducting any necessary expenses incurred) realized by tenant from any such sublease or assignment; and (c) landlord's reasonable attorneys' fees and costs incurred in connection with negotiation, review, and processing of the transfer. All such sums payable will be payable to landlord at the time the next payment of monthly rent is due.

9.4   Prohibited Transfers. The transfer of a majority of the issued and outstanding capital stock of any corporate tenant or subtenant of this lease, or a majority of the total interest in any partnership tenant or subtenant, however accomplished, and whether in a single transaction or in a series of related or unrelated transactions, will be deemed an assignment of this lease or of such sublease requiring landlord's consent in each instance. For purposes of this Article 9, the transfer of outstanding capital stock of any corporate tenant will not include any sale of such stock by persons other than those deemed "insiders" within the meaning of the Securities Exchange Act of 1934, as amended, effected through the "over-the-counter market" or through any recognized stock exchange.

9.5   Permitted Transfer. Landlord consents to an assignment of this lease or sublease of all or part of the premises to a wholly-owned subsidiary of tenant or the parent of tenant or to any corporation into or with which tenant may be merged or consolidated; provided that tenant promptly provides landlord with a fully executed copy of such assignment or sublease and that tenant is not released from liability under the lease.

9.6   Remedies. If tenant believes that landlord has unreasonably withheld its consent pursuant to this Article 9, tenant's sole remedy will be to seek a declaratory judgment that landlord has unreasonably withheld its consent or an order of specific performance or mandatory injunction of the landlord's agreement to give its consent; however, tenant may recover damages if a court of competent jurisdiction determines that landlord has acted arbitrarily and capriciously in evaluating the proposed assignee's or subtenant's creditworthiness, identity, and business character and the proposed use and lawfulness of the use.

ARTICLE 10   RULES AND REGULATIONS

Tenant and its employees, agents, licensees, and visitors will at all times observe faithfully, and comply strictly with, the rules and regulations set forth in Exhibit D. Landlord may from time to time reasonably amend, delete, or modify existing rules and regulations, or adopt reasonable new rules and regulations for the use, safety, cleanliness, and care of the premises, the building, and the project, and the comfort, quiet, and convenience of occupants of the project. Modifications or additions to the rules and regulations will be effective upon 30 days' prior written notice to tenant from landlord. In the event of any breach of any rules or regulations or any amendments or additions to such rules and regulations, landlord will have all remedies that this lease provides for default by tenant, and will in addition have any remedies available at law or in equity, including the right to enjoin any breach of such rules and regulations. Landlord will not be liable to tenant for violation of such rules and regulations by any other tenant, its employees, agents, visitors, or licensees or any other person. In the event of any conflict between the provisions of this lease and the rules and regulations, the provisions of this lease will govern.

ARTICLE 11   COMMON AREAS

As used in this lease, the term "common areas" means, without limitation, the hallways, entryways, stairs, elevators, driveways, walkways, terraces, docks, loading areas, restrooms, trash facilities, and all other areas and facilities in the project that are provided and designated from time to time by landlord for the general nonexclusive use and convenience of tenant with landlord and other tenants of the project and their respective employees, invitees, licensees, or other visitors. Landlord grants tenant, its employees, invitees, licensees, and other visitors a nonexclusive license for the term to use the common areas in common with others entitled to use the common areas, subject to the terms and conditions of this lease. Without advance written notice to tenant, except with respect to matters covered by subsection (a) below, and without any liability to tenant in any respect, provided landlord will take no action permitted under this Article 11 in such a manner as to materially impair or adversely affect tenant's substantial benefit and enjoyment of the premises, landlord will have the right to:

(a)   Close off any of the common areas to whatever extent required in the opinion of landlord and its counsel to prevent a dedication of any of the common areas or the accrual of any rights by any person or the public to the common areas;

(b)   Temporarily close any of the common areas for maintenance, alteration, or improvement purposes; and

(c)   Change the size, use, shape, or nature of any such common areas, including erecting additional buildings on the common areas, expanding the existing building or other buildings to cover a portion of the common areas, converting common areas to a portion of the building or other buildings, or converting any portion of the building (excluding the premises) or other buildings to common areas. Upon erection of any additional buildings or change in common areas, the portion of the project upon which buildings or structures have been erected will no longer be deemed to be a part of the common areas. In the event of any such changes in the size or use of the building or common areas of the building or project, landlord will make an appropriate adjustment in the rentable area of the building or the building's pro rata share of exterior common areas of the project, as appropriate, and a corresponding adjustment to tenant's share of the operating expenses payable pursuant to Article 5 of this lease.

ARTICLE 12   LANDLORD'S SERVICES

12.1   Landlord's Repair and Maintenance. Landlord will maintain, repair and restore the common areas of the project, including lobbies, stairs, elevators, corridors, and restrooms, the windows in the building, the mechanical, plumbing and electrical equipment serving the building, and the structure of the building in reasonably good order and condition.

12.2   Landlord's Other Services.

(a)   Landlord will furnish the premises with those services customarily provided in comparable office buildings in the vicinity of the project, including without limitation (1) electricity for lighting and the operation of low-wattage office machines (such as desktop micro-computers, desktop calculators, and typewriters) during business hours (as that term is defined below), although landlord will not be obligated to furnish more power to the premises than is proportionally allocated to the premises under the building design; (2) heat and air conditioning reasonably required for the comfortable occupation of the premises during business hours; (3) access and elevator service; (4) lighting replacement during business hours (for building standard lights, but not for any special tenant lights, which will be replaced at tenant's sole cost and expense); (5) restroom supplies; (6) window washing with reasonable frequency, as determined by landlord; and (7) daily cleaning service on weekdays. Landlord may provide, but will not be obligated to provide, any such services (except access and elevator service) on holidays or weekends.

(b)   Tenant will have the right to purchase for use during business hours and non-business hours the services described in clauses (a)(1) and (2) in excess of the amounts landlord has agreed to furnish so long as (1) tenant gives landlord reasonable prior written notice of its desire to do so; (2) the excess services are reasonably available to landlord and to the premises; and (3) tenant pays as additional rent (at the time the next payment of monthly rent is due) the cost of such excess service from time to time charged by landlord; subject to the procedures established by landlord from time to time for providing such additional or excess services.

(c)   The term "business hours" means 7:00 a.m. to 6:00 p.m. on Monday through Friday, except holidays (as that term is defined below), and 8:00 a.m. to 12:00 noon on Saturdays, except holidays. The term "holidays" means New Year's Day, Memorial Day, Independence Day, Labor Day, Thanksgiving Day, and Christmas Day.

12.3   Tenant's Costs. Whenever equipment or lighting (other than building standard lights) is used in the premises by tenant and such equipment or lighting affects the temperature otherwise normally maintained by the design of the building's air conditioning system, landlord will have the right, after prior written notice to tenant, to install supplementary air conditioning facilities in the premises or otherwise modify the ventilating and air conditioning system serving the premises; and the cost of such facilities, modifications, and additional service will be paid by tenant as additional rent. If landlord reasonably believes that tenant is using more power than landlord furnishes pursuant to Section 12.2, landlord may install separate meters of tenant's power usage, and tenant will pay for the cost of such excess power as additional rent, together with the cost of installing any risers, meters, or other facilities that may be necessary to furnish or measure such excess power to the premises.

12.4   Limitation on Liability. Landlord will not be in default under this lease or be liable to tenant or any other person for direct or consequential damage, or otherwise, for any failure to supply any heat, air conditioning, elevator, cleaning, lighting, security; for surges or interruptions of electricity; or for other services landlord has agreed to supply during any period when landlord uses reasonable diligence to supply such services. Landlord will use reasonable efforts to diligently remedy any interruption in the furnishing of such services. Landlord reserves the right temporarily to discontinue such services at such times as may be necessary by reason of accident; repairs, alterations or improvements; strikes; lockouts; riots; acts of God; governmental preemption in connection with a national or local emergency; any rule, order, or regulation of any governmental agency; conditions of supply and demand that make any product unavailable; landlord's compliance with any mandatory governmental energy conservation or environmental protection program, or any voluntary governmental energy conservation program at the request of or with consent or acquiescence of tenant; or any other happening beyond the control of landlord. Landlord will not be liable to tenant or any other person or entity for direct or consequential damages resulting from the admission to or exclusion from the building or project of any person. In the event of invasion, mob, riot, public excitement, strikes, lockouts, or other circumstances rendering such action advisable in landlord's sole opinion, landlord will have the right to prevent access to the building or project during the continuance of the same by such means as landlord, in its sole discretion, may deem appropriate, including without limitation locking doors and closing parking areas and other common areas. Landlord will not be liable for damages to person or property or for injury to, or interruption of, business for any discontinuance permitted under this Article 12, nor will such discontinuance in any way be construed as an eviction of tenant or cause an abatement of rent or operate to release tenant from any of tenant's obligations under this lease.

ARTICLE 13   TENANT'S CARE OF THE PREMISES

Tenant will maintain the premises (including tenant's equipment, personal property, and trade fixtures located in the premises) in their condition at the time they were delivered to tenant, reasonable wear and tear excluded. Tenant will immediately advise landlord of any damage to the premises or the project. All damage or injury to the premises, the project, or the fixtures, appurtenances, and equipment in the premises or the project that is caused by tenant, its agents, employees, or invitees may be repaired, restored, or replaced by landlord, at the expense of tenant. Such expense (plus 15% of such expense for landlord's overhead) will be collectible as additional rent and will be paid by tenant within 10 days after delivery of a statement for such expense.

ARTICLE 14   ALTERATIONS

14.1   General.

(a)   During the term, tenant will not make or allow to be made any alterations, additions, or improvements to or of the premises or any part of the premises, or attach any fixtures or equipment to the premises, without first obtaining landlord's written consent. All such alterations, additions, and improvements consented to by landlord, and capital improvements that are required to be made to the project as a result of the nature of tenant's use of the premises:

(1)   Will be performed by contractors approved by landlord and subject to conditions specified by landlord (which may include requiring the posting of a mechanic's or materialmen's lien bond); and

(2)   At landlord's option, will be made by landlord for tenant's account, and tenant will reimburse landlord for their cost (including 15% for landlord's overhead) within 10 days after receipt of a statement of such cost.

(b)   Subject to tenant's rights in Article 16, all alterations, additions, fixtures, and improvements, whether temporary or permanent in character, made in or upon the premises either by tenant or landlord, will immediately become landlord's property and at the end of the term will remain on the premises without compensation to tenant, unless when consenting to such alterations, additions, fixtures, or improvements, landlord has advised tenant in writing that such alterations, additions, fixtures, or improvements must be removed at the expiration or other termination of this lease.

14.2   Free-Standing Partitions. Tenant will have the right to install free-standing work station partitions, without landlord's prior written consent, so long as no building or other governmental permit is required for their installation or relocation; however, if a permit is required, landlord will not unreasonably withhold its consent to such relocation or installation. The free-standing work station partitions for which tenant pays will be part of tenant's trade fixtures for all purposes under this lease. All other partitions installed in the premises are and will be landlord's property for all purposes under this lease.

14.3   Removal. If landlord has required tenant to remove any or all alterations, additions, fixtures, and improvements that are made in or upon the premises pursuant to this Article 14 prior to the expiration date, tenant will remove such alterations, additions, fixtures, and improvements at tenant's sole cost and will restore the premises to the condition in which they were before such alterations, additions, fixtures, improvements, and additions were made, reasonable wear and tear excepted.

ARTICLE 15   MECHANICS' LIENS

Tenant will pay or cause to be paid all costs and charges for work (a) done by tenant or caused to be done by tenant, in or to the premises, and (b) for all materials furnished for or in connection with such work. Tenant will indemnify landlord against and hold landlord, the premises, and the project free, clear, and harmless of and from all mechanics' liens and claims of liens, and all other liabilities, liens, claims, and demands on account of such work by or on behalf of tenant, other than work performed by landlord pursuant to the workletter. If any such lien, at any time, is filed against the premises or any part of the project, tenant will cause such lien to be discharged of record within 10 days after the filing of such lien, except that if tenant desires to contest such lien, it will furnish landlord, within such 10-day period, security reasonably satisfactory to landlord of at least 150% of the amount of the claim, plus estimated costs and interest, or comply with such statutory procedures as may be available to release the lien. If a final judgment establishing the validity or existence of a lien for any amount is entered, tenant will pay and satisfy the same at once. If tenant fails to pay any charge for which a mechanics' lien has been filed, and has not given landlord security as described above, or has not complied with such statutory procedures as may be available to release the lien, landlord may, at its option, pay such charge and related costs and interest, and the amount so paid, together with reasonable attorneys' fees incurred in connection with such lien, will be immediately due from tenant to landlord as additional rent. Nothing contained in this lease will be deemed the consent or agreement of landlord to subject landlord's interest in the project to liability under any mechanics' or other lien law. If tenant receives written notice that a lien has been or is about to be filed against the premises or the project, or that any action affecting title to the project has been commenced on account of work done by or for or materials furnished to or for tenant, it will immediately give landlord written notice of such notice. At least 15 days prior to the commencement of any work (including but not limited to any maintenance, repairs, alterations, additions, improvements, or installations) in or to the premises, by or for tenant, tenant will give landlord written notice of the proposed work and the names and addresses of the persons supplying labor and materials for the proposed work. Landlord will have the right to post notices of nonresponsibility or similar written notices on the premises in order to protect the premises against any such liens.

ARTICLE 16   END OF TERM

At the end of this lease, tenant will promptly quit and surrender the premises broom-clean, in good order and repair, ordinary wear and tear excepted. If tenant is not then in default, tenant may remove from the premises any trade fixtures, equipment, and movable furniture placed in the premises by tenant, whether or not such trade fixtures or equipment are fastened to the building; tenant will not remove any trade fixtures or equipment without landlord's prior written consent if such fixtures or equipment are used in the operation of the building, or if the removal of such fixtures or equipment will result in impairing the structural strength of the building. Whether or not tenant is in default, tenant will remove such alterations, additions, improvements, trade fixtures, equipment, and furniture as landlord has requested in accordance with Article 14. Tenant will fully repair any damage occasioned by the removal of any trade fixtures, equipment, furniture, alterations, additions, and improvements. All trade fixtures, equipment, furniture, inventory, effects, alterations, additions, and improvements on the premises after the end of the term will be deemed conclusively to have been abandoned and may be appropriated, sold, stored, destroyed, or otherwise disposed of by landlord without written notice to tenant or any other person and without obligation to account for them. Tenant will pay landlord for all expenses incurred in connection with the removal of such property, including but not limited to the cost of repairing any damage to the building or premises caused by the removal of such property. Tenant's obligation to observe and perform this covenant will survive the expiration or other termination of this lease.

ARTICLE 17   EMINENT DOMAIN

If all of the premises are taken by exercise of the power of eminent domain (or conveyed by landlord in lieu of such exercise) this lease will terminate on a date (the "termination date") which is the earlier of the date upon which the condemning authority takes possession of the premises or the date on which title to the premises is vested in the condemning authority. If more than 25% of the rentable area of the premises is so taken, tenant will have the right to cancel this lease by written notice to landlord given within 20 days after the termination date. If less than 25% of the rentable area of the premises is so taken, or if the tenant does not cancel this lease according to the preceding sentence, the monthly rent will be abated in the proportion of the rentable area of the premises so taken to the rentable area of the premises immediately before such taking, and tenant's share will be appropriately re-calculated. If 25% or more of the building or the project is so taken, landlord may cancel this lease by written notice to tenant given within 30 days after the termination date. In the event of any such taking, the entire award will be paid to landlord and tenant will have no right or claim to any part of such award; however, tenant will have the right to assert a claim against the condemning authority in a separate action, so long as landlord's award is not otherwise reduced, for tenant's moving expenses and leasehold improvements owned by tenant.

ARTICLE 18   DAMAGE AND DESTRUCTION

(a)   If the premises or the building are damaged by fire or other insured casualty, landlord will give tenant written notice of the time which will be needed to repair such damage, as determined by landlord in its reasonable discretion, and the election (if any) which landlord has made according to this Article 18. Such notice will be given before the 30th day (the "notice date") after the fire or other insured casualty.

(b)   If the premises or the building are damaged by fire or other insured casualty to an extent which may be repaired within 120 days after the notice date, as reasonably determined by landlord, landlord will promptly begin to repair the damage after the notice date and will diligently pursue the completion of such repair. In that event this lease will continue in full force and effect except that monthly rent will be abated on a pro rata basis from the date of the damage until the date of the completion of such repairs (the "repair period") based on the proportion of the rentable area of the premises tenant is unable to use during the repair period.

(c)   If the premises or the building are damaged by fire or other insured casualty to an extent that may not be repaired within 120 days after the notice date, as reasonably determined by landlord, then (1) landlord may cancel this lease as of the date of such damage by written notice given to tenant on or before the notice date or (2) tenant may cancel this lease as of the date of such damage by written notice given to landlord within 10 days after landlord's delivery of a written notice that the repairs cannot be made within such 120-day period. If neither landlord nor tenant so elects to cancel this lease, landlord will diligently proceed to repair the building and premises and monthly rent will be abated on a pro rata basis during the repair period based on the proportion of the rentable area of the premises tenant is unable to use during the repair period.

(d)   Notwithstanding the provisions of subparagraphs (a), (b), and (c) above, if the premises or the building are damaged by uninsured casualty, or if the proceeds of insurance are insufficient to pay for the repair of any damage to the premises or the building, landlord will have the option to repair such damage or cancel this lease as of the date of such casualty by written notice to tenant on or before the notice date.

(e)   If any such damage by fire or other casualty is the result of the willful conduct or negligence or failure to act of tenant, its agents, contractors, employees, or invitees, there will be no abatement of monthly rent as otherwise provided for in this Article 18. Tenant will have no rights to terminate this lease on account of any damage to the premises, the building, or the project, except as set forth in this lease.

ARTICLE 19   SUBORDINATION

19.1   General. This lease and tenant's rights under this lease are subject and subordinate to any ground or underlying lease, mortgage, indenture, deed of trust, or other lien encumbrance (each a "superior lien"), together with any renewals, extensions, modifications, consolidations, and replacements of such superior lien, now or after the date affecting or placed, charged, or enforced against the land, the building, or all or any portion of the project or any interest of landlord in them or landlord's interest in this lease and the leasehold estate created by this lease (except to the extent any such instrument expressly provides that this lease is superior to such instrument). This provision will be self-operative and no further instrument of subordination will be required in order to effect it. Notwithstanding the foregoing, tenant will execute, acknowledge, and deliver to landlord, within 20 days after written demand by landlord, such documents as may be reasonably requested by landlord or the holder of any superior lien to confirm or effect any such subordination.

19.2   Attornment and Nondisturbance. Tenant agrees that in the event that any holder of a superior lien succeeds to landlord's interest in the premises, tenant will pay to such holder all rents subsequently payable under this lease. Further, tenant agrees that in the event of the enforcement by the holder of a superior lien of the remedies provided for by law or by such superior lien, tenant will, upon request of any person or party succeeding to the interest of landlord as a result of such enforcement, automatically become the tenant of and attorn to such successor in interest without change in the terms or provisions of this lease. Such successor in interest will not be bound by:

(a)   Any payment of rent for more than one month in advance, except prepayments in the nature of security for the performance by tenant of its obligations under this lease;

(b)   Any amendment or modification of this lease made without the written consent of such successor in interest (if such consent was required under the terms of such superior lien);

(c)   Any claim against landlord arising prior to the date on which such successor in interest succeeded to landlord's interest; or

(d)   Any claim or offset of rent against the landlord.

Upon request by such successor in interest and without cost to landlord or such successor in interest, tenant will, within 20 days after written demand, execute, acknowledge, and deliver an instrument or instruments confirming the attornment, so long as such instrument provides that such successor in interest will not disturb tenant in its use of the premises in accordance with this lease.

ARTICLE 20   ENTRY BY LANDLORD

Landlord, its agents, employees, and contractors may enter the premises at any time in response to an emergency and at reasonable hours to:

(a)   Inspect the premises;

(b)   Exhibit the premises to prospective purchasers, lenders, or tenants;

(c)   Determine whether tenant is complying with all its obligations in this lease;

(d)   Supply cleaning service and any other service to be provided by landlord to tenant according to this lease;

(e)   Post written notices of nonresponsibility or similar notices; or

(f)   Make repairs required of landlord under the terms of this lease or make repairs to any adjoining space or utility services or make repairs, alterations, or improvements to any other portion of the building; however, all such work will be done as promptly as reasonably possible and so as to cause as little interference to tenant as reasonably possible.

Tenant, by this Article 20, waives any claim against landlord, its agents, employees, or contractors for damages for any injury or inconvenience to or interference with tenant's business, any loss of occupancy or quiet enjoyment of the premises, or any other loss occasioned by any entry in accordance with this Article 20. Landlord will at all times have and retain a key with which to unlock all of the doors in, on, or about the premises (excluding tenant's vaults, safes, and similar areas designated in writing by tenant in advance). Landlord will have the right to use any and all means landlord may deem proper to open doors in and to the premises in an emergency in order to obtain entry to the premises, provided that landlord will promptly repair any damages caused by any forced entry. Any entry to the premises by landlord in accordance with this Article 20 will not be construed or deemed to be a forcible or unlawful entry into or a detainer of the premises or an eviction, actual or constructive, of tenant from the premises or any portion of the premises, nor will any such entry entitle tenant to damages or an abatement of monthly rent, additional rent, or other charges that this lease requires tenant to pay.

ARTICLE 21   INDEMNIFICATION, WAIVER, AND RELEASE

21.1   Indemnification. Except for any injury or damage to persons or property on the premises that is proximately caused by or results proximately from the negligence or deliberate act of landlord, its employees, or agents, and subject to the provisions of Section 6.4, tenant will neither hold nor attempt to hold landlord, its employees, or agents liable for, and tenant will indemnify and hold harmless landlord, its employees, and agents from and against, any and all demands, claims, causes of action, fines, penalties, damages (including consequential damages), liabilities, judgments, and expenses (including without limitation reasonable attorneys' fees) incurred in connection with or arising from:

(a) the use or occupancy or manner of use or occupancy of the premises by tenant or any person claiming under tenant;

(b) any activity, work, or thing done or permitted by tenant in or about the premises, the building, or the project;

(c) any breach by tenant or its employees, agents, contractors, or invitees of this lease; and

(d) any injury or damage to the person, property, or business of tenant, its employees, agents, contractors, or invitees entering upon the premises under the express or implied invitation of tenant.

If any action or proceeding is brought against landlord, its employees, or agents by reason of any such claim for which tenant has indemnified landlord, tenant, upon written notice from landlord, will defend the same at tenant's expense, with counsel reasonably satisfactory to landlord.

21.2 Waiver and Release. Tenant, as a material part of the consideration to landlord for this lease, by this Section 21.2 waives and releases all claims against landlord, its employees, and agents with respect to all matters for which landlord has disclaimed liability pursuant to the provisions of this lease.

ARTICLE 22 SECURITY DEPOSIT

Tenant has deposited the security deposit with landlord as security for the full, faithful, and timely performance of every provision of this lease to be performed by tenant. If tenant defaults with respect to any provision of this lease, including but not limited to the provisions relating to the payment of rent, landlord may use, apply, or retain all or any part of the security deposit for the payment of any rent, or any other sum in default, or for the payment of any other amount landlord may spend or become obligated to spend by reason of tenant's default, or to compensate landlord for any other loss or damage landlord may suffer by reason of tenant's default. If any portion of the security deposit is so used, applied, or retained, tenant will within 5 days after written demand deposit cash with landlord in an amount sufficient to restore the security deposit to its original amount. Landlord will not be required to keep the security deposit separate from its general funds, and tenant will not be entitled to interest on the security deposit. The security deposit will not be deemed a limitation on landlord's damages or a payment of liquidated damages or a payment of the monthly rent due for the last month of the term. If tenant fully, faithfully, and timely performs every provision of this lease to be performed by it, the security deposit or any balance of the security deposit will be returned to tenant within 60 days after the expiration of the term. Landlord may deliver the funds deposited under this lease by tenant to the purchaser of the building in the event the building is sold, and after such time landlord will have no further liability to tenant with respect to the security deposit.

ARTICLE 23   QUIET ENJOYMENT

Landlord covenants and agrees with tenant that so long as tenant pays the rent and observes and performs all the terms, covenants, and conditions of this lease on tenant's part to be observed and performed, tenant may peaceably and quietly enjoy the premises subject, nevertheless, to the terms and conditions of this lease, and tenant's possession will not be disturbed by anyone claiming by, through, or under landlord.

ARTICLE 24   EFFECT OF SALE

A sale, conveyance, or assignment of the building or the project will operate to release landlord from liability from and after the effective date of such sale, conveyance, or assignment upon all of the covenants, terms, and conditions of this lease, express or implied, except those liabilities that arose prior to such effective date, and, after the effective date of such sale, conveyance, or assignment, tenant will look solely to landlord's successor in interest in and to this lease. This lease will not be affected by any such sale, conveyance, or assignment, and tenant will attorn to landlord's successor in interest to this lease, so long as such successor in interest assumes landlord's obligations under the lease from and after such effective date.

ARTICLE 25   DEFAULT

25.1   Events of Default. The following events are referred to, collectively, as "events of default" or, individually, as an "event of default":

(a)   Tenant defaults in the due and punctual payment of rent, and such default continues for 5 days after written notice from landlord; however, tenant will not be entitled to more than 1 written notice for monetary defaults during any 12-month period, and if after such written notice any rent is not paid when due, an event of default will be considered to have occurred without further notice;

(b)   Tenant vacates or abandons the premises;

(c)   This lease or the premises or any part of the premises are taken upon execution or by other process of law directed against tenant, or are taken upon or subject to any attachment by any creditor of tenant or claimant against tenant, and said attachment is not discharged or disposed of within 15 days after its levy;

(d)   Tenant files a petition in bankruptcy or insolvency or for reorganization or arrangement under the bankruptcy laws of the United States or under any insolvency act of any state, or admits the material allegations of any such petition by answer or otherwise, or is dissolved or makes an assignment for the benefit of creditors;

(e)   Involuntary proceedings under any such bankruptcy law or insolvency act or for the dissolution of tenant are instituted against tenant, or a receiver or trustee is appointed for all or substantially all of the property of tenant, and such proceeding is not dismissed or such receivership or trusteeship vacated within 60 days after such institution or appointment;

(f)   Tenant fails to take possession of the premises on the commencement date of the term; or

(g)   Tenant breaches any of the other agreements, terms, covenants, or conditions that this lease requires tenant to perform, and such breach continues for a period of 30 days after written notice from landlord to tenant or, if such breach cannot be cured reasonably within such 30-day period, if tenant fails to diligently commence to cure such breach within 30 days after written notice from landlord and to complete such cure within a reasonable time thereafter.

25.2   Landlord's Remedies. If any one or more events of default set forth in Section 25.1 occurs then landlord has the right, at its election:

(a)   To give tenant written notice of landlord's intention to terminate this lease on the earliest date permitted by law or on any later date specified in such notice, in which case tenant's right to possession of the premises will cease and this lease will be terminated, except as to tenant's liability, as if the expiration of the term fixed in such notice were the end of the term;

(b)   Without further demand or notice, to reenter and take possession of the premises or any part of the premises, repossess the same, expel tenant and those claiming through or under tenant, and remove the effects of both or either, using such force for such purposes as may be necessary, without being liable for prosecution, without being deemed guilty of any manner of trespass, and without prejudice to any remedies for arrears of monthly rent or other amounts payable under this lease or as a result of any preceding breach of covenants or conditions; or

(c)   Without further demand or notice to cure any event of default and to charge tenant for the cost of effecting such cure, including without limitation reasonable attorneys' fees and interest on the amount so advanced at the rate set forth in Section 27.22, provided that landlord will have no obligation to cure any such event of default of tenant.

Should landlord elect to reenter as provided in subsection (b), or should landlord take possession pursuant to legal proceedings or pursuant to any notice provided by law, landlord may, from time to time, without terminating this lease, relet the premises or any part of the premises in landlord's or tenant's name, but for the account of tenant, for such term or terms (which may be greater or less than the period which would otherwise have constituted the balance of the term) and on such conditions and upon such other terms (which may include concessions of free rent and alteration and repair of the premises) as landlord, in its reasonable discretion, may determine, and landlord may collect and receive the rent. Landlord will in no way be responsible or liable for any failure to relet the premises, or any part of the premises, or for any failure to collect any rent due upon such reletting. No such reentry or taking possession of the premises by landlord will be construed as an election on landlord's part to terminate this lease unless a written notice of such intention is given to tenant. No written notice from landlord under this Section or under a forcible or unlawful entry and detainer statute or similar law will constitute an election by landlord to terminate this lease unless such notice specifically so states. Landlord reserves the right following any such reentry or reletting to exercise its right to terminate this lease by giving tenant such written notice, in which event this lease will terminate as specified in such notice.

25.3   Certain Damages. In the event that landlord does not elect to terminate this lease as permitted in Section 25.2(a), but on the contrary elects to take possession as provided in Section 25.2(b), tenant will pay to landlord monthly rent and other sums as provided in this lease that would be payable under this lease if such repossession had not occurred, less the net proceeds, if any, of any reletting of the premises after deducting all of landlord's reasonable expenses in connection with such reletting, including without limitation all repossession costs, brokerage commissions, attorneys' fees, expenses of employees, alteration and repair costs, and expenses of preparation for such reletting. If, in connection with any reletting, the new lease term extends beyond the existing term, or the premises covered by such new lease include other premises not part of the premises, a fair apportionment of the rent received from such reletting and the expenses incurred in connection with such reletting as provided in this Section will be made in determining the net proceeds from such reletting, and any rent concessions will be equally apportioned over the term of the new lease. Tenant will pay such rent and other sums to landlord monthly on the day on which the monthly rent would have been payable under this lease if possession had not been retaken, and landlord will be entitled to receive such rent and other sums from tenant on each such day.

25.4   Continuing Liability After Termination. If this lease is terminated on account of the occurrence of an event of default, tenant will remain liable to landlord for damages in an amount equal to monthly rent and other amounts that would have been owing by tenant for the balance of the term, had this lease not been terminated, less the net proceeds, if any, of any reletting of the premises by landlord subsequent to such termination, after deducting all of landlord's expenses in connection with such reletting, including without limitation the expenses enumerated in Section 25.3. Landlord will be entitled to collect such damages from tenant monthly on the day on which monthly rent and other amounts would have been payable under this lease if this lease had not been terminated, and landlord will be entitled to receive such monthly rent and other amounts from tenant on each such day. Alternatively, at the option of landlord, in the event this lease is so terminated, landlord will be entitled to recover against tenant as damages for loss of the bargain and not as a penalty:

(a)   The worth at the time of award of the unpaid rent that had been earned at the time of termination;

(b)   The worth at the time of award of the amount by which the unpaid rent that would have been earned after termination until the time of award exceeds the amount of such rental loss that tenant proves could have been reasonably avoided;

(c) The worth at the time of award of the amount by which the unpaid rent for the balance of the term of this lease (had the same not been so terminated by landlord) after the time of award exceeds the amount of such rental loss that tenant proves could be reasonably avoided;

(d) Any other amount necessary to compensate landlord for all the detriment proximately caused by tenant's failure to perform its obligations under this lease or which in the ordinary course of things would be likely to result therefrom.

The "worth at the time of award" of the amounts referred to in clauses (a) and (b) above is computed by adding interest at the per annum interest rate described in Section 27.22 on the date on which this lease is terminated from the date of termination until the time of the award. The "worth at the time of award" of the amount referred to in clause (c) above is computed by discounting such amount at the discount rate of the Federal Reserve Bank of [city], [state], at the time of award plus 1%.

25.5 Cumulative Remedies. Any suit or suits for the recovery of the amounts and damages set forth in Sections 25.3 and 25.4 may be brought by landlord, from time to time, at landlord's election, and nothing in this lease will be deemed to require landlord to await the date upon which this lease or the term would have expired had there occurred no event of default. Each right and remedy provided for in this lease is cumulative and is in addition to every other right or remedy provided for in this lease or now or after the lease date existing at law or in equity or by statute or otherwise, and the exercise or beginning of the exercise by landlord of any one or more of the rights or remedies provided for in this lease or now or after the lease date existing at law or in equity or by statute or otherwise will not preclude the simultaneous or later exercise by landlord of any or all other rights or remedies provided for in this lease or now or after the lease date existing at law or in equity or by statute or otherwise. All costs incurred by landlord in collecting any amounts and damages owing by tenant pursuant to the provisions of this lease or to enforce any provision of this lease, including reasonable attorneys' fees from the date any such matter is turned over to an attorney, whether or not one or more actions are commenced by landlord, will also be recoverable by landlord from tenant.

25.6 Waiver of Redemption. Tenant waives any right of redemption arising as a result of landlord's exercise of its remedies under this Article 25.

ARTICLE 26   PARKING

Tenant will be entitled to use the parking spaces during the term subject to the rules and regulations set forth in Exhibit D, and any amendments or additions to them. The parking charges set forth in Section 1.1(r), if any, will be due and payable in advance at the same time and place as monthly rent. The parking spaces will be unassigned, nonreserved, and nondesignated. Landlord reserves the right to adjust the parking charges in landlord's sole discretion at any time after 30 days' prior written notice.

ARTICLE 27   MISCELLANEOUS

27.1   No Offer. This lease is submitted to tenant on the understanding that it will not be considered an offer and will not bind landlord in any way until tenant has duly executed and delivered duplicate originals to landlord and landlord has executed and delivered one of such originals to tenant.

27.2   Joint and Several Liability. If tenant is composed of more than one signatory to this lease, each signatory will be jointly and severally liable with each other signatory for payment and performance according to this lease. The act of, written notice to, written notice from, refund to, or signature of any signatory to this lease (including without limitation modifications of this lease made by fewer than all such signatories) will bind every other signatory as though every other signatory had so acted, or received or given the written notice or refund, or signed.

27.3   No Construction Against Drafting Party. Landlord and tenant acknowledge that each of them and their counsel have had an opportunity to review this lease and that this lease will not be construed against landlord merely because landlord has prepared it.

27.4   Time of the Essence. Time is of the essence of each and every provision of this lease.

27.5   No Recordation. Tenant's recordation of this lease or any memorandum or short form of it will be void and a default under this lease.

27.6   No Waiver. The waiver by landlord of any agreement, condition, or provision contained in this lease will not be deemed to be a waiver of any subsequent breach of the same or any other agreement, condition, or provision contained in this lease, nor will any custom or practice that may grow up between the parties in the administration of the terms of this lease be construed to waive or to lessen the right of landlord to insist upon the performance by tenant in strict accordance with the terms of this lease. The subsequent acceptance of rent by landlord will not be deemed to be a waiver of any preceding breach by tenant of any agreement, condition, or provision of this lease, other than the failure of tenant to pay the particular rent so accepted, regardless of landlord's knowledge of such preceding breach at the time of acceptance of such rent.

27.7   Limitation on Recourse. Tenant specifically agrees to look solely to landlord's interest in the project for the recovery of any judgments from landlord. It is agreed that landlord (and its shareholders, venturers, and partners, and their shareholders, venturers, and partners and all of their officers, directors, and employees) will not be personally liable for any such judgments. The provisions contained in the preceding sentences are not intended to and will not limit any right that tenant might otherwise have to obtain injunctive relief against landlord or relief in any suit or action in connection with enforcement or collection of amounts that may become owing or payable under or on account of insurance maintained by landlord.

27.8   Estoppel Certificates. At any time and from time to time but within 10 days after prior written request by landlord, tenant will execute, acknowledge, and deliver to landlord, promptly upon request, a certificate certifying (a) that this lease is unmodified and in full force and effect or, if there have been modifications, that this lease is in full force and effect, as modified, and stating the date and nature of each modification; (b) the date, if any, to which rent and other sums payable under this lease have been paid; (c) that no written notice of any default has been delivered to landlord which default has not been cured, except as to defaults specified in said certificate; (d) that there is no event of default under this lease or an event which, with notice or the passage of time, or both, would result in an event of default under this lease, except for defaults specified in said certificate; and (e) such other matters as may be reasonably requested by landlord. Any such certificate may be relied upon by any prospective purchaser or existing or prospective mortgagee or beneficiary under any deed of trust of the building or any part of the project. Tenant's failure to deliver such a certificate within such time will be conclusive evidence of the matters set forth in it.

27.9   Waiver of Jury Trial. Landlord and tenant by this Section 27.9 waive trial by jury in any action, proceeding, or counterclaim brought by either of the parties to this lease against the other on any matters whatsoever arising out of or in any way connected with this lease, the relationship of landlord and tenant, tenant's use or occupancy of the premises, or any other claims (except claims for personal injury or property damage), and any emergency statutory or any other statutory remedy.

27.10   No Merger. The voluntary or other surrender of this lease by tenant or the cancellation of this lease by mutual agreement of tenant and landlord or the termination of this lease on account of tenant's default will not work a merger, and will, at landlord's option, (a) terminate all or any subleases and subtenancies or (b) operate as an assignment to landlord of all or any subleases or subtenancies. Landlord's option under this Section 27.10 will be exercised by written notice to tenant and all known sublessees or subtenants in the premises or any part of the premises.

27.11   Holding Over. Tenant will have no right to remain in possession of all or any part of the premises after the expiration of the term. If tenant remains in possession of all or any part of the premises after the expiration of the term, with the express or implied consent of landlord: (a) such tenancy will be deemed to be a periodic tenancy from month-to-month only; (b) such tenancy will not constitute a renewal or extension of this lease for any further term; and (c) such tenancy may be terminated by landlord upon the earlier of 30 days' prior written notice or the earliest date permitted by law. In such event, monthly rent will be increased to an amount equal to 150% of the monthly rent payable during the last month of the term, and any other sums due under this lease will be payable in the amount and at the times specified in this lease. Such month-to-month tenancy will be subject to every other term, condition, and covenant contained in this lease.

27.12   Notices. Any notice, request, demand, consent, approval, or other communication required or permitted under this lease must be in writing and will be deemed to have been given when personally delivered, sent by facsimile with receipt acknowledged, deposited with any nationally recognized overnight carrier that routinely issues receipts, or deposited in any depository regularly maintained by the United States Postal Service, postage prepaid, certified mail, return receipt requested, addressed to the party for whom it is intended at its address set forth in Section 1.1. Either landlord or tenant may add additional addresses or change its address for purposes of receipt of any such communication by giving 10 days' prior written notice of such change to the other party in the manner prescribed in this Section 27.12.

27.13   Severability. If any provision of this lease proves to be illegal, invalid, or unenforceable, the remainder of this lease will not be affected by such finding, and in lieu of each provision of this lease that is illegal, invalid, or unenforceable a provision will be added as a part of this lease as similar in terms to such illegal, invalid, or unenforceable provision as may be possible and be legal, valid, and enforceable.

27.14   Written Amendment Required. No amendment, alteration, modification of, or addition to the lease will be valid or binding unless expressed in writing and signed by landlord and tenant. Tenant agrees to make any modifications of the terms and provisions of this lease required or requested by any lending institution providing financing for the building, or project, as the case may be, provided that no such modifications will materially adversely affect tenant's rights and obligations under this lease.

27.15   Entire Agreement. This lease, the exhibits and addenda, if any, contain the entire agreement between landlord and tenant. No promises or representations, except as contained in this lease, have been made to tenant respecting the condition or the manner of operating the premises, the building, or the project.

27.16   Captions. The captions of the various articles and sections of this lease are for convenience only and do not necessarily define, limit, describe, or construe the contents of such articles or sections.

27.17   Notice of Landlord's Default. In the event of any alleged default in the obligation of landlord under this lease, tenant will deliver to landlord written notice listing the reasons for landlord's default and landlord will have 30 days following receipt of such notice to cure such alleged default or, in the event the alleged default cannot reasonably be cured within a 30-day period, to commence action and proceed diligently to cure such alleged default. A copy of such notice to landlord will be sent to any holder of a mortgage or other encumbrance on the building or project of which tenant has been notified in writing, and any such holder will also have the same time periods to cure such alleged default.

27.18   Authority. Tenant and the party executing this lease on behalf of tenant represent to landlord that such party is authorized to do so by requisite action of the board of directors or partners, as the case may be, and agree upon request to deliver to landlord a resolution or similar document to that effect.

27.19   Brokers. Landlord and tenant respectively represent and warrant to each other that neither of them has consulted or negotiated with any broker or finder with regard to the premises except the broker named in Section 1.1, if any. Each of them will indemnify the other against and hold the other harmless from any claims for fees or commissions from anyone with whom either of them has consulted or negotiated with regard to the premises except the broker. Landlord will pay any fees or commissions due the broker.

27.20   Governing Law. This lease will be governed by and construed pursuant to the laws of the state in which the project is located.

27.21   Late Payments. Any rent that is not paid when due will accrue interest at a late rate charge of the Prime Rate plus 5% per annum (but in no event in an amount in excess of the maximum rate allowed by applicable law) from the date on which it was due until the date on which it is paid in full with accrued interest.

27.22   No Easements for Air or Light. Any diminution or shutting off of light, air, or view by any structure that may be erected on lands adjacent to the building will in no way affect this lease or impose any liability on landlord.

27.23   Tax Credits. Landlord is entitled to claim all tax credits and depreciation attributable to leasehold improvements in the premises. Promptly after landlord's demand, landlord and tenant will prepare a detailed list of the leasehold improvements and fixtures and their respective costs for which landlord or tenant has paid. Landlord will be entitled to all credits and depreciation for those items for which landlord has paid by means of any tenant finish allowance or otherwise. Tenant will be entitled to any tax credits and depreciation for all items for which tenant has paid with funds not provided by landlord.

27.24   Relocation of the Premises. Landlord reserves the right to relocate the premises to substantially comparable space within the project, pursuant to this Section 27.24. Landlord will give tenant a written notice of its intention to relocate the premises, and tenant will complete such relocation within 60 days after receipt of such written notice. If the space to which landlord proposes to relocate tenant is not substantially comparable to the premises, tenant may so notify landlord, and if landlord fails to offer space satisfactory to tenant, tenant may terminate this lease effective as of the 30th day after the date of landlord's initial written notice. If tenant does relocate within the project, then effective on the date of such relocation this lease will be amended by deleting the description of the original premises and substituting for it a description of such comparable space. Landlord agrees to reimburse tenant for its actual reasonable moving costs to such other space within the project, the reasonable costs of reprinting stationery, and the costs of rewiring the new premises for telephone and computers comparably to the original premises.

27.25 Financial Reports. Within 15 days after landlord's request, tenant will furnish tenant's most recent audited financial statements (including any notes to them) to landlord, or, if no such audited statements have been prepared, such other financial statements (and notes to them) as may have been prepared by an independent certified public accountant or, failing those, tenant's internally prepared financial statements. Tenant will discuss its financial statements with landlord and will give landlord access to tenant's books and records in order to enable landlord to verify the financial statements. Landlord will not disclose any aspect of tenant's financial statements that tenant designates to landlord as confidential except (a) to landlord's lenders or prospective purchasers of the project, (b) in litigation between landlord and tenant, and (c) if required by court order.

27.26 Landlord's Fees. Whenever tenant requests landlord to take any action or give any consent required or permitted under this lease, tenant will reimburse landlord for all of landlord's reasonable costs incurred in reviewing the proposed action or consent, including without limitation reasonable attorneys', engineers' or architects' fees, within 10 days after landlord's delivery to tenant of a statement of such costs. Tenant will be obligated to make such reimbursement without regard to whether landlord consents to any such proposed action.

27.27 Binding Effect. The covenants, conditions, and agreements contained in this lease will bind and inure to the benefit of landlord and tenant and their respective heirs, distributees, executors, administrators, successors, and, except as otherwise provided in this lease, their assigns.

Landlord and tenant have executed this lease as of the day and year first above written.

LANDLORD:
[name]

By [name]
Its [position]

TENANT:
[name]

[corporate seal]
ATTEST:

By [name]

By [name]
Its [position]

Its Secretary

STATE OF [state]   )
) ss.
COUNTY OF [county]   )

The foregoing instrument was acknowledged before me on [date], 19[00], by [name], as [position] of [landlord], a [entity].
Witness my hand and official seal.

                                                  [name]
                                                  Notary Public

My commission expires [date]

STATE OF [state]   )

) ss.

COUNTY OF [county]   )

The foregoing instrument was acknowledged before me on [date], 19[00], by [name], as [position] of [tenant], a [entity].
Witness my hand and official seal.

                                                  [name]
                                                  Notary Public

My commission expires [date]

EXHIBIT A
The Premises

EXHIBIT B
Legal Description of the Land

EXHIBIT C
Workletter

This workletter is dated [date], 19[00], between [name] ("landlord") and [name] ("tenant").

RECITALS

A.   This workletter is attached to and forms a part of that certain office lease dated [date], 19[00] ("lease"), pursuant to which landlord has leased to tenant office space in the building to be known as [* * *].

B.   Landlord desires to make certain improvements to the premises, and tenant desires to have landlord make such initial improvements, prior to occupancy, upon the terms and conditions contained in this workletter.

1.   Definitions. In this workletter, some defined terms are used. They are:

(a)   Tenant's Representative: [name].

(b)   Landlord's Representative: [name].

(c)   Tenant Finish Allowance: $[amount] per usable square foot (non-cash), which equals $[amount] and is to be applied by landlord to the cost of the improvements.

(d)   Programming Information: Information provided by tenant, including the nature of the tenant's business, manner of operation, number and types of rooms, special equipment and functional requirements, anticipated growth, interactions among groups, and any other programming requirements the tenant may have.

(e)   Programming Information Submission Date: The date tenant will submit to landlord the information necessary for the preparation of the space plan.

(f)   Final Space Plan: A drawing of the premises clearly showing the layout and relationship of all departments and offices, depicting partitions, door locations, types of electrical/data/telephone outlets, and delineation of furniture and equipment.

(g)   Estimated Construction Costs: A preliminary estimate of the costs of the improvements that are depicted on the space plan, including all architectural, engineering, contractor, and any other costs as can be determined from the space plan.

(h)   Working Drawings: Construction documents detailing the improvements and conforming to codes, complete in form and content and containing sufficient information and detail to allow for competitive bidding or negotiated pricing by contractor(s) selected and engaged by landlord.

(i)   Construction Schedule: A schedule depicting the relative time frames for various activities related to the construction of the improvements in the premises.

(j)   Tenant Cost Proposal: A final estimate of costs of the improvements that are depicted on the working drawings, including all architectural, engineering, contractor, and any other costs, and clearly indicating the dollar amount, if any, that is to be paid by tenant pursuant to paragraph 7.

(k) Maximum Approved Cost: The sum of the tenant finish allowance and any additional amount that tenant has agreed to pay for the improvements to the premises.

(l) Improvements: The work is inclusive of the following:

(1) The development of space plans and working drawings, including supporting engineering studies (i.e., structural design or analysis, lighting or acoustical evaluations, or others as determined by landlord's architect);

(2) All construction work necessary to augment the base building, creating the details and partitioning shown on the space plan. The work will create finished ceilings, walls, and floor surfaces, as well as complete HVAC, lighting, electrical, and fire protection systems.

The improvements will NOT include personal property items, such as decorator items or services, artwork, plants, furniture, equipment, or other fixtures not permanently affixed to the premises.

(m) Cost of the Improvements: The cost includes but is not limited to the following:

(1) All architectural and engineering fees and expenses;

(2) All contractor and construction manager costs and fees;

(3) All permits and taxes;

(4) A coordination and administration fee to landlord, pursuant to paragraph 4(d).

(n) Change Order: Any change, modification, or addition to the space plan or working drawings after tenant has approved the same.

(o) Base Building: Those elements of the core and shell construction that are completed in preparation for the improvements to the premises. This includes building structure, envelope, and systems as indicated on Schedule 1, "base building definition," attached hereto. This defines the existing conditions to which improvements are added.

(p) Building Standard: Component elements utilized in the design and construction of the improvements that have been pre-selected by the landlord to ensure uniformity of quality, function, and appearance throughout the building. These elements include but are not limited to ceiling systems, doors, hardware, walls, floor coverings, finishes, window coverings, light fixtures, and HVAC components. A list of building standard elements is attached hereto as Schedule 2.

2. Representatives. Landlord appoints landlord's representative to act for landlord in all matters associated with this workletter. Tenant appoints tenant's representative to act for tenant in all matters associated with this workletter. All inquiries, requests, instructions, authorizations, and other communications with respect to the matters covered by this workletter will be made to landlord's representative or tenant's representative, as the case

may be. Tenant will not make any inquiries of or requests to, and will not give any instructions or authorizations to, any employee or agent of landlord, including, without limitation, landlord's architect, engineers, and contractors or any of their agents or employees, with regard to matters associated with this workletter. Either party may change its representative under this workletter at any time by providing 3 days' prior written notice to the other party.

3.   Project Design and Construction. All work will be performed by designers and contractors selected and engaged by landlord.

4.   Cost Responsibilities.

(a)   Landlord: Landlord will pay up to the amount of the tenant finish allowance for the cost of the improvements.

(b)   Tenant: Tenant will pay for:

(1)   Tenant-initiated changes to the space plan or working drawings after tenant's approval;

(2)   Tenant-initiated change orders, modifications, or additions to the improvements after tenant's approval of the working drawings;

(3)   All costs in excess of the tenant finish allowance that are not included in (1) or (2) immediately above;

(4)   The cost of the landlord's overhead for coordination and administration at a rate of 15% of the total cost to the landlord of clauses (1), (2), and (3) above.

(5)   Tenant will not be entitled to any credit for any portion of the tenant finish allowance which is not used.

5.   Landlord's Approval. Landlord, in its sole discretion, may withhold its approval of any space plan, working drawings, or change order that:

(a)   Exceeds or adversely affects the structural integrity of the building, or any part of the heating, ventilating, air conditioning, plumbing, mechanical, electrical, communication, or other systems of the building;

(b)   Is not approved by the holder of any mortgage or deed of trust encumbering the building at the time the work is proposed;

(c)   Would not be approved by a prudent owner of property similar to the building;

(d)   Violates any agreement which affects the building or binds the landlord;

(e)   Landlord reasonably believes will increase the cost of operation or maintenance of any of the systems of the building;

(f)   Landlord reasonably believes will reduce the market value of the premises or the building at the end of the term;

(g)   Does not conform to applicable building code or is not approved by any governmental, quasi-governmental, or utility authority with jurisdiction over the premises; or

(h)   Does not conform to the building standard.

6.　Schedule of Improvement Activities.

(a)　On or before the programming information submission date, tenant will cooperate with and submit to landlord the programming information necessary for landlord's architect to prepare the proposed space plan.

(b)　Landlord's architect will expeditiously prepare a space plan and forward it to tenant. Tenant will give landlord written notice whether or not tenant approves the proposed space plan within 5 days after its receipt. If tenant's notice objects to the proposed space plan, the notice will set forth how the proposed space plan is inconsistent with the programming information and how the proposed space plan must be changed in order to overcome tenant's objections. Landlord will resubmit a revised space plan to tenant and it will be treated as though it was the first proposed space plan prepared pursuant to this paragraph.

(c)　After tenant approval of the space plan (the "final space plan"), landlord will promptly cause to be prepared, a preliminary estimate of the cost of the improvements as set forth in the final space plan (the "estimated construction cost"). If the estimated construction cost is less than the tenant finish allowance, the estimated construction cost will be deemed approved without a required response from the tenant. If the estimated construction cost is more than the tenant finish allowance, landlord will so notify tenant in writing and tenant will establish the maximum approved cost by either:

(1)　Agreeing in writing to pay the amount by which the estimated construction cost exceeds the tenant finish allowance; or

(2)　Agreeing to have the final space plan revised by landlord's architect in order to assure that the estimated construction cost is either:

(A)　No more than the tenant finish allowance; or

(B)　Exceeds the tenant finish allowance by an amount which tenant agrees to pay pursuant to clause (1) immediately above.

Landlord expects tenant to give immediate attention to establishing the maximum approved cost and by responding to landlord within 2 business days. Upon tenant's timely fulfillment of its obligations in either clause (1) or clause (2) immediately above, the maximum approved cost will be established.

(d)　Upon establishment of the maximum approved cost, landlord will cause to be prepared and delivered to tenant the working drawings, the construction schedule, and the tenant cost proposal for the improvements in accordance with the final space plan. If the tenant cost proposal is less than the maximum approved cost, landlord will take steps necessary to commence construction of the improvements to the premises.

If the tenant cost proposal is more than the maximum approved cost, landlord will so notify tenant in writing and tenant will either (1) agree in writing to pay the amount by which the tenant cost proposal exceeds the maximum approved cost or (2) request landlord to revise the working drawings in order to assure that the tenant cost proposal is no more than the maximum approved cost.

Landlord expects tenant to give immediate attention to the cost proposal approval process and to respond to landlord within 3 business days.

(e) Following approval of the working drawings and the tenant cost proposal, landlord will cause application to be made to the appropriate governmental authorities for necessary approvals and building permits. Upon receipt of the necessary approvals and permits, landlord will begin construction of the improvements.

7.   Payment by Tenant. The amount payable by tenant will be billed periodically, as the work proceeds, and tenant agrees to pay the same within 15 business days following delivery of each such invoice.

8.   Change Orders. Tenant may authorize changes to the improvements during construction only by written instructions to landlord's representative on a form approved by landlord. All such changes will be subject to landlord's prior written approval in accordance with paragraph 5. Prior to commencing any change, landlord will prepare and deliver to tenant, for tenant's approval, a change order setting forth the total cost of such change, which will include associated architectural, engineering, construction contractor's costs and fees, completion schedule changes, and the cost of landlord's overhead. If tenant fails to approve such change order within 5 business days after delivery by landlord, tenant will be deemed to have withdrawn the proposed change and landlord will not proceed to perform the change. Upon landlord's receipt of tenant's approval, landlord will proceed with the change.

9.   Completion and Commencement Date. Tenant's obligation for payment of rent pursuant to the lease will commence on the commencement date; however, the commencement date and the date for the payment of rent may be delayed on a day-by-day basis for each day the substantial completion of the improvements are delayed by landlord or its contractors or agents. The payment of rent will not be delayed by a delay of substantial completion due to tenant. The following are some examples of delays which will not affect the commencement date and the date rent is to commence under the lease:

(a)   Late submissions of programming information;

(b)   Change orders requested by tenant;

(c)   Delays in obtaining non-building standard construction materials requested by tenant;

(d)   Tenant's failure to approve timely any item requiring tenant's approval; and

(e)   Delays by tenant according to paragraph 6.

In the event that substantial completion of the improvements is delayed by landlord, its contractors, or agents, the commencement date will be the date of substantial completion of the improvements, subject only to the completion of landlord's punch-list items (that is, those items that do not materially interfere with tenant's use and enjoyment of the premises). Landlord and tenant will confirm the commencement date in accordance with Section 3.1 of the lease.

10. Condition of the Premises.

(a) Prior to the commencement date, tenant will conduct a walk-through inspection of the premises with landlord and prepare a punch-list of items needing additional work by landlord. Other than the items specified in the punch-list and "latent defects" (as defined below), by taking possession of the premises tenant will be deemed to have accepted the premises in their condition on the date of delivery of possession and to have acknowledged that landlord has installed the improvements as required by this workletter and that there are no items needing additional work or repair. The punch-list will not include any damage to the premises caused by tenant's move-in or early access, if permitted. Damage caused by tenant will be repaired or corrected by landlord at tenant's expense. Tenant acknowledges that neither landlord nor its agents or employees have made any representations or warranties as to the suitability or fitness of the premises for the conduct of tenant's business or for any other purpose, nor has landlord or its agents or employees agreed to undertake any alterations or construct any tenant improvements to the premises except as expressly provided in this lease and this workletter. If tenant fails to submit a punch-list to landlord prior to the commencement date, it will be deemed that there are no items needing additional work or repair. Landlord's contractor will complete all reasonable punch-list items within 30 days after the walk-through inspection or as soon as practicable after such walk-through.

(b) A "latent defect" is a defect in the condition of the premises caused by landlord's failure to construct the improvements in a good and workmanlike manner and in accordance with the working drawings, which defect would not ordinarily be observed during a walk-through inspection. If tenant notifies landlord of a latent defect within one year following the commencement date, then landlord, at its expense, will repair such latent defect as soon as practicable. Except as set forth in this paragraph 10, landlord will have no obligation or liability to tenant for latent defects.

11. Adjustments Upon Completion. As soon as practicable, upon completion of the improvements in accordance with this workletter, landlord will notify tenant of the rentable area of the premises, the rentable area of the building, monthly rent, and tenant's share, if such information was not previously determinable by landlord. Tenant, within 10 days of landlord's written request, will execute a certificate confirming such information.

EXHIBIT D
RULES AND REGULATIONS

1. Landlord may from time to time adopt appropriate systems and procedures for the security or safety of the building, any persons occupying, using, or entering the building, or any equipment, finishings, or contents of the building, and tenant will comply with landlord's reasonable requirements relative to such systems and procedures.

2. The sidewalks, halls, passages, exits, entrances, elevators, and stairways of the building will not be obstructed by any tenants or used by any of them for any purpose other than for ingress to and egress from their respective premises. The halls, passages, exits, entrances, elevators, escalators, and stairways are not for the general public, and landlord will in all cases retain the right to control and prevent access to such halls, passages, exits, entrances, elevators, and stairways of all persons whose presence in the judgment of landlord would be prejudicial to the safety, character, reputation, and interests of the building and its tenants, provided that nothing contained in these rules and regulations will be construed to prevent such access to persons with whom any tenant normally deals in the ordinary course of its business, unless such persons are engaged in illegal activities. No tenant and no employee or invitee of any tenant will go upon the roof of the building except such roof or portion of such roof as may be contiguous to the premises of a particular tenant and may be designated in writing by landlord as a roof deck or roof garden area. No tenant will be permitted to place or install any object (including without limitation radio and television antennas, loudspeakers, sound amplifiers, microwave dishes, solar devices, or similar devices) on the exterior of the building or on the roof of the building.

3. No sign, placard, picture, name, advertisement, or written notice visible from the exterior of tenant's premises will be inscribed, painted, affixed, or otherwise displayed by tenant on any part of the building or the premises without the prior written consent of landlord. Landlord will adopt and furnish to tenant general guidelines relating to signs inside the building on the office floors. Tenant agrees to conform to such guidelines. All approved signs or lettering on doors will be printed, painted, affixed, or inscribed at the expense of the tenant by a person approved by landlord. Other than draperies expressly permitted by landlord and building standard mini-blinds, material visible from outside the building will not be permitted. In the event of the violation of this rule by tenant, landlord may remove the violating items without any liability, and may charge the expense incurred by such removal to the tenant or tenants violating this rule.

4. No cooking will be done or permitted by any tenant on the premises, except in areas of the premises which are specially constructed for cooking and except that use by the tenant of microwave ovens and Underwriters' Laboratory approved equipment for brewing coffee, tea, hot chocolate, and similar beverages will be permitted, provided that such use is in accordance with all applicable federal, state, and city laws, codes, ordinances, rules, and regulations.

5. No tenant will employ any person or persons other than the cleaning service of landlord for the purpose of cleaning the premises, unless otherwise agreed to by landlord in writing. Except with the written consent of landlord, no person or persons other than those approved by landlord will be permitted to enter the building for the purpose of cleaning it. No tenant will cause any unnecessary labor by reason of such tenant's carelessness or indifference in the preservation of good order and cleanliness. Should tenant's actions result in any increased expense for any required cleaning, landlord reserves the right to assess tenant for such expenses.

6. The toilet rooms, toilets, urinals, wash bowls and other plumbing fixtures will not be used for any purposes other than those for which they were constructed, and no sweepings, rubbish, rags, or other foreign substances will be thrown in such plumbing fixtures. All damages resulting from any misuse of the fixtures will be borne by the tenant who, or whose servants, employees, agents, visitors, or licensees, caused the same.

7. No tenant will in any way deface any part of the premises or the building of which they form a part. In those portions of the premises where carpet has been provided directly or indirectly by landlord, tenant will at its own expense install and maintain pads to protect the carpet under all furniture having casters other than carpet casters.

8. No tenant will alter, change, replace, or rekey any lock or install a new lock or a knocker on any door of the premises. Landlord, its agents, or employees will retain a pass (master) key to all door locks on the premises. Any new door locks required by tenant or any change in keying of existing locks will be installed or changed by landlord following tenant's written request to landlord and will be at tenant's expense. All new locks and rekeyed locks will remain operable by landlord's pass (master) key. Landlord will furnish each tenant, free of charge, with two (2) keys to each door lock on the premises and two (2) building/area access cards. Landlord will have the right to collect a reasonable charge for additional keys and cards requested by any tenant. Each tenant, upon termination of its tenancy, will deliver to landlord all keys and access cards for the premises and building that have been furnished to such tenant.

9. The elevator designated for freight by landlord will be available for use by all tenants in the building during the hours and pursuant to such procedures as landlord may determine from time to time. The persons employed to move tenant's equipment, material, furniture, or other property in or out of the building must be acceptable to landlord. The moving company must be a locally recognized professional mover, whose primary business is the performing of relocation services, and must be bonded and fully insured. A certificate or other verification of such insurance must be received and approved by landlord prior to the start of any moving operations. Insurance must be sufficient, in landlord's sole opinion, to cover all personal liability, theft or damage to the project, including but not limited to floor coverings, doors, walls, elevators, stairs, foliage, and landscaping. Special care must be taken to prevent damage to foliage and landscaping during adverse weather. All moving operations will

be conducted at such times and in such a manner as landlord will direct, and all moving will take place during non-business hours unless landlord agrees in writing otherwise. Tenant will be responsible for the provision of building security during all moving operations, and will be liable for all losses and damages sustained by any party as a result of the failure to supply adequate security. Landlord will have the right to prescribe the weight, size, and position of all equipment, materials, furniture, or other property brought into the building. Heavy objects will, if considered necessary by landlord, stand on wood strips of such thickness as is necessary to properly distribute the weight. Landlord will not be responsible for loss of or damage to any such property from any cause, and all damage done to the building by moving or maintaining such property will be repaired at the expense of tenant. Landlord reserves the right to inspect all such property to be brought into the building and to exclude from the building all such property which violates any of these rules and regulations or the lease of which these rules and regulations are a part. Supplies, goods, materials, packages, furniture, and all other items of every kind delivered to or taken from the premises will be delivered or removed through the entrance and route designated by landlord, and landlord will not be responsible for the loss or damage of any such property unless such loss or damage results from the negligence of landlord, its agents, or employees.

10. No tenant will use or keep in the premises or the building any kerosene, gasoline, or inflammable or combustible or explosive fluid or material or chemical substance other than limited quantities of such materials or substances reasonably necessary for the operation or maintenance of office equipment or limited quantities of cleaning fluids and solvents required in tenant's normal operations in the premises. Without landlord's prior written approval, no tenant will use any method of heating or air conditioning other than that supplied by landlord. No tenant will use or keep or permit to be used or kept any foul or noxious gas or substance in the premises.

11. Landlord will have the right, exercisable upon written notice and without liability to any tenant, to change the name and street address of the building.

12. Landlord will have the right to prohibit any advertising by tenant mentioning the building that, in landlord's reasonable opinion, tends to impair the reputation of the building or its desirability as a building for offices, and upon written notice from landlord, tenant will refrain from or discontinue such advertising.

13. Tenant will not bring any animals (except "Seeing Eye" dogs) or birds into the building, and will not permit bicycles or other vehicles inside or on the sidewalks outside the building except in areas designated from time to time by landlord for such purposes.

14. All persons entering or leaving the building between the hours of 6 p.m. and 7 a.m. Monday through Friday, and at all hours on Saturdays, Sundays, and holidays will comply with such off-hour regulations as landlord may establish and modify from time to time. Landlord reserves the right to limit reasonably or restrict access to the building during such time periods.

15. Each tenant will store all its trash and garbage within its premises. No material will be placed in the trash boxes or receptacles if such material is of such nature that it may not be disposed of in the ordinary and customary manner of removing and disposing of trash and garbage without being in violation of any law or ordinance governing such disposal. All garbage and refuse disposal will be made only through entryways and elevators provided for such purposes and at such times as landlord designates. Removal of any furniture or furnishings, large equipment, packing crates, packing materials, and boxes will be the responsibility of each tenant and such items may not be disposed of in the building trash receptacles nor will they be removed by the building's janitorial service, except at landlord's sole option and at the tenant's expense. No furniture, appliances, equipment, or flammable products of any type may be disposed of in the building trash receptacles.

16. Canvassing, peddling, soliciting, and distributing handbills or any other written materials in the building are prohibited, and each tenant will cooperate to prevent the same.

17. The requirements of the tenants will be attended to only upon application by written, personal, or telephone notice at the office of the building. Employees of landlord will not perform any work or do anything outside of their regular duties unless under special instructions from landlord.

18. A directory of the building will be provided for the display of the name and location of tenants only and such reasonable number of the principal officers and employees of tenants as landlord in its sole discretion approves, but landlord will not in any event be obligated to furnish more than one (1) directory strip for each 2,500 square feet of rentable area in the premises. Any additional name(s) that tenant desires to place in such directory must first be approved by landlord, and if so approved, tenant will pay to landlord a charge, set by landlord, for each such additional name. All entries on the building directory display will conform to standards and style set by landlord in its sole discretion. Space on any exterior signage will be provided in landlord's sole discretion. No tenant will have any right to the use of any exterior sign.

19. Tenant will see that the doors of the premises are closed and locked and that all water faucets, water apparatus, and utilities are shut off before tenant or tenant's employees leave the premises, so as to prevent waste or damage, and for any default or carelessness in this regard tenant will make good all injuries sustained by other tenants or occupants of the building or landlord. On multiple-tenancy floors, all tenants will keep the doors to the building corridors closed at all times except for ingress and egress.

20. Tenant will not conduct itself in any manner that is inconsistent with the character of the building as a first quality building or that will impair the comfort and convenience of other tenants in the building.

21. Neither landlord nor any operator of the parking areas within the project, as the same are designated and modified by landlord, in its sole discretion,

from time to time (the "parking areas") will be liable for loss of or damage to any vehicle or any contents of such vehicle or accessories to any such vehicle, or any property left in any of the parking areas, resulting from fire, theft, vandalism, accident, conduct of other users of the parking areas and other persons, or any other casualty or cause. Further, tenant understands and agrees that: (a) landlord will not be obligated to provide any traffic control, security protection or operator for the parking areas; (b) tenant uses the parking areas at its own risk; and (c) landlord will not be liable for personal injury or death, or theft, loss of, or damage to property. Tenant waives and releases landlord from any and all liability arising out of the use of the parking areas by tenant, its employees, agents, invitees, and visitors, whether brought by any of such persons or any other person.

22. Tenant (including tenant's employees, agents, invitees, and visitors) will use the parking spaces solely for the purpose of parking passenger model cars, small vans, and small trucks and will comply in all respects with any rules and regulations that may be promulgated by landlord from time to time with respect to the parking areas. The parking areas may be used by tenant, its agents, or employees, for occasional overnight parking of vehicles. Tenant will ensure that any vehicle parked in any of the parking spaces will be kept in proper repair and will not leak excessive amounts of oil or grease or any amount of gasoline. If any of the parking spaces are at any time used (a) for any purpose other than parking as provided above; (b) in any way or manner reasonably objectionable to landlord; or (c) by tenant after default by tenant under the lease, landlord, in addition to any other rights otherwise available to landlord, may consider such default an event of default under the lease.

23. Tenant's right to use the parking areas will be in common with other tenants of the project and with other parties permitted by landlord to use the parking areas. Landlord reserves the right to assign and reassign, from time to time, particular parking spaces for use by persons selected by landlord, provided that tenant's rights under the lease are preserved. Landlord will not be liable to tenant for any unavailability of tenant's designated spaces, if any, nor will any unavailability entitle tenant to any refund, deduction, or allowance. Tenant will not park in any numbered space or any space designated as: RESERVED, HANDICAPPED, VISITORS ONLY, or LIMITED TIME PARKING (or similar designation).

24. If the parking areas are damaged or destroyed, or if the use of the parking areas is limited or prohibited by any governmental authority, or the use or operation of the parking areas is limited or prevented by strikes or other labor difficulties or other causes beyond landlord's control, tenant's inability to use the parking spaces will not subject landlord or any operator of the parking areas to any liability to tenant and will not relieve tenant of any of its obligations under the lease and the lease will remain in full force and effect.

25. Tenant has no right to assign or sublicense any of its rights in the parking spaces, except as part of a permitted assignment or sublease of the lease; however, tenant may allocate the parking spaces among its employees.

26. No act or thing done or omitted to be done by landlord or landlord's agent during the term of the lease in connection with the enforcement of these rules and regulations will constitute an eviction by landlord of any tenant nor will it be deemed an acceptance of surrender of the premises by any tenant, and no agreement to accept such termination or surrender will be valid unless in a writing signed by landlord. The delivery of keys to any employee or agent of landlord will not operate as a termination of the lease or a surrender of the premises unless such delivery of keys is done in connection with a written instrument executed by landlord approving the termination or surrender.

27. In these rules and regulations, tenant includes the employees, agents, invitees, and licensees of tenant and others permitted by tenant to use or occupy the premises.

28. Landlord may waive any one or more of these rules and regulations for the benefit of any particular tenant or tenants, but no such waiver by landlord will be construed as a waiver of such rules and regulations in favor of any other tenant or tenants, nor prevent landlord from enforcing any such rules and regulations against any or all of the tenants of the building after such waiver.

29. These rules and regulations are in addition to, and will not be construed to modify or amend, in whole or in part, the terms, covenants, agreements, and conditions of the lease.

EXHIBIT E
COMMENCEMENT DATE CERTIFICATE

This commencement date certificate is entered into by landlord and tenant pursuant to Section 3.1 of the lease.

1.   DEFINITIONS. In this certificate the following terms have the meanings given to them:

(a)   Landlord: [name]

(b)   Tenant: [name]

(c)   Lease: Office lease dated [date] between landlord and tenant.

(d)   Premises: Suite [number].

(e)   Building Address: [address]

2.   CONFIRMATION OF LEASE COMMENCEMENT: Landlord and tenant confirm that the commencement date of the lease is [date] and the expiration date is [date] and that Sections 1.1(k) and (l) are accordingly amended.

Landlord and tenant have executed this commencement date certificate as of the dates set forth below.

TENANT: LANDLORD:

[name]   [name]

By [name]   By [name]

Its [position]   Its [position]

Date [date]   Date [date]

§ 1.2 Shopping Center Lease

SHOPPING CENTER LEASE

between

[landlord's name]

and

[tenant's name]

Date: [date], 19[00]

Shopping Center Lease
Table of Contents

Article 1 Basic Lease Information
Article 2 Agreement
Article 3 Term, Delivery, and Acceptance of Premises
    3.1 General
    3.2 Failure to Deliver Possession
    3.3 Early Access
    3.4 Condition of the Premises
Article 4 Monthly Base Rent
    4.1 General
    4.2 Annual Monthly Base Rent Adjustment
Article 5 Common Area Operating Expenses
    5.1 General
    5.2 Estimated Payments
    5.3 Annual Settlement
    5.4 Proration Upon Termination
    5.5 Other Taxes
    5.6 Additional Rent
Article 6 Insurance
    6.1 Landlord's Insurance
    6.2 Tenant's Insurance
    6.3 Forms of Policies
    6.4 Waiver of Subrogation
    6.5 Adequacy of Coverage
Article 7 Utilities
Article 8 Use, Operation of Business, Financial Statements
    8.1 Use—General
    8.2 Operation of Tenant's Business
    8.3 Manner of Conducting Business
    8.4 Financial Statements
Article 9 Requirements of Law, Fire Insurance
    9.1 General
    9.2 Toxic Materials

9.3 Certain Insurance Risks
9.4 Tenant's Insurance Payments
Article 10 Assignment and Subletting
10.1 General
10.2 Limitation on Remedies
Article 11 Common Areas
Article 12 Landlord's Services
12.1 Landlord's Repair and Maintenance
12.2 Landlord's Other Services
12.3 Limitation on Liability
12.4 Grand Opening Fund
12.5 Promotional Fund
Article 13 Tenant's Repairs
Article 14 Alterations
Article 15 Mechanics' Liens
Article 16 End of Term
Article 17 Eminent Domain
Article 18 Damage and Destruction
Article 19 Subordination
19.1 General
19.2 Attornment
Article 20 Entry by Landlord
Article 21 Indemnification, Waiver, and Release
21.1 Indemnification
21.2 Waiver and Release
Article 22 Security Deposit
Article 23 Quiet Enjoyment
Article 24 Effect of Sale
Article 25 Default
25.1 Events of Default
25.2 Landlord's Remedies
25.3 Certain Damages
25.4 Continuing Liability After Termination
25.5 Cumulative Remedies
Article 26 Rules and Regulations
Article 27 Signs
Article 28 Miscellaneous
28.1 No Offer
28.2 Joint and Several Liability
28.3 No Construction Against Drafting Party
28.4 Time of the Essence
28.5 No Recordation
28.6 No Waiver
28.7 Limitation on Recourse
28.8 Estoppel Certificates
28.9 Waiver of Jury Trial
28.10 No Merger

28.11 Holding Over
28.12 Notices
28.13 Severability
28.14 Written Amendment Required
28.15 Entire Agreement
28.16 Captions
28.17 Notice of Landlord's Default
28.18 Authority
28.19 Brokers
28.20 Governing Law
28.21 Force Majeure
28.22 Late Payments
28.23 No Easements for Air or Light
28.24 Tax Credits
28.25 Relocation of the Premises
28.26 Landlord's Fees
28.27 Binding Effect
Exhibit A: Legal Description of the Shopping Center
Exhibit B: The Premises
Exhibit C: Workletter
Exhibit D: Rules and Regulations
Exhibit E: Sign Criteria

SHOPPING CENTER LEASE

THIS SHOPPING CENTER LEASE is entered into by landlord and tenant described in the following basic lease information on the date that is set forth for reference only in the following basic lease information.

Landlord and tenant agree:

ARTICLE 1   BASIC LEASE INFORMATION

In addition to the terms which are defined elsewhere in this lease, the following defined terms are used in this lease:

(a)   LEASE DATE: [date].

(b)   TENANT: [name].

(c)   TENANT'S TRADE NAME: [trade name].

(d)   TENANT'S ADDRESS: [address]
with a copy at the
same time to:
(if none, so state) [* * *]

(e)   LANDLORD: [name].

(f) LANDLORD'S ADDRESS: [address]
with a copy at the
same time to:
(if none, so state) [* * *]

(g) SHOPPING CENTER ADDRESS: [address]

(h) COMMENCEMENT DATE: [date], or as extended pursuant to Section 3.02.

(i) EXPIRATION DATE: [date].

(j) SECURITY DEPOSIT: $[amount].

(k) FIRST MONTH'S MONTHLY BASE RENT: $[amount].

(l) MONTHLY BASE RENT: [amount] per month commencing on the commencement date, subject to adjustment annually in accordance with Section 4.02.

(m) LEASABLE AREA OF THE PREMISES: [number] square feet.

(n) LEASABLE AREA OF THE SHOPPING CENTER: [number] square feet.

(o) TENANT'S PRO RATA SHARE (of (n) above): [number] % (determined from time to time by landlord, by dividing the leasable area of the premises by the leasable area of the shopping center and multiplying the resulting quotient (to the second decimal place) by one hundred).

(p) USE PERMITTED: [* * *].

(q) MINIMUM BUSINESS HOURS:
Monday–Friday 10:00 a.m. to 9:00 p.m.
Saturday 10:00 a.m. to 5:00 p.m.
Sunday 12:00 p.m. to 5:00 p.m.

(r) BROKER:
(if none, so state) [* * *]

(s) GUARANTOR:
(if none, so state) [* * *]

(t) ADDITIONAL RENT: any amounts, including without limitation operating expenses that this lease requires tenant to pay in addition to monthly base rent.

(u) LAND: the land on which the shopping center is located and which is more particularly described on Exhibit A to this lease.

(v)   PREMISES: the premises shown on Exhibit B to this lease and known as Unit [number], [name] Shopping Center. The area of the premises and the shopping center will be determined by landlord and will be conclusive in the absence of fraud or manifest error. The premises do not include, and landlord reserves, the exterior walls and roof of the premises, the land beneath the premises, the pipes and ducts, conduits, wires, fixtures, and equipment above the suspended ceiling or structural elements that serve the premises or the shopping center; however, landlord has the right to enter the premises in order to install, inspect, maintain, use, repair, and replace those areas and items described in the preceding sentence.

(w)   SHOPPING CENTER: the shopping center consisting of the land and all improvements built on the land, including without limitation the parking lot, parking structure (if any), walkways, driveways, fences, and landscaping.

(x)   RENT: the monthly base rent and additional rent.

These exhibits are attached to this lease and are made parts of this lease:

    EXHIBIT A—Legal Description of the Shopping Center
    EXHIBIT B—The Premises
    EXHIBIT C—Workletter
    EXHIBIT D—Rules and Regulations
    EXHIBIT E—Sign Criteria

ARTICLE 2   AGREEMENT

Landlord leases the premises to tenant, and tenant leases the premises from landlord, according to this lease.

ARTICLE 3   TERM, DELIVERY, AND ACCEPTANCE OF PREMISES

3.1   General. The duration of this lease will be the "term." The term will commence on the commencement date and will expire on the expiration date.

3.2   Failure to Deliver Possession. If for any reason landlord cannot deliver possession of the premises to tenant on the commencement date, (a) this lease will not be void or voidable, (b) landlord will not be liable to tenant for any resultant loss or damage, and (c) unless landlord is unable to deliver possession of the premises to tenant on the commencement date because of tenant's delays, rent will be waived for the period between the commencement date and the date on which landlord delivers possession of the premises to tenant. If delivery of possession of the premises is delayed beyond the commencement date and tenant is not responsible for delays in completion of the premises, (i) the commencement date will be extended automatically, one day for each day after the commencement date and before delivery of possession; and (ii) landlord and tenant will execute a certificate of the commencement date. Landlord will construct or install in the premises the improvements to be constructed or installed by landlord according to Exhibit C. Landlord will be deemed to have delivered possession of the premises to tenant on the tenth (10th) day after landlord gives tenant written notice either that landlord has substantially completed the improvements or that landlord will have substantially completed the improvements within ten (10) days after such notice, in either case subject only to the completion of landlord's "punch-list" items which do not materially interfere with tenant's use and enjoyment of the premises.

3.3 Early Access. If tenant is permitted access to the premises prior to the commencement date for the purpose of installing fixtures or any other purpose permitted by landlord, such early entry will be at tenant's sole risk and subject to all the terms and provisions of this lease as though the commencement date had occurred, except for the payment of monthly base rent, which will commence on the commencement date. Tenant, its agents, or employees will not interfere with or delay landlord's completion of construction of the improvements and all rights of tenant under this Section 3.3 will be subject to the requirements of all applicable building codes and zoning requirements so as not to interfere with landlord's obtaining a certificate of occupancy for the premises. Landlord may impose such additional conditions on tenant's early entry as landlord, in its sole discretion, deems appropriate, and will further have the right to require that tenant execute an early entry agreement containing such conditions prior to tenant's early entry.

3.4 Condition of the Premises. Prior to the commencement date, tenant will conduct a walk-through inspection of the premises with landlord and prepare a punch-list of items needing additional work by landlord. Other than the items specified in the punch-list, by taking possession of the premises tenant will be deemed to have accepted the premises in their condition on the date of delivery of possession. The punch-list will not include any damage to the premises caused by tenant's move-in or early access, if permitted. Damage caused by tenant will be repaired or corrected by landlord, at tenant's expense. Tenant acknowledges that neither landlord nor its agents or employees have made any representations or warranties as to the suitability or fitness of the premises for the conduct of tenant's business or for any other purpose, nor has landlord or its agents or employees agreed to undertake any alterations or construct any improvements to the premises except as expressly provided in this lease and Exhibit C to this lease. If tenant fails to submit a punch-list to landlord prior to the commencement date, it will be deemed that there are no items needing additional work or repair. Landlord's contractor will complete all reasonable punch-list items within thirty (30) days after the walk-through inspection or as soon as practicable after such walk-through.

ARTICLE 4 MONTHLY BASE RENT

4.1 General. Throughout the term of this lease, tenant will pay monthly base rent to landlord as rent for the premises. Monthly base rent will be paid in advance on or before the first day of each calendar month of the term. If the term commences on a day other than the first day of a calendar month or ends on a day other than the last day of a calendar month, then monthly base rent will be appropriately prorated by landlord for such month. If the term commences on a day other than the first day of a calendar month, then the prorated monthly base rent for such month will be paid on or before the first day of the term. Monthly base rent will be paid to landlord, without notice or demand, and without deduction or offset, in lawful money of the United States of America at landlord's address, or to such other person or at such other place as landlord may from time to time designate in writing.

4.2   Annual Monthly Base Rent Adjustment. The monthly base rent will be increased on each January 1 during the term by the greater of (a) six percent (6%), or (b) the percentage increase in the price index as defined and determined according to the further provisions of this Section 4.2.

In this Section 4.2,

(i)   "Base year" means the full calendar year during which the term of this lease commences.

(ii)   "Lease year" means any full calendar year during the term after the base year.

(iii)   "Price index" means the Consumer Price Index published by the Bureau of Labor Statistics of the United States Department of Labor, Denver-Boulder, Colorado, All Items and Major Group Figures for Urban Wage Earners and Clerical Workers (1982–84 = 100).

(iv)   "Price index for a lease year" means the average of the price indexes for the months of such year during which the price index is published.

(A)   If the price index published nearest to or in December in any lease year during the term of this lease is greater than the price index for the preceding lease year, then the monthly base rent payable on January 1 of the succeeding lease year will be the sum of (1) the monthly base rent effective in that December, plus (2) the product of the percentage difference between the price index published nearest to or in December and the price index for the preceding lease year multiplied by the monthly base rent for that December. The adjusted monthly base rent will be payable until it is readjusted pursuant to the terms of this Section 4.2.

(B)   If a substantial change is made in the price index, then the price index will be adjusted to the figure that would have been used had the manner of computing the price index in effect at the date of this lease not been altered. If the price index (or a successor or substitute index) is not available, a reliable governmental or other nonpartisan publication evaluating the information used in determining the price index will be used. No adjustments will be made due to any revision that may be made in the price index for any month.

(C)   Statements of any adjustment on account of the price index, to be furnished by landlord under this Section 4.2, will consist of data prepared by landlord. The statements thus furnished to tenant will constitute a final determination as between landlord and tenant of the relevant adjustment.

The monthly base rent in Article 1(l) will not be reduced.

Landlord's delay or the failure of landlord, beyond January of any year, in computing or billing for these adjustments will not impair the continuing obligation of tenant to pay rent adjustments.

Tenant's obligation to pay rent as adjusted by this Section 4.2 will continue up to the expiration of this lease and will survive any earlier termination of this lease.

ARTICLE 5   COMMON AREA OPERATING EXPENSES

5.1   General. In addition to monthly base rent, tenant will pay tenant's pro rata share of the operating expenses paid, payable, or incurred by landlord according to an accrual method of accounting in each calendar year or partial calendar year during the term.

As used in this lease, the term "operating expenses" means:

(a)   all costs of management, operation, and maintenance of the shopping center (any of which may be furnished by an affiliate of landlord), including without limitation: cleaning, window washing, landscaping, lighting, heating, air conditioning, maintaining, painting, repairing, and replacing (except to the extent proceeds of insurance or condemnation awards are available) any common areas; maintaining, repairing, replacing, cleaning, lighting, removing snow and ice, painting, and landscaping of all vehicle parking areas and other outdoor common areas, including any shopping center pylon and sign; providing security; seasonal holiday decorations; removing trash from the common areas; providing public liability, property damage, fire, extended coverage, and such other insurance as landlord deems appropriate; total compensation and benefits (including premiums for workmen's compensation and other insurance) paid to or on behalf of employees; personal property taxes; supplies; fire protection and fire hydrant charges; steam, water, and sewer charges; gas, electricity, and telephone utility charges; licenses and permit fees; supplying music to the common areas; depreciation of equipment used in operating and maintaining the common areas and rent paid for leasing such equipment; real property taxes (and any tax levied in whole or in part in lieu of real property taxes); that part of office rent or rental value of space in the shopping center used by landlord to manage, operate, and maintain the shopping center; and any other costs, charges, and expenses that under generally accepted accounting principles would be regarded as maintenance and operating expenses; and ten percent (10%) of all costs and expenses included within the preceding provisions of paragraph (a); and

(b)   the cost (amortized over such reasonable period as landlord will determine) together with interest on the unamortized balance of any capital improvements (i) that are made to the shopping center by landlord during the term and that are intended to reduce other operating expenses, or (ii) that are made to the shopping center by landlord after the lease date and which are required under any governmental law or regulation that was not applicable to the shopping center at the time it was constructed and are not a result of tenant's unique use of the premises. The cost of any capital improvements which are required to be made to the shopping center after the lease date as a result of tenant's unique use of the premises will be made by landlord at tenant's sole cost and expense.

Operating expenses will not include depreciation on the shopping center (other than depreciation on personal property, equipment, window coverings on exterior windows provided by landlord, and carpeting in public corridors and common areas), costs of improvements made for other tenants of the shopping center, real estate brokers' commissions, mortgage interest, and capital items other than those referred to in clause (b).

5.2   Estimated Payments.   In addition to monthly base rent, tenant will pay to landlord in advance on the first day of each month during the term one-twelfth ($^1/_{12}$) of tenant's pro rata share of estimated operating expenses paid, payable, or incurred during the subject calendar year or partial calendar year (the "estimated operating expenses"). The estimated operating expenses are subject to revision according to the further provisions of this Section 5.2 and Section 5.3. During December of each calendar year or as soon after December as practicable, landlord will give tenant written notice of landlord's reasonable estimate of the amounts payable under Section 5.1 for the ensuing calendar year. On or before the first day of each month during the ensuing calendar year, tenant will pay to landlord in advance one-twelfth ($^1/_{12}$) of such reasonable estimated amount; however, if such notice is not given in December, tenant will continue to pay on the basis of the prior year's estimate until the month after such notice is given; provided that in the month tenant first pays landlord's new estimate tenant will pay to landlord the difference between the new estimate and the amount payable under the prior year's estimate for each month which has elapsed since December. If at any time or times it reasonably appears to landlord that the amount payable under Section 5.1 for the current calendar year will vary from landlord's estimate, landlord may, by written notice to tenant, revise landlord's estimate for such year, and subsequent payments by tenant for such year will be based upon landlord's reasonably revised estimate.

5.3   Annual Settlement.   Within ninety (90) days after the close of each calendar year or as soon after such ninety (90) day period as practicable, landlord will deliver to tenant a statement of amounts payable under Section 5.1 for such calendar year prepared and certified by landlord. Such certified statement will be final and binding upon landlord and tenant unless tenant objects to it in writing to landlord within thirty (30) days after it is given to tenant. If such statement shows an amount owing by tenant that is less than the estimated payments previously made by tenant for such calendar year, the excess will be held by landlord and credited against the next payment of rent; however, if the term has ended and tenant was not in default at its end, landlord will refund the excess to tenant. If such statement shows an amount owing by tenant that is more than the estimated payments previously made by tenant for such calendar year, tenant will pay the deficiency to landlord within thirty (30) days after the delivery of such statement.

5.4   Proration Upon Termination.   If, for any reason other than the default of tenant, this lease ends on a day other than the last day of a calendar year, the amount of increase (if any) in operating expenses payable by tenant applicable to the calendar year in which this lease ends will be calculated on the basis of actual expenses for the period up to the lease termination date.

5.5   Other Taxes. Tenant will reimburse landlord upon demand for any and all taxes payable by landlord (other than net income taxes) whether or not now customary or within the contemplation of landlord and tenant:

(a)   upon, measured by or reasonably attributable to the cost or value of tenant's merchandise, equipment, furniture, fixtures and other personal property located in the premises or by the cost or value of any leasehold improvements made in or to the premises by or for tenant, regardless of whether title to such improvements is in tenant or landlord;

(b)   upon or measured by rent, including without limitation any gross income tax or excise tax levied by the federal government or any other governmental body with respect to the receipt of rent;

(c)   upon or with respect to the possession, leasing, operation, management, maintenance, alteration, repair, use, or occupancy by tenant of the premises or any portion of the premises;

(d)   upon this transaction or any document to which tenant is a party creating or transferring an interest or an estate in the premises.

If it is not lawful for tenant to reimburse landlord, the rent payable to landlord under this lease will be revised to yield to landlord the same net rental after the imposition of any such tax upon landlord as would have been payable to landlord prior to the imposition of any such tax.

Tenant will pay promptly when due all sales, merchandise or personal property taxes on tenant's personal property in the premises and any other taxes payable by tenant that if not paid might give rise to a lien on the premises or the tenant's interest in the premises.

5.6   Additional Rent. Amounts payable by tenant according to this Article 5 will be payable as rent, without deduction or offset. If tenant fails to pay any amounts due according to this Article 5, landlord will have all the rights and remedies available to it on account of tenant's failure to pay rent.

ARTICLE 6   INSURANCE

6.1   Landlord's Insurance. At all times during the term of this lease, landlord will carry and maintain (a) fire and extended coverage insurance covering the shopping center, parking structure (if any), and the shopping center's equipment and common area furnishings, and (b) comprehensive general insurance in such amounts as landlord determines from time to time in its reasonable discretion. Tenant will reimburse landlord, as an operating expense, for the costs of all such insurance in accordance with Article 5.

6.2   Tenant's Insurance. At all times during the term of this lease, tenant will carry and maintain, at tenant's expense, the following insurance, in the amounts specified below or such other amounts as landlord may from time to time reasonably request, with insurance companies and on forms satisfactory to landlord:

(a)   Comprehensive general liability insurance, with an aggregate limit of not less than $3,000,000. All such insurance will specifically include, without limitation, contractual liability coverage for the performance by tenant of the indemnity agreements set forth in Article 21 of this lease.

(b)   Fire and extended coverage insurance covering all leasehold improvements in the premises and all of tenant's merchandise, equipment, trade fixtures, appliances, furniture, furnishings, and personal property from time to time in, on, or upon the premises, in an amount not less than the full replacement cost without deduction for depreciation from time to time during the term of this lease, providing protection against all perils included within the classification of fire, extended coverage, vandalism, malicious mischief, special extended peril (all risk), boiler, flood, glass breakage, and sprinkler leakage. All policy proceeds will be used for the repair or replacement of the property damaged or destroyed; however, if this lease ceases under the provisions of Article 18, tenant will be entitled to any proceeds resulting from damage to tenant's merchandise, equipment, trade fixtures, appliances, furniture, and personal property, and landlord will be entitled to all other proceeds.

(c)   Workmen's compensation insurance insuring against and satisfying tenant's obligations and liabilities under the workmen's compensation laws of the state in which the premises are located.

(d)   Such other insurance (including without limitation plate glass insurance), in such amounts as landlord or its lender may reasonably require of tenant upon thirty (30) days' prior written notice.

6.3   Forms of Policies. All policies of liability insurance which tenant is obligated to maintain according to this lease (other than any policy of workmen's compensation insurance) will name landlord and such other persons or firms as landlord specifies from time to time as additional insureds. Original or copies of original policies (together with copies of the endorsements naming landlord and any others specified by landlord as additional insureds) and evidence of the payment of all premiums of such policies will be delivered to landlord prior to tenant's occupancy of the premises and from time to time at least thirty (30) days prior to the expiration of the term of each such policy. All liability policies maintained by tenant will contain a provision that landlord and any other additional insureds, although named as an insured, will nevertheless be entitled to recover under such policies for any loss sustained by landlord and such other additional insureds, its agents, and employees as a result of the acts or omissions of tenant. All such policies maintained by tenant will provide that they may not be terminated or amended except after thirty (30) days' prior written notice to landlord. All policies maintained by tenant will be written as primary policies, not contributing with and not supplemental to the coverage that landlord may carry. No insurance required to be maintained by tenant by this Article 6 will be subject to more than a $250 deductible limit without landlord's prior written consent.

6.4 Waiver of Subrogation. Landlord and tenant each waive any and all rights to recover against the other or against any other tenant or occupant of the shopping center, or against the officers, directors, shareholders, partners, joint venturers, employees, agents, customers, invitees, or business visitors of such other party or of such other tenant or occupant of the shopping center, for any loss or damage to such waiving party arising from any cause covered by any insurance required to be carried by such party pursuant to this Article 6 or any other insurance actually carried by such party. Landlord and tenant from time to time will cause their respective insurers to issue appropriate waiver of subrogation rights endorsements to all policies of insurance carried in connection with the shopping center or the premises or the contents of the shopping center or the premises. Tenant agrees to cause all other occupants of the premises claiming by, under, or through tenant to execute and deliver to landlord such a waiver of claims and to obtain such waiver of subrogation rights endorsements.

6.5 Adequacy of Coverage. Landlord, its agents and employees make no representation that the limits of liability specified to be carried by tenant pursuant to this Article 6 are adequate to protect tenant. If tenant believes that any of such insurance coverage is inadequate, tenant will obtain, at tenant's sole expense, such additional insurance coverage as tenant deems adequate.

ARTICLE 7   UTILITIES

Tenant will pay all initial utility deposits and fees and all monthly service charges for water, electricity, sewage, gas, telephone, and any other utility services furnished to the premises and the improvements on the premises during the term of this lease. If any such services are not separately metered or billed to tenant but rather are billed to and paid by landlord, tenant will pay to landlord tenant's pro rata share of the cost of such services in accordance with Article 5.

ARTICLE 8   USE, OPERATION OF BUSINESS, FINANCIAL STATEMENTS

8.1 Use—General. The premises will be used for the purposes described in Article 1(p) and for no other purpose. Tenant will not: do or permit to be done in or about the premises, nor bring to, keep, or permit to be brought or kept in the premises, anything that is prohibited by or will in any way conflict with any law, statute, ordinance, or governmental rule or regulation that is now in force or that may be enacted or promulgated after the lease date; do or permit anything to be done in or about the premises that will in any way obstruct or interfere with the rights of other tenants of the shopping center, or injure or annoy them; use or allow the premises to be used for any improper, immoral, unlawful, or objectionable purpose; cause, maintain, or permit any nuisance in, on, or about the premises. Landlord has not promised tenant that tenant will have the exclusive right in the shopping center to the use tenant is allowed in Article 1(p).

8.2   Operation of Tenant's Business. Tenant will operate tenant's business in the premises so as to maximize the gross sales produced by such operation, and will carry in the premises at all times a stock of merchandise of such size, character, quantity, and quality as is reasonably designed to produce the greatest gross sales. Tenant will carry on its business diligently and continuously at the premises through the term of this lease and will keep the premises open for business on all business days in accordance with the schedule of business hours specified in the basic lease information. If landlord from time to time establishes a different schedule of business hours for the shopping center, tenant will remain open during such revised business hours.

8.3   Manner of Conducting Business. Tenant's business in the premises will be conducted only under the trade name specified in Article 1. Tenant will not use or permit the premises to be used under any other trade name without landlord's prior written consent. Tenant will maintain an adequate number of capable employees and sufficient inventory in order to achieve the greatest possible gross sales. Tenant's local advertising will refer to the business conducted at the premises and will mention the name of the shopping center. Tenant acknowledges that the identity of tenant, the specific character of tenant's business, the anticipated use of the premises, and the relationship between such use and other uses within the shopping center have been material considerations to landlord's entry into this lease. Any material change in the character of tenant's business or use will constitute a default under this lease.

Tenant will not, without the consent of landlord, use the name of the shopping center for any purpose other than as the address of the business to be conducted by tenant in the premises, nor will tenant do or permit the doing of anything in connection with tenant's business or advertising that in the judgment of landlord may reflect unfavorably on landlord or the shopping center or confuse or mislead the public as to any relationship between landlord and tenant.

Tenant will not (a) use or permit the use of any portion of the premises for the conduct in or on the premises of what is commonly known in the retail trade as an outlet store or second-hand store, or army, navy, or government surplus store; (b) advertise any distress, fire, bankruptcy, liquidation, relocation or closing, or going out of business sale unless such advertisements are true and landlord gives its prior written consent; (c) warehouse and stock within the premises any goods, wares, or merchandise other than those tenant intends to offer for sale in the premises; or (d) use or permit the use on the premises of any pinball machines, video games, or other devices or equipment for amusement or recreation, or any vending machines, newspaper racks, pay telephones, or other coin-operated devices.

8.4   Financial Statements. Within sixty (60) days of the end of each calendar year during the lease term, tenant will deliver to landlord (a) a financial statement (including balance sheet and statement of profits and losses) for tenant's most recently completed fiscal year, certified by tenant's chief financial officer, and (b) copies of the past year's sales tax returns filed by tenant with respect to business conducted from the premises.

ARTICLE 9 REQUIREMENTS OF LAW, FIRE INSURANCE

9.1 General. Tenant, at its expense, will comply with all applicable governmental laws, orders and regulations, and with any direction of any public officer or officers, according to law, that will impose any violation, order or duty upon landlord or tenant with respect to the premises or their use or occupancy.

9.2 Toxic Materials. Tenant will not store, use, or dispose of any hazardous, toxic, corrosive, explosive, reactive, or radioactive matter in, on, or about the premises or the shopping center.

9.3 Certain Insurance Risks. Tenant will not do or permit to be done any act or thing upon the premises which would (a) jeopardize or be in conflict with fire insurance policies covering the shopping center and fixtures and property in the shopping center; (b) increase the rate of fire insurance applicable to the shopping center to an amount higher than it otherwise would be for the general use as a shopping center; or (c) subject landlord to any liability or responsibility for injury to any person or persons or to property by reason of any business or operation being carried on upon the premises; however, this Section 9.3 will not prevent tenant's use of the premises for the purposes stated in Article 8.

9.4 Tenant's Insurance Payments. If, as a result of any act or omission or violation of this lease by tenant, the rate of fire insurance applicable to the shopping center or any other insurance carried by landlord is increased to an amount higher than it otherwise would have been, tenant will reimburse landlord for the increased cost of landlord's insurance premiums. Such reimbursement will be rent payable upon the first day of the month following landlord's delivery to tenant of a statement showing payment by landlord for such increased insurance premiums. In any action or proceeding in which landlord and tenant are parties, a schedule or "make up" of rates for the shopping center or premises issued by the body making fire insurance rates for the premises will be presumptive evidence of the facts stated and of the several items and charges in the fire insurance rate then applicable to the premises.

ARTICLE 10 ASSIGNMENT AND SUBLETTING

10.1 General. Tenant, for itself, its heirs, distributees, executors, administrators, legal representatives, successors, and assigns, covenants that it will not assign, mortgage, or encumber this lease, nor sublease, nor permit the premises or any part of the premises to be used or occupied by others, without the prior written consent of landlord in each instance, which consent may be withheld for any reason. The transfer of control or of a majority of the issued and outstanding capital stock of any corporate tenant or subtenant of this lease or a majority interest in any partnership tenant or subtenant, however accomplished, and whether in a single transaction or in a series of transactions, will be an assignment of this lease or of such sublease requiring landlord's prior written consent in each instance. The transfer of outstanding capital stock of any corporate tenant, for purposes of this Article 10, will not include any sale of such stock by persons other than those deemed "insiders" within the meaning of the Securities Exchange Act of 1934, as amended, so long as such sale is effected through the "over-the-counter market" or through any recognized stock exchange.

Any assignment or sublease in violation of this Section 10.1 will be void. If this lease is assigned, or if the premises or any part of the premises are subleased or occupied by anyone other than tenant, landlord may, after default by tenant, collect rent from the assignee, subtenant, or occupant, and apply the net amount collected to rent. No assignment, sublease, occupancy, or collection will be deemed (a) a waiver of the provisions of this Section 10.1; (b) the acceptance of the assignee, subtenant, or occupant as tenant; or (c) release tenant from the further performance by tenant of covenants on the part of tenant contained in this lease. The consent by landlord to an assignment or sublease will not be construed to relieve tenant from obtaining landlord's prior written consent in writing to any further assignment or sublease. No permitted subtenant will assign or encumber its sublease or further sublease all or any portion of its subleased space, or otherwise permit the subleased space or any part of its subleased space to be used or occupied by others, without landlord's prior written consent in each instance.

10.2   Limitation on Remedies. Tenant will not be entitled to make, nor will tenant make, any claim, and tenant by this Section 10.2 waives any claim, for money damages (nor will tenant claim any money damages by way of set-off, counterclaim, or defense) based upon any claim or assertion by tenant that landlord has unreasonably withheld or unreasonably delayed its consent or approval to a proposed assignment or subletting as provided for in this Article 10. Tenant's sole remedy will be an action or proceeding to enforce any such provision, or for specific performance, injunction, or declaratory judgment.

ARTICLE 11   COMMON AREAS

As used in this lease, the term "common areas" means, without limitation, any hallways, entryways, stairs, elevators, driveways, walkways, terraces, docks, loading areas, trash facilities, and all other areas and facilities in the shopping center that are provided and designated from time to time by landlord for the general nonexclusive use and convenience of tenant with other tenants of the shopping center and their respective employees, customers, invitees, licensees, or other visitors. Landlord grants tenant, its employees, invitees, licensees, and other visitors a nonexclusive license for the term to use the common areas in common with others entitled to use the common areas including, without limitation, landlord and other tenants of the shopping center, and their respective employees, customers, invitees, licensees, and visitors, and other persons authorized by landlord, subject to the terms and conditions of this lease. Without advance notice to tenant, except with respect to matters covered by subsection (a) below, and without any liability to tenant in any respect, landlord will have the right to:

(a)   establish and enforce reasonable rules and regulations concerning the maintenance, management, use and operation of the common areas;

(b)   close off any of the common areas to whatever extent required in the opinion of landlord and its counsel to prevent a dedication of any of the common areas or the accrual of any rights by any person or the public to the common areas, provided such closure does not deprive tenant of the substantial benefit and enjoyment of the premises;

(c)   temporarily close any of the common areas for maintenance, alteration, or improvement purposes;

(d)   select, appoint, or contract with any person for the purpose of operating and maintaining the common areas, subject to such terms and at such rates as landlord deems reasonable and proper;

(e)   change the size, use, shape, or nature of any such common areas, provided such change does not deprive tenant of the substantial benefit and enjoyment of the premises. So long as tenant is not thus deprived of the substantial use and benefit of the premises, landlord will also have the right at any time to change the arrangement or location of, or both, or to regulate or eliminate the use of, any concourse, parking spaces, garage, or any elevators, stairs, toilets, or other public conveniences in the shopping center, without incurring any liability to tenant or entitling tenant to any abatement of rent, and such action will not constitute an actual or constructive eviction of tenant; and

(f)   erect one or more additional buildings on the common areas, expand the existing shopping center to cover a portion of the common areas, convert common areas to a portion of the shopping center, or convert any portion of the shopping center to common areas. Upon erection or change of location of the buildings, the portion of the shopping center upon which buildings or structures have been erected will no longer be deemed to be a part of the common areas. In the event of any such changes in the size or use of the shopping center or common areas, landlord will make an appropriate adjustment in the leasable area of the shopping center and in tenant's pro rata share payable pursuant to Article 5 of this lease.

ARTICLE 12   LANDLORD'S SERVICES

12.1   Landlord's Repair and Maintenance. Landlord will maintain, repair, restore, repaint, and replace the common areas of the shopping center, including without limitation landscaping, asphalt, the corridors and restrooms, the windows in the common areas, and the mechanical, plumbing, and electrical equipment serving the common areas, in reasonably good order and condition, except for (a) any damage occasioned by the negligent or willful acts or omissions of tenant, tenant's agents, employees, or invitees; (b) any damage occasioned by the failure of tenant to perform or comply with any terms, conditions, or covenants in this lease; (c) ordinary wear and tear; and (d) any structural alterations or improvements required by tenant's use and occupancy of the premises, which damage will be repaired by landlord at tenant's expense. As a condition precedent to all obligations of landlord to repair, restore and maintain under this Section 12.1, tenant must notify landlord in writing of the need for such repairs, restoration, or maintenance.

Tenant will reimburse landlord for tenant's pro rata share of the costs landlord incurs in performing its repair and maintenance obligations with respect to the shopping center. Reimbursement by tenant to landlord for tenant's share of such costs will be made within thirty (30) days of receipt of a statement for such changes. If landlord fails to commence the making of repairs within thirty (30) days after such notice, and the failure to repair has materially interfered with tenant's use of the premises, tenant's sole right and remedy for such failure on the part of the landlord will be to cause such repairs to be made and to charge landlord the reasonable cost of such repairs. If the repair is necessary to end or avert an emergency, and if landlord after receiving notice from tenant of such necessity fails to commence repair as soon as reasonably possible, tenant may do so at landlord's cost, without waiting thirty (30) days.

12.2   Landlord's Other Services. Landlord will keep the common areas (a) in a clean and orderly condition and free of snow, ice, and debris, and (b) properly lighted and landscaped. Landlord will not be in default under this lease or be liable for any damages directly or indirectly resulting from, nor will the rent be abated by reason of, (i) the installation, use, or interruption of use of any equipment in connection with the furnishing of any of such services; (ii) failure to furnish or delay in furnishing any such services, when such failure or delay is caused by accident or any condition beyond the reasonable control of landlord or by the making of necessary repairs or improvements to the premises or to the shopping center; or (iii) the limitation, curtailment, rationing, or restrictions on use of water, electricity, gas, or any other form of energy serving the premises or the shopping center. Landlord will use reasonable efforts to remedy diligently any interruption in the furnishing of such services.

12.3   Limitation on Liability. Landlord will not be liable to tenant or any other person for direct or consequential damage or otherwise for any failure to supply any heat, air conditioning, elevator, cleaning, lighting, security, or other service landlord has agreed to supply during any period when landlord uses reasonable diligence to supply such services. Landlord reserves the right to discontinue temporarily such services, or any of them, at such times as may be necessary by reason of accident; unavailability of employees; repairs, alterations, or improvements; strikes; lockouts; riots; acts of God; governmental preemption in connection with a national or local emergency; any rule, order, or regulation of any governmental agency; conditions of supply and demand that make any product unavailable; landlord's compliance with any mandatory governmental energy conservation or environmental protection program, or any voluntary governmental energy conservation program at the request of or with consent or acquiescence of tenant; or any other happening beyond the control of landlord. Landlord will not be liable to tenant or any other person or entity for direct or consequential damages resulting from the admission to or exclusion from the shopping center of any person. In the event of invasion, mob, riot, public excitement, or other circumstances rendering such action advisable in landlord's sole opinion, landlord will have the right to prevent access to or from the shopping center during the continuance of the same by such means as landlord, in its sole discretion, may deem appropriate, including without limitation locking doors and closing parking areas and other common areas. Landlord will not be liable for damages to person or property or for injury to, or interruption of, business for any discontinuance permitted under this Article 12, nor will such discontinuance in any way be construed as an eviction of tenant or cause an abatement of rent or operate to release tenant from any of tenant's obligations under this lease.

12.4   Grand Opening Fund. Landlord will arrange a grand opening promotion for the shopping center. The grand opening will be held at the shopping center on a date between the ninetieth (90th) and one hundred eightieth (180th) day after the first tenant of the shopping center occupies its premises. Landlord will contribute ten cents ($0.10) for each leasable square foot of the shopping center that is occupied by tenants who have accepted their premises and begun to pay rent for them as of the fifteenth (15th) day before the grand opening. If the grand opening promotion costs more than landlord's contribution, the excess cost will be treated as an operating expense. Landlord will be solely responsible for all aspects of arranging the grand opening promotion, including without limitation selecting the date of the grand opening (subject to the limitations in the first sentence of this paragraph), decorating the shopping center, and advertising the grand opening. Tenant will cooperate with landlord and will abide by special rules and regulations promulgated by landlord in order to ensure a successful grand opening.

12.5   Promotional Fund. Landlord will arrange occasional promotions of the shopping center. Landlord will make contributions to a promotional fund, on a monthly basis, in an amount equal to two cents ($.02) per square foot of leasable square foot of the shopping center leased for that month. Landlord's contribution will remain landlord's property and may be contributed to an interest-bearing account for the benefit of landlord. If the promotions cost more than landlord's contributions, the excess may be treated as an operating expense or deferred and paid from future promotion fund contributions. Excess costs treated as operating expenses payable by tenants will not exceed ten cents ($.10) per square foot of leasable square foot of the shopping center in any one calendar year. Although landlord will consult with a representative of the tenants in the shopping center, landlord will be solely responsible for all aspects of the occasional promotions, including without limitation selecting the date, time, and manner of the promotions, decorating the shopping center, and advertising the promotions. Tenant will cooperate with landlord and will abide by special rules and regulations promulgated by landlord in order to assure the success of the promotions.

ARTICLE 13   TENANT'S REPAIRS

(a)   Tenant will at all times during the term of this lease keep and maintain at its own cost and expense, in good order, condition, and repair, the premises (including, without limitation, all improvements, fixtures, and equipment on the premises), and will make all repairs and replacements, interior and exterior, above or below ground, and ordinary or extraordinary.

(b) Tenant's obligation to keep and maintain the premises in good order, condition, and repair includes without limitation all plumbing and sewage facilities in the premises; floors (including floor coverings); doors, locks, and closing devices; window casements and frames; glass and plate glass; grilles; all electrical facilities and equipment; HVAC systems and equipment and all other appliances and equipment of every kind and nature; and all landscaping upon, within, or attached to the premises. In addition, tenant will at its sole cost and expense install or construct any improvements, equipment, or fixtures required by any governmental authority or agency as a consequence of tenant's use and occupancy of the premises. Tenant will replace any damaged plate glass within forty-eight (48) hours of the occurrence of such damage.

(c) Landlord will assign to tenant, and tenant will have the benefit of, any guarantee or warranty to which landlord is entitled under any purchase, construction, or installation contract relating to a component of the premises that tenant is obligated to repair and maintain. Tenant will have the right to call upon the contractor to make such adjustments, replacements, or repairs as are required to be made by the contractor under such contract.

(d) Landlord may at landlord's option employ and pay a firm satisfactory to landlord, engaged in the business of maintaining systems, to perform periodic inspections of the HVAC systems serving the premises, and to perform any necessary work, maintenance, or repair of them. In that event, tenant will reimburse landlord for all reasonable amounts paid by landlord in connection with such employment.

(e) Upon the expiration or termination of this lease, tenant will surrender the premises to landlord in good order, condition, and repair, ordinary wear and tear excepted. To the extent allowed by law, tenant waives the right to make repairs at landlord's expense under the provisions of any laws permitting repairs by a tenant at the expense of a landlord.

ARTICLE 14   ALTERATIONS

Tenant will not make or cause to be made any alterations, additions, or improvements to or of the premises or any part of the premises, or attach any fixture or equipment to the premises, without first obtaining landlord's written consent. Any alterations, additions, or improvements to the premises consented to by landlord will be made by tenant at tenant's sole cost and expense according to plans and specifications approved by landlord, and any contractor or person selected by tenant to make them must first be approved by landlord. Landlord may require, at its option, that tenant provide landlord at tenant's sole cost and expense a lien and completion bond, or payment and performance bond, in an amount equal to twice the estimated cost of any contemplated alterations, fixtures, and improvements, to insure landlord against any liability for mechanics' or materialmen's liens and to ensure the completion of such work. All alterations, additions, fixtures, and improvements, whether temporary or permanent in character, made in or upon the premises either by tenant or landlord (other than furnishings, trade fixtures, and equipment installed by tenant), will be landlord's property and, at the end of the term of this lease, will remain on the premises without compensation to tenant. If landlord requests, tenant will remove all such alterations, fixtures, and improvements from the premises and return the premises to the condition in which they were delivered to tenant. Upon such removal tenant will immediately and fully repair any damage to the premises occasioned by the removal.

ARTICLE 15   MECHANICS' LIENS

Tenant will pay or cause to be paid all costs and charges for work done by it or caused to be done by it in or to the premises and for all materials furnished for or in connection with such work. Tenant will indemnify landlord against, and hold landlord, the premises, and the shopping center free, clear, and harmless of and from, all mechanics' liens and claims of liens, and all other liabilities, liens, claims, and demands, on account of such work. If any such lien, at any time, is filed against the premises or any part of the shopping center, tenant will cause such lien to be discharged of record within ten (10) days after the filing of such lien, except that if tenant desires to contest such lien, it will furnish landlord, within such ten (10) day period, security reasonably satisfactory to landlord of at least one hundred fifty percent (150%) of the amount of the claim, plus estimated costs and interest. If a final judgment establishing the validity or existence of a lien for any amount is entered, tenant will pay and satisfy the same at once. If tenant fails to pay any charge for which a mechanics' lien has been filed, and has not given landlord security as described above, landlord may, at its option, pay such charge and related costs and interest, and the amount so paid, together with reasonable attorneys' fees incurred in connection with such lien, will be immediately due from tenant to landlord. Nothing contained in this lease will be deemed the consent or agreement of landlord to subject landlord's interest in the shopping center to liability under any mechanics' or other lien law. If tenant receives notice that a lien has been or is about to be filed against the premises or the shopping center, or that any action affecting title to the shopping center has been commenced on account of work done by or for or materials furnished to or for tenant, it will immediately give landlord written notice of such notice. At least fifteen (15) days prior to the commencement of any work (including, but not limited to, any maintenance, repairs, alterations, additions, improvements, or installations) in or to the premises, by or for tenant, tenant will give landlord written notice of the proposed work and the names and addresses of the persons supplying labor and materials for the proposed work. Landlord will have the right to post notices of nonresponsibility or similar notices on the premises in order to protect the premises against any such liens.

ARTICLE 16   END OF TERM

At the end of this lease, tenant will promptly quit and surrender the premises in good order, condition, and repair, ordinary wear and tear excepted. If tenant is not then in default, tenant may remove from the premises any trade fixtures, equipment, and movable furniture placed in the premises by tenant, whether or not such trade fixtures or equipment are fastened to the shopping center; tenant will not remove any trade fixtures or equipment without landlord's written consent if such fixtures or equipment are used in the operation of the shopping center or improvements or if the removal of such fixtures or equipment will result in impairing the structural strength of the shopping center or improvements. Whether or not tenant is in default, tenant will remove such alterations, additions, improvements, trade fixtures, equipment, and furniture as landlord has requested in accordance with Article 14. Tenant will fully repair any damage occasioned by the removal of any trade fixtures, equipment, furniture, alterations, additions, and improvements. All trade fixtures, equipment, furniture, inventory, effects, alterations, additions, and improvements not so removed will be deemed conclusively to have been abandoned and may be appropriated, sold, stored, destroyed, or otherwise disposed of by landlord without notice to tenant or any other person and without obligation to account for them; and tenant will pay landlord for all expenses incurred in connection with such property, including but not limited to the cost of repairing any damage to the shopping center or premises caused by the removal of such property. Tenant's obligation to observe and perform this covenant will survive the expiration or other termination of this lease.

ARTICLE 17   EMINENT DOMAIN

(a)   The term "total taking" means the taking of the fee title or landlord's master leasehold estate by right of eminent domain or other authority of law, or a voluntary transfer under the threat of the exercise of the right of eminent domain or other authority, to so much of the premises or a portion of the shopping center as is necessary for tenant's occupancy that the premises are not suitable for tenant's intended use. The term "partial taking" means a taking of only a portion of the premises or the shopping center that does not constitute a total taking.

(b)   If a total taking occurs during the term of this lease, this lease will terminate as of the date of the taking. The phrase "date of the taking" means the date of taking actual physical possession by the condemning authority or such earlier date as the condemning authority gives notice that it is deemed to have taken possession.

(c)   If a partial taking occurs during the term of this lease, either landlord or tenant may cancel this lease by written notice given within thirty (30) days after the date of the taking, and this lease will terminate as to the portion of the premises taken on the date of the taking. If the lease is not so terminated, this lease will continue in full force and effect as to the remainder of the premises. The monthly base rent payable by tenant for the balance of the term will be abated in the proportion that the leasable area of the premises taken bears to the leasable area of the premises immediately prior to such taking, and landlord will make all necessary repairs or alterations to make the remaining premises a complete architectural unit.

(d)   If more than forty percent (40%) of the common areas in the shopping center dedicated to customer parking are acquired or condemned under power of eminent domain or other authority of law, or a voluntary transfer under the threat of an exercise of the right of eminent domain or other authority, then the term of this lease will terminate as of the date of the taking unless landlord takes reasonable steps to provide other parking facilities substantially equal to the previously existing ratio between the common parking areas and the leasable area of the shopping center, and such parking facilities are provided by landlord within ninety (90) days from the date of the taking. If landlord provides such other parking facilities, then this lease will continue in full force.

(e) All compensation and damages awarded for the taking of the premises, any portion of the premises, or the whole or any portion of the common areas or shopping center will belong to landlord. Tenant will not have any claim or be entitled to any award for diminution in value of its rights under this lease or for the value of any unexpired term of this lease; however, tenant may make its own claim for any separate award that may be made by the condemnor for tenant's loss of business or for the taking of or injury to tenant's improvements, or on account of any cost or loss tenant may sustain in the removal of tenant's trade fixtures, equipment, and furnishing, or as a result of any alterations, modifications, or repairs that may be reasonably required by tenant to put the remaining portion of the premises not so condemned in a suitable condition for the continuance of tenant's occupancy.

(f) If this lease is terminated pursuant to the provisions of this Article 17, then all rentals and other charges payable by tenant to landlord under this lease will be paid up to the date of the taking, and any rentals and other charges paid in advance and allocable to the period after the date of the taking will be repaid to tenant by landlord. Landlord and tenant will then be released from all further liability under this lease.

ARTICLE 18   DAMAGE AND DESTRUCTION

(a) If the premises or the portion of the shopping center necessary for tenant's occupancy is damaged or destroyed during the term of this lease by any casualty insurable under standard fire and extended coverage insurance policies, landlord will repair or rebuild the premises to substantially the condition in which the premises were immediately prior to such destruction.

(b) Landlord's obligation under this Article 18 will not exceed the lesser of (i) with respect to the premises, the scope of building-standard improvements installed by landlord in the original construction of the premises or (ii) the extent of proceeds received by landlord of any insurance policy maintained by landlord.

(c) The monthly base rent will be abated proportionately during any period in which, by reason of any damage or destruction not occasioned by the negligence or willful misconduct of tenant or tenant's employees or invitees, there is a substantial interference with the operation of the business of tenant. Such abatement will be proportional to the measure of business in the premises that tenant may be required to discontinue. The abatement will continue for the period commencing with such destruction or damage and ending with the completion by the landlord of such work, repair, or reconstruction as landlord is obligated to do.

(d) If the premises, or the portion of the shopping center necessary for tenant's occupancy, is damaged or destroyed (i) to the extent of ten percent (10%) or more of the then-replacement value of either, (ii) in the last three (3) years of the term of this lease, (iii) by a cause or casualty other than those covered by fire and extended coverage insurance, or (iv) to the extent that it would take, in landlord's opinion, in excess of ninety (90) days to complete the requisite repairs, then landlord may either terminate this lease or elect to repair or restore the damage or destruction. If this lease is not terminated pursuant to the preceding sentence, this lease will remain in full force and effect. Landlord and tenant waive the provisions of any law that would dictate automatic termination or grant either of them an option to terminate in the event of damage or destruction. Landlord's election to terminate under this paragraph will be exercised by written notice to tenant given within sixty (60) days after the damage or destruction. Such notice will set forth the effective date of the termination of this lease.

(e) Upon the completion of any such work, repair, or restoration by landlord, tenant will repair and restore all other parts of the premises, including without limitation non-building-standard leasehold improvements and all trade fixtures, equipment, furnishings, signs, and other improvements originally installed by tenant. Tenant's work will be subject to the requirements of Article 14.

(f) During any period of reconstruction or repair of the premises, tenant will continue the operation of its business in the premises to the extent reasonably practicable.

ARTICLE 19 SUBORDINATION

19.1 General. This lease and tenant's rights under this lease are subject and subordinate to any ground or underlying lease, first mortgage, indenture, first deed of trust, or other first lien encumbrance, together with any renewals, extensions, modifications, consolidations, and replacements of such first lien encumbrance, now or after the lease date, affecting or placed, charged, or enforced against the land or all or any portion of the shopping center or any interest of landlord in them or landlord's interest in this lease and the leasehold estate created by this lease (except to the extent any such instrument expressly provides that this lease is superior to such instrument). This provision will be self-operative and no further instrument of subordination will be required in order to effect it. Nevertheless, tenant will execute, acknowledge and deliver to landlord, at any time and from time to time, upon demand by landlord, such documents as may be requested by landlord, any ground or underlying lessor, or any mortgagee, to confirm or effect any such subordination. If tenant fails or refuses to execute, acknowledge, and deliver any such document within twenty (20) days after written demand, landlord, its successors, and assigns will be entitled to execute, acknowledge, and deliver any and all such documents for and on behalf of tenant as attorney-in-fact for tenant. Tenant by this Section

19.1 constitutes and irrevocably appoints landlord, its successors, and assigns as tenant's attorney-in-fact to execute, acknowledge, and deliver any and all documents described in this Section 19.1 for and on behalf of tenant, as provided in this Section 19.1.

19.2 Attornment. Tenant agrees that if any holder of any ground or underlying lease, mortgage, deed of trust, or other encumbrance encumbering any part of the shopping center succeeds to landlord's interest in the premises, tenant will pay to such holder all rents subsequently payable under this lease. Further, tenant agrees that in the event of the enforcement by the trustee or the beneficiary under or holder or owner of any such mortgage, deed of trust, or land or ground lease of the remedies provided for by law or by such mortgage, deed of trust, or land or ground lease, tenant will, upon request of any person or party succeeding to the interest of landlord as a result of such enforcement, automatically become the tenant of and attorn to such successor in interest without change in the terms or provisions of this lease. Such successor in interest will not be bound by (a) any payment of monthly base rent or rent for more than one month in advance, except prepayments in the nature of security for the performance by tenant of its obligations under this lease, or (b) any amendment or modification of this lease made without the written consent of such trustee, beneficiary, holder, owner, or such successor in interest. Upon request by such successor in interest and without cost to landlord or such successor in interest, tenant will execute, acknowledge, and deliver an instrument or instruments confirming the attornment. If tenant fails or refuses to execute, acknowledge, and deliver any such document within twenty (20) days after written demand, such successor in interest will be entitled to execute, acknowledge, and deliver any and all such documents for and on behalf of tenant as attorney-in-fact for tenant. Tenant by this Section 19.2 constitutes and irrevocably appoints such successor in interest as tenant's attorney-in-fact to execute, acknowledge, and deliver any and all documents described in this Section 19.2 for and on behalf of tenant, as provided in this Section 19.2.

ARTICLE 20 ENTRY BY LANDLORD

Landlord, its agents, employees, and contractors may enter the premises at any time in response to an emergency and at reasonable hours to (a) inspect the same, (b) exhibit the same to prospective purchasers, lenders, or tenants, (c) determine whether tenant is complying with all its obligations in this lease, (d) supply any service that this lease obligates landlord to provide to tenant, (e) post notices of nonresponsibility or similar notices, or (f) make repairs required of landlord under the terms of this lease or make repairs to any adjoining space or utility services or make repairs, alterations, or improvements to any other portion of the shopping center; however, all such work will be done as promptly as reasonably possible and so as to cause as little interference to tenant as reasonably possible. Tenant by this Article 20 waives any claim against landlord, its agents, employees, or contractors for damages for any injury or inconvenience to or interference with tenant's business, any loss of occupancy or quiet enjoyment of the premises, or any other loss occasioned by such entry. Landlord will at all times have and retain a key with which to unlock all of the doors in, on, or about the premises (excluding tenant's vaults, safes, and similar areas designated in writing by tenant in advance). Landlord will have the right to use any and all means landlord may deem proper to open doors in and to the premises in an emergency in order to obtain entry to the premises. Any entry to the premises obtained by landlord by any means permitted under this article will not under any circumstances be construed or deemed to be a forcible or unlawful entry into or a detainer of the premises or an eviction, actual or constructive, of tenant from the premises or any portion of the premises, nor will any such entry entitle tenant to damages or an abatement of monthly base rent, additional rent, or other charges that this lease requires tenant to pay.

ARTICLE 21   INDEMNIFICATION, WAIVER, AND RELEASE

21.1   Indemnification. Tenant will neither hold nor attempt to hold landlord or its employees or agents liable for, and tenant will indemnify and hold harmless landlord, its employees, and agents from and against, any and all demands, claims, causes of action, fines, penalties, damages (including consequential damages), liabilities, judgments, and expenses (including without limitation attorneys' fees) incurred in connection with or arising from:

(a)   the use or occupancy or manner of use or occupancy of the premises by tenant or any person claiming under tenant;

(b)   any activity, work, or thing done, permitted, or suffered by tenant in or about the premises or the shopping center;

(c)   any acts, omissions, or negligence of tenant or any person claiming under tenant or the contractors, agents, employees, invitees, or visitors of tenant or any such person;

(d)   any breach, violation, or nonperformance by tenant or any person claiming under tenant or the employees, agents, contractors, invitees, or visitors of tenant or any such person of any term, covenant, or provision of this lease or any law, ordinance, or governmental requirement of any kind;

(e)   except for loss of use of all or any portion of the premises or tenant's property located within the premises that is proximately caused by or results proximately from the negligence of landlord, any injury or damage to the person, property, or business of tenant or its employees, agents, contractors, invitees, visitors, or any other person entering upon the premises or the shopping center under the express or implied invitation of tenant.

If any action or proceeding is brought against landlord or its employees by reason of any such claim, tenant, upon notice from landlord, will defend the same at tenant's expense with counsel reasonably satisfactory to landlord.

21.2   Waiver and Release. Tenant, as a material part of the consideration to landlord for this lease, by this Section 21.2 waives and releases all claims against landlord, its employees, and agents with respect to all matters for which landlord has disclaimed liability pursuant to the provisions of this lease. Tenant agrees that landlord, its agents, and its employees will not be liable for any loss, injury, death, or damage (including consequential damages) to persons, property, or tenant's business occasioned by theft; act of God; public enemy; injunction; riot; strike; insurrection; war; court order; requisition; order of governmental body or authority; fire; explosion; falling objects; steam, water, rain or snow; leak or flow of water (including fluid from the elevator system), rain or snow from or into part of the shopping center or from the roof, street, subsurface, or from any other place, or by dampness, or from the breakage, leakage, obstruction, or other defects of the pipes, sprinklers, wires, appliances, plumbing, air conditioning, or lighting fixtures of the shopping center; or from construction, repair, or alteration of any other premises in the shopping center or the premises; or from any acts or omissions of any other tenant, occupant, or visitor of the shopping center; or from any cause beyond landlord's control.

ARTICLE 22   SECURITY DEPOSIT

Tenant has deposited the security deposit with landlord as security for the full, faithful, and timely performance of every provision of this lease to be performed by tenant. If tenant defaults with respect to any provision of this lease, including but not limited to the provisions relating to the payment of rent, landlord may use, apply, or retain all or any part of the security deposit for the payment of any rent, or any other sum in default, or for the payment of any other amount landlord may spend or become obligated to spend by reason of tenant's default, or to compensate landlord for any other loss or damage landlord may suffer by reason of tenant's default. If any portion of the security deposit is so used, applied, or retained, tenant will within ten (10) days after written demand deposit cash with landlord in an amount sufficient to restore the security deposit to its original amount. Landlord will not be required to keep the security deposit separate from its general funds and tenant will not be entitled to interest on the security deposit. The security deposit will not be deemed a limitation on landlord's damages or a payment of liquidated damages or a payment of the monthly base rent due for the last month of the term. If tenant fully, faithfully, and in a timely manner performs every provision of this lease to be performed by it, the security deposit or any balance of the security deposit will be returned to tenant within sixty (60) days after the expiration of the term. Landlord may deliver the funds deposited under this lease by tenant to the purchaser of the shopping center in the event the shopping center is sold, and after such time landlord will have no further liability to tenant with respect to the security deposit.

ARTICLE 23   QUIET ENJOYMENT

Landlord covenants and agrees with tenant that so long as tenant pays the rent and observes and performs all the terms, covenants, and conditions of this lease on tenant's part to be observed and performed, tenant may peaceably and quietly enjoy the premises subject, nevertheless, to the terms and conditions of this lease, and tenant's possession will not be disturbed by anyone claiming by, through, or under landlord.

ARTICLE 24   EFFECT OF SALE

A sale, conveyance, or assignment of the shopping center will operate to release landlord from liability from and after the effective date of such sale, conveyance, or assignment upon all of the covenants, terms, and conditions of this lease, express or implied, except those which arose prior to such effective date, and, after the effective date of such sale, conveyance, or assignment, tenant will look solely to landlord's successor in interest in and to this lease. This lease will not be affected by any such sale, conveyance, or assignment, and tenant will attorn to landlord's successor in interest to this lease.

ARTICLE 25   DEFAULT

25.1   Events of Default. The following events are referred to collectively as "events of default" or individually as an "event of default":

(a)   Tenant defaults in the due and punctual payment of rent, and such default continues for five (5) days after notice from landlord; however, tenant will not be entitled to more than one (1) notice for monetary defaults during any twelve (12) month period, and if after such notice any rent is not paid when due, an event of default will be considered to have occurred without further notice;

(b)   Tenant vacates or abandons the premises;

(c)   This lease or the premises or any part of the premises are taken upon execution or by other process of law directed against tenant, or are taken upon or subject to any attachment at the instance of any creditor or claimant against tenant, and the attachment is not discharged or disposed of within fifteen (15) days after its levy;

(d)   Tenant files a petition in bankruptcy or insolvency or for reorganization or arrangement under the bankruptcy laws of the United States or under any insolvency act of any state, or admits the material allegations of any such petition by answer or otherwise, or is dissolved or makes an assignment for the benefit of creditors;

(e)   Involuntary proceedings under any such bankruptcy law or insolvency act or for the dissolution of tenant are instituted against tenant, or a receiver or trustee is appointed for all or substantially all of the property of tenant, and such proceeding is not dismissed or such receivership or trusteeship vacated within sixty (60) days after such institution or appointment;

(f)   Tenant fails to take possession of the premises on the commencement date of the term; or

(g)   Tenant breaches any of the other agreements, terms, covenants, or conditions that this lease requires tenant to perform, and such breach continues for a period of thirty (30) days after notice from landlord to tenant; or if such breach cannot be cured reasonably within such thirty (30) day period and tenant fails to commence and proceed diligently to cure such breach within a reasonable time period.

25.2   Landlord's Remedies. If any one or more events of default set forth in Section 25.1 occurs then landlord has the right, at its election:

(a)   to give tenant written notice of landlord's intention to terminate this lease on the earliest date permitted by law or on any later date specified in such notice, in which case tenant's right to possession of the premises will cease and this lease will be terminated, except as to tenant's liability, as if the expiration of the term fixed in such notice were the end of the term; or

(b)   without further demand or notice, to reenter and take possession of the premises or any part of the premises, repossess the same, expel tenant and those claiming through or under tenant, and remove the effects of both or either, using such force for such purposes as may be necessary, without being liable for prosecution, without being deemed guilty of any manner of trespass, and without prejudice to any remedies for arrears of monthly base rent or other amounts payable under this lease or as a result of any preceding breach of covenants or conditions; or

(c)   without further demand or notice, to cure any event of default and to charge tenant for the cost of effecting such cure, including without limitation attorneys' fees and interest on the amount so advanced at the rate set forth in Section 26.22, provided that landlord will have no obligation to cure any such event of default of tenant.

Should landlord elect to reenter as provided in subsection (b), or should landlord take possession pursuant to legal proceedings or pursuant to any notice provided by law, landlord may, from time to time, without terminating this lease, relet the premises or any part of the premises in landlord's or tenant's name, but for the account of tenant, for such term or terms (which may be greater or less than the period which would otherwise have constituted the balance of the term) and on such conditions and upon such other terms (which may include concessions of free rent and alteration and repair of the premises) as landlord, in its sole discretion, may determine, and landlord may collect and receive the rent. Landlord will in no way be responsible or liable for any failure to relet the premises or any part of the premises, or for any failure to collect any rent due upon such reletting. No such reentry or taking possession of the premises by landlord will be construed as an election on landlord's part to terminate this lease unless a written notice of such intention is given to tenant. No notice from landlord under this Section or under a forcible or unlawful entry and detainer statute or similar law will constitute an election by landlord to terminate this lease unless such notice specifically so states. Landlord reserves the right following any such reentry or reletting to exercise its right to terminate this lease by giving tenant such written notice, in which event this lease will terminate as specified in such notice.

25.3   Certain Damages. If landlord does not elect to terminate this lease as permitted in subsection (a) of Section 25.2, but on the contrary elects to take possession as provided in subsection (b) of Section 25.2, tenant will pay to landlord: monthly base rent and other sums as provided in this lease that would be payable under this lease if such repossession had not occurred, less the net proceeds, if any, of any reletting of the premises after deducting all landlord's expenses in connection with such reletting, including without limitation all repossession costs, brokerage commissions, attorneys' fees, expenses of employees, alteration and repair costs, and expenses of preparation for such reletting. If, in connection with any reletting, the new lease term extends beyond the existing term, or the premises covered by such new lease include other premises not part of the premises, a fair apportionment of the rent received from such reletting and the expenses incurred in connection with such reletting as provided in this Section will be made in determining the net proceeds from such reletting, and any rent concessions will be equally apportioned over the term of the new lease. Tenant will pay such rent and other sums to landlord monthly on the day on which the monthly base rent would have been payable under this lease if possession had not been retaken, and landlord will be entitled to receive such rent and other sums from tenant on each such day.

25.4   Continuing Liability After Termination. If this lease is terminated on account of the occurrence of an event of default, tenant will remain liable to landlord for damages in an amount equal to monthly base rent and other amounts that would have been owing by tenant for the balance of the term, had this lease not been terminated, less the net proceeds, if any, of any reletting of the premises by landlord subsequent to such termination, after deducting all landlord's expenses in connection with such reletting, including without limitation the expenses enumerated in Section 25.3. Landlord will be entitled to collect such damages from tenant monthly on the day on which monthly base rent and other amounts would have been payable under this lease if this lease had not been terminated, and landlord will be entitled to receive such monthly base rent and other amounts from tenant on each such day. Alternatively, at the option of landlord, in the event this lease is so terminated, landlord will be entitled to recover against tenant, as damages for loss of the bargain and not as a penalty, an aggregate rent that, at the time of such termination of this lease, represents the excess of the aggregate of monthly base rent and all other rent payable by tenant that would have accrued for the balance of the term over the aggregate rental value of the premises (such rental value to be computed on the basis of a tenant paying not only a rent to landlord for the use and occupation of the premises, but also such other charges as are required to be paid by tenant under the terms of this lease) for the balance of such term, both discounted to present value at the lesser of eight percent (8%) or the discount rate of the New York Federal Reserve Bank on the date of the event of default.

25.5   Cumulative Remedies. Any suit or suits for the recovery of the amounts and damages set forth in Sections 25.3 and 25.4 may be brought by landlord, from time to time, at landlord's election, and nothing in this lease will be deemed to require landlord to await the date upon which this lease or the term would have expired had there occurred no event of default. Each right and remedy provided for in this lease is cumulative and is in addition to every other right or remedy provided for in this lease or now or after the lease date existing at law or in equity or by statute or otherwise, and the exercise or beginning of the exercise by landlord of any one or more of the rights or remedies provided for in this lease or now or after the lease date existing at law or in equity or by statute or otherwise will not preclude the simultaneous or later exercise by landlord of any or all other rights or remedies provided for in this lease or now or after the lease date existing at law or in equity or by statute or otherwise. All costs incurred by landlord in collecting any amounts and damages owing by tenant pursuant to the provisions of this lease or to enforce any provision of this lease, including reasonable attorneys' fees from the date any such matter is turned over to an attorney, whether or not one or more actions are commenced by landlord, will also be recoverable by landlord from tenant.

ARTICLE 26   RULES AND REGULATIONS

Tenant and its employees, agents, licensees, and visitors will at all times observe faithfully, and comply strictly with, the rules and regulations set forth on Exhibit D. Landlord may from time to time amend, delete, or modify existing rules and regulations, or adopt new rules and regulations, for the use, safety, cleanliness, and care of the premises and the shopping center and the comfort, quiet, and convenience of occupants of the shopping center. Modifications or additions to the rules and regulations will be effective upon notice to tenant from landlord. In the event of any breach of any rules or regulations or any amendments or additions to such rules and regulations, landlord will have all remedies that this lease provides for default by tenant, and will, in addition, have any remedies available at law or in equity, including the right to enjoin any breach of such rules and regulations. Landlord will not be liable to tenant for violation of such rules and regulations by any other tenant, its employees, agents, visitors, licensees, or any other person. In the event of any conflict between the provisions of this lease and the rules and regulations, the provisions of this lease will govern.

ARTICLE 27   SIGNS

(a)   Tenant will purchase and install one sign in the sign box provided by landlord on the front of the premises. Installation will be made only by a licensed electrician approved in advance by landlord and will be completed on the earlier of the date on which tenant opens for business or within thirty (30) days after the date of commencement of this lease. The sign will conform to landlord's sign criteria attached to this lease as Exhibit E. Tenant will maintain, repair, and replace the sign as required by landlord during this lease. At the end of this lease, the sign will immediately become the property of landlord.

(b)   Tenant will keep the display windows and signs of the premises well-lighted until 10:00 p.m. each night or such shorter period as may be prescribed by any applicable policies or regulations adopted by any utility or governmental agency, and will maintain adequate night lights within the premises after that hour or period.

(c)   Without the prior written consent of landlord, tenant will not place or permit to be placed any sign, advertising material, or lettering upon the exterior of the premises or any sign, advertising material, or lettering upon the exterior or interior surface of any door or show window or at any point inside the premises from which it may be visible from outside the premises. Upon request of landlord, tenant will immediately remove any sign, advertising material, or lettering at tenant's expense. Tenant will comply with such regulations as may from time to time be promulgated by landlord governing signs, advertising material, or lettering of all tenants in the retail area; however, tenant will not be required to change any sign or lettering that was in compliance with applicable regulations at the time it was installed or placed in, on, or about the premises.

ARTICLE 28   MISCELLANEOUS

28.1   No Offer. This lease is submitted to tenant on the understanding that it will not be considered an offer and will not bind landlord in any way until (a) tenant has duly executed and delivered duplicate originals to landlord and (b) landlord has executed and delivered one of such originals to tenant.

28.2   Joint and Several Liability. If tenant is composed of more than one signatory to this lease, each signatory will be jointly and severally liable with each other signatory for payment and performance according to this lease.

28.3   No Construction Against Drafting Party. Landlord and tenant acknowledge that each of them and their counsel have had an opportunity to review this lease and that this lease will not be construed against landlord merely because landlord's counsel has prepared it.

28.4   Time of the Essence. Time is of the essence of each and every provision of this lease.

28.5   No Recordation. Tenant's recordation of this lease or any memorandum or short form of it will be void and a default under this lease.

28.6   No Waiver. The waiver by landlord of any agreement, condition, or provision contained in this lease will not be deemed to be a waiver of any subsequent breach of the same or any other agreement, condition, or provision contained in this lease, nor will any custom or practice that may grow up between the parties in the administration of the terms of this lease be construed to waive or lessen the right of landlord to insist upon the performance by tenant in strict accordance with the terms of this lease. The subsequent acceptance of rent by landlord will not be deemed to be a waiver of any preceding breach by tenant of any agreement, condition, or provision of this lease, other than the failure of tenant to pay the particular rent so accepted, regardless of landlord's knowledge of such preceding breach at the time of acceptance of such rent.

28.7   Limitation on Recourse. Tenant specifically agrees to look solely to landlord's interest in the shopping center for the recovery of any judgments from landlord, it being agreed that landlord (and its shareholders, venturers, and partners, and their shareholders, venturers, and partners, and all of their officers, directors, and employees) will never be personally liable for any such judgments. The provision contained in the preceding sentence is not intended to and will not limit any right that tenant might otherwise have to obtain injunctive relief against landlord or to pursue any suit or action in connection with enforcement or collection of amounts that may become owing or payable under or on account of insurance maintained by landlord.

28.8 Estoppel Certificates. At any time and from time to time but within ten (10) days after written request by landlord, tenant will execute, acknowledge, and deliver to landlord a certificate certifying (a) that this lease is unmodified and in full force and effect or, if there have been modifications, that this lease is in full force and effect, as modified, and stating the date and nature of each modification; (b) the date, if any, to which rent and other sums payable under this lease have been paid; (c) that no notice has been received by landlord of any default which has not been cured, except as to defaults specified in the certificate; and (d) such other matters as may be reasonably requested by landlord. Any such certificate may be relied upon by any prospective purchaser or existing or prospective mortgagee or beneficiary under any deed of trust of the shopping center or any part of the shopping center.

28.9 Waiver of Jury Trial. Landlord and tenant by this Section 28.9 waive trial by jury in any action, proceeding, or counterclaim brought by either of the parties to this lease against the other on any matters whatsoever arising out of or in any way connected with this lease, the relationship of landlord and tenant, tenant's use or occupancy of the premises, or any other claims (including without limitation claims for personal injury or property damage), and any emergency statutory or any other statutory remedy.

28.10 No Merger. The voluntary or other surrender of this lease by tenant or the cancellation of this lease by mutual agreement of tenant and landlord or the termination of this lease on account of tenant's default will not work a merger, and will, at landlord's option, (a) terminate all or any subleases and subtenancies, or (b) operate as an assignment to landlord of all or any subleases or subtenancies. Landlord's option under this Section 28.10 will be exercised by notice to tenant and all known sublessees or subtenants in the premises or any part of the premises.

28.11 Holding Over. Tenant will have no right to remain in possession of all or any part of the premises after the expiration of the term. If tenant remains in possession of all or any part of the premises after the expiration of the term, with the express or implied consent of landlord: (a) such tenancy will be deemed to be a periodic tenancy from month-to-month only; (b) such tenancy will not constitute a renewal or extension of this lease for any further term; and (c) such tenancy may be terminated by landlord upon the earlier of thirty (30) days prior written notice or the earliest date permitted by law. In such event, monthly base rent will be increased to an amount equal to one hundred fifty percent (150%) of the monthly base rent payable during the last month of the term, and any other sums due under this lease will be payable in the amount and at the times specified in this lease. Such month-to-month tenancy will be subject to every other term, condition, and covenant contained in this lease.

28.12   Notices. Any notice, request, demand, consent, approval, or other communication required or permitted under this lease must be in writing and will be deemed to have been given when personally delivered or deposited in any depository regularly maintained by the United States Postal Service, postage prepaid, certified mail, return receipt requested, addressed to the party for whom it is intended at its address set forth in Article 1. Either landlord or tenant may add additional addresses or change its address for purposes of receipt of any such communication by giving ten (10) days prior written notice of such change to the other party in the manner prescribed in this Section 28.12.

28.13   Severability. If any provision of this lease proves to be illegal, invalid, or unenforceable, the remainder of this lease will not be affected by such finding, and in lieu of each provision of this lease that is illegal, invalid, or unenforceable a provision will be added as a part of this lease as similar in terms to such illegal, invalid, or unenforceable provision as may be possible and be legal, valid and enforceable.

28.14   Written Amendment Required. No amendment, alteration, modification of, or addition to the lease will be valid or binding unless expressed in writing and signed by the party or parties to be bound by such change. Tenant agrees to make any modifications of the terms and provisions of this lease required or requested by any lending institution providing financing for the shopping center, provided that no such modifications will materially adversely affect tenant's rights and obligations under this lease.

28.15   Entire Agreement. This lease, the exhibits, and addenda, if any, contain the entire agreement between landlord and tenant and may be amended only by subsequent written agreement. No promises or representations, except as contained in this lease, have been made to tenant respecting the condition of the premises or the manner of operating the shopping center.

28.16   Captions. The captions of the various articles and sections of this lease are for convenience only and do not necessarily define, limit, describe, or construe the contents of such articles or sections.

28.17   Notice of Landlord's Default. In the event of any alleged default in the obligation of landlord under this lease, tenant will deliver to landlord written notice and landlord will have thirty (30) days following receipt of such notice to cure such alleged default or, in the event the alleged default cannot reasonably be cured within a thirty (30) day period, to commence action to cure such alleged default. A copy of such notice will be sent to any holder of a mortgage or other encumbrance on the shopping center or the premises of which tenant has been notified in writing, and such holder will also have the same time periods to cure such alleged default.

28.18   Authority. Tenant and the party executing this lease on behalf of tenant represent to landlord that such party is authorized to do so by requisite action of the board of directors or partners, as the case may be, and agree upon request to deliver to landlord a resolution or similar document to that effect.

28.19 Brokers. Landlord and tenant respectively represent and warrant to each other that neither of them has consulted or negotiated with any broker or finder with regard to the premises except the broker named in Article 1(r), if any. Each of them will indemnify the other against and hold the other harmless from any claims for fees or commissions from anyone with whom either of them has consulted or negotiated with regard to the premises except the broker. Landlord will pay any fees or commissions due the broker.

28.20 Governing Law. This lease will be governed by and construed pursuant to the laws of the state in which the shopping center is located.

28.21 Force Majeure. Landlord will have no liability to tenant, nor will tenant have any right to terminate this lease or abate rent or assert a claim of partial or total actual or constructive eviction, because of landlord's failure to perform any of its obligations in the lease if the failure is due to reasons beyond landlord's reasonable control, including without limitation strikes or other labor difficulties; inability to obtain necessary governmental permits and approvals (including building permits or certificates of occupancy); unavailability or scarcity of materials; war; riot; civil insurrection; accidents; acts of God; and governmental preemption in connection with a national emergency. If landlord fails to perform its obligations because of any reasons beyond landlord's reasonable control (including those enumerated above), the period for tenant's performance will be extended day for day for the duration of the cause of landlord's failure.

28.22 Late Payments. Any payment of rent, including monthly base rent, that is not received within ten (10) days after it is due will be subject to a late charge equal to five percent (5%) of the unpaid payment or $100.00, whichever is greater. This amount is in compensation of landlord's additional cost of processing late payments. In addition, any rent that is not paid when due, including monthly base rent, will accrue interest at a late rate charge of one and one-half percent (1 1/2%) per month (but in no event in an amount in excess of the maximum rate allowed by applicable law) from the date on which it was due until the date on which it is paid in full with accrued interest.

28.23 No Easements for Air or Light. Any diminution or shutting off of light, air, or view by any structure that may be erected on lands adjacent to the shopping center will in no way affect this lease or impose any liability on landlord.

28.24 Tax Credits. Landlord is entitled to all local, state, and federal income tax benefits (including without limitation investment tax credits, energy credits, and rehabilitation credits) available as a result of leasehold improvements for which landlord has paid, or lent money, or guaranteed payment. Promptly after landlord's demand, tenant will give landlord a detailed list of the leasehold improvements and fixtures and their respective costs for which tenant has paid without a loan or guarantee by landlord, and tenant will be entitled to tax benefits attributable to such listed improvements. Landlord will be entitled to all other such tax benefits for all other leasehold improvements.

28.25   Relocation of the Premises. Landlord reserves the unrestricted and unconditional right to relocate the premises to substantially comparable space within the shopping center. Landlord will give tenant a written notice of its intention to relocate the premises, and tenant will complete such relocation within thirty (30) days after receipt of such written notice. If the furnishings of the space to which landlord proposes to relocate tenant are not substantially the same as those of the premises, or if the monthly base rent of the new space is not substantially the same as the prior monthly base rent, tenant may so notify landlord, and if landlord fails to offer space satisfactory to tenant, tenant may terminate this lease effective as of the thirtieth (30th) day after landlord's initial notice. Upon tenant's peaceable vacation and abandonment of the premises, landlord will pay to tenant a sum equal to one monthly installment of the monthly base rent payable under this lease. If tenant does relocate within the shopping center, then effective on the date of such relocation this lease will be amended by deleting the description of the original premises and substituting for it a description of such comparable space. Landlord agrees to reimburse tenant for its actual moving costs to such other space within the shopping center, to the extent such costs are reasonable.

28.26   Landlord's Fees. Whenever tenant requests landlord to take any action or give any consent required or permitted under this lease, tenant will reimburse landlord for all of landlord's costs incurred in reviewing the proposed action or consent, including without limitation reasonable attorneys', engineers', architects', accountants', and other professional fees, within ten (10) days after landlord's delivery to tenant of a statement of such costs. Tenant will be obligated to make such reimbursement without regard to whether landlord consents to any such proposed action.

28.27   Binding Effect. The covenants, conditions, and agreements contained in this lease will bind and inure to the benefit of landlord and tenant and their respective heirs, distributees, executors, administrators, successors, and, except as otherwise provided in this lease, their assigns.

Landlord and tenant have executed this lease as of the day and year first above written.

LANDLORD:

[name]

By: [name]

TENANT:

[name]

[corporate seal]

ATTEST:

BY: [name]

Its [title]

By: [name]

Its Secretary

EXHIBIT A
Legal Description of the Shopping Center

EXHIBIT B
The Premises

EXHIBIT C
Workletter

EXHIBIT D
Rules and Regulations

EXHIBIT E
Sign Criteria

§ 1.3 Single Tenant Lease

SINGLE TENANT BUILDING LEASE

between

[landlord's name]

and

[tenant's name]

Date: [date], 19[00]

TABLE OF CONTENTS

1. Agreement
2. Premises
3. Term
    (a) Initial Term
    (b) Option to Extend
4. Rent
5. Taxes
    (a) Obligation for Payment
    (b) Taxes Payable in Installments
    (c) Taxes for Period other than Term
    (d) Other Impositions
    (e) Right to Contest Taxes
    (f) Estimated Payments
    (g) Final Settlement
6. Utilities
7. Insurance
    (a) "All-Risk" Coverage
    (b) General Liability
    (c) Other Matters
    (d) Additional Insureds
    (e) Waiver
8. Use
9. Compliance with Laws (Generally)
    (a) Tenant's Obligations
    (b) Tenant's Obligations with Respect to Environmental Laws
    (c) Right to Contest Laws
10. Assignments and Subleases
11. Signs
12. Repairs and Maintenance
13. Alterations
14. End of Term
15. Damage and Destruction
    (a) General
    (b) Landlord's Inspection

    (c)   Landlord's Costs
    (d)   No Rent Abatement
    (e)   Damage During Last Three Years
16. Condemnation
    (a)   Total Taking
    (b)   Partial Taking
    (c)   Tenant's Award
    (d)   Allocation of an Award for a Total Taking
17. Subordination
    (a)   General
    (b)   Attornment
18. Landlord's Access
19. Indemnification, Waiver and Release
    (a)   Indemnification
    (b)   Waiver and Release
20. Security Deposit
21. Covenant of Quiet Enjoyment
22. Limitation on Tenant's Recourse
23. Default
    (a)   Cure
    (b)   Events of Default
    (c)   Remedies
24. Arbitration
25. Miscellaneous
    (a)   Recordation
    (b)   Holding Over
    (c)   Estoppel Certificates
    (d)   No Waiver
    (e)   Authority
    (f)   Notices
    (g)   Attorneys' Fees
    (h)   Waiver of Jury Trial
    (i)   Binding Effect

SINGLE TENANT BUILDING LEASE

THIS SINGLE TENANT BUILDING LEASE is made on [date], 19[00], by [name of landlord] ("landlord"), and [name of tenant] ("tenant").

1.   AGREEMENT

Landlord leases the premises (as that term is defined in paragraph 2) to tenant, and tenant leases the premises from landlord, according to this lease.

2.   PREMISES

The premises are the land and building commonly known as [address], City of [city], County of [county], State of [state], and more particularly described as:

Lot [no.]
Block [no.]
[name] Subdivision
according to the plat recorded [date],
19[00], in book [no.], page [no.] of maps,
City of [city]
County of [county]
State of [state]

The premises include the heating, ventilating, and air conditioning systems and the mechanical, electrical, and plumbing systems serving the premises.

3.   TERM

(a)   Initial Term. The term of this lease will be five years, beginning on January 1, 19[00], and expiring on December 31, 19[00].

(b)   Option to Extend. Tenant may extend the term until the fifth anniversary of the expiration date by written notice of its election to do so given to landlord at least one year prior to the expiration date. The terms and conditions of the lease applicable at the expiration date will govern the extended term; however, tenant will have no further right to extend the term and the monthly rent will be the fair market rent for the premises on the expiration date. If landlord and tenant are unable to agree upon the fair market rent prior to the expiration date, the question will be submitted to arbitration according to paragraph 24. In that event, tenant will continue to pay rent according to the lease until the arbitration decision is rendered; at that time, landlord and tenant will make appropriate adjustments as of the expiration date. Tenant will not have any rights under this paragraph 3(b) if (1) an event of default exists on the expiration date or on the date on which the tenant gives its notice, or (2) tenant exercises its rights less than one year before the expiration date.

4.   RENT

Tenant will pay landlord $[amount] (the "monthly rent") in equal consecutive monthly installments on or before the first day of each month during the term of this lease. The monthly rent will be paid in advance at the address specified for landlord in paragraph 25(f) or such other place as landlord designates, without prior demand and without any abatement, deduction or setoff. If the commencement date occurs on a day other than the first day of a calendar month, or if the expiration date occurs on a day other than the last day of a calendar month, then the monthly rent for the fractional month will be prorated on a daily basis.

5.   TAXES

(a)   Obligation for Payment. Tenant will pay all taxes (collectively the "tax"), including without limitation real estate and personal property taxes and assessments assessed, levied, confirmed, or imposed during the term of this lease, whether or not now customary or within the contemplation of landlord and tenant:

(1)   upon, measured by, or reasonably attributable to the cost or value of tenant's equipment, furniture, fixtures, and other personal property located in the premises, or by the cost or value of any leasehold improvements made in or to the premises by or for tenant, regardless of whether title to the improvements is in tenant or landlord;

(2)   upon or measured by the monthly rent, including without limitation any gross receipts tax or excise tax levied by the federal government or any other governmental body with respect to the receipt of monthly rent;

(3)   upon or with respect to the possession, leasing, operation, management, maintenance, alteration, repair, use, or occupancy by tenant of the premises or any portion of the premises;

(4)   upon this transaction or any document to which tenant is a party creating or transferring an interest or an estate in the premises;

(5)   upon the premises and all personal property, furniture, fixtures, and equipment, and all replacements, improvements, or additions to them, whether owned by landlord or tenant; and

(6)   based in whole or in part on a monthly rent, whether made in addition to or in substitution for any other tax.

(b)   Taxes Payable in Installments. Unless landlord has exercised its rights under paragraph 5(f) and if, by law, any tax may at the option of the taxpayer be paid in installments (whether or not interest accrues on the unpaid balance of the tax), tenant may exercise the option to pay the tax (and any accrued interest on the unpaid balance of the tax) in installments; in that event, tenant will pay the installments that become due during the term of this lease as they become due and before any fine, penalty, further interest, or cost may be added to them.

(c)   Taxes for Period Other Than Term. Any tax, including taxes that have been converted into installment payments, relating to a fiscal period of the taxing authority, a part of which period is included within the term and a part of which is included in a period of time prior to the commencement or after the end of the term, whether or not such tax or installments are assessed, levied, confirmed, imposed upon or in respect of, or become a lien upon the premises, or become payable, during the term, will be adjusted between landlord and tenant as of the commencement or end of the term, so that tenant will pay that portion of the tax or installment which the part of the fiscal period included in the term bears to the fiscal period, and landlord will pay the remainder.

(d)   Other Impositions. Tenant will not be obligated to pay local, state, or federal net income taxes assessed against landlord; local, state, or federal capital levy of landlord; or sales, excise, franchise, gift, estate, succession, inheritance, or transfer taxes of landlord.

(e)   Right to Contest Taxes. Tenant will have the right to contest the amount or validity, in whole or in part, of any tax by appropriate proceedings diligently conducted in good faith, only after paying the tax or posting such security as landlord may reasonably require in order to protect the premises against loss or forfeiture. Upon the termination of those proceedings, tenant will pay the amount of the tax or part of the tax as finally determined, the payment of which may have been deferred during the prosecution of the proceedings, together with any costs, fees, interest, penalties, or other related liabilities. Landlord will not be required to join in any contest or proceedings unless the provisions of any law or regulations then in effect require that the proceedings be brought by or in the name of landlord. In that event, landlord will join in the proceedings or permit them to be brought in its name; however, landlord will not be subjected to any liability for the payment of any costs or expenses in connection with any contest or proceedings, and tenant will indemnify landlord against and save landlord harmless from any of those costs and expenses.

(f)   Estimated Payments. If any lender requires landlord to do so, then, in each December during the term or as soon after December as practicable, landlord will give tenant written notice of its estimate of amounts payable under paragraph 5 for the ensuing calendar year. On or before the first day of each month during the ensuing calendar year, tenant will pay to landlord one-twelfth ($^{1}/_{12}$th) of the estimated amounts; however, if notice is not given in December, tenant will continue to pay on the basis of the prior year's estimate until the month after notice is given. If at any time or times it appears to landlord that the amounts payable under paragraph 5 for the current calendar year will vary from its estimate by more than ten percent (10%), landlord will, by written notice to tenant, revise its estimate for the year, and subsequent payments by tenant for such year will be based upon the revised estimate.

(g)   Final Settlement. Within ninety (90) days after the close of each calendar year or as soon after the ninety-day period as practicable, landlord will deliver to tenant a statement of amounts payable under paragraph 5 for the calendar year, prepared by certified public accountants designated by landlord or prepared by landlord and certified by one of its officers. The certified statement will be final and binding upon landlord and tenant. If the statement shows an amount owing by tenant that is less than the estimated payments previously made by tenant for the calendar year, the statement will be accompanied by a refund of the excess by landlord to tenant. If the statement shows an amount owing by tenant that is more than the estimated payments previously made by tenant for the calendar year, tenant will pay the deficiency to landlord within thirty (30) days after the delivery of the statement.

6.   UTILITIES

Tenant will pay the appropriate suppliers for all water, gas, electricity, light, heat, telephone, power, and other utilities and communications services used by tenant on the premises during the term, whether or not the services are billed directly to tenant. Tenant will also procure, or cause to be procured, without cost to landlord, any and all necessary permits, licenses, or other authorizations required for the lawful and proper installation and maintenance upon the premises of wires, pipes, conduits, tubes, and other equipment and appliances for use in supplying any of the services to and upon the premises. Landlord, upon request of tenant, and at the sole expense and liability of tenant, will join with tenant in any application required for obtaining or continuing any of the services.

7. INSURANCE

(a) "All-Risk" Coverage. Tenant will, at its sole expense, obtain and keep in force, during the term of this lease, "all-risk" coverage insurance (including earthquake and flood insurance) naming landlord and tenant as their interests may appear and other parties that landlord or tenant may designate as additional insureds in the customary form in the City of [city] for buildings and improvements of similar character, on all buildings and improvements now or after this date located on the premises. The amount of the insurance will be designated by landlord no more frequently than once every twelve (12) months, will be set forth on an "agreed amount endorsement" to the policy of insurance, will not be less than the agreed value of the buildings and improvements, and will be subject to arbitration pursuant to paragraph 24 if landlord and tenant do not agree with regard to such value. Landlord and tenant agree that the value of the existing building on the premises is [amount] dollars ($[0000]).

(b) General Liability. Tenant will, at its sole expense, obtain and keep in force during the term of this lease commercial general liability insurance with a combined single limit of not less than [amount] dollars ($[0000]) for injury to or death of any one person, for injury to or death of any number of persons in one occurrence, and for damage to property, insuring against any and all liability of landlord and tenant, including without limitation coverage for contractual liability, broad form property damage, host liquor liability, and non-owned automobile liability, with respect to the premises or arising out of the maintenance, use, or occupancy of the premises. The insurance will insure the performance by tenant of the indemnity agreement as to liability for injury to or death of persons and damage to property set forth in paragraph 19. The insurance will be noncontributing with any insurance that may be carried by landlord and will contain a provision that landlord, although named as an insured, will nevertheless be entitled to recover under the policy for any loss, injury, or damage to landlord, its agents, and employees, or the property of such persons. The limits and coverage of all the insurance will be adjusted by agreement of landlord and tenant during every third lease year during the term of this lease in conformity with the then prevailing custom of insuring liability in the City of [city], and any disagreement regarding the adjustment will be submitted to arbitration in the manner provided in paragraph 24.

(c) Other Matters. All insurance required in this paragraph and all renewals of it will be issued by companies authorized to transact business in the State of [state], and rated at least A+ Class X by Best's Insurance Reports (property liability) or approved by landlord. All insurance policies will be subject to approval by landlord and any lender as to form and substance; will expressly provide that the policies will not be canceled or altered without thirty (30) days' prior written notice to landlord and any lender, in the case of "all-risk" coverage insurance, and to landlord, in the case of general liability insurance; and will, to the extent obtainable, provide that no act or omission of tenant which would otherwise result in forfeiture or reduction of the insurance will affect or limit the obligation of the insurance company to pay the amount of any loss sustained. Tenant may satisfy its obligation under this paragraph by appropriate endorsements of its blanket insurance policies.

(d) Additional Insureds. All policies of liability insurance that tenant is obligated to maintain according to this lease (other than any policy of workmen's compensation insurance) will name landlord and such other persons or firms as landlord specifies from time to time as additional insureds. Original or copies of original policies (together with copies of the endorsements naming landlord, and any others specified by landlord, as additional insureds) and evidence of the payment of all premiums of such policies will be delivered to landlord prior to tenant's occupancy of the premises and from time to time at least thirty (30) days prior to the expiration of the term of each policy. All public liability, property damage liability, and casualty policies maintained by tenant will be written as primary policies, not contributing with and not in excess of coverage that landlord may carry. No insurance required to be maintained by tenant by this paragraph will be subject to any deductible without landlord's prior written consent.

(e) Waiver. Landlord and tenant waive all rights to recover against each other or against any other tenant or occupant of the building, or against the officers, directors, shareholders, partners, joint venturers, employees, agents, customers, invitees, or business visitors of each of theirs or of any other tenant or occupant of the building, for any loss or damage arising from any cause covered by any insurance required to be carried by each of them pursuant to this paragraph 7 or any other insurance actually carried by each of them. Landlord and tenant will cause their respective insurers to issue appropriate waiver of subrogation rights endorsements to all policies of insurance carried in connection with the building or the premises or the contents of either of them. Tenant will cause all other occupants of the premises claiming by, under, or through tenant to execute and deliver to landlord a waiver of claims similar to the waiver in this paragraph and to obtain such waiver of subrogation rights endorsements.

8. USE

The premises will be used only for:

[description]

9. COMPLIANCE WITH LAWS (GENERALLY)

(a) Tenant's Obligations. Tenant will not use or occupy, or permit any portion of the premises to be used or occupied:

(1) in violation of any law, ordinance, order, rule, regulation, certificate of occupancy, or other governmental requirement;

(2) for any disreputable business or purpose; or

(3)   in any manner or for any business or purpose that creates risks of fire or other hazards, or that would in any way violate, suspend, void, or increase the rate of fire or liability or any other insurance of any kind at any time carried by landlord upon all or any part of the building in which the premises are located or its contents.

Tenant will comply with all laws, ordinances, orders, rules, regulations, and other governmental requirements relating to the use, condition, or occupancy of the premises, and all rules, orders, regulations, and requirements of the board of fire underwriters or insurance service office, or any other similar body, having jurisdiction over the building in which the premises are located.

(b)   Tenant's Obligations with Respect to Environmental Laws.

(1)   Tenant and the premises will remain in compliance with all applicable laws, ordinances, and regulations (including consent decrees and administrative orders) relating to public health and safety and protection of the environment, including those statutes, laws, regulations, and ordinances identified in subparagraph (7), all as amended and modified from time to time (collectively, "environmental laws"). All governmental permits relating to the use or operation of the premises required by applicable environmental laws are and will remain in effect, and tenant will comply with them.

(2)   Tenant will not permit to occur any release, generation, manufacture, storage, treatment, transportation, or disposal of "hazardous material," as that term is defined in subparagraph (7), on, in, under, or from the premises. Tenant will promptly notify landlord, in writing, if tenant has or acquires notice or knowledge that any hazardous material has been or is threatened to be released, discharged, disposed of, transported, or stored on, in, under, or from the premises; and if any hazardous material is found on the premises, tenant, at its own cost and expense, will immediately take such action as is necessary to detain the spread of and remove the hazardous material to the complete satisfaction of landlord and the appropriate governmental authorities.

(3)   Tenant will immediately notify landlord and provide copies upon receipt of all written complaints, claims, citations, demands, inquiries, reports, or notices relating to the condition of the premises or compliance with environmental laws. Tenant will promptly cure and have dismissed with prejudice any of those actions and proceedings to the satisfaction of landlord. Tenant will keep the premises free of any lien imposed pursuant to any environmental laws.

(4)   Landlord will have the right at all reasonable times and from time to time to conduct environmental audits of the premises, and tenant will cooperate in the conduct of those audits. The audits will be conducted by a consultant of landlord's choosing, and if any hazardous material is detected or if a violation of any of the warranties, representations, or covenants contained in this paragraph is discovered, the fees and expenses of such consultant will be borne by tenant and will be paid as additional rent under this lease on demand by landlord.

(5)   If tenant fails to comply with any of the foregoing warranties, representations, and covenants, landlord may cause the removal (or other cleanup

acceptable to landlord) of any hazardous material from the premises. The costs of hazardous material removal and any other cleanup (including transportation and storage costs) will be additional rent under this lease, whether or not a court has ordered the cleanup, and those costs will become due and payable on demand by landlord. Tenant will give landlord, its agents, and employees access to the premises to remove or otherwise clean up any hazardous material. Landlord, however, has no affirmative obligation to remove or otherwise clean up any hazardous material, and this lease will not be construed as creating any such obligation.

(6) Tenant agrees to indemnify, defend (with counsel reasonably acceptable to landlord and at tenant's sole cost), and hold landlord and landlord's affiliates, shareholders, directors, officers, employees, and agents free and harmless from and against all losses, liabilities, obligations, penalties, claims, litigation, demands, defenses, costs, judgments, suits, proceedings, damages (including consequential damages), disbursements, or expenses of any kind (including attorneys' and experts' fees and expenses and fees and expenses incurred in investigating, defending, or prosecuting any litigation, claim, or proceeding) that may at any time be imposed upon, incurred by, or asserted or awarded against landlord or any of them in connection with or arising from or out of:

(A) any hazardous material on, in, under, or affecting all or any portion of the premises;

(B) any misrepresentation, inaccuracy, or breach of any warranty, covenant, or agreement contained or referred to in this paragraph;

(C) any violation or claim of violation by tenant of any environmental law; or

(D) the imposition of any lien for the recovery of any costs for environmental cleanup or other response costs relating to the release or threatened release of hazardous material.

This indemnification is the personal obligation of tenant and will survive termination of this lease. Tenant, its successors, and assigns waive, release, and agree not to make any claim or bring any cost recovery action against landlord under CERCLA, as that term is defined in subparagraph (7), or any state equivalent or any similar law now existing or enacted after this date. To the extent that landlord is strictly liable under any such law, regulation, ordinance, or requirement, tenant's obligation to landlord under this indemnity will also be without regard to fault on the part of tenant with respect to the violation or condition that results in liability to landlord.

(7) For purposes of this lease, "hazardous material" means:

(A) "hazardous substances" or "toxic substances" as those terms are defined by the Comprehensive Environmental Response, Compensation, and Liability Act (CERCLA), 42 U.S.C. § 9601, et seq., or the Hazardous Materials Transportation Act, 49 U.S.C. § 1802, both as amended to this date and as amended after this date;

(B) "hazardous wastes," as that term is defined by the Resource Conservation and Recovery Act (RCRA), 42 U.S.C. § 6902, et seq., as amended to this date and as amended after this date;

(C) any pollutant, contaminant, or hazardous, dangerous, or toxic chemical, material, or substance within the meaning of any other applicable federal, state, or local law, regulation, ordinance, or requirement (including consent decrees and administrative orders) relating to or imposing liability or standards of conduct concerning any hazardous, toxic, or dangerous waste substance or material, all as amended to this date or as amended after this date;

(D) crude oil or any fraction of it that is liquid at standard conditions of temperature and pressure (60 degrees Fahrenheit and 14.7 pounds per square inch absolute);

(E) any radioactive material, including any source, special nuclear, or by-product material as defined at 42 U.S.C. § 2011, et seq., as amended to this date or as amended after this date;

(F) asbestos in any form or condition; and

(G) polychlorinated biphenyls (PCB's) or substances or compounds containing PCB's.

(c) Right to Contest Laws. Tenant will have the right to contest by appropriate proceedings diligently conducted in good faith in the name of tenant, or, with the prior consent of the landlord, in the name of landlord, or both, without cost or expense to landlord, the validity or application of any law, ordinance, order, rule, regulation, or legal requirement of any nature. If compliance with any law, ordinance, order, rule, regulation, or requirement may legally be delayed pending the prosecution of any proceeding, without incurring any lien, charge, or liability of any kind against the premises, or tenant's interest in the premises, and without subjecting tenant or landlord to any liability, civil or criminal, for failure so to comply, tenant may delay compliance until the final determination of the proceeding. Even if a lien, charge, or liability may be incurred by reason of delay, tenant may contest and delay, so long as (1) the contest or delay does not subject landlord to criminal liability and (2) tenant furnishes to landlord security, reasonably satisfactory to landlord, against any loss or injury by reason of any contest or delay. Landlord will not be required to join any proceedings referred to in this paragraph unless the provision of any applicable law, rule, or regulation at the time in effect requires that the proceedings be brought by or in the name of landlord, or both. In that event landlord will join the proceedings or permit them to be brought in its name if tenant pays all related expenses.

10. ASSIGNMENTS AND SUBLEASES

Without landlord's prior written consent, which landlord agrees will not be unreasonably withheld or delayed, tenant will neither assign this lease in whole or in part nor sublease all or part of the premises.

11. SIGNS

Tenant may install signs on the premises in accordance with federal, state, and local statutes, laws, ordinances, and codes.

12.   REPAIRS AND MAINTENANCE

Tenant will, at its sole cost and expense, maintain the premises and make repairs, restorations, and replacements to the premises, including without limitation the heating, ventilating, air conditioning, mechanical, electrical, elevator, and plumbing systems, structural roof, walls, and foundations, and the fixtures and appurtenances to the premises as and when needed to preserve them in good working order and condition and regardless of whether the repairs, restorations, and replacements are ordinary or extraordinary, foreseeable or unforeseeable, capital or noncapital, or the fault or not the fault of tenant, its agents, employees, invitees, visitors, or contractors. All repairs, restorations, and replacements will be in quality and class equal to the original work or installations. If tenant fails to make repairs, restorations, or replacements, landlord may make them at the expense of tenant and the expense will be collectible as additional rent to be paid by tenant within fifteen (15) days after delivery of a statement for the expense.

13.   ALTERATIONS

Tenant will not make any alterations, additions, or improvements to the premises without landlord's prior written consent; however, landlord's prior written consent will not be necessary for any alteration, addition, or improvement which:

(a)   costs less than [amount] dollars ($[0000]) including labor and materials;

(b)   does not change the general character of the premises, or reduce the fair market value of the premises below its fair market value prior to the alteration, addition, or improvement;

(c)   is made with due diligence, in a good and workmanlike manner, and in compliance with the laws, ordinances, orders, rules, regulations, certificates of occupancy, or other governmental requirements described in paragraph 9;

(d)   is promptly and fully paid for by tenant; and

(e)   is made under the supervision of an architect or engineer reasonably satisfactory to landlord and in accordance with plans and specifications and cost estimates approved by landlord.

Landlord may designate a supervising architect to assure compliance with the provisions of this paragraph, and if it does, tenant will pay the supervising architect's charges. Subject to tenant's rights in paragraph 14, all alterations, additions, fixtures, and improvements, whether temporary or permanent in character, made in or upon the premises by tenant, will immediately become landlord's property and at the end of the term of this lease will remain on the premises without compensation to tenant. By notice given to tenant no less than ninety (90) days prior to the end of this lease, landlord may require that any alterations, additions, fixtures, and improvements made in or upon the premises be removed by tenant. In that event, tenant will remove the alterations, additions, fixtures, and improvements at tenant's sole cost and will restore the premises to the condition in which they were before the alterations, additions, improvements, and additions were made, reasonable wear and tear excepted.

14.   END OF TERM

At the end of this lease, tenant will surrender the premises in good order and condition, ordinary wear and tear excepted. If tenant is not then in default, tenant may remove from the premises any trade fixtures, equipment, and movable furniture placed in the premises by tenant, whether or not the trade fixtures or equipment are fastened to the building. Tenant will not remove any trade fixtures or equipment without landlord's prior written consent if the trade fixtures or equipment are used in the operation of the building or if the removal of the fixtures or equipment will impair the structure of the building. Whether or not tenant is then in default, tenant will remove alterations, additions, improvements, trade fixtures, equipment, and furniture that landlord has requested be removed in accordance with paragraph 13. Tenant will fully repair any damage occasioned by the removal of any trade fixtures, equipment, furniture, alterations, additions, and improvements. All trade fixtures, equipment, furniture, alterations, additions, and improvements not so removed will conclusively be deemed to have been abandoned by tenant and may be appropriated, sold, stored, destroyed, or otherwise disposed of by landlord without notice to tenant or to any other person and without obligation to account for them. Tenant will pay landlord all expenses incurred in connection with landlord's disposition of such property, including without limitation the cost of repairing any damage to the building or premises caused by removal of the property. Tenant's obligation to observe and perform this covenant will survive the end of this lease.

15.   DAMAGE AND DESTRUCTION

(a)   General. If the premises are damaged or destroyed by reason of fire or any other cause, tenant will immediately notify landlord and will promptly repair or rebuild the building at tenant's expense, so as to make the building at least equal in value to the building existing immediately prior to the occurrence and as nearly similar to it in character as is practicable and reasonable. Landlord will apply and make available to pay to tenant the net proceeds of any fire or other casualty insurance paid to landlord, after deduction of any costs of collection, including attorneys' fees, for repairing or rebuilding as the same progresses. Payments will be made against properly certified vouchers of a competent architect in charge of the work and approved by landlord. Landlord will contribute, out of the insurance proceeds, towards each payment to be made by or on behalf of tenant for the repairing or rebuilding of the building, under a schedule of payments to be made by tenant and not unreasonably objected to by landlord, an amount in the proportion to the payment by tenant as the total net amount received by landlord from insurers bears to the total estimated cost of the rebuilding or repairing. Landlord, however, may withhold from each amount so to be paid by landlord fifteen percent (15%) of the amount until the work of repairing or rebuilding is completed and proof has been furnished to landlord that no lien or liability has attached or will attach to the premises or to landlord in connection with the repairing or rebuilding. Upon the completion of rebuilding and the furnishing of that proof, the balance of the net proceeds of the insurance will be paid to tenant. If the proceeds of insurance are paid to the holder of any mortgage on landlord's interest in the premises, landlord will make available net proceeds of the insurance in accordance with the provisions of this paragraph. Before beginning repairs or rebuilding, or letting any contracts in connection with repairs or rebuilding, tenant will submit for landlord's approval, which approval landlord will not unreasonably withhold or delay, complete and detailed plans and specifications for the repairs or rebuilding. Promptly after receiving landlord's approval of those plans and specifications, tenant will begin the repairs or rebuilding and will prosecute the repairs or rebuilding to completion with diligence, subject, however, to strikes, lockouts, acts of God, embargoes, governmental restrictions, and other causes beyond tenant's reasonable control. Tenant will obtain and deliver to landlord a temporary or final certificate of occupancy before the premises are reoccupied for any purpose. The repairs or rebuilding will be completed free and clear of mechanics' or other liens, and in accordance with the building codes and all applicable laws, ordinances, regulations, or orders of any state, municipal, or other public authority affecting the repairs or rebuilding, and also in accordance with all requirements of the insurance rating organization, or similar body, and of any liability insurance company insuring landlord against liability for accidents related to the premises. Any remaining proceeds of insurance after the restoration will be tenant's property.

(b)   Landlord's Inspection. During the progress of repairs or rebuilding, landlord and its architects and engineers may from time to time inspect the building and will be furnished, if required by them, with copies of all plans, shop drawings, and specifications relating to the repairs or rebuilding. Tenant will keep all plans, shop drawings, and specifications at the building, and landlord and its architects and engineers may examine them at all reasonable times. If, during repairs or rebuilding, landlord and its architects and engineers determine that the repairs or rebuilding are not being done in accordance with the approved plans and specifications, landlord will give prompt notice in writing to tenant, specifying in detail the particular deficiency, omission, or other respect in which landlord claims the repairs or rebuilding do not accord with the approved plans and specifications. Upon the receipt of that notice, tenant will cause corrections to be made to any deficiencies, omissions, or such other respect. Tenant's obligations to supply insurance according to paragraph 7 will be applicable to any repairs or building under this paragraph.

(c)   Landlord's Costs. The charges of any architect or engineer of landlord employed to pass upon any plans and specifications and to supervise and approve any construction, or for any services rendered by the architect or engineer to landlord as contemplated by any of the provisions of this lease, will be paid by tenant as a cost of the repair or rebuilding. The fees of such architect or engineer will be those customarily paid for comparable services.

(d)   No Rent Abatement. Monthly rent and additional rent will not abate pending the repairs or rebuilding except to the extent to which landlord receives a net sum as proceeds of any rent insurance.

(e)   Damage During Last Three Years. If at any time during the last three years of the term (as extended according to paragraph 3) the building is so damaged by fire or otherwise that the cost of restoration exceeds fifty percent (50%) of the replacement value of the building (exclusive of foundations) immediately prior to the damage, either landlord or tenant may, within thirty (30) days after such damage, give notice of its election to terminate this lease and, subject to the further provisions of this paragraph, this lease will cease on the tenth (10th) day after the delivery of that notice. Monthly rent will be apportioned and paid to the time of termination. If this lease is so terminated, tenant will have no obligation to repair or rebuild, and the entire insurance proceeds will belong to landlord.

16.   CONDEMNATION

(a)   Total Taking. If, by exercise of the right of eminent domain or by conveyance made in response to the threat of the exercise of such right (in either case a "taking"), all of the premises are taken, or if so much of the premises are taken that the premises (even if the restorations described in paragraph 16(b) were to be made) cannot be used by tenant for the purposes for which they were used immediately before the taking, this lease will end on the earlier of the vesting of title to the premises in the condemning authority or the taking of possession of the premises by the condemning authority (in either case the "ending date"). If this lease ends according to this paragraph 16(a), prepaid rent will be appropriately prorated to the ending date. The award in a taking subject to this paragraph 16(a) will be allocated according to paragraph 16(d).

(b)   Partial Taking. If, after a taking, so much of the premises remains that the premises can be used for substantially the same purposes for which they were used immediately before the taking:

(1)   this lease will end on the ending date as to the part of the premises which is taken;

(2)   prepaid rent will be appropriately allocated to the part of the premises which is taken and prorated to the ending date;

(3)   beginning on the day after the ending date, rent for so much of the premises as remains will be reduced in the proportion of the floor area of the building remaining after the taking to the floor area of the building before the taking;

(4)   at its cost, tenant will restore so much of the premises as remains to a sound architectural unit substantially suitable for the purposes for which it was used immediately before the taking, using good workmanship and new first class materials, all according to paragraph 13;

(5)   upon the completion of restoration according to clause (6), landlord will pay tenant the lesser of the net award made to landlord on account of the taking (after deducting from the total award attorneys', appraisers', and other

costs incurred in connection with obtaining the award, and amounts paid to the holders of mortgages affecting the premises), or tenant's actual out-of-pocket cost of restoring the premises; and

(6)   landlord will keep the balance of the net award.

(c)   Tenant's Award. In connection with any taking subject to paragraph 16(a) or 16(b), tenant may prosecute its own claim by separate proceedings against the condemning authority for damages legally due to it (such as the loss of fixtures which tenant was entitled to remove and moving expenses) only so long as tenant's award does not diminish or otherwise adversely affect landlord's award.

(d)   Allocation of an Award for a Total Taking. If this lease ends according to paragraph 16(a), the condemnation award will be paid in the order in this paragraph 16(d) to the extent it is sufficient:

(1)   First, landlord will be reimbursed for its attorneys' fees, appraisal fees, and other costs incurred in prosecuting the claim for the award.

(2)   Second, any lender whose loan is secured by the premises will be paid the principal balance of its loan, plus accrued and unpaid interest, and any other charges due on payment.

(3)   Third, landlord will be paid the value at the time of the award of lost rent and the reversion to the extent they exceed the amount paid to landlord's lender.

(4)   Fourth, tenant will be paid its adjusted book value as of the date of the taking of its improvements (excluding trade fixtures) made to the premises. In computing its adjusted book value, improvements will be conclusively presumed to have been depreciated or amortized for federal income tax purposes over their useful lives with a reasonable salvage value.

(5)   Fifth, the balance will be divided equally between landlord and tenant.

17.   SUBORDINATION

(a)   General. This lease and tenant's rights under this lease are subject and subordinate to any ground lease or underlying lease, first mortgage, first deed of trust, or other first lien encumbrance or indenture, together with any renewals, extensions, modifications, consolidations, and replacements of them, which now or at any subsequent time affect the premises, any interest of landlord in the premises, or landlord's interest in this lease and the estate created by this lease (except to the extent that any such instrument expressly provides that this lease is superior to it). This provision will be self-operative and no further instrument of subordination will be required in order to effect it. Nevertheless, tenant will execute, acknowledge and deliver to landlord, at any time and from time to time, upon demand by landlord, any documents as may be requested by landlord, any ground landlord or underlying lessor, or any mortgagee, or any holder of a deed of trust or other instrument described in this paragraph, to confirm or effect the subordination. If tenant fails or refuses to execute, acknowledge, and deliver any such document within twenty (20) days after written demand, landlord, its successors, and assigns will be entitled to execute, acknowledge, and deliver the document on behalf of tenant as tenant's as attorney-in-fact. Tenant constitutes and irrevocably appoints landlord, its successors, and assigns, as tenant's attorney-in-fact to execute, acknowledge, and deliver on behalf of tenant any documents described in this paragraph.

(b)   Attornment. If any holder of any mortgage, indenture, deed of trust, or other similar instrument described in subparagraph (a) succeeds to landlord's interest in the premises, tenant will pay to it all rents subsequently payable under this lease. Tenant will, upon request of anyone so succeeding to the interest of landlord, automatically become the tenant of, and attorn to, the successor in interest without change in this lease. The successor in interest will not be bound by (1) any payment of rent for more than one month in advance, (2) any amendment or modification of this lease made without its written consent, (3) any claim against landlord arising prior to the date on which the successor succeeded to landlord's interest, or (4) any claim or offset of rent against the landlord. Upon request by the successor in interest and without cost to landlord or the successor in interest, tenant will execute, acknowledge, and deliver an instrument or instruments confirming the attornment. The instrument of attornment will also provide that the successor in interest will not disturb tenant in its use of the premises in accordance with this lease. If tenant fails or refuses to execute, acknowledge, and deliver the instrument within twenty (20) days after written demand, the successor in interest will be entitled to execute, acknowledge, and deliver the document on behalf of tenant as tenant's as attorney-in-fact. Tenant constitutes and irrevocably appoints the successor in interest as tenant's attorney-in-fact to execute, acknowledge, and deliver on behalf of tenant any document described in this paragraph.

18.   LANDLORD'S ACCESS

Landlord, its agents, employees, and contractors may enter the premises at any time in response to an emergency, and at reasonable hours to (a) inspect the premises, (b) exhibit the premises to prospective purchasers, lenders, or tenants, (c) determine whether tenant is complying with its obligations in this lease, (d) supply any other service which this lease requires landlord to provide, (e) post notices of nonresponsibility or similar notices, or (f) make repairs which this lease requires landlord to make; however, all work will be done as promptly as reasonably possible and so as to cause as little interference to tenant as reasonably possible. Tenant waives any claim on account of any injury or inconvenience to tenant's business, interference with tenant's business, loss of occupancy or quiet enjoyment of the premises, or any other loss occasioned by the entry. Landlord will at all times have a key with which to unlock all of the doors in the premises (excluding tenant's vaults, safes, and similar areas designed in writing by tenant in advance). Landlord will have the right to use any means landlord may deem proper to open doors in the premises and to the premises in an emergency in order to enter the premises. No entry to the premises by landlord by any means will be a forcible or unlawful entry into the premises or a detainer of the premises or an eviction, actual or constructive, of tenant from the premises, or any part of the premises, nor will any entry entitle tenant to damages or an abatement of rent or other charges which this lease requires tenant to pay.

19. INDEMNIFICATION, WAIVER AND RELEASE

(a) Indemnification. Tenant will indemnify landlord, its agents, and employees against, and hold landlord, its agents, and employees harmless from, any and all demands, claims, causes of action, fines, penalties, damages (including consequential damages), losses, liabilities, judgments, and expenses (including without limitation attorneys' fees and court costs) incurred in connection with or arising from:

(1)   the use or occupancy of the premises by tenant or any person claiming under tenant;

(2)   any activity, work, or thing done or permitted or suffered by tenant in or about the premises;

(3)   any acts, omissions, or negligence of tenant, any person claiming under tenant, or the employees, agents, contractors, invitees, or visitors of tenant or any person;

(4)   any breach, violation, or nonperformance by tenant, any person claiming under tenant, or the employees, agents, contractors, invitees, or visitors of tenant, or any person of any term, covenant, or provision of this lease or any law, ordinance, or governmental requirement of any kind; or

(5)   except for loss of use of all or any portion of the premises or tenant's property located within the premises that is proximately caused by or results proximately from the negligence of landlord, any injury or damage to the person, property, or business of tenant or its employees, agents, contractors, invitees, visitors, or any other person entering upon the premises under the express or implied invitation of tenant.

If any action or proceeding is brought against landlord, its employees, or agents by reason of any claim, tenant, upon notice from landlord, will defend the claim at tenant's expense with counsel reasonably satisfactory to landlord.

(b) Waiver and Release. Tenant waives and releases all claims against landlord, its employees, and agents with respect to all matters for which landlord has disclaimed liability pursuant to the provisions of this lease. In addition, tenant agrees that landlord, its agents, and employees will not be liable for any loss, injury, death, or damage (including consequential damages) to persons, property, or tenant's business occasioned by theft; act of God; public enemy; injunction; riot; strike; insurrection; war; court order; requisition; order of governmental body or authority; fire; explosion; falling objects; steam, water, rain or snow; leak or flow of water (including water from the elevator system), rain or snow from the premises or into the premises or from the roof, street, subsurface, or from any other place, or by dampness, or from the breakage, leakage, obstruction, or other defects of the pipes, sprinklers, wires, appliances, plumbing, air conditioning, or lighting fixtures of the building; or from construction, repair, or alteration of the premises or from any acts or omissions of any visitor of the premises; or from any cause beyond landlord's control.

20.   SECURITY DEPOSIT

Tenant has deposited [amount] dollars ($[0000]) with landlord as security for tenant's payment of rent and performance of its other obligations under this lease, and any renewals or extensions of this lease. If tenant defaults in its payment of rent or performance of its other obligations under this lease, landlord may use all or part of the security deposit for the payment of rent or any other amount in default, or for the payment of any other amount which landlord may spend or become obligated to spend by reason of tenant's default, or for the payment to landlord of any other loss or damage which landlord may suffer by reason of tenant's default. If landlord so uses any portion of the security deposit, tenant will restore the security deposit to its original amount within five (5) days after written demand from landlord. Landlord will not be required to keep the security deposit separate from its general funds, and tenant will not be entitled to interest on the security deposit. The security deposit will not be a limitation on landlord's damages or other rights under this lease, or a payment of liquidated damages, or an advance payment of the rent. If tenant pays the rent and performs all of its other obligations under this lease, landlord will return the unused portion of the security deposit to tenant within sixty (60) days after the end of the term; however, if landlord has evidence that the security deposit has been assigned to an assignee of the lease, landlord will return the security deposit to the assignee. Landlord may deliver the security deposit to the purchaser of the premises and be discharged from further liability with respect to it.

21.   COVENANT OF QUIET ENJOYMENT

So long as tenant pays the rent and performs all of its obligations in this lease, tenant's possession of the premises will not be disturbed by landlord, or anyone claiming by, through or under landlord, or by the holders of the mortgages described in paragraph 17.

22.   LIMITATION ON TENANT'S RECOURSE

Tenant's sole recourse against landlord, and any successor to the interest of landlord in the premises, is to the interest of landlord, and any successor, in the premises. Tenant will not have any right to satisfy any judgment which it may have against landlord, or any successor, from any other assets of landlord, or any successor.

In this paragraph the terms "landlord" and "successor" include the shareholders, venturers, and partners of landlord and successor and the officers, directors, and employees of landlord and successor. The provisions of this paragraph are not intended to limit tenant's right to seek injunctive relief or specific performance, or tenant's right to claim the proceeds of insurance (if any) specifically maintained by landlord for tenant's benefit.

23. DEFAULT

(a)   Cure. If tenant fails to pay when due amounts payable under this lease or to perform any of its other obligations under this lease within the time permitted for its performance, then landlord, after ten (10) days' written notice to tenant (or, in case of any emergency, upon notice or without notice as may be reasonable under the circumstances) and without waiving any of its rights under this lease, may (but will not be required to) pay the amount or perform the obligation.

All amounts so paid by landlord and all costs and expenses incurred by landlord in connection with the performance of any obligations (together with interest at the prime rate from the date of landlord's payment of the amount or incurring of each cost or expense until the date of full repayment by tenant) will be payable by tenant to landlord on demand. In the proof of any damages that landlord may claim against tenant arising out of tenant's failure to maintain insurance, landlord will not be limited to the amount of the unpaid insurance premium but will also be entitled to recover as damages for the breach the amount of any uninsured loss (to the extent of any deficiency in the insurance required by the provisions of this lease), damages, costs and expenses of suit, including attorneys' fees, arising out of damage to, or destruction of, the premises occurring during any period for which tenant has failed to provide the insurance.

(b)   Events of Default. The following occurrences are "events of default":

(1)   Tenant defaults in the due and punctual payment of rent, and the default continues for five (5) days after notice from landlord; however, tenant will not be entitled to more than one (1) notice for default in payment of rent during any twelve-month period, and if, within twelve (12) months after any notice, any rent is not paid when due, an event of default will have occurred without further notice;

(2)   Tenant vacates or abandons the premises;

(3)   This lease or the premises or any part of the premises is taken upon execution or by other process of law directed against tenant, or is taken upon or subjected to any attachments by any creditor of tenant or claimant against tenant, and the attachment is not discharged within fifteen (15) days after its levy;

(4)   Tenant files a petition in bankruptcy or insolvency or for reorganization or arrangement under the bankruptcy laws of the United States or under any insolvency act of any state, or is dissolved, or makes an assignment for the benefit of creditors;

(5)   Involuntary proceedings under any bankruptcy laws or insolvency act or for the dissolution of tenant are instituted against tenant, or a receiver or trustee is appointed for all or substantially all of tenant's property, and the proceeding is not dismissed or the receivership or trusteeship is not vacated within sixty (60) days after institution or appointment;

(6)   Tenant fails to take possession of the premises on the commencement date of the term; or

(7)   Tenant breaches any of the other agreements, terms, covenants, or conditions that this lease requires tenant to perform, and the breach continues for a period of thirty (30) days after notice by landlord to tenant.

(c)   Remedies. If any one or more events of default set forth in paragraph 23(b) occurs, then landlord may, at its election, either:

(1)   give tenant written notice of its intention to terminate this lease on the date of the notice or on any later date specified in the notice, and, on the date specified in the notice, tenant's right to possession of the premises will cease and the lease will be terminated, except as to tenant's liability set forth in this paragraph 23(c)(1), as if the date fixed in the notice were the end of the term of this lease. If this lease is terminated pursuant to the provisions of this subparagraph (1), tenant will remain liable to landlord for damages in an amount equal to the rent and other sums that would have been owing by tenant under this lease for the balance of the term if this lease had not been terminated, less the net proceeds, if any, of any reletting of the premises by landlord subsequent to the termination, after deducting all landlord's expenses in connection with reletting, including without limitation the expenses set forth in paragraph 23(c)(2). Landlord will be entitled to collect damages from tenant monthly on the days on which the rent and other amounts would have been payable under this lease if this lease had not been terminated, and landlord will be entitled to receive damages from tenant on each day. Alternatively, at the option of landlord, if this lease is terminated, landlord will be entitled to recover from tenant:

(A)   the worth at the time of award of the unpaid rent which had been earned at the time of termination;

(B)   the worth at the time of award of the amount by which the unpaid rent which would have been earned after termination until the time of award exceeds the amount of rent loss that tenant proves could reasonably have been avoided;

(C)   the worth at the time of award of the amount by which the unpaid rent for the balance of the term of this lease after the time of award exceeds the amount of rent loss that tenant proves could reasonably be avoided; and

(D)   any other amount necessary to compensate landlord for all the detriment proximately caused by tenant's failure to perform its obligations under this lease or which in the ordinary course of things would be likely to result from the failure.

The "worth at the time of award" of the amount referred to in clauses (A) and (B) is computed by allowing interest at the highest rate permitted by law. The "worth at the time of award" of the amount referred to in clause (C) is computed by discounting the amount at the discount rate of the Federal Reserve Bank of [name] at the time of award.

or

(2)   without demand or notice, re-enter and take possession of the premises or any part of the premises; repossess the premises as of the landlord's former estate; expel the tenant from the premises and those claiming through or under tenant; and remove the effects of both or either, without

being deemed guilty of any manner of trespass and without prejudice to any remedies for arrears of rent or preceding breach of covenants or conditions. If landlord elects to re-enter as provided in this paragraph 23(c)(2), or if landlord takes possession of the premises pursuant to legal proceedings or pursuant to any notice provided by law, landlord may, from time to time, without terminating this lease, relet the premises or any part of the premises, either alone or in conjunction with other portions of the building of which the premises are a part, in landlord's or tenant's name but for the account of tenant, for the term or terms (which may be greater or less than the period which would otherwise have constituted the balance of the term of this lease) and on such terms and conditions (which may include concessions of free rent, and the alteration and repair of the premises) as landlord, in its uncontrolled discretion, may determine. Landlord may collect and receive the rents for the premises. Landlord will not be responsible or liable for any failure to relet the premises, or any part of the premises, or for any failure to collect any rent due upon the reletting. No re-entry or taking possession of the premises by landlord will be construed as an election on landlord's part to terminate this lease unless a written notice of the intention is given to tenant. No notice from landlord under this lease or under a forcible entry and detainer statute or similar law will constitute an election by landlord to terminate this lease unless the notice specifically says so. Landlord reserves the right following any re-entry or reletting, or both, to exercise its right to terminate this lease by giving tenant written notice, and in that event the lease will terminate as specified in the notice. If landlord elects to take possession of the premises according to this paragraph 23(c)(2) without terminating the lease, tenant will pay landlord the rent and other sums which would be payable under this lease if the repossession had not occurred, less the net proceeds, if any, of any reletting of the premises after deducting all of landlord's expenses incurred in connection with the reletting, including without limitation all repossession costs, brokerage commissions, legal expenses, attorneys' fees, expenses of employees, alteration, remodeling and repair costs, and expenses of preparation for the reletting. If, in connection with any reletting, the new lease term extends beyond the existing term, or the premises covered by the reletting include areas that are not part of the premises, a fair apportionment of the rent received from the reletting and the expenses incurred in connection with the reletting will be made in determining the net proceeds received from reletting. In addition, in determining the net proceeds from reletting, any rent concessions will be apportioned over the term of the new lease. Tenant will pay the amounts to landlord monthly on the days on which the rent and all other amounts owing under this lease would have been payable if possession had not been retaken, and landlord will be entitled to receive the rent and other amounts from tenant on each day.

24. ARBITRATION

These procedures will govern any arbitration according to this lease:

(a) Arbitration will be commenced by a written demand made by landlord or tenant upon the other. The written demand will contain a statement of the question to be arbitrated and the name and address of the arbitrator appointed by the demandant. Within ten (10) days after its receipt of the written demand, the other will give the demandant written notice of the name and address of its arbitrator. Within ten (10) days after the date of the appointment of the second arbitrator, the two arbitrators will meet. If the two arbitrators are unable to resolve the question in dispute within ten (10) days after their first meeting, they will select a third arbitrator. The third arbitrator will be designated as chairman and will immediately give landlord and tenant written notice of its appointment. The three arbitrators will meet within ten (10) days after the appointment of the third arbitrator. If they are unable to resolve the question in dispute within ten (10) days after their first meeting, the third arbitrator will select a time, date, and place for a hearing and will give landlord and tenant thirty (30) days' prior written notice of it. The date for the hearing will not be more than sixty (60) days after the date of appointment of the third arbitrator. The first two arbitrators may be partial. The third arbitrator must be neutral. All of the arbitrators must have these qualifications: [state the qualifications of the arbitrators.]

(b)   At the hearing, landlord and tenant will each be allowed to present testimony and tangible evidence and to cross-examine each other's witnesses. The arbitrators may make additional rules for the conduct of the hearing or the preparation for it. The arbitrators will render their written decision to landlord and tenant not more than thirty (30) days after the last day of the hearing.

(c)   If the one of whom arbitration is demanded fails to appoint its arbitrator within the time specified, or if the two arbitrators appointed are unable to agree on an appointment of the third arbitrator within the time specified, either landlord or tenant may petition a justice of the [court] Court of the State of [state] to appoint a third arbitrator. The petitioner will give the other five (5) days' written notice before filing its petition.

(d)   The arbitration will be governed by the Arbitration Law of the State of [state], and, when not in conflict with that law, by the general procedures in the Commercial Arbitration Rules of the American Arbitration Association.

(e)   The arbitrators will not have power to add to, modify, detract from, or alter in any way the provisions of this lease or any amendments or supplements to this lease. The written decision of at least two arbitrators will be conclusive and binding upon landlord and tenant. No arbitrator is authorized to make an award of punitive or exemplary damages.

(f)   Landlord and tenant will each pay for the services of its appointees, attorneys, and witnesses, plus one-half (1/2) of all other proper costs relating to the arbitration.

(g)   The decision of the arbitrators will be final and non-appealable, and may be enforced according to the laws of the State of [state].

25.   MISCELLANEOUS

(a)   Recordation. Tenant's recordation of this lease or any memorandum or short form of it will be void and a default under this lease.

(b)   Holding Over. If tenant remains in possession of the premises after the end of this lease, tenant will occupy the premises as a tenant from month to month, subject to all conditions, provisions, and obligations of this lease in effect on the last day of the term.

(c)   Estoppel Certificates. Within no more than [number] ([000]) days after written request by landlord, tenant will execute, acknowledge, and deliver to landlord a certificate stating:

(1)   that this lease is unmodified and in full force and effect, or, if the lease is modified, the way in which it is modified accompanied by a copy of the modification agreement;

(2)   the date to which rental and other sums payable under this lease have been paid;

(3)   that no notice has been received by tenant of any default which has not been cured, or, if the default has not been cured, what tenant intends to do in order to effect the cure, and when it will do so;

(4)   that tenant has accepted and occupied the premises;

(5)   that tenant has no claim or offset against landlord, or, if it does, stating the date of the assignment and assignee (if known to tenant); and

(6)   other matters as may be reasonably requested by landlord.

Any certificate may be relied upon by any prospective purchaser of the premises and any prospective mortgagee or beneficiary under any deed of trust or mortgage encumbering the premises. If landlord submits a completed certificate to tenant, and if tenant fails to object to its contents within ten (10) days after its receipt of the completed certificate, the matters stated in the certificate will conclusively be deemed to be correct. Furthermore, tenant irrevocably appoints landlord as tenant's attorney-in-fact to execute and deliver on tenant's behalf any completed certificate to which tenant does not object within ten (10) days after its receipt.

(d)   No Waiver. No waiver of any condition or agreement in this lease by either landlord or tenant will imply or constitute a further waiver by such party of the same or any other condition or agreement. No act or thing done by landlord or landlord's agents during the term of this lease will be deemed an acceptance of a surrender of the premises, and no agreement to accept the surrender will be valid unless in writing signed by landlord. The delivery of tenant's keys to any employee or agent of landlord will not constitute a termination of this lease unless landlord has entered into a written agreement to that effect. No payment by tenant, or receipt from landlord, of a lesser amount than the rent or other charges stipulated in this lease will be deemed to be anything other than a payment on account of the earliest stipulated rent. No endorsement or statement on any check or any letter accompanying any check or payment as rent will be deemed an accord and satisfaction. Landlord will accept the check for payment without prejudice to landlord's right to recover the balance of the rent or to pursue any other remedy available to landlord. If this lease is assigned, or if the premises or any part of the premises are sublet or occupied by anyone other than tenant, landlord may collect rent from the assignee, subtenant, or occupant and apply the net amount collected to the rent reserved in this lease. No collection will be deemed a waiver of the covenant in this lease against assignment and subletting; the acceptance of the assignee, subtenant, or occupant as tenant; or a release of tenant from the complete performance by tenant of its covenants in this lease.

(e)   Authority. If tenant signs this lease as a corporation, each of the persons executing this lease on behalf of tenant warrants to landlord that tenant is a duly authorized and existing corporation, that tenant is qualified to do business in the state in which the premises are located, that tenant has full right and authority to enter into this lease, and that each and every person signing on behalf of tenant is authorized to do so. Upon landlord's request, tenant will provide evidence satisfactory to landlord confirming these representations.

(f)   Notices. Any notice, request, demand, consent, approval, or other communication required or permitted under this lease will be written and will be deemed to have been given (1) when personally delivered, (2) when served pursuant to the Federal Rules of Civil Procedure, or (3) on the [number] ([000]) day after it is deposited in any depository regularly maintained by the United States postal service, postage prepaid, certified or registered mail, return receipt requested, addressed to:

Landlord: [name]
                [address]

with a copy at the same
time to: [name]
                [address]

Tenant   [name]
                [address]

with a copy at the same
time to: [name]
                [address]

Either landlord or tenant may change its address or addressee for purposes of this paragraph by giving ten (10) days' prior notice according to this paragraph. Any notice from landlord to tenant will be deemed to have been given if delivered to the premises, addressed to tenant, whether or not tenant has vacated or abandoned the premises.

(g)   Attorneys' Fees. If landlord and tenant litigate any provision of this lease or the subject matter of this lease, the unsuccessful litigant will pay to the successful litigant all costs and expenses, including reasonable attorneys' fees and court costs, incurred by the successful litigation at trial and on any appeal. If, without fault, either landlord or tenant is made a party to any litigation instituted by or against the other, the other will indemnify the faultless one against all loss, liability, and expense, including reasonable attorneys' fees and court costs, incurred by it in connection with the litigation.

(h)   Waiver of Jury Trial. Landlord and tenant waive trial by jury in any action, proceeding, or counterclaim brought by either of them against the other on all matters arising out of this lease or the use and occupancy of the premises (except claims for personal injury or property damage). If landlord commences any summary proceeding for nonpayment of rent, tenant will not interpose (and waives the right to interpose) any counterclaim in any proceeding.

(i)   Binding Effect. This lease will inure to the benefit of, and will be binding upon, landlord's successors and assigns. This lease will inure to the benefit of, and will be binding upon, the tenant's successors and assigns so long as the succession or assignment is permitted by paragraph 10.

Landlord and tenant have executed this lease as of the first date in this lease.

LANDLORD:

[name]

APPROVED AS TO LEGAL FORM:

By [attorney]   By [attorney]

Date [date]   Its [position]

TENANT:

[name]

ATTEST:

By [name]   By [name]

Its Secretary   Its [position]

Date [date]   Date [date]

[corporate seal]

STATE OF [state]   )
) ss.
COUNTY OF [county]   )

The foregoing instrument was acknowledged before me on [date], 19[00], by [name], as [position] of [business], a [entity].

Witness my hand and official seal.

[name]

Notary Public

My commission expires: [date]

§ 1.4   Office Lease (A Tenant's Response to Landlord's Form)*

OFFICE LEASE
BASIC LEASE INFORMATION

Date: [date]

Lessor: [name]

Lessee: [name]

	Lease Reference
Premises:	Paragraph 1(c)
Rentable Area of Premises:	Paragraph 1(c)
Lessee's Percentage Share:	Paragraph 1(d)
Base Year:	Paragraph 1(e)
Term Commencement:	Paragraph 2
Term Expiration:	Paragraph 2
Base Rent:	Paragraph 3(a)
Security Deposit:	Paragraph 29
Lessee's Address for Notices:	Paragraph 31
Number of Parking Stalls:	Paragraph 36

---

*This special section presents a tenant's response to a landlord's office lease. The office lease was prepared by Reverdy Johnson, Esq., Pettit & Martin, San Francisco, California, who graciously consented to its use. The exhibits to the office lease have been omitted, and the focus of the tenant's comments is on the body of the lease itself.

For the purposes of this lease, the tenant has been assumed to be a full-floor user. As a result, no comments have been addressed to the maintenance of other parts of the tenant's floor, as might have been the case if the tenant were the user of only part of a floor. The tenant has also been assumed to be an accounting firm. For that reason, it has made an objection in paragraph 2(a) to any possible obligation to take possession of the premises between March 1 and May 15, that is, "tax season." Although opening dates are usually a concern for retail tenants, they are infrequently a concern for office tenants. However, accountants are an exception to the general rule.

No effort has been made to rewrite the business deal which has been presumed to have been agreed to by the landlord and tenant. For example, the tenant has not asked for any renewal options or expansion rights in the comments shown in the lease, since it has been assumed that those rights were not part of the business arrangement between them.

In preparing its responses, the tenant has no reason to believe that it will get everything for which it asks. All of the tenant's requests have compromise or "fallback" positions which may be reached in the course of negotiation. In some instances, the condition of the market makes it improbable that the tenant will be given any of its requests, while other market conditions will sometimes enable the tenant to get whatever it wants.

Tenant's proposed additions shown in [   ] and proposed deletions shown in ⟨   ⟩.

Initial Parking Stall Rent:	Paragraph 36
Exhibit(s) and Addendum:	Paragraph 37
Allowance Area:	Exhibit B, Paragraph 2
Date for Delivery of Instructions:	Exhibit B, Paragraph 7

The provisions of the Lease identified above are those provisions where references to particular Basic Lease Information appear. Each such reference shall incorporate the applicable Basic Lease Information. In the event of any conflict between any Basic Lease Information and the Lease, the latter shall control.

LESSEE   LESSOR

By [name]   By [name]
 Its [* * *]   Its [* * *]

By [name]   By [name]
 Its [* * *]   Its [* * *]

Date of Execution   Date of Execution
by Lessee [date]   by Lessor [date]

TABLE OF CONTENTS

Paragraph:

   1. Definitions
   2. Term; Completion of Improvements
   3. Rental
   4. Escalation Rent Payments
   5. Use
   6. Services
   7. Taxes and Impositions Payable by Lessee
   8. Alterations
   9. Liens
  10. Condition of Premises; Repairs
  11. Destruction or Damage
  12. Insurance
  13. Waiver of Subrogation
  14. Indemnification
  15. Compliance with Legal Requirements
  16. Assignment and Subletting
  17. Entry by Lessor
  18. Default

Tenant's proposed additions shown in [ ] and proposed deletions shown in 〈 〉.

19. Continuation after Default
20. Lessor's Right to Cure Defaults
21. Attorneys' Fees
22. Eminent Domain
23. Subordination
24. No Merger
25. Sale
26. Estoppel Certificate
27. No Light, Air or View Easement
28. Holding Over
29. Security Deposit
30. Waiver
31. Notices and Consents
32. Complete Agreement
33. Corporate Authority
34. Limitation of Liability to Building
35. Miscellaneous
36. Parking
37. Exhibits

Exhibits

A   Floor Plan(s)
B   Initial Improvement of the Premises

OFFICE LEASE

THIS LEASE, dated [date], 19[00], for purposes of reference only, is made and entered into by and between [name], a [* * *] ("Lessor"), and [name] a [* * *] ("Lessee").

WITNESSETH

Lessor hereby leases to Lessee, and Lessee hereby leases from Lessor the premises described in paragraph 1(c) below for the term and subject to the terms, convenants, agreements and conditions hereinafter set forth, to each and all of which Lessor and Lessee hereby mutually agree.

1.   Definitions. Unless the context otherwise specifies or requires, the following terms shall have the meanings herein specified:

(a)   The term "Building" shall mean the land and building located at [address], California.

(b)   The term "Tenant Improvements" shall have the meaning defined in paragraph 1 of Exhibit B attached hereto.

(c)   The term "premises" shall mean the portion of the Building located on the floor(s) specified in the Basic Lease Information that is identified as the premises on the floor plans attached hereto as part of Exhibit A, together with the appurtenant right to the use, in common with others, of lobbies [parking areas, telephone and electric closets, truck docks, restrooms,] entrances,

---

Tenant's proposed additions shown in [   ] and proposed deletions shown in ⟨   ⟩.

stairs, elevators, accessways, platforms, passageways, pipes, ducts, conduits, wires and appurtenant facilities, and all [other] public portions and facilities of the Building. [Lessee may install at its expense microwave, satellite, or other antennae communication systems in the premises or on the roof of the Building; if it decides to do so, Lessor will enable Lessee to install wires, conduits, and appurtenant facilities in the common areas of the Building at no cost to Lessee (other than the cost of installation).] The premises contain the number of square feet of rentable area specified in the Basic Lease Information. The perimeter walls and other structural elements of the Building located within the premises, and any space in the premises used for shafts, stacks, pipes, conduits, ducts, utility facilities or other building facilities and the use thereof and access thereto through the premises for the purposes of operation, maintenance and repairs, are reserved to Lessor: [Lessor's entry in the premises in order to use or have access to such reserved areas is subject to paragraph 17 below.]

(d)   The term "Lessee's percentage share" shall mean the percentage figure specified in the Basic Lease Information. ⟨Lessor and Lessee acknowledge that⟩ Lessee's percentage share has been obtained by dividing the rentable area of the premises as specified in the Basic Lease Information by the total rentable area of the Building, which Lessor ⟨and Lessee estimate⟩ [represents] to be 266,502 square feet, and multiplying such quotient by one hundred. In the event the actual rentable area of the Building is more ⟨or less⟩ than 266,502 square feet [or becomes more than 266,502 square feet as a result of the conversion of common area to rentable area] or in the event the rentable area of the premises is changed from that specified in the Basic Lease Information, Lessee's percentage share shall be appropriately adjusted and for the purposes of paragraph 4 below Lessee's percentage share shall be determined [as a weighted average] in accordance with the number of days during such calendar year when each such percentage share was in effect. ⟨Notwithstanding the foregoing, if any tenant space within the Building, including space for retail or restaurant uses, is leased on a basis where the tenant is separately responsible for paying the cost of services that would otherwise be included in Operating Expenses, such as janitorial or utility services, the rentable area of such tenant space shall be excluded from the rentable area of the Building for the purpose of determining Lessee's percentage share of the balance of the cost of such services that is included in Operating Expenses.⟩

(e)   Unless otherwise provided herein, the term "Base Year" shall mean the calendar year specified in the Basic Lease Information [or the calendar year in which the term of this Lease commences, whichever is later].

(f)   The term "Operating Expenses" shall mean (1) all costs of operation, maintenance, and repair of the Building, including, without limitation, wages, salaries, and payroll tax and insurance burden of employees; janitorial, maintenance, guard and other services; customary management fees and administrative office rent or rental value; power, water, waste disposal and other utility services; materials, tools, equipment and supplies, whether purchased or rented; maintenance and repairs; insurance; and depreciation on personal

---

Tenant's proposed additions shown in [   ] and proposed deletions shown in ⟨   ⟩.

property; and (2) [the annual amortization on a straight-line basis with a reasonable salvage value of] the cost of any capital improvements made to the Building after the Base Year that ⟨are reasonably anticipated to⟩ reduce other operating expenses [(and only to the extent of the reduction if the annual amortization exceeds the reduction)] or that are required under any governmental law or regulation that was not applicable to the Building [on the commencement date of the term of this Lease] ⟨at the time of substantial shell completion⟩ [and does not become applicable to the Building because of changes which Lessor makes to the Building or any part of it,] such cost to be amortized over such reasonable useful life as Lessor shall determine together with interest on the unamortized balance at the rate [which would be charged to the most creditworthy borrowers] ⟨of 10% per annum or such higher rate as may have been paid by Lessor⟩ on funds borrowed for the purpose of constructing such capital improvements; provided, however, that Operating Expenses shall not include Property Taxes, depreciation [or amortization on any buildings or equipment except as allowed by clause (2) immediately above,] cost of tenants' improvements, real estate brokers' commissions, interest, capital items other than those referred to in clause (2) above, and any expense for which Lessor is [entitled to be] ⟨directly⟩ reimbursed by tenants or other parties. Actual Operating Expenses for both the Base Year and each subsequent calendar year shall be adjusted to equal Lessor's reasonable estimate of Operating Expenses had ⟨the total⟩ [90% of the rentable area of the Building been occupied. Operating Expenses will be set forth in a written statement furnished by Lessor to Lessee setting forth in reasonable detail the amounts and components of Operating Expenses. That statement will be certified by an executive officer of Lessor. Lessor will furnish Lessee such information as Lessee reasonably requires in order to verify Operating Expenses. Lessee's payment of Escalation Rent will not preclude Lessee from questioning the truth, correctness, or completeness of the Operating Expenses. Lessee and its authorized representatives will have the right to audit Lessor's books and records with regard to the Operating Expenses.]

(g)   The term "Base Operating Expenses" shall mean the Operating Expenses paid or incurred by Lessor in the Base Year.

(h)   The term "Property Taxes" shall mean all real property taxes or assessments (and any tax or assessment to the extent levied or assessed in lieu thereof) levied or assessed against the Building and all reasonable real estate tax consultant expenses and attorneys' fees incurred for the purpose of maintaining an equitable assessed valuation of the Building.

(i)   The term "Base Property Taxes" shall mean the amount of Property Taxes for the tax year ending June 30 of the Base Year. [Landlord represents to Tenant that such Property Taxes were not abated and that the Building was assessed as a fully completed structure in the Base Year.]

2.   Term; Completion of Improvements.

(a)   The term of this Lease shall commence and, unless sooner terminated as hereinafter provided, shall end on the dates respectively specified in the Basic Lease Information. If Lessor, for any reason whatsoever, cannot deliver

Tenant's proposed additions shown in [   ] and proposed deletions shown in ⟨   ⟩.

possession of the premises to Lessee at the commencement of said term, as above specified, this Lease shall not be void or voidable, nor shall Lessor be liable to Lessee for any loss or damage resulting therefrom, but in that event, subject to any contrary provisions in Exhibit B attached hereto and made a part hereof, rental shall be waived for the period between commencement of the term and the time when Lessor can deliver possession; [however, if Lessor does not deliver possession of the premises on or before [date], 19[00], regardless of the reason for its failure to do so, Lessee may cancel this Lease without liability by notice given on or before [date], 19[00].] No delay in delivery of possession shall operate to extend the term hereof [unless, within thirty days after delivery of possession, Lessee gives notice of its election to extend the term of this Lease by a period equal to the period beginning on the commencement date in the Basic Lease Information and ending on the date of delivery of possession. Lessee shall not be obligated to take possession of the premises between March 1 and May 15.]

(b) In the event the premises are ready for occupancy prior to the date referred to in subparagraph (a) above for the commencement of the term, Lessee [may elect] ⟨shall have the right⟩ to take early occupancy of the premises on such date as ⟨Lessor and⟩ Lessee shall [designate] ⟨agree⟩, and, [if Lessee does take early occupancy,] notwithstanding the provisions of subparagraph (a) above, the term of the Lease shall commence upon such occupancy.

(c) Prior to the commencement date of the term hereof [specified in the Basic Lease Information,] Lessor shall complete the Tenant Improvements to be constructed or installed in the premises. The Tenant Improvements shall be deemed completed and possession of the premises delivered when [an occupancy certificate has been issued with respect to the premises and] Lessor has substantially completed the Tenant Improvements, subject only to the completion of minor items which do not materially impair the usability of the Tenant Improvements by Lessee [and whose completion will not materially impair Lessee's use of the premises,] and Lessee shall accept the premises upon [the third day after its receipt of] notice from Lessor that the Tenant Improvements have been so completed.

3. Rental.

(a) Lessee shall pay to Lessor throughout the term of this Lease as rental for the premises the sum specified in the Basic Lease Information as the Base Rent, provided that the rental payable during each calendar year subsequent to the Base Year shall be the Base Rent, increased by Lessee's percentage share of the total dollar increase, if any, in Operating Expenses paid ⟨or incurred⟩ by Lessor in each such year subsequent to the Base Year over the Base Operating Expenses, and also increased by Lessee's percentage share of the total dollar increase, if any, in Property Taxes paid by Lessor in each such year over the Base Property Taxes. [If Lessee's percentage share of Operating Expenses in any year are less than Lessee's percentage share of the Base Operating Expenses or if Lessee's percentage share of Property Taxes in any year are less than Lessee's percentage share of Base Property Taxes, then Lessee's rental for the subject year will be the increase in Property Taxes or Operating

Expenses (as the case may be) reduced by the amount by which Base Operating Expenses or Base Property Taxes exceed the actual Operating Expenses or Property Taxes, as the case may be.] The increased rental due pursuant to this paragraph (a) is hereinafter referred to as "Escalation Rent."

(b)   Rental shall be paid to Lessor ⟨on or before the first day of the term hereof and⟩ on or before the first day of each and every ⟨successive⟩ calendar month ⟨thereafter⟩ during the term hereof. In the event the term commences on a day other than the first day of a calendar month or ends on a day other than the last day of a calendar month, then the monthly rental for the first fractional month and the monthly rental for the last fractional month of the term hereof shall be appropriately prorated on the basis of a 30-day month [and will be paid on the first day of the first and last full months of the term.]

(c)   Lessee hereby acknowledges that late payment by Lessee to Lessor of rent and other sums due hereunder after the expiration of any applicable grace period will cause Lessor to incur costs not contemplated by this Lease, the exact amount of which will be extremely difficult to ascertain. Such costs include, but are not limited to, processing and accounting charges, and late charges which may be imposed on Lessor by the terms of any mortgage or trust deed covering the premises. Accordingly, if any installment of rent or any other sums due from Lessee shall not be received by Lessor when due or if a grace period is applicable, prior to the expiration of the grace period, [without notice Lessor may apply the deposit described in paragraph 29 below to the payment of such rent or other sums and, if Lessee fails to replenish such deposit within 10 days after notice of its application or if such rent or other sums exceed the deposit, or both,] Lessee shall pay to Lessor a late charge equal to 6% of such [deposit or] overdue amount, [or both.] The parties hereby agree that such late charge represents a fair and reasonable estimate of the costs Lessor will incur by reason of late payment by Lessee. Acceptance of such late charge by Lessor shall in no event constitute a waiver of Lessee's default with respect to such overdue amount or prevent Lessor from exercising any of the other rights and remedies granted hereunder.

(d)   Any amount due to Lessor, if not paid when due, shall bear interest from the date due until paid at the rate of 10% per annum or [Lessor's cost of funds from the time such amount was due until it is fully paid, whichever is less;] ⟨if a higher rate is legally permissible, at the highest rate legally permitted⟩, provided that interest shall not be payable on late charges incurred by Lessee or on any amounts upon which late charges are paid by Lessee to the extent such interest would cause the total interest to be in excess of that legally permitted. Payment of interest shall not excuse or cure any default hereunder by Lessee.

(e)   All payments due from Lessee to Lessor shall be made to Lessor, without deduction or offset, in lawful money of the United States of America at Lessor's address for notices hereunder or to such other person or at such other place as Lessor may from time to time designate in writing to Lessee [or at Lessor's office, or its managing agent's office, in the Building.]

Tenant's proposed additions shown in [   ] and proposed deletions shown in ⟨   ⟩.

4.　Escalation Rent Payments. Escalation Rent shall be paid monthly [according to Lessor's reasonable good faith estimate,] ⟨on an estimated basis⟩, with subsequent annual reconciliation, in accordance with the following procedures:

(a)　During December of the Base Year and during December of each subsequent calendar year, or as soon thereafter as practicable, Lessor shall give Lessee notice of its estimate of any Escalation Rent due under paragraph 3(a) above for the ensuing calendar year. On or before the first day of each month during the ensuing calendar year, Lessee shall pay to Lessor $1/12$th of such estimated Escalation Rent, provided that if such notice is not given in December, Lessee shall continue to pay on the basis of the prior year's estimate until the month after such notice is given. If at any time or times it appears to Lessor that the Escalation Rent for the current calendar year will vary from its estimate by more than 5%, Lessor may, by notice to Lessee, revise its estimate for such year, and subsequent payments by Lessee for such year shall be based upon such revised estimate.

(b)　Within 90 days after the close of each calendar year or as soon after such 90-day period as practicable, Lessor shall deliver to Lessee a statement of the actual Escalation Rent for such calendar year [and, at Lessee's request, supporting documentation.] If on the basis of such statement Lessee owes an amount that is less than the estimated payments for such calendar year previously made by Lessee, Lessor shall refund such excess to Lessee within 30 days after delivery of the statement. If on the basis of such statement Lessee owes an amount that is more than the estimated payments for such calendar year previously made by Lessee, Lessee shall pay the deficiency to Lessor within 30 days after delivery of the statement.

(c)　If the term of this Lease shall commence in a calendar year subsequent to the Base Year and on a day other than the first day of such calendar year, or if the term of this Lease shall end on a day other than the last day of the calendar year, the amount of the Escalation Rent that is applicable to the calendar year in which the term commences or in which the term ends shall be prorated on the basis which the number of days from the commencement of the term to the end of the calendar year in which the term commences bears to 365, or the number of days from the commencement of the calendar year in which the terms ends to the end of the term bears to 365, as the case may be. The termination of this Lease shall not affect the obligation of Lessor and Lessee pursuant to subparagraph (b) above to be performed after such termination.

5.　Use. The premises shall be used for general office purposes [and incidental uses for which Tenant Improvements or Tenant Extra Improvements are made and the sale of computer software and other products developed by Lessee] and no other. Lessee shall not do or permit to be done in or about the premises, nor bring or keep or permit to be brought or kept therein, anything which is prohibited by or will in any way conflict with any law, statute, ordinance or governmental rule or regulation now in force or which may hereafter be enacted or promulgated and [govern Lessee's use of the premises,] or

---

Tenant's proposed additions shown in [ ] and proposed deletions shown in ⟨ ⟩.

which is prohibited by ⟨the standard form of⟩ [Lessor's] fire insurance policy [on the Building,] or will in any way increase the existing rate of or affect any fire or other insurance upon the building or any of its contents, or cause a cancellation of any insurance policy [of Lessor] covering the Building or any part thereof or any of its contents. Lessee shall not do or permit anything to be done in [or about] the premises which will in any way obstruct or interfere with the rights of other tenants or owners in the Building, or injure or annoy them, or use or allow the premises to be used for any ⟨improper, immoral,⟩ unlawful ⟨or objectionable⟩ purpose, nor shall Lessee cause, maintain or permit any nuisance in, on or about the premises or commit or suffer to be committed any waste in, on or about the premises.

6.   Services.

(a)   Lessor shall furnish the premises with (1) electricity for lighting and the operation of office machines, (2) heat and air conditioning [sufficient to maintain temperature in the premises between 68°F and 78°F,] (3) elevator service, (4) [initial] lighting replacement [bulbs and ballasts] (for recessed ceiling-mounted fluorescent fixtures), (5) restroom supplies, (6) window washing with reasonable frequency, [and] (7) security services and daily janitor service, [and (8) heated and chilled water to serve the premises for restroom and drinking use] ⟨during the times and in the manner such services are customarily furnished in comparable office buildings in the commercial district in which the Building is located⟩ [from 7:00 a.m. to 7:00 p.m., Mondays through Fridays, and from 8:00 a.m. to 1:00 p.m., Saturdays. The Building may be closed on Sundays and on the following holidays: New Year's Day, Memorial Day, Independence Day, Labor Day, Thanksgiving Day, and Christmas Day; however Lessee's access to the premises pursuant to this paragraph will not be impaired on those days.] Lessor shall not be in default hereunder or be liable for any damages directly or indirectly resulting from, nor shall the rental herein reserved be abated by reason of (i) the installation, use or interruption of use of any equipment in connection with the furnishing of any of the foregoing services, (ii) failure to furnish or delay in furnishing any such services when such failure or delay is caused by accident or any condition beyond the reasonable control of Lessor or by the making of necessary repairs or improvements to the premises or to the Building, or (iii) [so long as the condition is generally prevailing and does not arise from any default by Lessor,] the limitation, curtailment, rationing or restrictions on use of water, electricity, gas or any other form of energy serving the premises or the Building. Lessor shall use reasonable efforts diligently to remedy any interruption in the furnishing of such services.

(b)   Whenever heat generating machines or equipment other than [normal desktop] office equipment or lighting other than recessed ceiling-mounted fluorescent fixtures are used in the premises by Lessee which [substantially] affect the temperature otherwise maintained by the air conditioning system, Lessor shall have the right to install supplementary air conditioning facilities in the premises or otherwise modify the ventilating and air conditioning system serving the premises, and the cost of such facilities and modifications shall be borne by Lessee. Lessee shall also pay as additional rent the cost of providing all cooling energy to the premises in excess of that required for

---

Tenant's proposed additions shown in [   ] and proposed deletions shown in ⟨   ⟩.

normal office use or during hours requested by Lessee when air conditioning is not otherwise furnished by Lessor. If Lessee installs lighting requiring power in excess of that required for normal office use in the Building or if Lessee installs equipment requiring power in excess of that required for ⟨normal desk-top⟩ office equipment or ⟨normal⟩ copying equipment, Lessee shall pay for the actual cost of such excess power as additional rent, together with the [actual] cost of installing any additional risers or other facilities that may be necessary to furnish such excess power to the premises.

(c) [Lessee, its assignees, subtenants and their employees, agents, contractors, licensees, and guests will have access to the premises at all times, 24 hours per day, every day of the year. Lessor may require a reasonable identification from visitors to the premises outside hours when services are furnished pursuant to this paragraph.]

7.   Taxes and Impositions Payable by Lessee. In addition to the monthly rental and other charges to be paid by Lessee hereunder, Lessee shall pay or reimburse Lessor for any and all of the following, whether or not now customary or in the contemplation of the parties hereto [but not arising out of any fault or special status of Lessor:] taxes (other than local, state and federal personal or corporate income taxes measured by the net income of Lessor from all sources and other than estate or inheritance taxes), assessments (including, without limitation, all assessments for public improvements services or benefits, irrespective of when commenced or completed), excises, levies, business taxes, license, permit, inspection and other authorization fees, transit development fees, assessments or charges for housing funds, service payments in lieu of taxes and any other fees or charges of any kind which are assessed, levied, charged, confirmed or imposed by any public authority (a) upon, measured by or reasonably attributable to (1) the cost or value of Lessee's equipment, furniture, fixtures and other personal property located in the premises, (2) the cost or value of the Tenant Extra Improvements, or (3) the cost or value of any other leasehold improvements made in or to the premises by or for Lessee [with respect to which Lessor represents that there are no presently effective taxes or other costs pursuant to this paragraph;] (b) upon or measured by the monthly rental payable hereunder, including, without limitation, any gross income tax or excise tax levied by any governmental body with respect to the receipt of such rental; (c) upon, with respect to or by reason of the development, possession, leasing, operation, management, maintenance, alteration, repair, use or occupancy of the premises or any portion thereof; (d) upon [this transaction or] any document to which Lessee is a party creating or transferring an interest or an estate in the premises. In the event that it shall not be lawful for Lessee so to remiburese Lessor, the rental payable to Lessor under this Lease shall be revised to net Lessor the same net rental after imposition of any such tax or other charge upon Lessor as would have been payable to Lessor prior to the imposition of any such tax or other charge.

8.   Alterations.

(a) Following the construction or installation of the Tenant Improvements in the premises pursuant to Exhibit B, Lessee may make such alterations,

---

Tenant's proposed additions shown in [   ] and proposed deletions shown in ⟨   ⟩.

additions or improvements thereto or may install such fixtures or equipment in the premises as Lessee shall desire, provided that no such work shall be undertaken without first obtaining Lessor's consent, which consent shall not be unreasonably withheld. At the time such consent is requested, Lessee shall furnish to Lessor a description of the proposed work, an estimate of the cost thereof and such information as shall reasonably be requested by Lessor substantiating Lessee's ability to pay for such work. Within a reasonable period following completion of such work Lessee shall furnish to Lessor "as built" plans showing the changes made to the Tenant Improvements as initially constructed or installed.

(b)   Any alterations, additions or improvements (except the initial Tenant Improvements covered by Exhibit B) to the premises shall be made by Lessee at Lessee's sole cost and expense, and any contractor or other person selected by Lessee to make the same shall be subject to Lessor's prior approval, which approval shall not be unreasonably withheld. Lessee's contractor and its subcontractors shall employ union labor to the extent necessary to insure, so far as may be possible, the progress of the alterations, additions or improvements and the performance of any other work or the provision of any services in the Building without interruption on account of strikes, work stoppage or similar causes of delay. All alterations, additions and improvements [(except Lessee's trade fixtures)] shall immediately become Lessor's property and, at the end of the term hereof, shall remain on the premises without compensation to Lessee.

(c)   So long as the Tenant Improvements in the premises at the end of the term are of the same general character, quantity and configuration as the Tenant Improvements initially constructed or installed in the premises [as modified by alterations made pursuant to subparagraphs (a) and (b),] Lessee shall have no obligation to make any changes in the then existing Tenant Improvements [and alterations;] otherwise, at Lessor's request, Lessee shall take such action at Lessee's expense as shall be necessary to restore the Tenant Improvements to their condition as initially constructed or installed.

(d)   [Any additions and alterations to the premises will be the property of Lessee during the term of this Lease, and Lessee may claim any tax credits and depreciate such property. At the end of the term of this Lease, all such additions and alterations will be and remain part of the Building and the property of Lessor.]

9.   Liens. Lessee shall keep the premises and the Building free from any liens or similar encumbrances arising out of any work performed, materials furnished or obligations incurred by Lessee ⟨and Lessee shall indemnify and hold Lessor harmless from and against any claims, liabilities, judgments or costs, including attorneys' fees, in connection therewith⟩. In the event that Lessee shall not, within 10 days following notice from Lessor as to the imposition of any such lien, cause the same to be released by filing of a bond, by payment or by such other means as shall be satisfactory to Lessor, Lessor shall have, in addition to all other remedies provided herein and by law, the right but not the obligation to cause the same to be released by such means as it shall deem proper, including payment of the claim giving rise to such lien. All

Tenant's proposed additions shown in [   ] and proposed deletions shown in ⟨   ⟩.

sums paid by Lessor for such purpose, and all expenses incurred by it in connection therewith, shall be payable to Lessor by Lessee on demand. Lessor shall have the right to post and keep posted on the premises any notices that may be provided by law or which Lessor may deem to be proper for the protection of Lessor, the premises and the Building from such liens. In the event that any lien is filed against the premises or the Building as a result of work done [at Lessee's request] or materials furnished to Lessee, Lessee shall discharge the same at Lessee's expense within 30 days thereafter by the filing of a bond, by payment or by such other means satisfactory to Lessor.

10. Condition of Premises; Repairs. By entry hereunder Lessee accepts the premises as being in the condition in which Lessor is obligated to deliver the premises subject only to the completion or correction of items on ⟨Lessor's architect's⟩ the punch list [and latent defects.] Lessee shall, at all times during the term hereof and at Lessee's sole cost and expense, ⟨keep⟩ [repair any damage which it does to] the premises and every part thereof, including all improvements and fixtures, whether installed by Lessor or Lessee, ⟨in good condition and repair,⟩ ordinary wear and tear, damage thereto by fire, earthquake, act of God or the elements excepted, Lessee hereby waiving all rights to make repairs at the expense of Lessor or in lieu thereof to vacate the premises as provided by California Civil Code Section 1942 or any other law, statute or ordinance now or hereafter in effect. Subject to the provisions of paragraph 8(c) above, Lessee shall at the end of the term hereof surrender to Lessor the premises and all alterations, additions and improvements thereto in the same condition as when received or when first installed, ordinary wear and tear, and damage by fire, earthquake, act of God or the elements excepted. Lessor has no obligation and has made no promise to alter, remodel, improve, repair, decorate or paint the premises or any part thereof, except as specifically herein set forth. No representations respecting the condition of the premises or the Building have been made by Lessor to Lessee, except as specifically herein set forth. [Lessor will, at its cost (except as provided in this Lease), maintain in good repair and working order and make all repairs, replacements, and restorations to the Building and all parts of the Building which are required in the normal maintenance operation and use of the Building, including, without limitation, the structural elements, mechanical, plumbing, and electrical systems, walkways, paths, landscaping, exterior walls and roof, and interior walls, floors, and ceilings.]

11. Destruction or Damage.

(a) In the event the premises or the portion of the Building necessary for Lessee's use and enjoyment of the premises are damaged by fire, earthquake, act of God, the elements or other casualty, Lessor shall forthwith repair the same, subject to the provisions of this paragraph hereinafter set forth, if such repairs can, in Lessor's opinion, be made within a period of 120 days after [such damage] ⟨commencement of the repair work⟩. This Lease shall remain in full force and effect except that an abatement of rental shall be allowed Lessee ⟨for such part of the premises as shall be rendered unusable by Lessee in the conduct of its business⟩ [to the extent that the value of the premises is reduced] during the time such part is so unusable.

Tenant's proposed additions shown in [ ] and proposed deletions shown in ⟨ ⟩.

(b)   As soon as is reasonably possible following the occurrence of any damage [but no more than thirty days thereafter,] Lessor shall notify Lessee of the estimated time required for the repair or restoration of the premises or the portion of the Building necessary for Lessee's occupancy. If the estimated time is in excess of a period of 120 days after [such damage] ⟨commencement of the repair work⟩, Lessor or Lessee may elect, upon notice to the other within 30 days after Lessor's notice of estimated time is given, to terminate this Lease effective on the date of such damage or destruction; [however, a condition of Lessor's termination of this Lease will be that it also terminates other tenants whose premises are similarly affected.] If neither party so elects to terminate this Lease, this Lease shall continue in full force and effect, but the rent shall be partially abated as hereinabove in this paragraph provided, and Lessor shall immediately proceed to repair such damage.

(c)   A total destruction of the Building [or the premises] shall automatically terminate this Lease. Lessee waives California Civil Code Sections 1932(2) and 1933(4) providing for termination of hiring upon destruction of the thing hired.

12.   Insurance. Lessee shall secure and maintain in force during the term of this Lease comprehensive general liability insurance with a combined single limit for personal injury and property damage in an amount not less than $1,000,000, and employer's liability and workers compensation insurance as required by law. Lessee's comprehensive general liability insurance policy shall insure the performance by Lessee of the indemnity agreement set forth in paragraph 14, and shall be endorsed to provide that (i) it may not be cancelled or altered in such a manner as adversely to affect the coverage afforded thereby without 30 days' prior written notice to Lessor, (ii) Lessor is named as additional insured, (iii) the insurer acknowledges acceptance of the mutual waiver of claims by Lessor and Lessee pursuant to paragraph 13 below, and (iv) such insurance is primary with respect to Lessor and that any other insurance maintained by Lessor is excess and noncontributing with such insurance. If, in the opinion of Lessor's insurance adviser, based on a substantial increase in recovered liability claims generally, the specified amounts of coverage are no longer adequate, such coverage shall be appropriately increased. Prior to the commencement of the term, Lessee shall deliver to Lessor a duplicate of such policy or a certificate thereof with endorsements, and at least 30 days prior to the expiration of such policy or any renewal thereof, Lessee shall deliver to Lessor a replacement or renewal binder, followed by a duplicate policy or certificate within a reasonable time thereafter. If Lessee fails to obtain such insurance or to furnish Lessor any such duplicate policy, certificate or binder as herein required, Lessor may, at its election, without notice to Lessee and without any obligation so to do, procure and maintain such coverage and Lessee shall reimburse Lessor on demand as additional rent for any premium so paid by Lessor. Lessee shall have the right to provide all insurance required herein for the premises and for Lessee and Lessor pursuant to blanket policies so long as such coverage is expressly afforded by such policies. [Lessor will maintain at all times during the term of this Lease: (a) all-risk insurance in an amount not less than the actual replacement cost (exclusive of

foundations and excavations) of the Building as calculated annually according to the applicable insurance policies, and (b) personal, public liability and property damage occurring in, on, or about the Building and adjoining streets and sidewalks in such amounts as are customary for properties comparable to the Building. Lessee will be named as an additional insured on the liability policy.]

13. Waiver of Subrogation. Lessor hereby waives all claims against Lessee, including the officers, directors, partners, employees, agents or representatives of Lessee, for loss or damage [to the Building or any part of it, and Lessor will deliver to Lessee proof that Lessor's insurer of the Building has consented to such waiver] ⟨to the extent that such loss or damage is insured against under any valid and collectible insurance policy insuring Lessor or would have been insured against but for any deductible amount under any such policy, and⟩ Lessee waives all claims against Lessor, including the officers, directors, partners, employees, agents, or representatives of Lessor, for loss or damage to the extent such loss or damage is insured against under any valid and collectible insurance policy insuring Lessee or required to be maintained by Lessee under this Lease, or would have been insured against but for any deductible amount under any such policy.

14. Indemnification. Lessee hereby waives all claims against Lessor for damage to any property or injury to or death of any person in, upon or about the premises or the Building arising at any time and from any cause, and Lessee shall hold Lessor harmless from and defend Lessor against all claims for damage to any property or injury to or death of any person arising from (a) the use of the premises by Lessee, except such as is caused by the sole negligence or willful misconduct of Lessor, its agents, employees or contractors, or (b) the negligence or willful misconduct of Lessee, its employees, agents or contractors in, upon or about those portions of the Building other than the premises. The foregoing indemnity obligation of Lessee shall include reasonable attorneys' fees, investigation costs and all other reasonable costs and expenses incurred by Lessor from the first notice that any claim or demand is to be made or may be made. The provisions of this paragraph 14 shall survive the termination of the Lease with respect to any damage, injury or death occurring prior to such termination. [Lessee's liability under this paragraph will not exceed $ amount.]

15. Compliance with Legal Requirements. Lessee shall at its sole cost and expense promptly comply with all laws, statutes, ordinances and governmental rules, regulations or requirements now in force or which may hereafter be in force, with any [presently effective] direction or occupancy certificate issued pursuant to any law by any public officer, as well as the provisions of all recorded documents affecting the premises [on the date of this Lease,] insofar as any thereof (a) relate to or affect the condition, use or occupancy of the premises, [and (b) apply solely as a result of the nature of Lessee's use of the premises (as opposed to the uses of other tenants of the Building), and (c) require costs which cannot be included in Operating Expenses,] excluding requirements of structural changes or capital improvements not related to or

---

affected by improvements made by or for Lessee or Lessee's acts. [At its cost, Lessor will comply with all laws, statutes, ordinances, rules, regulations or requirements (whether or not now in effect or foreseeable), or direction or occupancy certificate in effect on the commencement date of the term of this Lease with respect to which Lessee would otherwise incur any cost pursuant to the terms of this paragraph.]

16. Assignment and Subletting.

(a)   Lessee shall not assign this Lease or any interest herein or sublet the premises or any part thereof without the prior consent of Lessor, which consent shall not be unreasonably withheld; Lessee shall not hypothecate this Lease or any interest herein or permit the use of the premises by any party other than Lessee without the prior consent of Lessor, which consent may be withheld by Lessor in its absolute discretion. This Lease shall not, nor shall any interest herein, be assignable as to the interest of Lessee by operation of law without the consent of Lessor. Any of the foregoing acts without such consent shall be void and shall, at the option of Lessor, terminate this Lease. In connection with each consent requested by Lessee, Lessee shall submit to Lessor the terms of the proposed transaction, the identity of the parties to the transaction, the proposed documentation for the transaction, current financial statements of any proposed assignee or sublessee, and all other information reasonably requested by Lessor concerning the proposed transaction and the parties involved therein.

(b)   Without limiting the other instances in which it may be reasonable for Lessor to withhold its consent to an assignment or subletting, Lessor and Lessee acknowledge that it shall be reasonable for Lessor to withhold its consent in the following instances:

(1)   ⟨if at the time consent is requested or at any time prior to the granting of consent, Lessee is in default under the Lease or would be in default under the Lease but for the pendency of any grace or cure period under paragraph 18 below;⟩

(2)   if the proposed assignee or sublessee is a governmental agency [whose number of visitors is proportionately substantially greater than the volume of visitors of any other tenant in the Building;

(3)   if in Lessor's reasonable judgment the use of the premises by the proposed assignee or sublessee would involve occupancy by other than primarily executive or professional personnel, would entail any alterations which would lessen the value of ⟨the leasehold improvements in⟩ the premises, would result in ⟨more than⟩ a ⟨reasonable⟩ greater number of occupants per floor than any other floor in the Building] or would require increased services by Lessor [unless the assignee or sublessee gives Lessor reasonably adequate assurances of its ability to pay for such increased services according to this Lease;]

(4)   if, in Lessor's reasonable judgment, the financial worth of the proposed assignee or sublessee does not meet the credit standards applied by Lessor for other tenants under leases with comparable terms, or the character, reputation

or business of the proposed assignee or sublessee is not consistent with the quality of the other tenancies in the Building; and

(5)   in the case of a subletting of less than the entire premises, if the subletting ⟨would result in the division of the premises into more than two subparcels, would create a subparcel of a configuration that is not suitable for normal leasing purposes, or⟩ would require access to be provided through space leased or held for lease to another tenant or improvements to be made outside of the premises.

(c)   If at any time or from time to time during the term of this Lease, Lessee desires to sublet all or any part of the premises, Lessee shall give notice to Lessor setting forth the terms of the proposed subletting and the space so proposed to be sublet. Lessor shall have the option, exercisable by notice given to Lessee within 20 days after Lessee's notice is given, either to sublet from Lessee such space at the rental and other terms set forth in Lessee's notice, or, if the proposed subletting is for the entire premises for a sublet term ending within the last year of the term of this Lease, to terminate this Lease. If Lessor does not exercise such option, Lessee shall be free to sublet such space to any third party on the same terms set forth in the notice given to Lessor, subject to obtaining Lessor's prior consent as hereinabove provided.

(d)   Notwithstanding the provisions of paragraphs (a) and (b) above, Lessee may assign this Lease or sublet the premises or any portion thereof, without Lessor's consent and without extending any option to Lessor pursuant to paragraph (c) above, to any corporation which controls, is controlled by or is under common control with Lessee, to any corporation resulting from the merger or consolidation with Lessee, or to any person or entity which acquires all the assets of Lessee as a going concern of the business that is being conducted on the premises, provided that notice of such assignment or subletting is given to Lessor.

(e)   No sublessee (other than Lessor if it exercises its option pursuant to subparagraph (c) above) shall have a right further to sublet and any assignment by a sublessee of its sublease shall be subject to Lessor's prior consent in the same manner as if Lessee were entering into a new sublease.

(f)   In the case of an assignment, one-half of any sums or other economic consideration received by Lessee ⟨as a result of⟩ [reasonably attributed to] such assignment [by Lessee] shall be paid to Lessor after first deducting the unamortized cost of leasehold improvements paid for by Lessee, [the amounts paid to Lessor pursuant to this Lease during any period immediately preceding the assignment in which the premises were vacant, Lessee's costs of moving from the premises to the new location of its business,] and the cost of any real estate commissions incurred in connection with such assignment.

(g)   In the case of a subletting, one-half of any sums or economic consideration received by Lessee ⟨as a result of⟩ [reasonably attributed to] such subletting [by Lessee] shall be paid to Lessor after first deducting (1) the rental due hereunder, prorated to reflect only rental allocable to the sublet portion of the premises, (2) the cost of leasehold improvements made to the sublet

---

portion of the premises at Lessee's cost, amortized over [their useful lives] ⟨the term of this Lease⟩ except for leasehold improvements made for the specific benefit of the sublessee, which shall be amortized over the term of the sublease, and (3) the cost of any real estate commissions incurred in connection with such subletting, amortized over the term of the sublease [or deducted from such other economic consideration received by Lessee, and (4) the amounts paid to Lessor pursuant to this Lease during any period immediately preceding the subletting in which the premises were vacant, and (5) Lessee's cost of moving from the premises to the new location of its business.]

(h) [Regardless of Lessor's consent, no subletting (except a subletting to lessor pursuant to paragraph (c) above)] or assignment shall release Lessee or Lessee's obligation or alter the primary liability of Lessee to pay the rental and to perform all other obligations to be performed by Lessee hereunder. The acceptance of rental by Lessor from any other person shall not be deemed to be a waiver by Lessor of any provision hereof. Consent to one assignment or subletting shall not be deemed consent to any subsequent assignment or subletting. In the event of default by any assignee of Lessee or any successor of Lessee in the performance of any of the terms hereof, Lessor may proceed directly against Lessee without the necessity of exhausting remedies against such assignee or successor. Lessor may consent to subsequent assignments or subletting of this Lease or amendments or modifications to this Lease with assignees of Lessee, without notifying Lessee, or any successor of Lessee, and without obtaining its or their consent thereto and such action shall not relieve Lessee of liability under this Lease.

(i)   In the event Lessee shall assign or sublet the premises or request the consent of Lessor to any assignment or subletting [(except a subletting pursuant to paragraph (b) above)] or if Lessee shall request the consent of Lessor for any act that Lessee proposes to do, then Lessee shall pay Lessor's reasonable attorneys' fees incurred in connection therewith.

17.   Entry by Lessor. Lessor may enter the premises at reasonable hours and upon reasonable prior notice, except in case of an emergency, to (a) inspect the same, (b) exhibit the same to prospective purchasers or lenders or, within the last ⟨twelve⟩ [three] months of the term, to prospective tenants, (c) determine whether Lessee is complying with all its obligations hereunder, (d) supply janitor service and any other service to be provided by Lessor to Lessee hereunder, (e) post notices of nonresponsibility, and (f) make repairs required of Lessor under the terms hereof or repairs to any adjoining space or utility services or make repairs, alterations or improvements to any other portion of the Building, provided, however, that all such work shall be done as promptly as reasonably possible [and after six o'clock p.m. on weekdays, or on weekends] and so as to cause as little interference to Lessee as reasonably possible [and the premises shall be restored to their condition prior to such entry.] Lessor shall at all times have and retain a key with which to unlock all of the doors in, on or about the premises (excluding Lessee's vaults, safes and similar areas designated in writing by Lessee in advance) [for entry pursuant to this

paragraph;] and Lessor shall have the right to use any and all means which Lessor may deem proper to open said doors in an emergency in order to obtain entry to the premises. [An emergency subject to this paragraph is a situation which immediately threatens the Building or its occupants.]

18. Default.

(a)   The following events shall constitute events of default under this Lease:

(1)   a default by Lessee in the payment when due of any rent or other sum payable hereunder and the continuation of such default for a period of 10 days after notice that the same is due, provided that if Lessee has failed three or more times in any twelve-month period to pay any rent or other sum within 10 days after [such notice] ⟨the due date⟩, no grace period shall thereafter be applicable hereunder;

(2)   a default by Lessee in the performance of any of the other terms, covenants, agreements or conditions contained herein and, if the default is curable, the continuation of such default for a period of 10 days after notice by Lessor or beyond the time reasonably necessary for cure if the default is of a nature to require more than 10 days to remedy, provided that if Lessee has defaulted in the performance of the same obligation three or more times in any twelve-month period and notice of such default has been given by Lessor in each instance no cure period shall thereafter be applicable hereunder;

(3)   the bankruptcy or insolvency of Lessee, any transfer by Lessee in fraud of creditors, assignment by Lessee for the benefit of creditors, or the commencement of any proceedings of any kind by or against Lessee under any provision of the Federal Bankruptcy Code or under any other insolvency, bankruptcy or reorganization act unless, in the event any such proceedings are involuntary, Lessee is discharged from the same within 60 days thereafter;

(4)   the appointment of a receiver for a substantial part of the assets of Lessee;

(5)   the abandonment of the premises; and

(6)   the levy upon this Lease or any estate of Lessee hereunder by any attachment or execution and the failure to have such attachment or execution vacated within 30 days thereafter.

(b)   Upon the occurrence of any event of default by Lessee hereunder, Lessor may, at its option and without any further notice or demand, in addition to any other rights and remedies given hereunder or by law, do any of the following:

(1)   Lessor shall have the right, so long as such default continues, to give notice of termination to Lessee, and on the date specified in such notice this Lease shall terminate.

(2)   In the event of any such termination of the Lease, Lessor may then or at any time thereafter by judicial process, re-enter the premises and remove therefrom all persons and property and again repossess and enjoy the premises, without prejudice to any other remedies that Lessor may have by reason of Lessee's default or of such termination.

Tenant's proposed additions shown in [   ] and proposed deletions shown in ⟨   ⟩.

(3)   In the event of any such termination of this Lease, and in addition to any other rights and remedies Lessor may have, Lessor shall have all of the rights and remedies of a landlord provided by Section 1951.2 of the California Civil Code. The amount of damages which Lessor may recover in event of such termination shall include, without limitation, (i) the worth at the time of award (computed by discounting such amount at the discount rate of the Federal Reserve Bank of San Francisco at the time of award plus one percent) of the amount by which the unpaid rent for the balance of the term after the time of award exceeds the amount of rental loss that Lessee proves could be reasonably avoided, (ii) all legal expenses and other related costs incurred by Lessor following Lessee's default, (iii) all costs incurred by Lessor in restoring the premises to good order and condition, or in remodeling, renovating or otherwise preparing the premises for reletting, and (iv) all costs (including, without limitation, any brokerage commissions) incurred by Lessor in reletting the premises.

(4)   For the purpose of determining the unpaid rent in the event of a termination of this Lease or the rent due hereunder in the event of a reletting of the premises, the monthly rent reserved in this Lease shall be deemed to be the sum of the rental due under paragraph 3 above and the amounts last payable pursuant to paragraph 4 above.

(5)   After terminating this Lease, Lessor may remove any and all personal property located in the premises and place such property in a public or private warehouse or elsewhere at the sole cost and expense of Lessee. In the event that Lessee shall not immediately pay the cost of storage of such property after the same has been stored for a period of 30 days or more, Lessor may sell any or all thereof at a public or private sale in such manner and at such times and places as Lessor in its sole discretion may deem proper, without notice to or demand upon Lessee. Lessee waives all claims for damages that may be caused by Lessor's removing or storing or selling the property as herein provided, and Lessee shall indemnify and hold Lessor free and harmless from and against any and all losses, costs and damages, including without limitation all costs of court and attorneys' fees of Lessor occasioned thereby. Lessee hereby appoints Lessor as Lessee's attorney-in-fact with the rights and powers necessary in order to effectuate the provisions of this subparagraph (5).

(c)   The remedies provided for in this Lease are in addition to any other remedies available to Lessor at law or in equity, by statute or otherwise, including, without limitation, the right of Lessor to seek any declaratory or immediate, temporary or permanent injunctive or other equitable relief and specifically enforce this Lease or restrain or enjoin a violation or breach of any provision hereof.

19. Continuation after Default. Even though Lessee has breached this Lease and abandoned the premises, this Lease shall continue in effect for so long as Lessor does not terminate Lessee's right to possession, and Lessor may enforce all its rights and remedies under this Lease, including the right to recover rental as it becomes due under this Lease. Acts of maintenance or

Tenant's proposed additions shown in [   ] and proposed deletions shown in 〈   〉.

preservation or efforts to relet the premises or the appointment of a receiver upon initiative of Lessor to protect Lessor's interest under this Lease shall not constitute a termination of Lessee's right to possession.

20. Lessor's Right to Cure Defaults. All agreements and provisions to be performed by Lessee under any of the terms of this Lease shall be at its sole cost and expense and without any abatement of rental, except as otherwise provided herein. If Lessee shall fail to pay any sum of money, other than rental, required to be paid by it hereunder or shall fail to perform any other act on its part to be performed hereunder and such failure shall continue for 30 days after notice thereof by Lessor, or such longer period as may be allowed hereunder, Lessor may, but shall not be obligated so to do, and without waiving or releasing Lessee from any obligations of Lessee make any such payment or perform any such other act on Lessee's part to be made or performed as in this Lease provided. All sums so paid by Lessor and all necessary incidental costs shall be deemed additional rent hereunder and shall be payable to Lessor on demand, and Lessor shall have (in addition to any other right or remedy of Lessor) the same rights and remedies in the event of the non-payment thereof by Lessee as in the case of default by Lessee in the payment of rental.

21. Attorneys' Fees. In the event of any action or proceeding brought by either party against the other under this Lease, the prevailing party shall be entitled to recover for the fees its attorneys in such action or proceeding such amount as the court may adjudge reasonable.

22. Eminent Domain. If all or any part of the premises shall be taken as a result of the exercise of the power of eminent domain, this Lease shall terminate as to the part so taken as of the date of taking, and, in the case of a partial taking, [either Lessor or] Lessee shall have the right to terminate this Lease as to the balance of the premises by notice to the other within 30 days after ⟨such⟩ [the] date [on which the condemning authority takes possession,] provided, however, that a condition to the exercise by Lessee of such right to terminate shall be that the portion of the premises taken shall be of such extent and nature as substantially to handicap, impede or impair Lessee's use of the balance of the premises for Lessee's purposes [before such taking. If Lessee does not elect to terminate this Lease as to the balance of the premises, Lessor will restore, rebuild, and replace the balance of the premises (including, without limitation, the installation of demising walls and heating, ventilating and air-conditioning systems) so that the balance of the premises are as usable by Lessee for Lessee's purposes as they were before such taking.] In the event of any taking, Lessor shall be entitled to any and all compensation, damages, income, rent, awards, or any interest therein whatsoever which may be paid or made in connection therewith, and Lessee shall have no claim against Lessor for the value of any unexpired term of this Lease or otherwise, provided that Lessee shall be entitled to any and all compensation, income, rent or awards paid for or on account of Tenant Improvements [(including Tenant Extra Improvements)] that have been paid for by Lessee, to the extent of Lessee's unamortized cost of such Tenant Improvements based upon

---

Tenant's proposed additions shown in [   ] and proposed deletions shown in ⟨   ⟩.

[Lessee's book value of them] ⟨an amortization period of the term of this Lease⟩. In the event of a partial taking of the premises which does not result in a termination of this Lease the monthly rental thereafter to be paid shall be equitably reduced on a square footage basis [and will be fully abated until the balance of the premises are restored, rebuilt, and replaced according to this paragraph.]

23. Subordination. [Upon the satisfaction of the condition set forth in the last sentence of this paragraph,] this Lease shall be subordinate to any ground lease, mortgage, deed of trust, or any other hypothecation for security now or hereafter placed upon the Building and to any and all advances made on the security thereof and to all renewals, modifications, consolidations, replacements and extensions thereof. Notwithstanding the foregoing if any mortgagee, trustee or ground lessor shall elect to have this Lease prior to the lien of its mortgage or deed of trust or prior to its ground lease, and shall give notice thereof to Lessee, this Lease shall be deemed prior to such mortgage, deed of trust, or prior to its ground lease whether this Lease is dated prior or subsequent to the date of said mortgage, deed of trust or ground lease or the date of recording thereof. In the event any mortgage or deed of trust to which this Lease is subordinate is foreclosed or a deed in lieu of foreclosure is given to the mortgagee or beneficiary, Lessee shall attorn to the purchaser at the foreclosure sale or to the grantee under the deed in lieu of foreclosure; in the event any ground lease to which this Lease is subordinate is terminated, Lessee shall attorn to the ground lessor. Lessee agrees to execute any documents required to effectuate such subordination, to make this Lease prior to the lien of any mortgage or deed of trust or ground lease, or to evidence such attornment. [As a condition to the subordination of this Lease, Lessor will deliver to Lessee an agreement by which the holder of any instrument to which this Lease is subordinate agrees that Lessee's rights under this Lease will not be affected by such holder's succession to Lessor's interest in the Building or premises.]

24. No Merger. The voluntary or other surrender of this Lease by Lessee, or a mutual cancellation thereof, shall not work a merger [(except those made pursuant to paragraph 16 above which Lessor will recognize after such surrender or cancellation),] and shall, at the option of Lessor terminate all or any existing subleases or subtenancies, or may, at the option of Lessor, operate as an assignment to it of any or all such subleases or subtenancies.

25. Sale. In the event the original Lessor hereunder, or any successor owner of the Building, shall sell or convey the Building, all liabilities and obligations on the part of the original Lessor, or such successor owner under this Lease accruing thereafter shall terminate, and thereupon all such liabilities and obligations shall be binding upon the new owner. Lessee agrees to attorn and pay rent to such new owner.

26. Estoppel Certificate. At any time and from time to time but on not less than 10 days prior notice ⟨by Lessor⟩, [Lessor and] Lessee shall execute, acknowledge and deliver to [the other] ⟨Lessor⟩, promptly upon request, a certificate certifying (a) that this Lease is unmodified and in full force and effect

Tenant's proposed additions shown in [   ] and proposed deletions shown in ⟨   ⟩.

(or, if there have been modifications, that this Lease is in full force and effect, as modified, and stating the date and nature of each modification), (b) the date, if any, to which rental and other sums payable hereunder have been paid, (c) that no notice has been received of any default which has not been cured, except as to defaults specified in said certificate and (d) such other matters as may be reasonably requested ⟨by Lessor⟩. Any such certificate may be relied upon by any prospective purchaser, mortgagee or beneficiary under any deed of trust of the Building or any part thereof.

27. No Light, Air or View Easement. Any diminution or shutting off of light, air or view by any structure which may be erected on lands adjacent to the Building shall in no way affect this Lease or impose any liability on Lessor.

28. Holding Over. If, ⟨without⟩ [after receipt of Lessor's written] objection ⟨by Lessor⟩, Lessee holds possession of the premises after expiration of the term of this Lease, Lessee shall become a tenant from month to month upon the terms herein specified but at a monthly rental equal to the then fair rental value of the premises ⟨but not less than the monthly rental paid by Lessee at the expiration of the term of this Lease⟩ pursuant to all the provisions of paragraphs 3 and 4, payable in advance on or before the first day of each month. Each party shall give the other written notice at least one month prior to the date of termination of such monthly tenancy of its intention to terminate such tenancy.

29. Security Deposit. Lessee has deposited with Lessor the sum specified in the Basic Lease Information (the "deposit"). The deposit shall be held by Lessor as security for the faithful performance by Lessee of all the provisions of this Lease to be performed or observed by Lessee. [If an event of default under paragraph 18 occurs] ⟨Lessee fails to pay rent or other charges due hereunder, or otherwise defaults with respect to any provision of this Lease,⟩ Lessor may use, apply or retain all or any portion of the deposit for the payment of any rent or other charge in default or the payment of any other sum to which Lessor may become obligated by Lessee's default ⟨, or to compensate Lessor for any loss or damage which Lessor may suffer thereby⟩. If Lessor so uses or applies all or any portion of the deposit, then within ten days after demand therefor Lessee shall deposit cash with Lessor in an amount sufficient to restore the deposit to the full amount thereof, and Lessee's failure to do so shall be a material breach of this Lease. Lessor shall not be required to keep the deposit separate from its general accounts. If Lessee performs all of Lessee's obligations hereunder, the deposit, or so much thereof as has not theretofore been applied by Lessor, shall be returned, ⟨without payment of⟩ [with interest and [* * *] Bank's fluctuating passbook interest rate] ⟨or other increment⟩ for its use, to Lessee (or, at Lessor's option, to the last assignee, if any, of Lessee's interest hereunder) at the expiration of the term hereof, and after Lessee has vacated the premises. No trust relationship is created herein between Lessor and Lessee with respect to the deposit.

Tenant's proposed additions shown in [ ] and proposed deletions shown in ⟨ ⟩.

30. Waiver. The waiver by Lessor or Lessee of any agreement, condition or provision herein contained shall not be deemed to be a waiver of any subsequent breach of the same or any other agreement, condition or provision herein contained, nor shall any custom or practice which may grow up between the parties in the administration of the terms hereof be construed to waive or to lessen the right of Lessor or Lessee to insist upon the performance by Lessee or Lessor in strict accordance with said terms; [however, no claims regarding this Lease may be maintained after the separation of the applicable statute of limitations]. The subsequent acceptance of rental hereunder by Lessor or payment of rent by Lessee shall not be deemed to be a waiver of any preceding breach by Lessee or Lessor of any agreement, condition or provision of this Lease, other than the failure of Lessee to pay the particular rental so accepted, regardless of Lessor's or Lessee's knowledge of such preceding breach at the time of acceptance or payment of such rental.

31. Notices and Consents. All notices, consents, demands and other communications from one party to the other given pursuant to the terms of this Lease shall be in writing and shall be deemed to have been fully given the second day after deposit in the United States mail, postage prepaid, and addressed as follows: to Lessee at the address specified in the Basic Lease Information ⟨or⟩ [and] to such other place as Lessee may from time to time designate in a notice to Lessor; to Lessor at the address specified in the Basic Lease Information, or to such other place as Lessor may from time to time designate in a notice to Lessee.

32. Complete Agreement. There are no oral agreements between Lessor and Lessee affecting this Lease, and this Lease supersedes and cancels any and all previous negotiations, arrangements, brochures, agreements and understandings, if any, between Lessor and Lessee or displayed by Lessor to Lessee with respect to the subject matter of this Lease, or the Building. Lessee acknowledges that there are no representations between Lessor or any agent of Lessor and Lessee other than those contained in this Lease and all reliance with respect to any representations is solely upon the representations contained herein. All implied warranties are excluded, including implied warranties of merchantability and fitness, if any.

33. Corporate Authority. If Lessee signs as a corporation, each of the persons executing this Lease on behalf of Lessee does hereby covenant and warrant that Lessee is a duly authorized and existing corporation, that Lessee has and is qualified to do business in California, that the corporation has full right and authority to enter into this Lease, and that each person signing on behalf of the corporation is authorized to do so.

34. Limitation of Liability to Building. The liability of Lessor to Lessee for any default by Lessor under this Lease or arising in connection with Lessor's operation, management, leasing, repair, renovation, alteration, or any other matter relating to the Building or the premises shall be limited to the interest of Lessor in the Building. Lessee agrees to look solely to Lessor's interest in the Building

for the recovery of any judgment against Lessor, and Lessor shall not be personally liable for any such judgment or deficiency after execution thereon. The limitations of liability contained in this paragraph 34 shall apply equally and inure to the benefit of Lessor, its successors and their respective, present and future partners of all tiers, beneficiaries, officers, directors, trustees, shareholders, agents and employees, and their respective heirs, successors and assigns. Under no circumstances shall any present or future general partner of Lessor (if Lessor is a partnership) or individual trustee or beneficiary (if Lessor or any partner of Lessor is a trust) have any liability for the performance of Lessor's obligations under this Lease.

35. Miscellaneous. The words "Lessor" and "Lessee" as used herein shall include the plural as well as the singular. If there be more than one Lessee, the obligations hereunder imposed upon Lessee shall be joint and several. Time is of the essence of this Lease and each and all of its provisions. Submission of this instrument for examination or signature by Lessee does not constitute a reservation of or option for lease, and it is not effective as a lease or otherwise until execution and delivery by both Lessor and Lessee. The agreements, conditions and provisions herein contained shall, subject to the provisions as to assignment, apply to and bind the heirs, executors, administrators, successors and assigns of the parties hereto. If any provision of this Lease shall be determined to be illegal or unenforceable, such determination shall not affect any other provision of this Lease and such other provisions shall remain in full force and effect. This Lease shall be governed by and construed pursuant to the laws of the State of California.

36. Parking.

(a)   Lessor shall lease to Lessee and Lessee shall lease from Lessor for the term of this Lease the number of stalls in the automobile parking facilities within the Building that is specified in the Basic Lease Information. All parking stalls leased by Lessee shall be for the exclusive use of Lessee's employees [and will be marked "RESERVED FOR * * *",] and such use shall be in accordance with such reasonable rules and regulations as shall be adopted with respect to such parking facilities ⟨, including regulations governing whether parking is on a reserved stall or nonassigned stall basis⟩.

(b)   The rental for the stalls leased by Lessee as of the commencement of the term of this Lease shall be the sum per month per stall that is specified in the Basic Lease Information. Such rental shall be subject to being modified thereafter to equal to the then prevailing rental rate, as such rate varies from time to time, for comparable parking privileges in [other privately owned parking garages in office buildings in the commercial district in which] the Building ⟨is located⟩.

(c)   Rental for all parking stalls leased by Lessee shall be paid at the same time and in the same manner as monthly rental due pursuant to paragraph 3.

37. Exhibits. The exhibits and addendum, if any, specified in the Basic Lease Information are attached to this Lease and by this reference made a part hereof.

Tenant's proposed additions shown in [   ] and proposed deletions shown in ⟨   ⟩.

IN WITNESS WHEREOF, the parties have executed this Lease on the respective dates indicated below.

LESSEE   LESSOR

By [* * *]   By [* * *]
  Its [* * *]   Its [* * *]

By [* * *]   By [* * *]
  Its [* * *]   Its [* * *]

Date of Execution   Date of Execution
by Lessee: [* * *]   by Lessor: [* * *]

§ 1.5   Office Lease (Space Users Network Office Building Lease)*

OFFICE BUILDING LEASE

between

[name]

as Landlord

and

[name]

as Tenant

[date], 19[* *]

This is a legal and binding contract and significantly affects your legal rights and obligations.

You should consult independent legal counsel of your choice BEFORE using or signing this document.

Space Users Network, a national association of space users
(Revised 1987)

[Additional copies may be obtained by writing to Space Users Network at Post Office Box 71989, Los Angeles, California 90071-0989 or by calling 1-800-442-4SUN (in California) and 1-800-441-4SUN (outside California).]

OFFICE BUILDING LEASE

THIS OFFICE BUILDING LEASE ("Lease") is made and entered into as of the [* *] day of [month], 19[00] by and between [name], a [* * *] ("Landlord"), as

---

* Copyright © by Space Users Network. Reprinted with permission.

Tenant's proposed additions shown in [ ] and proposed deletions shown in ⟨ ⟩.

the landlord and owner of that certain office building complex ("Building") located or to be located at [address], and [name], a [* * *] ("Tenant"), as the tenant and expected occupant of certain office space ("Space") located or to be located in the Building.

On the full terms and conditions ("Terms and Conditions") which follow the summary ("Summary") on the next page, and as summarized in the Summary, Landlord hereby leases the Space to Tenant and Tenant hereby leases the Space from Landlord.

To confirm the agreements, rights and obligations of the parties, both those which are expressed in this Lease as well as those which arise as a matter of law because of it, Landlord and Tenant have both signed one or more copies of this Lease in the county and state in which the Building is located as of the date and year stated above on this page.

[This is a legal and binding contract and significantly affects your legal rights and obligations. You should consult independent legal counsel of your choice BEFORE using or signing this document.]

By [name]   By [name]

By [name]   By [name]
                 Landlord   Tenant

GUARANTEE

As a material inducement to Landlord to make and enter into the Lease, and for other valuable consideration, receipt of which is hereby acknowledged, the party or parties executing this guarantee ("Guarantor") hereby unconditionally guarantees, or hereby jointly and severally unconditionally guarantee, the full, complete and timely performance of each and all of the obligations of Tenant under the Lease. This guarantee is independent of each and all of the obligations of Tenant under the Lease and separate action or actions may be brought and prosecuted against Guarantor, whether action is brought under the Lease, whether Tenant is joined in any such action or actions and/or whether Landlord has first pursued or exhausted any other remedy or remedies to which it may be entitled. Guarantor hereby authorizes Landlord, without notice or demand and without affecting the liability of Guarantor hereunder, from time to time, to compromise, extend or otherwise change or modify any or all of the terms or conditions of the Lease. Guarantor hereby waives all presentments, demands for performance, notices of nonperformance, protests, notices of protest, notices of dishonor and notices of acceptance of this guarantee.

By [name]   By [name]

By [name]   By [name]
                 Guarantor   Guarantor

As to any party who is an individual, such individual should sign above the first line and such individual's name should be neatly printed or typed below such line. As to any party which is an entity, the authorized representative, or representatives, of such entity should sign above the second line, or the second and third lines, such entity's name should be neatly printed or typed above the first line and the name, or names, of such representative, or representatives, should be neatly printed or typed below the second line, or the second and third lines. The address of each party should be neatly printed or typed on the lines below the signature of such party. *All* inserts, deletions and other changes on this and/or any other page or pages should be initialed by *all* parties and/or representatives *in each instance* in the left or right margin directly adjacent to such insert, deletion or other change.

SUMMARY

1.   Clarification. This summary ("Summary") relates to and is a part of the Office Building Lease ("Lease") to which it is attached, including the terms and conditions ("Terms and Conditions") which follow this Summary. The parties to the Lease are the landlord ("Landlord"), the tenant ("Tenant") and, as a guarantor, any guarantor or guarantors ("Guarantor") who sign the Lease just above this Summary. No brokers have acted for any party except [* * *] on behalf of Landlord and [* * *] on behalf of Tenant. This Summary highlights some of the more significant provisions of the Lease, but does not cover all of the provisions of the Lease and should only be read in conjunction with the Terms and Conditions.

2.   Definitions. The terms specifically defined anywhere in the Lease, including in Section 2 of the Terms and Conditions, shall have the same meaning throughout the Lease. In particular, the Lease pertains to the office space ("Space"), and potentially to the additional office space ("Additional Space"), in the office building complex ("Building") defined in Sections 7, 8 and 9, respectively, of this Summary and, subject to verification as provided in Section 5.2.6 of the Terms and Conditions, the usable square footage of the Space ("Usable Space Footage") and the rentable square footage of the Space ("Rentable Space Footage"), the rentable square footage of the Building ("Rentable Building Footage") and the ratio of the Rentable Space Footage to the Rentable Building Footage ("Tenant Share") defined in Sections 7, 9 and 10, respectively, of this Summary. The Lease also includes any additional provisions ("Additional Provisions") inserted at the end of the Terms and Conditions.

3.   Term. The Lease shall govern the relationship of the parties beginning with the agreed effective date of its execution, which is specified in the opening sentence of the Lease. The term ("Term") of the Lease, however, which significantly impacts the relationship of the parties in several material respects, including the payment of rent ("Rent"), shall not commence until the date ("Commencement Date") on which Landlord, following the required prior written notice specified in Section 3.1 of the Terms and Conditions, tenders possession of the Space to Tenant in the condition contemplated by Section 4 of the Terms and Conditions. The Commencement Date shall not

be sooner than [date], 19[00] ("Estimated Commencement Date") and shall not be later than [date], 19[00] ("Latest Commencement Date"). Subject to earlier termination of the initial term ("Initial Term") of the Lease pursuant to Sections 7.3, 8.10 or 9 of the Terms and Conditions, the Initial Term shall terminate ("Initial Termination Date") [* * *] [(* *)] years after the Commencement Date. The base year ("Base Year") of the Lease means the one (1) year period commencing [date], 19[00]. As specified in Section 3.3 of the Terms and Conditions, Tenant shall have [* * *] [(* *)] successive [* * *] [(* *)] year options to extend the Term, in each case exercisable in writing delivered to Landlord not less than [* * *] [(* *)] months nor more than [* * *] [(* *)] months before when the Term would otherwise have expired, and the applicable percentage of fair market rental value of the Space shall be [* * *] percent [(* *%).]

4.   Construction. The provisions of Section 4 of the Terms and Conditions shall apply to the Space only if the Space is not being leased "as is" and only if the "blanks" in this Section 4 of the Summary are each filled in and initialled both by Landlord and Tenant. If the Space is to be improved as contemplated in Section 4 of the Terms and Conditions, (i) Tenant shall cause to be reasonably prepared and delivered to Landlord the preliminary space plan ("Space Plan") referred to in Section 4.2 of the Terms and Conditions within [* * *] [(* *)] days after the effective date of execution of the Lease, (ii) Landlord shall, concurrently with such delivery, pay to Tenant a space planning allowance ("Space Planning Allowance") equal to [* * *] ($ [amount]) per rentable square foot of the Space multiplied by the Rentable Space Footage, (iii) Tenant shall cause to be reasonably prepared and delivered to Landlord detailed engineering and working drawings and specifications ("Buildout Drawings") referred to in Section 4.2 of the Terms and Conditions within [* * *] [(* *)] days after approval of the Space Plan pursuant to Section 4.2 of the Terms and Conditions, (iv) Landlord shall, concurrently with such delivery, pay to Tenant a buildout drawings allowance ("Buildout Drawings Allowance") equal to [* * *] ($ [amount]) per rentable square foot of the Space multiplied by the Rentable Space Footage, (v) Landlord shall cause to be reasonably prepared and delivered to Tenant a construction agreement ("Buildout Agreement") and buildout cost breakdown ("Buildout Cost Breakdown") referred to in Section 4.3 of the Terms and Conditions within [* * *] [(* *)] days after approval of the Buildout Drawings pursuant to Section 4.2 of the Terms and Conditions and (vi) Landlord shall, in discharge of the first dollar costs of the buildout ("Buildout") contemplated by Section 4 of the Terms and Conditions, and pursuant to either the Buildout Agreement or the written alternative ("Buildout Alternative") referred to in Section 4.3 of the Terms and Conditions, as the case may be, pay on Tenant's behalf a buildout allowance ("Buildout Allowance") equal to [* * *] ($ [amount]) per rentable square foot of the Space multiplied by the Rentable Space Footage.

5.   Rent and Security Deposit. Base rent ("Base Rent") payable under Section 5.1 of the Terms and Conditions shall, through the first [* * *] [(* *)] full calendar months of the Initial Term following the Commencement Date,

be [* * *] Dollars ($ [amount]) per rentable square foot of the Space and shall thereafter, subject to adjustment during any Optional Term as required under Section 3.3 of the Terms and Conditions, be [* * *] Dollars ($ [amount]) per rentable square foot of the Space, in each case multiplied by the Rentable Space Footage. Section 5.2 of the Terms and Conditions provides for the likely payment of certain described escalation rent ("Escalation Rent") tied to increases in the permitted costs and expenses ("Operating Costs") of the Building after the Base Year. A security deposit ("Security Deposit") in the amount of [* * *] Dollars ($ [amount]), payable in installments of [* * *] Dollars ($ [amount]) on [* * *], 19[00], [* * *] Dollars ($ [amount]) on [* * *], 19[00] and [* * *] Dollars ($ [amount]) on [* * *], 19[00], shall be held and administered pursuant to Section 5.4 of the Terms and Conditions.

6.   Operations. Tenant shall not use the Space for any purpose other than [* * *]. The numbers of exclusive and/or nonexclusive parking spaces ("Parking Spaces") referred to in Section 6.3 (viii) of the Terms and Conditions shall be [* * *] [(* *)] and [* * *] [(* *)], respectively.

7.   Space. The Space which is the subject of the Lease is located on the [* * *] [(* *)] floor of the Building and is known as, or shall be known as, Suite [* * *]. The Usable Space Footage and the Rentable Space Footage are approximately [* * *] [(* *)] square feet and [* * *] [(* *)] square feet, respectively. The Space may be further identified in any diagram ("Space Diagram") initialled both by Landlord and Tenant.

8.   Additional Space. The Additional Space which may potentially also be the subject of the Lease is located on the [* * *] [(* *)] floor of the Building and, if not contiguous to the Space, shall be known as Suite [* * *]. The Additional Space may be further identified in any diagram ("Additional Space Diagram") initialled both by Landlord and Tenant. In accordance with the provisions of Section 8.2 of the Terms and Conditions, Tenant shall have the options, (i) not less frequently than every [* * *] [(* *)] years and (ii) otherwise as available from time to time on not less than [* * *] [(* *)] days nor more than [* * *] [(* *)] days prior written notice delivered by Landlord to Tenant, respectively effective on the corresponding anniversary date of the effective date of the Lease or on the date specified in such notice, and exercisable in writing delivered to Landlord by Tenant not less than [* * *] [(* *)] days nor more than [* * *] [(* *)] days before such effective date, to lease pursuant to this Lease any or all of the Additional Space in increments of not less than [* * *] [(* *)] rentable square feet. In respect of such pending options to expand, Landlord shall not, in the meanwhile, lease, or agree to lease, any or all of the Additional Space to any third parties except for terms not to exceed [* * *] [(* *)] months and rentable square footages not to exceed [* * *] [(* *)] rentable square feet.

9.   Building. The Building is that office building complex commonly known as [* * *] and located at [* * *]. The Rentable Building Footage is approximately [* * *] [(* *)] square feet.

10. Tenant Share. The Tenant Share is approximately [* * *] percent [(* *%)].

TERMS AND CONDITIONS
TABLE OF CONTENTS

Section		Heading	Page
1		Clarification	1
2		Definitions	1
3		Term	2
	3.1	Initial Term	2
	3.2	Optional Term	2
	3.3	Option(s) to Extend Term	3
4		Construction	3
	4.1	Base Building	3
	4.2	Space Plan and Buildout Drawings	3
	4.3	Buildout Cost and Documentation	3
	4.4	Buildout	3
5		Rent and Security Deposit	3
	5.1	Base Rent	3
	5.2	Escalation Rent	3
	5.2.1	Purpose	3
	5.2.2	General Approach	3
	5.2.3	Specific Inclusions	4
	5.2.4	Specific Exclusions	4
	5.2.5	Payment	4
	5.2.6	Review	4
	5.3	Additional Rent	4
	5.4	Security Deposit	4
6		Operations	4
	6.1	Use	4
	6.2	Alterations and Improvements	5
	6.3	Services	5
	6.4	Maintenance and Repairs	5
7		Liability	5
	7.1	Indemnification	5
	7.2	Insurance	5
	7.2.1	Landlord	5
	7.2.2	Tenant	5
	7.3	Damage and Destruction	5
8		Title	5
	8.1	Space	5
	8.2	Option(s) to Expand Space	5
	8.3	Quiet Enjoyment	6
	8.4	Access	6
	8.5	Estoppel Certificates	6
	8.6	Subordination and Nondisturbance	6
	8.7	Attornment	6
	8.8	Assignment and Subletting	6
	8.9	Transfer by Landlord	6

Section	Heading	Page
8.10	Condemnation	6
8.11	Surrender	6
9	Disputes	7
9.1	Exclusive Procedure	7
9.2	Arbitration Panel	7
9.3	Duty	7
9.4	Authority	7
9.5	Appeal	7
9.6	Compensation	7
10	Miscellaneous	7
10.1	Notice	7
10.2	Time	7
10.3	Entire Agreement	7
10.4	Applicable Law	7
10.5	Counterparts	7
10.6	Headings and Gender	8
10.7	Successors	8
—	Cleaning Specifications	9
—	Additional Provisions	10, 11

TERMS AND CONDITIONS

1.   Clarification

These terms and conditions ("Terms and Conditions") relate to and are a part of the Office Building Lease ("Lease") to which they are attached, just as if they were physically set forth before the signatures of the parties. The same is true as to the summary ("Summary") of these Terms and Conditions which immediately follows such signatures. These Terms and Conditions are intended to further, and not contradict, the Summary. In the event of any inconsistency or inconsistencies between the Summary and these Terms and Conditions, such inconsistency or inconsistencies shall be resolved in favor of the Summary. The parties shall at all times act prudently, fairly, equitably, reasonably, promptly and in good faith in dealing with one another under the Lease and shall not unreasonably withhold or delay any consents, approvals, authorizations, exercises of discretion, exercises of judgment or the like provided for in the Lease, all of which shall be communicated in writing. Without the necessity of any further consideration, the parties shall execute and deliver such other documents, and take such other action, as may be necessary to further the purposes of the Lease.

2.   Definitions

Except as the specific context might otherwise logically require in any particular situation or circumstance, the following terms shall have the following meanings in the Lease:

2.1 Additional Provisions. The term "Additional Provisions" shall mean any additional provisions inserted at the end of these Terms and Conditions.

2.2 Additional Rent. The term "Additional Rent" shall mean any payments referred to in Section 5.3 of these Terms and Conditions.

2.3 Additional Space. The term "Additional Space" shall mean the space described in Section 8 of the Summary.

2.4 Additional Space Diagram. The term "Additional Space Diagram" shall mean any diagram of the Additional Space referred to in Section 8 of the Summary.

2.5 Arbitration Panel. The term "Arbitration Panel" shall mean the panel of arbitrators described in Section 9.2 of these Terms and Conditions.

2.6 Adjusted Escalation Difference. The term "Adjusted Escalation Difference" shall mean any adjustment in the Escalation Difference which takes into account any prior Projected Escalation Rent Statement payments made on account of such Escalation Difference, all as referred to in Section 5.2.5 of these Terms and Conditions.

2.7 Base Building Drawings. The term "Base Building Drawings" shall mean the plans and specifications referred to in Section 4.1 of these Terms and Conditions.

2.8 Base Building Work. The term "Base Building Work" shall mean the work referred to in Section 4.1 of these Terms and Conditions.

2.9 Base Rent. The term "Base Rent" shall mean the amount of Rent referred to in and payable under Section 5.1 of these Terms and Conditions.

2.10 Base Year. The term "Base Year" shall mean the one (1) year period of time referred to in Section 3 of the Summary.

2.11 Base Year Operating Costs. The term "Base Year Operating Costs" shall mean Operating Costs for the Base Year, as referred to and used in Section 5.2.5 of these Terms and Conditions.

2.12 Building. The term "Building" shall mean that office building complex described in Section 9 of the Summary.

2.13 Buildout. The term "Buildout" shall mean that buildout of the Space referred to in Sections 4.2, 4.3 and 4.4 of these Terms and Conditions.

2.14 Buildout Agreement. The term "Buildout Agreement" shall mean the construction agreement referred to in Section 4.3 of these Terms and Conditions.

2.15 Buildout Allowance. The term "Buildout Allowance" shall mean the buildout allowance referred to in Section 4(vi) of the Summary.

2.16 Buildout Alternative. The term "Buildout Alternative" shall mean the alternative buildout proposal referred to in Section 4.3 of these Terms and Conditions.

2.17 Buildout Cost. The term "Buildout Cost" shall mean the buildout cost referred to in Section 4.3 of these Terms and Conditions.

2.18 Buildout Cost Breakdown. The term "Buildout Cost Breakdown" shall mean the buildout cost breakdown referred to in Section 4.3 of these Terms and Conditions.

2.19 Buildout Drawings. The term "Buildout Drawings" shall mean the detailed working and engineering drawings referred to in Section 4.2 of these Terms and Conditions.

2.20 Buildout Drawings Allowance. The term "Buildout Drawings Allowance" shall mean the buildout drawings allowance referred to in Section 4(iv) of the Summary.

2.21 Cleaning Specifications. The term "Cleaning Specifications" shall mean the cleaning specifications attached to and included near the end of these Terms and Conditions.

2.22 Commencement Date. The term "Commencement Date" shall mean the date referred to in Section 3.1 of these Terms and Conditions.

2.23 Dispute Date. The term "Dispute Date" shall mean the date referred to in Section 9.2 of these Terms and Conditions.

2.24 Escalation Difference. The term "Escalation Difference" shall mean the difference between Base Year Operating Costs and Operating Costs for any subsequently commencing calendar year during the Term, all as referred to in Section 5.2.5 of these Terms and Conditions.

2.25 Escalation Rent. The term "Escalation Rent" shall mean the amount of Rent referred to in and payable under Section 5.2 of these Terms and Conditions.

2.26 Escalation Rent Statement. The term "Escalation Rent Statement" shall mean the statement referred to as such in Section 5.2.5 of these Terms and Conditions.

2.27 Estimated Commencement Date. The term "Estimated Commencement Date" shall mean the earliest Commencement Date permitted under Section 3 of the Summary.

2.28 Guarantor. The term "Guarantor" shall mean the party or parties, if any, signing the guarantee of the Lease just before the Summary.

2.29 Initial Term. The term "Initial Term" shall mean the period referred to in Section 3.1 of these Terms and Conditions.

2.30 Initial Termination Date. The term "Initial Termination Date" shall mean the date of termination of the Initial Term referred to in Section 3.1 of these Terms and Conditions.

2.31 Landlord. The term "Landlord" shall mean the party or parties referred to as such at the outset of the Lease.

2.32 Latest Commencement Date. The term "Latest Commencement Date" shall mean the latest Commencement Date permitted under Section 3 of the Summary.

2.33 Lease. The term "Lease" shall mean the Office Building Lease to which these Terms and Conditions are attached.

2.34 Notice of Dispute. The term "Notice of Dispute" shall mean any notice referred to in and given under Section 9.2 of these Terms and Conditions.

2.35 Operating Costs. The term "Operating Costs" shall mean any permissible costs and expenses effectively defined in Sections 5.2.2, 5.2.3 and 5.2.4 of these Terms and Conditions.

2.36 Optional Term. The term "Optional Term" shall mean the period referred to in Section 3.2 of these Terms and Conditions.

2.37 Optional Termination Date. The term "Optional Termination Date" shall mean the date of termination of the Optional Term referred to in Section 3.2 of these Terms and Conditions.

2.38 Parking Spaces. The term "Parking Spaces" shall refer to the number of parking spaces specified in Section 6 of the Summary.

2.39 Projected Escalation Difference. The term "Projected Escalation Difference" shall mean any projected Escalation Difference as referred to in Section 5.2.5 of these Terms and Conditions.

2.40 Projected Escalation Rent Statement. The term "Projected Escalation Rent Statement" shall mean the statement referred to as such in Section 5.2.5 of these Terms and Conditions.

2.41 Property Taxes. The term "Property Taxes" shall mean the taxes and assessments referred to in Section 5.2.3 of these Terms and Conditions.

2.42 Regulations. The term "Regulations" shall mean any rules or regulations enacted by Landlord consistent with Section 6.1(iv)(a) of these Terms and Conditions.

2.43 Rent. The term "Rent" shall mean any dollar amounts referred to in and payable under Section 5 of these Terms and Conditions.

2.44 Rentable Building Footage. The term "Rentable Building Footage" shall mean the rentable square footage of the Building as stated in Section 9 of the Summary.

2.45 Rentable Space Footage. The term "Rentable Space Footage" shall mean the rentable square footage of the Space as stated in Section 7 of the Summary.

2.46 Security Deposit. The term "Security Deposit" shall mean any dollar deposits as stated in Section 5 of the Summary.

2.47 Space. The term "Space" shall mean the space described in Section 7 of the Summary.

2.48 Space Diagram. The term "Space Diagram" shall mean any diagram of the Space referred to in Section 7 of the Summary.

2.49 Space Plan. The term "Space Plan" shall mean the preliminary space plan described in Section 4.2 of these Terms and Conditions.

2.50 Space Planning Allowance. The term "Space Planning Allowance" shall mean the space planning allowance referred to in Section 4(ii) of the Summary.

2.51 Summary. The term "Summary" shall mean the summary of the Lease which immediately precedes these Terms and Conditions.

2.52 Taking. The term "Taking" shall mean the taking or sale of the Building, or any part thereof or interest therein, as described in Section 8.10 of the Terms and Conditions.

2.53 Tenant. The term "Tenant" shall mean the party or parties referred to as such at the outset of the Lease.

2.54 Tenant Share. The term "Tenant Share" shall mean the percentage stated in Section 10 of the Summary.

2.55 Term. The term "Term" shall mean the term of the Lease as referred to in Section 3 of the Summary and Section 3 of these Terms and Conditions.

2.56 Terms and Conditions. The term "Terms and Conditions" shall mean these terms and conditions of the Lease.

2.57 Usable Space Footage. The term "Usable Space Footage" shall mean the usable square footage of the Space as stated in Section 7 of the Summary.

3.   Term

3.1   Initial Term. The initial term ("Initial Term") of the Lease shall commence as of the date ("Commencement Date") on which Landlord tenders possession of the Space to Tenant in the condition contemplated by Section 4 of these Terms and Conditions, provided, however, that Landlord shall give Tenant neither less than thirty (30) days nor more than sixty (60) days prior written notice of the Commencement Date and the Commencement Date shall neither be sooner than the earliest date ("Estimated Commencement Date") specified in Section 3 of the Summary nor later than the latest date ("Latest Commencement Date") specified in Section 3 of the Summary. Tenant shall nevertheless be entitled to possession of the Space for all purposes other than the payment of Rent upon substantial completion of any Buildout as contemplated by Section 4 of these Terms and Conditions. The Initial Term shall terminate as of the date ("Initial Termination Date") specified in Section 3 of the Summary, or as sooner provided in Sections 7.3, 8.10 or 9 of these Terms and Conditions. If Landlord does not tender possession of the Space to Tenant on or before the Latest Commencement Date in the condition contemplated by Section 4 of these Terms and Conditions, the Lease shall automatically terminate and be null and void and of no further force or effect, in which event, so long as Landlord has continuously and diligently used its reasonable best efforts to tender possession of the Space to Tenant in the condition contemplated by Section 4 of these Terms and Conditions on or before the Latest Commencement Date, Landlord shall have no liability to Tenant, or anyone claiming under Tenant, for any loss or damage incurred or suffered by any of them as a result of the inability of Landlord to tender possession of the Space to Tenant in the condition contemplated by Section 4 of these Terms and Conditions on or before the Latest Commencement Date. Tenant shall not be liable to Landlord, or to anyone claiming under Landlord, for any loss or damage incurred or suffered by them as a result of any such termination of the Lease.

3.2   Optional Term. Any optional term ("Optional Term") of the Lease shall commence concurrently with the Initial Termination Date in accordance with the terms and conditions of any option or options to extend the Initial Term included below in Section 3.3 of these Terms and Conditions. Any Optional Term shall terminate as of the date ("Optional Termination Date") of expiration of such Optional Term, or as sooner provided in Section 7.3, 8.10 or 9 of these Terms and Conditions.

3.3 Option(s) to Extend Term. So long as Tenant is not then in default under the Lease, Tenant shall have the options, on the number of occasions, at the times and for the periods of time stated in Section 3 of the Summary, to extend the Term on each of these Terms and Conditions, provided, however, that the Base Rent during each such extension shall be the percentage of the fair market rental value of the Space at the date of exercise of each such option specified in Section 3 of the Summary. Such fair market rental value shall represent what a sophisticated, arms length, new (nonrenewal) tenant and Landlord would likely agree upon with respect to the Space, taking into account rental rate, free rent and other rent concessions, tenant buildout allowances and periods, base year escalation provisions, brokerage expenses and other lease up costs, including vacancy. In the event the parties are unable to agree on such fair market rental value within thirty (30) days after the exercise of any such option, that determination shall be made in accordance with the arbitration provisions of Section 9 of these Terms and Conditions, provided, however, (i) that the members of the Arbitration Panel shall be real estate brokers instead of lawyers, but otherwise qualified as set forth in Section 9 of these Terms and Conditions, (ii) that Landlord and Tenant shall each submit to the Arbitration Panel the dollar figure they each believe represents such fair market rental value within ten (10) days after the Arbitration Panel is selected or shall be deemed to have agreed with the dollar figure submitted by the other party and (iii) that the Arbitration Panel shall determine such fair market rental value by selecting whichever of Landlord's and Tenant's respective dollar figures the Arbitration Panel feels most closely approximates such fair market rental value.

4. Construction

4.1 Base Building. At its sole cost and expense, Landlord shall perform, or cause to be performed, all work ("Base Building Work") reasonably required to construct and maintain the Building in keeping with first class office buildings constructed in the community in which the Building is located and substantially completed not more than (2) years prior to and not more than one (1) year after substantial completion of the Building, including, specifically with respect to the Space, such prebuildout work as typically provided to full floor tenants in such buildings during such period of time, and including any and all work described in any plans and specifications ("Base Building Drawings") initialled on each page both by Landlord and Tenant.

4.2 Space Plan and Buildout Drawings. Within the number of days after the effective date of execution of the Lease specified in Section 4(i) of the Summary, Tenant shall cause to be reasonably prepared and delivered to Landlord a proposed preliminary space plan ("Space Plan") for buildout ("Buildout") of the Space. Upon receipt of such proposed Space Plan, Landlord shall concurrently pay to Tenant a space planning allowance ("Space Planning Allowance") in the amount specified in Section 4(ii) of the Summary. The proposed Space Plan shall be subject to approval by Landlord and shall be deemed so approved unless Landlord delivers written notice to Tenant specifying and explaining the reasons for any objections to the proposed Space Plan in reasonable detail within ten (10) days after such initial delivery of the proposed Space Plan or after any subsequent delivery of any revised Space Plan. In the event of any objections, the parties shall promptly meet and confer and endeavor to resolve such objections. Within the number of days after approval of the Space Plan specified in Section 4(iii) of the Summary, Tenant shall cause to be reasonably prepared and delivered to Landlord proposed detailed working and engineering drawings and specifications ("Buildout Drawings") for the Buildout of the Space reasonably consistent with the approved Space Plan. Upon receipt of such proposed Buildout Drawings, Landlord shall concurrently pay to Tenant a buildout drawings allowance ("Buildout Drawings Allowance") in the amount specified in Section 4(iv) of the Summary. The proposed Buildout Drawings shall be subject to approval by Landlord and shall be deemed so approved unless Landlord delivers written notice to Tenant specifying and explaining the reasons for any objections to the proposed Buildout Drawings in reasonable detail within fifteen (15) days after such initial delivery of the proposed Buildout Drawings or after any subsequent delivery of any revised Buildout Drawings. In the event of any objection, the parties shall promptly meet and confer and endeavor to resolve such objections.

4.3   Buildout Cost and Documentation.   Within the number of days after approval of the Buildout Drawings specified in Section 4(v) of the Summary, Landlord shall cause to be reasonably prepared and delivered to Tenant a proposed construction agreement ("Buildout Agreement") pertaining to the proposed Buildout of the Space, including the identity of the proposed interior general contractor, the proposed cost ("Buildout Cost") of the Buildout, the proposed time frame for substantially completing the Buildout and paying the Buildout Cost, the proposed terms and conditions of an institutional escrow arrangement under which the entire Buildout Cost would be deposited before Buildout commencement, the proposed definition of substantial completion of the Buildout and the proposed terms of Buildout warranty, and accompanied by a detailed, line item by line item breakdown ("Buildout Cost Breakdown") of the proposed Buildout Cost, including as to each line item the applicable unit prices and number of units. Landlord shall, in the manner specified in the Buildout Agreement, contribute toward the first dollar costs of the Buildout a buildout allowance ("Buildout Allowance") in the amount specified in Section 4(vi) of the Summary. The proposed Buildout Agreement, the proposed Buildout Cost and the proposed Buildout Cost Breakdown shall be subject to approval by Tenant and shall be deemed so approved unless Tenant delivers written notice to Landlord specifying and explaining the reasons for any objections to the proposed Buildout Agreement, the proposed Buildout Cost and/or the proposed Buildout Cost Breakdown in reasonable detail within fifteen (15) days after such initial delivery of such proposed items or after any subsequent delivery of any such revised items. In the event of any objections, the parties shall promptly meet and endeavor to resolve such objections, provided, however, in the event that Tenant, within such fifteen (15) days, identifies in writing ("Buildout Alternative") a reputable and experienced alternative interior general contractor willing to perform the Buildout for ninety-five percent (95%) or less of the proposed Buildout Cost on specified terms and conditions substantially along the lines of the proposed Buildout Agreement, or on other specified reasonable terms and conditions acceptable to Tenant and not materially less favorable to Landlord than the proposed Buildout Agreement, then Landlord shall be deemed to have approved such Buildout Alternative, and shall, within five (5) days after receipt of such proposed Buildout Alternative, sign all reasonable documentation consistent with the Buildout Alternative or resubmit the proposed Buildout Agreement, the proposed Buildout Cost and the proposed Buildout Cost Breakdown to Tenant, revised to reflect a Buildout Cost not greater than the proposed Buildout Cost included in the Buildout Alternative. Any such revised proposal so submitted to Tenant shall again be subject to Tenant's approval exactly as set forth in this Section 4.3 in connection with the initial proposal submitted to Tenant under this Section 4.3.

4.4 Buildout. Within ten (10) days after approval of the Buildout Agreement, the Buildout Cost and the Buildout Cost Breakdown, or the Buildout Alternative, as the case may be, Landlord shall cause the Buildout to be commenced and performed as agreed and Tenant shall cooperate with the Buildout in all contemplated and/or reasonable respects. Landlord shall be responsible for completion of the Buildout as so agreed and, at Tenant's written election, shall either enforce for Tenant's benefit and/or assign to Tenant all representations and warranties of the interior general contractor, all subcontractors and/or all materialmen contributing to the Buildout. In spite of any provision to the contrary in these Terms and Conditions, the Commencement Date shall not occur until substantial completion of the Buildout as that term is defined in the Buildout Agreement or under the Buildout Alternative.

5. Rent and Security Deposit

Promptly when due, and without offset or deduction, Tenant shall pay to Landlord as rent ("Rent"), and as a security deposit ("Security Deposit"):

5.1 Base Rent. Base rent ("Base Rent"), payable in advance on the Commencement Date and on the first day of each calendar month thereafter during the Term, shall equal the monthly amount or amounts specified in Section 5 of the Summary, prorated as to any partial or split months in the event that the Commencement Date is not on the first day of a calendar month and/or in the event that the Initial Termination Date and/or any Optional Termination Date is not on the last day of any calendar month.

5.2 Escalation Rent. Escalation rent ("Escalation Rent") shall be determined in accordance with the following terms and conditions:

5.2.1 Purpose. The purpose of Escalation Rent is to further the objective that Landlord will realize a fair and equitable return on its capital investment, as essentially defined by Base Rent, and that such return will neither be eroded nor inflated by any increases or decreases in the costs of operating the Building. The purpose of Escalation Rent is not to provide an additional source of revenue or profit to Landlord and the provisions of this Section 5.2 shall be interpreted and applied accordingly.

5.2.2   General Approach. Landlord shall at all times operate the Building in an efficient, economical and cost effective manner consistent with maintaining the Building on a par with comparable buildings in the community in which the Building is located and so as to reasonably minimize all Rent and Escalation Rent which Tenant is required to pay. Only reasonable and necessary direct out of pocket costs and expenses ("Operating Costs") of operation, maintenance and repair of the Building, computed in accordance with generally accepted accounting principles consistently applied, but only to the extent deductible on a current basis for federal income tax purposes, shall be considered in computing Escalation Rent, and only then to the extent that such dollar amounts are net of any insurance or condemnation awards receivable, any tenant or other reimbursements receivable and/or any other revenues or accounts receivable and pertain to matters or items provided to Tenant without obligation for any additional charge and which Landlord is not entitled to bill to any tenant or occupant. For the purpose of computing Escalation Rent, Operating Costs may be computed as if the Building was ninety-five percent (95%) occupied, but only to the extent of any such adjustment in the Base Year Operating Costs multiplied by a ratio the numerator of which is equal to the difference between ninety-five percent (95%) and any lower average occupancy percentage for the calendar year in question and the denominator of which is equal to the difference between ninety-five percent (95%) and any lower average occupancy percentage for the Base Year.

5.2.3   Specific Inclusions. Except as otherwise provided in this Section 5.2, Operating Costs shall include (i) the operation, maintenance and repair of all utility systems, services and the like and all other common areas of the Building, (ii) utility charges, (iii) insurance premiums, (iv) employee compensation and benefits directly attributable to the operation, maintenance and repair of the Building, (v) independent contractors engaged for the benefit of the Building, as distinguished from the benefit of Landlord, (vi) the reasonably amortized or depreciated cost of improvements and/or equipment intended to reduce Operating Costs, but, in each calendar year, only to the extent of any such reduction in such calendar year, and (vii) real property taxes ("Property Taxes"). Except as otherwise provided in this Section 5.2, Property Taxes shall mean all taxes and assessments from time to time levied and assessed against the Building and/or all taxes and assessments from time to time levied and assessed against the gross or net income of Landlord derived from the Building to the extent in lieu or substitution of what otherwise could and would have been a tax or assessment from time to time levied and assessed against the Building.

5.2.4   Specific Exclusions. Operating Costs shall exclude any costs or expenses not specifically authorized in this Section 5.2, including (i) any and all capital costs, except as permitted under Section 5.2.3(vi) of these Terms and Conditions, (ii) any and all depreciation or amortization of the Building, or any portion or component of the Building, or any equipment or other property, except as permitted under Section 5.2.3(vi) of these Terms and Conditions, (iii) any and all loan payments, principal or interest, or ground lease or similar payments, (iv) any and all leasing costs, including brokerage commissions, legal fees, vacancy costs and/or refurbishment or improvement expenses, (v) any and all collection costs, including legal fees and/or bad debt losses or reserves, (vi) any otherwise permissible fees or costs to the extent in excess of prevailing and competitive rates, (vii) any costs or expenses resulting from Landlord's violation of any agreement to which it is a party or any applicable laws or ordinances or governmental rules, regulations or orders, (viii) any documentary transfer taxes imposed in connection with the Lease or any other lease and (ix) any increase in Property Taxes attributable to or as a result of any sale, refinancing, transfer or change of ownership in the Building, or any portion of or interest in the Building, whether directly or otherwise.

     5.2.5 Payment. On or before April 1 of each year, Landlord shall deliver to Tenant a statement ("Projected Escalation Rent Statement") setting forth Tenant's share of the difference ("Projected Escalation Difference"), if any, between the projected Operating Costs for the current calendar year, together with sufficient detail and backup to substantiate such projection, and the Operating Costs for the Base Year ("Base Year Operating Costs") and a statement ("Escalation Rent Statement") setting forth Tenant's Share of the difference, ("Escalation Difference") if any, between the Operating Costs for the preceding calendar year, together with sufficient detail and backup to substantiate such amount, and the Base Year Operating Costs. In the event such Projected Escalation Difference is negative, the Projected Escalation Rent Statement shall be accompanied by Landlord's payment to Tenant in a prorated amount corresponding to the period which runs from the beginning of such calendar year to the end of the calendar month in which the Projected Escalation Rent Statement is delivered to Tenant, and the Base Rent for the remainder of such calendar year shall be reduced by one-twelfth ($1/12$th) of such negative Projected Escalation Difference. In the event such Projected Escalation Difference is positive, Tenant shall make payment to Landlord within thirty (30) days after Tenant's receipt of the Projected Escalation Rent Statement in a prorated amount corresponding to the period which runs from the beginning of such calendar year to the end of the calendar month in which such payment is made, and the Base Rent for the remainder of such calendar year shall be increased by one-twelfth ($1/12$th) of such positive Projected Escalation Difference. In the event such Escalation Difference, after first taking into account any Projected Escalation Rent Statement payments under this Section 5.2.5 for such preceding calendar year ("Adjusted Escalation Difference"), is negative, the Escalation Rent Statement shall be accompanied by Landlord's payment to Tenant in that amount. In the event such Adjusted Escalation Difference is positive, Tenant shall make payment to Landlord in that amount within thirty (30) days after Tenant's receipt of such Escalation Rent Statement. In the calendar year in which the Base Year ends, and in the calendar year in which the Term ends, Escalation Rent payable shall be prorated on the basis of the number of days in each such year respectively following the end of the Base Year and preceding expiration of the Term.

5.2.6 Review. Tenant shall be entitled from time to time to audit and verify the operations of the Building and/or the related books and records of Landlord to assure that the Operating Costs from time to time reported by Landlord are in keeping with the provisions of this Section 5.2. As to any calendar year, any such undertaking by Tenant must be initiated before the end of the following calendar year and, absent fraud or gross negligence on Landlord's part, the Operating Costs as timely reported by Landlord for such calendar year shall be deemed controlling upon the expiration of Tenant's audit and verification rights for such calendar year under this Section 5.2.6. In the event of any errors, the appropriate party shall make a correcting payment in full to the other party within thirty (30) days after the determination and communication to all parties of the amount of such error. In the event of any errors on the part of Landlord in excess of three percent (3%), Landlord shall also reimburse Tenant for all costs of such audit and verification reasonably incurred by Tenant within such thirty (30) day period. Within three (3) months of the Commencement Date, Tenant shall be entitled to verify the Rentable Building Footage, the Rentable Space Footage, the Usable Space Footage and/or the Tenant Share. In the event of any errors, these terms shall be restated to eliminate such errors. In the event of any errors in excess of three percent (3%), Landlord shall also reimburse Tenant for all costs of such verification reasonably incurred by Tenant within thirty (30) days after the determination and communication to all parties of the amount of such error. In the event of any dispute or difference between the parties under this Section 5.2.6, such dispute or difference shall be resolved pursuant to the provisions of Section 9 of these Terms and Conditions.

5.3 Additional Rent. Additional rent ("Additional Rent"), if any, shall equal the sum of all payments, other than the Base Rent and the Escalation Rent, to be made by Tenant under the Lease, payable within thirty (30) days after Landlord provides Tenant with written notice of the amount involved, together with reasonable detail and support of such amount.

5.4 Security Deposit. As consideration for the execution of the Lease by Landlord, Tenant shall deposit the Security Deposit with Landlord in the amount or amounts, and at the time or times, specified in Section 5 of the Summary. Any such deposit shall bear interest for the account of Tenant at reasonable rates from time to time available, distributable quarterly. In the event of any such determination under Section 9 of these Terms and Conditions, Landlord may apply the Security Deposit in reduction of any damages or losses incurred or suffered by Landlord as a result of such default or in reasonable performance of the defaulted obligations of Tenant, in which event Tenant shall within thirty (30) days after Landlord provides Tenant with notice to such effect, redeposit with Landlord the Security Deposit, or any portion of the Security Deposit, so applied. Upon termination of the Lease, Landlord shall promptly return to Tenant the Security Deposit, less any portion of the Security Deposit applied, but not refurbished, pursuant to this Section 5.4.

6.   Operations

6.1   Use. Except as otherwise expressly permitted in the Lease, or except upon the prior written consent of Landlord, Tenant shall be entitled to the exclusive use and occupancy of the Space and shall be entitled to the nonexclusive use of all common areas of the Building for all purposes intended, but (i) shall not use the Space for any purpose other than as specified in Section 6 of the Summary, (ii) shall not cause or permit any nuisance to, or waste of, the Space, or the posting or distribution of any signs, handbills, circulars, advertisements, or papers or other material or matters in or about the Space, (iii) shall not cause or permit the violation of any federal, state, county or municipal statutes, laws, ordinances, rules, regulations or orders now or in the future affecting the Space or the Building, (iv) shall not cause or permit the violation of (a) the Lease, including any rules or regulations ("Regulations") from time to time reasonably inacted and uniformly maintained as to all tenants by Landlord, but only so long as such Regulations do not impair or otherwise prejudice any of Tenant's rights under the Lease, or (b) any encumbrance or policy of insurance now or in the future affecting the Building, but only so long as such encumbrances and policies of insurance do not impair or otherwise prejudice any of Tenant's rights under the Lease, and (v) shall not permit to take any act which would in any way increase the rates of any policy of insurance now or in the future affecting the Building or unreasonably subject Landlord, or anyone claiming under Landlord, to any liability for injury to any person or any property as a result of such act.

6.2   Alterations and Improvements. Except as otherwise expressly provided in the Lease, and except upon the prior written consent of Landlord, Tenant shall not make or permit any alterations of or improvements to the Space and, upon expiration or sooner termination of the Lease, any such alterations and/or improvements shall belong to Landlord.

6.3   Services. Subject to the provisions of Section 5.2 of these Terms and Conditions, Landlord shall furnish to the Space all services and utilities reasonably and customarily provided in first class buildings in the community in which the Building is located, in such quality, magnitude and frequency as is not less than in keeping with that provided in such first class buildings, including (i) not less than four (4) watts per rentable square foot of electricity for customary lighting and commercially reasonable business machines, (ii) heat and air conditioning during customary week day and Saturday business hours, (iii) automatic and/or manual elevator service, (iv) lighting and lighting replacement for all lights located within any common areas of the Building, (v) customary lobby directory services, (vi) customary and reasonable custodial service not less favorable to Tenant than outlined in the Cleaning Specifications ("Cleaning Specifications") included below in these Terms and Conditions, (vii) a customary and reasonable life support and security system and (viii) the number of exclusive and/or nonexclusive parking spaces ("Parking Spaces") stated in Section 6 of the Summary. Except as otherwise provided elsewhere in these Terms and Conditions, no interruption in the furnishing of any such services or utilities beyond the control of Landlord shall constitute an actual or constructive eviction, excuse or release Tenant from any of its obligations under the Lease or cause Landlord to be liable to Tenant, or to anyone claiming under Tenant, for any loss or damage resulting from such interruption.

6.4   Maintenance and Repair. Subject to the provisions of Section 8.4 of these Terms and Conditions, Landlord shall maintain, repair, replace, restore and renew at all times during the Term the good condition, order and repair of the foundations and the structural soundness of the roof, floors and exterior walls of the Building, including the interior surfaces of such roof, floors and exterior walls, and the common areas of the Building, reasonable wear and tear and matters arising out of the default or negligence of Tenant, or anyone claiming under Tenant, hereby excepted. Tenant shall maintain, repair, replace, restore and renew at all times during the Term the good condition, order and repair of the Space, reasonable wear and tear, Building Systems running through or contained within the Space and matters arising out of the default or negligence of Landlord, or anyone claiming under Landlord, hereby excepted.

7.   Liability.

7.1   Indemnification. The parties shall indemnify and hold one another, and all those claiming under them, harmless from and against all liability, claims, losses, damages and costs and expenses, including reasonable attorneys' fees, as a result of the use or occupancy of, or the presence in or about, the Building, or any portion of the Building, including the Space, or the breach of any provision of the Lease. Except as otherwise expressly stated to the contrary in the additional provisions ("Additional Provisions") at the end of these Terms and Conditions, no party shall have any obligations to any broker except as specifically hired by such party.

7.2   Insurance.

7.2.1   Landlord. Landlord shall maintain in effect at all times during the Term such policies of insurance, in such amounts and subject to such deductibles, as are not less than in keeping with what is customarily provided in first class buildings in the community in which the Building is located, including insurance covering the Building against loss by fire, theft, vandalism, malicious mischief or any other peril or casualty customarily included in standard extended coverage insurance, to the extent of the full replacement value of the Building and insurance covering all liability in connection with the Building, with bodily injury limits of not less than One Million Dollars ($1,000,000) per person and with property damage deductibility of not more than Ten Thousand Dollars ($10,000) per accident and property damage limits of not less than One Million Dollars ($1,000,000) per accident. To the extent that such executory waiver does not constitute a violation of such policies of insurance and Tenant pays to Landlord an amount equal to any additional premiums imposed upon Landlord in connection with such executory waiver within thirty (30) days after Landlord provides Tenant with written notice of such amount, the liability of Tenant, and anyone claiming under Tenant, shall be secondary to the liability arising out of such policies of insurance.

7.2.2   Tenant. So long as available at premium rates reasonably in keeping with corresponding premium rates as of the date of execution of the Lease, Tenant shall maintain in effect at all times during the Term policies of insurance naming as the insured Landlord, Tenant and the beneficiaries of any encumbrances now or in the future affecting the Building and insuring the Space, and all fixtures, equipment and other personal property located within the Space, from and against loss by fire, theft, vandalism, malicious mischief or any other peril or casualty customarily included in standard extended coverage insurance to the extent of the full replacement value of such items, all liability in connection with the Space, with bodily injury limits of not less than One Million Dollars ($1,000,000) per person and with property damage deductibility of not more than Ten Thousand Dollars ($10,000) per accident and property damage limits of not less than One Million Dollars ($1,000,000) per accident, and all of Tenant's employees working in or about the Space for workman's compensation, with limits not less than required by applicable law. All such policies of insurance shall be issued by responsible insurance companies qualified to do business in the State in which the Building is located and first approved in writing by Landlord on forms satisfactory to Landlord, duplicate copies of which shall, upon the prior written request of Landlord, be deposited with Landlord, bearing endorsements that such policy shall not be cancelled or reduced in scope or amount of coverage except upon thirty (30) days' prior written notice to Landlord.

7.3   Damage and Destruction. In the event of any damage or destruction to the Building, or any portion of the Building, at any time during the Term, the parties shall promptly repair, replace, restore and renew the good condition, order and repair of the Building as respectively required of them pursuant to Section 6.4 of the Lease, provided, however, that either party may, in writing delivered to the other party within thirty (30) days after such damage or destruction, terminate the Lease as of the date of such damage or destruction, terminate the Lease as of the date of such damage or destruction if such repair, replacement, restoration or renewal would likely require more than six (6) months to complete or if such damage or destruction occurs within the final eighteen (18) months of the Term. During the period of any such repair, replacement, restoration or renewal, the obligation of Tenant to pay Rent shall be abated if the Space is effectively rendered unfit for its intended use by Tenant as a result of such damage or destruction.

8.   Title

8.1   Space. The Space which is the subject of the Lease is as described in Section 7 of the Summary.

8.2   Option(s) to Expand Space. So long as Tenant is not then in default under the Lease, Tenant shall have the option, on the number of occasions stated in Section 8 of the Summary, and otherwise during the Term as any or all of the additional space ("Additional Space") described in Section 8 of the Summary from time to time becomes available on the basis of such notice as specified in Section 8 of the Summary, without regard to the fact that Tenant may have previously elected not to exercise any such option, to expand the Space, on each of these Terms and Conditions, to include any or all of the Additional Space, but only in rentable square footage increments not less than stated in Section 8 of the Summary, with the result (i) that the Lease shall expire as to both the Space and any or all of the Additional Space exactly as it would have with respect to the Space alone if no such option had been exercised, (ii) that the Rent and Tenant Share shall prospectively be increased proportionately as any or all of the Additional Space from time to time taken bears to the Space, (iii) that the Space Planning Allowance, the Buildout Drawings Allowance and the Buildout Allowance for any or all of the Additional Space from time to time taken shall be calculated on the same per rentable square foot basis as in the case of the Space and (iv) that any free or reduced rent period, and any other rent concessions, for any Additional Space shall be the same as in the case of the Space multiplied by a ratio the numerator of which shall equal the remainder of the Term at the date of exercise of such option, taking into account any then exercised options to extend the Term, and the denominator of which shall equal the Term without taking into account the exercise or possible exercise of any options to extend the Term. In respect of such options to expand, Landlord shall not lease, or agree to lease, any or all of the Additional Space to any third parties except in rentable square footage and time increments not greater than set forth in Section 8 of the Summary.

8.3   Quiet Enjoyment. Except as otherwise expressly provided in the Lease, Tenant shall lawfully, peaceably and quietly have, hold, occupy and enjoy the Space during the Term, without hindrance or ejection by Landlord or by anyone claiming under Landlord.

8.4   Access. Upon reasonable prior written notice of not less than two (2) days, Landlord, and its employees and agents, shall be entitled to enter the Space and to make all repairs, replacements, restorations or renewals as may be reasonably necessary, provided, however, that such notice shall not be necessary to the extent required by emergency. To the extent possible, such access shall be confined to periods of time other than customary business hours. During any such periods of repair, replacement, restoration or renewal, the obligation of Tenant to pay Rent shall be abated if the Space is rendered unfit for its intended use by Tenant. During the last twelve (12) months of the Term, Landlord shall also be entitled to such access on such prior written notice for the purpose of showing the Space to prospective tenants.

8.5   Estoppel Certificates. Tenant shall execute, acknowledge and deliver to Landlord, from time to time during the Term within ten (10) days after Landlord provides Tenant with written notice to do so, an estoppel certificate certifying in writing that the Lease is in full force and effect, unmodified or modified solely as set forth in such estoppel certificate, including confirmation of the Commencement Date and the Initial Termination Date, the date or dates to which Rent has been paid and that Landlord has, as of the date of such estoppel certificate, fully and completely performed and complied with each of these Terms and Conditions, without exception or except as only set forth in such estoppel certificate. Any such estoppel certificate may be conclusively relied upon by any prospective purchaser or encumbrancer of the

Building. The failure of Tenant to so deliver such estoppel certificate in such period of time shall mean that the Lease is in full force and effect, without modification, that Rent has not been prepaid under the Lease except as expressly required in the Lease and that Landlord has, as of the date on which Tenant failed to deliver such estoppel certificate, fully and completely performed and complied with each of these Terms and Conditions, without exception.

8.6   Subordination and Nondisturbance. Without the necessity of any further consideration or action, Tenant shall subordinate all of its right, title and interest in the Lease to any encumbrance now or in the future affecting the Building, or any portion thereof, provided, however, that the beneficiary or beneficiaries of such encumbrance shall first agree in writing delivered to Tenant to recognize all of Tenant's right, title and interest in the Lease so long as Tenant performs and complies with each of these Terms and Conditions. Within ten (10) days after Landlord or such beneficiary or beneficiaries provides Tenant with written notice to do so, Tenant shall execute and deliver to Landlord such documents, and shall take such further action, as either Landlord or such beneficiary or beneficiaries may deem necessary or advisable to effect or maintain such subordination.

8.7   Attornment. Upon delivery of Tenant of the written election of the beneficiary or beneficiaries of any encumbrance now or in the future affecting the Building which is superior to the Lease that such encumbrance shall be deemed subordinate to the Lease, the Lease shall, without the necessity of any further consideration or action, be deemed superior to such encumbrance, whether the Lease was executed before or after the execution of such encumbrance, and the beneficiary or beneficiaries of such encumbrance shall have the same rights with respect to the Lease as if the Lease had been executed and delivered prior to execution and delivery of such encumbrance and had thereafter been assigned to such beneficiary or beneficiaries. If, by reason of Landlord's default under any encumbrance now or in the future affecting the Building, any of Landlord's right, title or interest in the Building is terminated, Tenant shall waive all rights at law or in equity now or hereafter in effect to terminate the Lease and surrender possession of the Space, shall atorn to the transferee, whether by foreclosure, judicial or trustees' sale, deed in lieu of foreclosure or otherwise, of any of Landlord's right, title or interest in or to the Building, shall recognize such transferee and its transferees as a landlord under the Lease and shall execute and deliver to Landlord and to such transferee and transferees, within ten (10) days after Landlord, such transferee or transferees provides Tenant with written notice to do so, such documents, and take such further action, as Landlord, such transferee or transferees may deem necessary or advisable to effect or maintain such attornment.

8.8   Assignment and Subletting. Tenant may neither sell, assign, transfer, convey, mortgage, hypothecate, pledge or encumber, by operation of law or otherwise, the Lease, or any of Tenant's right, title or interest in the Lease, or, in the event that Tenant is a partnership, corporation or other form of business or investment entity, more than fifty percent (50%) of the right, title or interest in such partnership, corporation or other form of business or investment entity existing as of the date of the Lease, either directly or by authorization or issuance of additional right, title or interest, in one (1) or more transactions, nor sublet the Space or any portion thereof, nor agree to do any such things, except upon the prior written consent of Landlord. Within ten (10) days after Landlord provides Tenant with written notice to do so, Tenant, and its assignees and sublessees, shall execute and deliver to Landlord such documents, and take such further action, as Landlord may deem necessary or advisable to effect or maintain such transaction or to protect Landlord's rights under the Lease. The consent to any particular assignment, subletting or other such transfer shall not be deemed a consent to any other assignment, subletting or other such transfer and shall not relieve Tenant of any of its obligations under the Lease, whether arising before or after such consent, provided, however, that the consent to any particular assignment shall relieve Tenant of its obligations under the Lease to the extent that the assignee in writing delivered to Landlord and Tenant expressly assumes such obligations. In the event of the consent to any particular subletting, and the termination of the Lease after such consent as a result of any default under the Lease by Tenant, Landlord shall recognize all of the subtenant's right, title and interest in such sublease as a direct lease with Landlord so long as such subtenant performs and complies with each of the terms and conditions of the sublease and the subtenant shall attorn to and recognize Landlord to the same extent as if the sublease were instead a direct lease between Landlord and the subtenant.

8.9   Transfer by Landlord. In the event of any sale, assignment, transfer, or conveyance of the Building and the Lease by Landlord, Landlord shall be relieved of its obligations under the Lease, both those arising before and after such transfer, to the extent that such transferee in writing delivered to Landlord and Tenant expressly assumes such obligations.

8.10 Condemnation. In the event of any taking or sale ("Taking") of the Building, or any portion of the Building or any interest in the Building, under the power or threat of eminent domain, the Lease shall terminate to the extent of such taking and the parties shall promptly repair, replace, restore and renew the good condition, order and repair of the remainder of the Building as respectively required of them pursuant to Section 6.4 of the Lease, provided, however, that either party may, in writing delivered to the other party within thirty (30) days after such Taking, terminate the Lease as of the date of such Taking if such repair, replacement, restoration or renewal of the Building is reasonably likely to require more than six (6) months, if such Taking occurs within the final eighteen (18) months of the Term or if the Taking includes any portion of the Space and Tenant concludes that the remainder of the Space is not sufficient for Tenant's intended use of the Space. In the event that any Taking of a portion of the Space does not result in a full and complete termination of the Lease, the obligation of Tenant to pay Rent shall be abated during the period of such Taking proportionately as the usable square footage of the Space so taken or sold bears to the total Usable Space Footage. All consideration, compensation, damages, income, rent, awards and interest which may be paid or made in connection with any Taking shall be divided between the parties as their respective interests may appear as determined by the condemning authority.

8.11 Surrender. Upon expiration of the Term, or sooner termination of the Lease, Tenant shall, at its sole cost and expense, reasonable wear and tear not resulting from the failure of Tenant to perform and comply with its obligations to maintain, repair, replace, restore or renew pursuant to Section 6.4 of the Lease hereby excepted, promptly undo and remove all fixtures, equipment and other personal property of Tenant, or anyone claiming under Tenant, within the Space and surrender up and deliver possession of the Space to Landlord.

9. Disputes

In the event of any dispute or disagreement between the parties under the Lease, the matter shall be resolved by arbitration as follows:

9.1 Exclusive Procedure. The provisions of this Section 9 contain the sole and exclusive method, means and procedure to resolve any and all disputes or disagreements, including whether any particular matter constitutes, or with the passage of time would constitute, a default. The parties hereby irrevocably waive any and all rights to the contrary and shall at all times conduct themselves in strict, full, complete and timely accordance with the provisions of this Section 9 and all attempts to circumvent the provisions of this Section 9 shall be absolutely null and void and of no force or effect whatsoever. As to any matter submitted to arbitration to determine whether it would, with the passage of time, constitute a default, such passage of time shall not commence to run until any such affirmative determination so long as it is simultaneously determined that the challenge of such matter as a potential default was made in good faith.

9.2 Arbitration Panel. Within ten (10) days after delivery of written notice ("Notice of Dispute") of the existence and nature of any dispute given by any party to the other party, the parties shall each (i) appoint one (1) lawyer actively engaged in the licensed and full time practice of law in the county in which the Building is located for a continuous period immediately preceding the date of delivery ("Dispute Date") of the Notice of Dispute of not less than ten (10) years, but who has at no time ever represented or acted on behalf of any of the parties and (ii) deliver written notice of the identity of such lawyer and a copy of his or her written acceptance of such appointment to the other parties hereto. In the event that any party fails to so act, such dispute shall automatically be deemed resolved against such party. Within ten (10) days after such appointment and notice, such lawyers shall appoint a third lawyer (together with the first two (2) lawyers, "Arbitration Panel") of such qualification and background and shall deliver written notice of the identity of such lawyer and a copy of his or her written acceptance of such appointment to each of the parties. In the event that agreement cannot be reached on the appointment of a third lawyer within such period, such appointment and notification shall be made as quickly as possible by any court of competent jurisdiction, by any licensing authority, agency or organization having jurisdiction over such lawyers, by any professional association of lawyers in existence for not less than ten (10) years at the time of such dispute or disagreement and the geographical membership boundaries of which extend to the county in which the Building is located or by any arbitration association or organization in existence for not less than ten (10) years at the time of such dispute or disagreement and the geographical boundaries of which extend to the county in which the Building is located, as determined by the party giving such Notice of Dispute and simultaneously confirmed in writing delivered by such party to the other party. Any such court, authority, agency, association or organization shall be entitled either to directly select such third lawyer or to designate in writing delivered to each of the parties an individual who shall do so.

9.3   Duty. Consistent with the provisions of this Section 9, the members of the Arbitration Panel shall utilize their utmost skill and shall apply themselves diligently so as to hear and decide, by majority vote, the outcome and resolution of any dispute or disagreement submitted to the Arbitration Panel as promptly as possible, but in any event on or before the expiration of thirty (30) days after the appointment of the members of the Arbitration Panel. None of the members of the Arbitration Panel shall have any liability whatsoever for any acts or omissions performed or omitted in good faith pursuant to the provisions of this Section 9. To that extent, the parties shall each indemnify and hold each of the members of the Arbitration Panel harmless from and against any and all claims, damages, losses, costs and expenses, including reasonable attorneys' fees, suffered or incurred in connection with any arbitration under this Section 9.

9.4   Authority. The Arbitration Panel (i) shall fix and establish any and all rules as it shall consider appropriate in its sole and absolute discretion to govern the proceedings before it, including any and all rules of discovery, procedure and/or evidence, and (ii) shall make and issue any and all orders, final or otherwise, and any and all awards, as a court of competent jurisdiction sitting at law or in equity could make and issue and as it shall consider appropriate in its sole and absolute discretion, including the awarding of monetary damages, whether special, general, compensatory, punitive or otherwise, the awarding of reasonable attorneys' fees and costs to the prevailing party as determined by the Arbitration Panel in its sole and absolute discretion and the issuance of injunctive relief.

9.5   Appeal. The decision of the Arbitration Panel shall be final and binding, may be confirmed and entered by any court of competent jurisdiction at the request of any party and may not be appealed to any court of competent jurisdiction or otherwise except upon a claim of fraud on the part of the Arbitration Panel.

9.6   Compensation. Each member of the Arbitration Panel (i) shall be compensated for any and all services rendered under this Section 9 at a rate of compensation equal to Two Hundred Fifty Dollars ($250.00) per hour and (ii) shall be reimbursed for any and all expenses incurred in connection with the rendering of such services, payable in full promptly upon conclusion of the proceedings before the Arbitration Panel. Such compensation and reimbursement shall be borne by the nonprevailing party as determined by the Arbitration Panel in its sole and absolute discretion.

10. Miscellaneous

10.1 Notice. All notices and other communications pertaining to the Lease shall be in writing and shall be deemed to have been given when delivered personally or two (2) days after being mailed, certified or registered mail, return receipt requested, postage prepaid, to the respective addresses set forth above immediately following the signatures of the parties or to such other address or addresses as any of the parties may from time to time in writing designate to the other party pursuant to this Section 10.1.

10.2 Time. Time is of the essence of the Lease with respect to every provision in which time is a factor.

10.3 Entire Agreement. The Lease, including the Summary and these Terms and Conditions, contains the entire agreement between the parties pertaining to the subject matter of the Lease, fully supersedes all prior agreements or understandings between the parties pertaining to the subject matter of the Lease and no change in, modification of or addition, amendment or supplement to the Lease shall be valid unless set forth in writing signed and dated by each of the parties following the signing of the Lease.

10.4 Applicable Law. The existence, validity, construction and operational effect of the Lease, including the Summary and these Terms and Conditions, and the rights and obligations of each of the parties shall be determined in accordance with the laws of the state in which the Building is located, provided, however, that (i) any provision of the Lease which may be prohibited by law or otherwise held invalid shall be ineffective only to the extent of such prohibition or invalidity and shall not invalidate or otherwise render ineffective any or all of the remaining provisions of the Lease, (ii) the Lease shall not be construed as creating either a partnership, an agency or an employment relationship between the parties, (iii) the failure of any party to insist at any time upon the strict performance of any provision of the Lease or to act upon any right or remedy available to such party, whether under the Lease or as a matter of law, shall not be interpreted as a waiver or a relinquishment of any such right or remedy unless specifically expressed in writing signed by such party and neither the receipt, acceptance nor application of any payment shall, without more, constitute such a writing and (iv) the obligation of any party to make any payment with respect to the Lease shall survive any earlier termination of the Lease.

10.5 Counterparts. The Lease may be executed in several counterparts and all such executed counterparts shall constitute one (1) agreement binding on all of the parties in spite of the fact that all of the parties have not signed the same counterpart.

10.6 Headings and Gender. The section headings used in the Lease are intended solely for convenience of reference and shall not in any way or manner amplify, limit, modify or otherwise be used in the interpretation of any of the provisions of the Lease. The masculine, feminine or neuter gender, and the singular or plural number, shall be deemed to include the others whenever the context so indicates or requires. The term "including" shall be deemed to mean "including, but not by way of limitation,".

10.7 Successors. Subject to the provisions of Section 8.8 of these Terms and Conditions, the Lease shall be binding upon and shall inure to the benefit of the successors and assigns of the parties.

CLEANING SPECIFICATIONS

1.   Premises Other Than Restrooms
   1.1 Nightly Services (Monday Through Friday)
      1.1.1   Spot clean all resilient and composition floors, including balconies.
      1.1.2   Sweep all resilient and composition floors with appropriately treated dust mop.
      1.1.3   Remove spots from all carpets and rugs.
      1.1.4   Vacuum all rugs and carpets.
      1.1.5   Dust all desks, chairs, files and all other office furniture, fixtures and low reach areas. (Papers, folders and the like on desks are not to be removed.)
      1.1.6   Clean and polish all glass desk tops and any other bright work.
      1.1.7   Dust company desk accessories, including telephones.
      1.1.8   Empty and clean all ash trays and sand urns.
      1.1.9   Properly position furniture in offices.
      1.1.10   Remove any trash from floors and empty, clean and reline all waste baskets and carry trash to pickup area outside the Premises.
      1.1.11   Spot clean doors, door knobs, door frames, glass partitions, windows, glass doors, walls, other vertical surfaces and counters.
      1.1.12   Spot clean around wall switches.
      1.1.13   Clean, sanitize and polish drinking fountain.
      1.1.14   Sweep stairways.
      1.1.15   Clean elevator cabs and door jambs.
      1.1.16   Secure doors and windows upon completion of work assignments.
      1.1.17   Secure all lights as soon as possible each night, other than for any from time to time designated in writing by Tenant to be left on.
      1.1.18   Sweep and dust with appropriately treated dust mop outer lobbies.
      1.1.19   Return all chairs and waste baskets to proper positions.
   1.2 Weekly Services
      1.2.1   Dust chairs, rugs, furniture, ledges, baseboards, moulding, window sills and other similar items.
      1.2.2   Perform low reach dusting.
      1.2.3   Remove fingerprints, smudges and the like from all woodwork, walls, glass desk tops, other bright work and partitions.
      1.2.4   Dust and wipe clean mini-blinds and/or other window treatments.

       1.2.5   Edge all rugs and carpets.

    1.3 Monthly Services

       1.3.1   Perform high reach dusting, including tops of door frames, door sashes, furniture ledges, empty closet shelving and tops of partitions.

       1.3.2   Dust picture frames (but not art work), wall hangings and exterior surfaces of lighting fixtures, damp dust air conditioning diffusers and return grills and thoroughly clean and polish glass.

       1.3.3   Brush down wall and ceiling vents.

       1.3.4   Thoroughly vacuum upholstered furniture and under and around all desks and office furniture.

       1.3.5   Wash, scrub, wax and/or spray buff as appropriate all resilient and composition floors and other horizontal surfaces, including balconies, so as to make all surfaces appear as refinished.

2.   RESTROOMS

    2.1 Nightly Services (Monday Through Friday)

       2.1.1   Remove any trash from floors and empty, clean and reline all waste paper receptacles and carry trash to pick up area outside the Premises.

       2.1.2   Empty and clean sanitary napkin containers and replace insert.

       2.1.3   Clean and polish all metal, enameled surfaces, flushometers, bright work and mirrors.

       2.1.4   Clean and polish all dispensers.

       2.1.5   Clean and disinfect wash basins, toilet seats, toilet bowls, urinals and other fixtures and wipe dry all wash basins.

       2.1.6   Disinfect underside and tops of toilet seats.

       2.1.7   Spot clean tile walls and toilet partitions so as to be unstreaked.

       2.1.8   Spot clean walls around wash basins so as to be unstreaked.

       2.1.9   Clean floors with a germicidal solution.

       2.1.10   Refill or restock soap, towel, tissue and seat cover dispensers and supplies, including sanitary napkin and tampon dispensers.

    2.2 Semiweekly Services

    Pour clean water down floor drains to prevent sewer gasses from escaping.

    2.3 Weekly Services

       2.3.1   Wash down ceramic tile walls and toilet compartment partitions.

       2.3.2   Vacuum all louvres and ventillating grills and dust light fixtures.

    2.4 Monthly Services

    Brush down vents and reseal all resilient and composition floors so as to make such floors appear as refinished.

3.   Floors

    3.1 Daily Services

    Damp mop and buff all resilient and composition floors and other surfaces.

    3.2 Monthly Services

    Clean and refinish all resilient and composition floors and other surfaces.

4.   Windows

4.1 Quarterly Services

Dust, wipe clean and/or vacuum all mini-blinds and/or other window treatments.

4.2 Bimonthly/Biannually Services

In keeping with the frequency at first class office buildings in the community in which the Building is located, but not less frequently than biannually and not more frequently than bimonthly, clean and dry so as to eliminate all streaks and water marks on all windows, inside and outside.

5.   Common Areas and Adjacencies

Maintain in keeping with first class office buildings in the community in which the Building is located.

6.   Supplies and Equipment

Landlord will furnish all the janitorial supplies and equipment necessary to perform the work as described herein, including, but not limited to, restroom supplies such as paper towels, hand soap, toilet tissue, toilet seat covers, deodorants and plastic liners.

ADDITIONAL PROVISIONS

CHAPTER 2

ADDITIONAL AGREEMENTS

§ 2.1   Guaranty of Lease

§ 2.2   Lease for Use of Storage Space

§ 2.3   Workletter

§ 2.4   Assignment—Form

§ 2.5   Sublease—Form

§ 2.6   Sublease (Another Form)

§ 2.7   Rules and Regulations for a Shopping Center

§ 2.8   Rules and Regulations for an Office Building

§ 2.9   Subordination—Nondisturbance, Attornment, Estoppel, and Subordination Agreement

§ 2.10   Estoppel, Subordination, Nondisturbance, and Attornment Agreement

§ 2.11   Estoppel Certificate Form

§ 2.12   Tenant Estoppel Certificate

§ 2.13   Memorandum of Lease

§ 2.14   Short Form Lease

§ 2.15   Commencement Date Certificate

§ 2.16   Lease Commencement Memorandum

§ 2.17   Basic Lease Information—Office Building

§ 2.18   Basic Lease Information—Shopping Center

§ 2.19   Basic Lease Information—Single Tenant Building

§ 2.20   Amendment to Office Lease

§ 2.21   Lease Summary

171

§ 2.1   Guaranty of Lease

FORM 2.1
GUARANTY OF LEASE

Landlord: [name]

Tenant: [name]

Lease: lease dated [date], 19[00]

Guarantor: [name]

Date: [date], 19[00]

Tenant wishes to enter into the lease with landlord. Landlord is unwilling to enter into the lease unless guarantor assures landlord of the full performance of tenant's obligations under the lease. Guarantor is willing to do so.

Accordingly, in order to induce landlord to enter into the lease with tenant, and for good and valuable consideration, the receipt and adequacy of which are acknowledged by guarantor:

1.   Guarantor unconditionally guarantees to landlord, and the successors and assigns of landlord, tenant's full and punctual performance of its obligations under the lease, including without limitation the payment of rent and other charges due under the lease. Guarantor waives notice of any breach or default by tenant under the lease. If tenant defaults in the performance of any of its obligations under the lease, upon landlord's demand, guarantor will perform tenant's obligations under the lease.

2.   Any act of landlord, or the successors or assigns of landlord, consisting of a waiver of any of the terms or conditions of the lease, or the giving of any consent to any matter related to or thing relating to the lease, or the granting of any indulgences or extensions of time to tenant, may be done without notice to guarantor and without affecting the obligations of guarantor under this guaranty.

3.   The obligations of guarantor under this guaranty will not be affected by landlord's receipt, application, or release of security given for the performance of tenant's obligations under the lease, nor by any modification of the lease, including without limitation the alteration, enlargement, or change of the premises described in the lease, except that in case of any such modification, the liability of the guarantor will be deemed modified in accordance with the terms of any such modification.

4.   The liability of guarantor under this guaranty will not be affected by:

(a)   the release or discharge of tenant from its obligations under the lease in any creditors', receivership, bankruptcy, or other proceedings, or the commencement or pendency of any such proceedings;

(b) the impairment, limitation, or modification of the liability of tenant or the estate of tenant in bankruptcy, or of any remedy for the enforcement of tenant's liability under the lease, resulting from the operation of any present or future bankruptcy code or other statute, or from the decision in any court;

(c) the rejection or disaffirmance of the lease in any such proceedings;

(d) the assignment or transfer of the lease or sublease of all or part of the premises described in the lease by tenant;

(e) any disability or other defense of tenant; or

(f) the cessation from any cause whatsoever of the liability of tenant under the lease.

5. Until all of tenant's obligations under the lease are fully performed, guarantor:

(a) waives any right of subrogation against tenant by reason of any payments or acts of performance by guarantor, in compliance with the obligations of guarantor under this guaranty;

(b) waives any other right that guarantor may have against tenant by reason of any one or more payments or acts in compliance with the obligations of guarantor under this guaranty; and

(c) subordinates any liability or indebtedness of tenant held by guarantor to the obligations of tenant to landlord under the lease.

6. This guaranty will apply to the lease, any extension or renewal of the lease, and any holdover term following the term of the lease, or any such extension or renewal.

7. This guaranty may not be changed, modified, discharged, or terminated orally or in any manner other than by an agreement in writing signed by guarantor and landlord.

8. Guarantor is primarily obligated under the lease. Landlord may, at its option, proceed against guarantor without proceeding against tenant or anyone else obligated under the lease or against any security for any of tenant's or guarantor's obligations.

9. Guarantor will pay on demand the reasonable attorneys' fees and costs incurred by landlord, or its successors and assigns, in connection with the enforcement of this guaranty.

10. Guarantor irrevocably appoints tenant as its agent for service of process related to this guaranty.

Guarantor has executed this guaranty as of the date.

[Signature block for guarantor]
[Acknowledgment]

[See Commercial Real Estate Leases: Preparation and Negotiation § 3.15.]

§ 2.2   Lease for Use of Storage Space

FORM 2.2
LEASE FOR USE OF STORAGE SPACE

THIS STORAGE SPACE LEASE is made on [date], 19[00], by [name] ("landlord") and [name] ("tenant").

1.   In consideration of the payment of rent and keeping and performance of the covenants and agreements by tenant in this lease, landlord leases to tenant approximately [* * *] square feet of storage space shown on the drawing marked Exhibit 1 attached to this lease and made a part of it (the "storage space"), numbered [* * *] and located in the basement of [* * *] (the "building").

2.   Tenant's right to use the storage space will commence as of 7:00 a.m. on [date], 19[00], and end simultaneously with the term of the lease (the "office building lease") between landlord and tenant with respect to office space (the "office space") in the building.

3.   The monthly rental for the storage space will be [* * *] ($[* * *]). All rent will be payable on the first day of each month until this storage space lease ends. The monthly rental will be payable in advance, without notice, setoff, abatement, or diminution, at the office of landlord in [* * *], [* * *], or at such place as landlord from time to time designates in writing.

4.   Tenant will use the storage space only for the storage of furniture, equipment, files, and supplies in a careful, safe, and proper manner. Tenant will not bring in or permit within the storage space property in excess of fifty (50) pounds per square foot, and will be fully liable for any damages or losses sustained by landlord as a result of any overloading by tenant. Tenant will pay landlord on demand for any damage to the storage space caused by misuse or abuse by tenant, its agents or employees, or any other person entering upon the storage space. The storage space will not be used for any purposes prohibited by the laws of the United States or the State of [state] or by the ordinances of the City and County of [* * *]. Tenant will not commit waste, nor permit waste to be committed, nor permit any nuisance in the storage space.

5.   Landlord agrees, without extra charge, during the period tenant occupies the storage space, to furnish electric lighting to and ingress and egress to and from the storage space during ordinary business hours as may, in the judgment of landlord, be reasonably required for its use. Tenant agrees that landlord will not be liable for failure to provide lighting or ingress and egress during any period when landlord uses reasonable diligence to supply them. Landlord reserves the right temporarily to discontinue electric service or ingress or egress at such times as may be necessary when, by reason of accident, unavailability of employees, repairs, alterations, or improvements, or whenever by reason of strikes, walkouts, riots, acts of God, or any other happening beyond the control of landlord, landlord is unable to provide them. Landlord will not be obligated to furnish heating or air conditioning to the storage space.

6.   Tenant agrees that all property of tenant kept or stored in the storage space will be at the sole risk of tenant and that landlord will not be liable for any injury or damage to the property. Taking possession of the storage space by tenant will be conclusive evidence that the storage space was in the condition agreed upon between landlord and tenant and acknowledgment by tenant that it accepts the storage space in its then "as is" condition, without any further improvement by landlord.

7.   If for any reason the office building lease ends before its expiration date, this storage space will, without further action of either party, terminate simultaneously. Tenant will vacate the storage space and leave the storage space in the same order and condition as when tenant took occupancy, ordinary wear and tear excepted.

8.   A default under the office building lease is a default under this lease, and landlord will have all of its rights and remedies provided in the office building lease in the event of such a default.

9.   All of the terms and conditions of the office building lease are incorporated by reference in this lease; for the purposes of this storage space lease the term "premises" used in the office building lease means the storage space.

10.   Tenant agrees to indemnify, defend, and save landlord harmless of and from all liability, loss, damages, costs, or expenses, including attorneys' fees, on account of injuries to the person or property of landlord or of any other tenant in the building or to any other person rightfully in said building for any purpose, when the injuries are caused by the negligence or misconduct of tenant, its agents, servants, or employees or any other person entering the storage space under express or implied invitation of tenant or when such injuries are the result of the violation of the provisions of this lease by any of them.

TENANT: LANDLORD:

[signature]   [signature]

By: [* * *]   By: [* * *]

Title: [* * *]   Title: [* * *]

[See Commercial Real Estate Leases: Preparation and Negotiation § 4.17.]

§ 2.3   Workletter

FORM 2.3
WORKLETTER

This workletter is dated [date], 19[00], between [name] ("landlord") and [name] ("tenant").

RECITALS

A.   This workletter is attached to and forms a part of the certain office lease dated [date], 19[00] ("the lease"), pursuant to which landlord had leased to tenant office space in the building to be known as [name].

B.   Landlord desires to make improvements to the premises, and tenant desires to have landlord make them, prior to occupancy, upon the terms and conditions contained in this workletter.

1.   Definitions. In this workletter, some defined terms are used. They are:

(a)   Tenant's representative: [name].

(b)   Landlord's representative: [name].

(c)   [Tenant finish] allowance: $[amount] per usable square foot, which equals $[amount] and is to be applied by landlord to the cost of the improvements. Tenant is not entitled to a cash allowance in any circumstance.

(d)   Programming information: information provided by tenant, including the nature of tenant's business, manner of operation, number and types of rooms, special equipment and functional requirements, anticipated growth, interactions among groups, and any other programming requirements tenant may have.

(e)   Programming information submission date: [date], 19[00].

(f)   Final space plan: a drawing of the premises clearly showing the layout and relationship of all departments and offices, depicting partitions, door locations, types of electrical and data and telephone outlets, and delineation of furniture and equipment. The final space plan will be preceded by preliminary space plans.

(g)   Estimated construction costs: a preliminary estimate of the costs of the improvements that are depicted on the space plan, including all architectural, engineering, contractor, and any other costs as can be determined from the space plan.

(h)   Working drawings: construction documents detailing the improvements and conforming to codes, complete in form and content and containing sufficient information and detail to allow for competitive bidding or negotiated pricing by contractors selected and engaged by landlord.

(i)   Construction schedule: a schedule depicting the relative time frames for various activities related to the construction of the improvements in the premises.

(j)   Tenant cost proposal: a final estimate of costs of the improvements that are depicted on the working drawings, including all architectural, engineering, contractor, and any other costs, and clearly indicating the cost, if any, that is to be paid by tenant pursuant to paragraph 7.

(k)   Maximum approved cost: the sum of the [tenant finish] allowance and any additional amount that tenant has agreed to pay for the improvements to the premises.

(l)   Improvements:

(1)   The development of space plans and working drawings, including supporting engineering studies (that is, structural design or analysis, lighting or acoustical evaluations, or others as determined by landlord's architect).

(2)   All construction work necessary to augment the base building, creating the details and partitioning shown on the space plan. The work will create finished ceilings, walls, and floor surfaces, as well as complete HVAC, lighting, electrical, and fire protection systems.

The improvements will NOT include personal property items, such as decorator items or services, art work, plants, furniture, equipment, or other fixtures not permanently affixed to the premises.

(m)   Cost of the improvements: the cost includes, but is not limited to, the following:

(1)   All architectural and engineering fees and expenses.

(2)   All contractor and construction manager costs and fees.

(3)   All permits and taxes.

(4)   A coordination and administration fee to landlord, pursuant to paragraph 4(d).

(n)   Change order: any change, modification, or addition to the final space plan or working drawings after tenant has approved the same.

(o)   Base building: those elements of the core and shell construction that are completed in preparation for the improvements to the premises. This includes building structure, envelope, and systems as indicated on Schedule 1, "base building definition," attached to this workletter. Base building defines the existing conditions to which improvements are added.

(p)   Building standard: component elements utilized in the design and construction of the improvements that have been pre-selected by the landlord to ensure uniformity of quality, function, and appearance throughout the building. These elements include, but are not limited to, ceiling systems, doors, hardware, walls, floor coverings, finishes, window coverings, light fixtures, and HVAC components. A list of building standard elements is attached to this workletter as Schedule 2.

2.   Representatives. Landlord appoints landlord's representative to act for landlord in all matters associated with this workletter. Tenant appoint tenant's representative to act for tenant in all matters associated with this workletter. All inquiries, requests, instructions, authorizations, and other communications with respect to the matters covered by this workletter will be made to landlord's representative or tenant's representative, as the case may be. Tenant will not make any inquiries of or requests to, and will not give any instructions or authorizations to, any employee or agent of landlord, including without limitation landlord's architect, engineers, and contractors, or any of their agents or employees, with regard to matters associated with this workletter. Either party may change its representative under this workletter at any time by providing 3 days' prior written notice to the other party.

3.   Project Design and Construction. All work will be performed by designers and contractors selected and engaged by landlord.

4.   Cost Responsibilities.

(a)   Landlord: Landlord will pay up to the amount of the [tenant finish] allowance for the cost of the improvements.

(b)   Tenant: Tenant will pay for:

(1)   Tenant-initiated changes to the final space plan or working drawings after tenant's approval.

(2)   Tenant-initiated change orders, modifications, or additions to the improvements after tenant's approval of the working drawings.

(3)   All costs in excess of the [tenant finish] allowance that are not included in (1) or (2).

(4)   The cost of the landlord's overhead for coordination and administration at a rate of 15% of the total cost to the landlord of (1), (2), and (3).

(5)   Tenant will not be entitled to any credit for any portion of the [tenant finish] allowance that is not used.

5.   Landlord's Approval. Landlord, in its sole discretion, may withhold its approval of any final space plan, working drawings, or change order that:

(a)   Exceeds or adversely affects the structural integrity of the building, or any part of the heating, ventilating, air conditioning, plumbing, mechanical, electrical, communication, or other systems of the building;

(b)   Is not approved by the holder of any mortgage or deed of trust encumbering the building at the time the work is proposed;

(c)   Would not be approved by a prudent owner of property similar to the building;

(d)   Violates any agreement that affects the building or binds landlord;

(e)   Landlord reasonably believes will increase the cost of operation or maintenance of any of the systems of the building;

(f)   Landlord reasonably believes will reduce the market value of the premises or the building at the end of the term;

(g)   Does not conform to applicable building code or is not approved by any governmental, quasi-governmental, or utility authority with jurisdiction over the premises; or

(h)   Does not conform to the building standard.

6.   Schedule of Improvement Activities.

(a)   On or before the programming information submission date, tenant will cooperate with and submit to landlord the programming information necessary for landlord's architect to prepare a preliminary space plan.

(b)   Landlord's architect will expeditiously prepare a preliminary space plan and forward it to tenant. Tenant will give landlord written notice whether or not tenant approves the preliminary space plan within 5 days after its receipt.

items needing additional work by landlord. Other than the items specified in the punch-list and latent defects (as defined below), by taking possession of the premises, tenant will be deemed to have accepted the premises in their condition on the date of delivery of possession and to have acknowledged that landlord has installed the improvements as required by this workletter and that there are no items needing additional work or repair. The punch-list will not include any damage to the premises caused by tenant's move-in or early access, if permitted. Damage caused by tenant will be repaired or corrected by landlord at tenant's expense. Tenant acknowledges that neither landlord nor its agents or employees have made any representations or warranties as to the suitability or fitness of the premises for the conduct of tenant's business or for any other purpose, nor has landlord or its agents or employees agreed to undertake any alterations or construct any tenant improvements to the premises except as expressly provided in this lease and this workletter. If tenant fails to submit a punch-list to landlord prior to the commencement date, it will be deemed that there are no items needing additional work or repair. Landlord's contractor will complete all reasonable punch-list items within 30 days after the walk-through inspection or as soon as practicable after such walk-through.

(b)   A "latent defect" is a defect in the condition of the premises, caused by landlord's failure to construct the improvements in a good and workmanlike manner and in accordance with the working drawings, which would not ordinarily be observed during a walk-through inspection. If tenant notifies landlord of a latent defect within one year following the commencement date, then landlord, at its expense, will repair the latent defect as soon as practicable. Except as set forth in this paragraph 10, landlord will have no obligation or liability to tenant for latent defects.

11. Adjustments upon Completion. As soon as practicable, upon completion of the improvements in accordance with this work-letter, landlord will notify tenant of the rentable area of the premises, the rentable area of the building, monthly rent, and tenant's share, if such information was not previously determinable by landlord. Tenant, within 10 days of landlord's written request, will execute a certificate confirming such information.

[See Commercial Real Estate Leases: Preparation and Negotiation § 5.5.]

§ 2.4   Assignment—Form

FORM 2.4
ASSIGNMENT—FORM

For valuable consideration, the receipt and adequacy of which are expressly acknowledged, assignor and assignee agree that:

1.   *Definitions.* In this assignment the following terms have the meanings given to them.

  (a)   Assignor: [name]

  (b)   Assignee: [name]

  (c)   Agreement: [* * *]

dated [date], 19[* *], between [* *], as [* * *], and assignor, as [* *]. A copy of the agreement is annexed to this assignment as Exhibit A and made a part of this agreement by this reference.

  (d)   Premises: [* * *]

  (e)   Security deposit: $[* * *]

  (f)   Date: [date], 19[* *]

  (g)   Delivery of possession: [date], 19[* *]

    2.   *Assignment and Delivery of the Premises.* Assignor assigns to assignee, effective as of the date, all of assignor's right, title, and interest in (a) the agreement, (b) the security deposit made pursuant to the agreement, and (c) the rent prepaid under the agreement. Assignor will deliver possession of the premises to assignee on the date or on such other date as may be set forth above for delivery of possession.

    3.   *Assumption and Acceptance of the Premises.* Assignee assumes and agrees to perform each and every obligation of assignor under the agreement, effective as of the date. Assignee will accept the premises in their condition as of the date.

    4.   *Assignor's Warranties.* Assignor warrants to assignee that (a) the agreement is in full force and effect and unmodified, (b) assignor's interest in the agreement is free and clear of any liens, encumbrances, or adverse interests of third parties, (c) assignor has full and lawful authority to assign its interest in the agreement, and (d) there is no default under the agreement or any circumstances which by lapse of time or after notice would be a default under the agreement. The warranties contained in this paragraph will be true as of the date of assignor's execution of this assignment and will be true as of the date. These warranties will survive the date.

    5.   *Mutual Indemnification.* Assignor will indemnify assignee against and hold assignee harmless from any and all loss, liability, and expense (including reasonable attorney's fees and court costs) arising out of any breach by assignor of its warranties contained in this assignment, and assignee will indemnify assignor against and will hold assignor harmless from any loss, liability, and expense (including reasonable attorney's fees and court costs) arising out of any breach by assignee of its agreements contained in this assignment after the date.

    6.   *Consent.* The effectiveness of this assignment is conditioned upon the endorsement of the consent below.

    7.   *Amendment of Agreement.* Assignor authorizes assignee to amend the agreement after the date, at assignee's sole discretion and without notice to or consent of assignor, and assignor agrees that no such amendment will limit or alter assignor's liability under the agreement, as it may be amended from time to time; however, no such amendment will increase the amount of rent for which assignor is obligated under the agreement.

8. *Joint and Several Liability.* The liability of assignor and assignee under the agreement will be joint and several. If the term "assignee" refers to more than one corporation, partnership, trust, association, individual, or other entity, their liability under this assignment will be joint and several.

9. *Entire Agreement.* This assignment embodies the entire agreement of assignor and assignee with respect to the subject matter of this assignment, and it supersedes any prior agreements, whether written or oral, with respect to the subject matter of this assignment. There are no agreements or understandings which are not set forth in this assignment. This assignment may be modified only by a written instrument duly executed by assignor and assignee.

10. *Binding Effect.* The terms and provisions of this assignment will inure to the benefit of, and will be binding upon, the successors, assigns, personal representatives, heirs, devisees, and legatees of assignor and assignee.

Assignor and assignee have executed this assignment on the respective dates set forth beneath their signatures below.

Assignor

[signature]

Date: [date], 19[00]

Assignee

[signature]

Date: [date], 19[00]

CONSENT

The undersigned consents to the foregoing assignment on the express conditions that (1) assignor will remain liable for the performance of each and every one of its obligations under the agreement, and (2) this consent will not be deemed a consent to any subsequent assignment, but rather any subsequent assignment will require the consent of the undersigned pursuant to the agreement.

[signature]

By: [* * *]

Date: [date], 19[00]

[See Commercial Real Estate Forms: Preparation and Negotiation § 12.14.]

§ 2.5   Sublease—Form

FORM 2.5
SUBLEASE—FORM

THIS SUBLEASE is made on [date], 19[00], by [name] ("sublandlord"), whose address is [* * *], and [name] ("subtenant"), whose address is [* * *].

RECITALS

[Name], as landlord ("landlord"), and subtenant, as tenant, entered into a lease dated [date], 19[00] (the "master lease"), with regard to Suite [* * *], [* * *] Street, [city], [state] (the "premises"). A copy of the master lease is attached to this sublease as Exhibit A. Sublandlord wishes to sublease to subtenant, and subtenant wishes to sublease from sublandlord, a portion of the premises known as Suite [* * *], [* * *] Street, [city], [state] (the "subleased premises"). The subleased premises are depicted on Exhibit B to this sublease. Accordingly, sublandlord and subtenant agree:

1.   Agreement. Sublandlord subleases the subleased premises to subtenant, and subtenant subleases the subleased premises from sublandlord, according to this sublease. The provision of the master lease (except paragraphs [* *], [* *], and [* *]) are incorporated into this sublease as the agreement of sublandlord and subtenant as though sublandlord was landlord under the master lease and subtenant was tenant under the master lease.

2.   Term. The term of this sublease will begin on [date], 19[00], and will end on [date], 19[00], inclusive. If sublandlord is unable to deliver possession of the subleased premises to subtenant because the present occupant of the subleased premises fails to vacate them on or before [date], 19[00], then subtenant's right to occupy, and obligation to pay rent for, the subleased premises will be delayed until sublandlord delivers possession of the subleased premises. The deferral of subtenant's obligations to pay such rent will be full satisfaction of all claims that subtenant may have as a result of such delayed delivery of possession.

3.   Rent. Subtenant will pay sublandlord as rent for the subleased premises $[amount] per month, in advance, without notice, demand, offset, or counterclaim, on the first day of each month. Rent will be paid at sublandlord's address. If the term of this sublease begins on other than the first day of a month or ends on other than the last day of a month, rent will be prorated on a per diem basis.

4.   Acceptance of the Premises. Subtenant accepts the subleased premises in their present condition. Sublandlord will not be obligated to make any alterations or improvements to the subleased premises on account of this sublease.

5.   Security Deposit. Subtenant has deposited with sublandlord the sum of [* * *] dollars ($[* * *]) that sublandlord will hold in accordance with paragraph [* *] of the master lease.

6.   Other Charges. During the term of this sublease, subtenant will pay to sublandlord [* * *] percent ([* *]%) any increase in sublandlord's rent pursuant to paragraphs [* *] and [* *] of the master lease. Such payments will be made as and when due under the master lease.

7.   Parking. Sublandlord agrees that, during the term of this sublease, subtenant will be entitled to use [* * *] ([* *]) of the parking spaces in the parking garage allocated by landlord to sublandlord pursuant to the master lease. Subtenant will pay the monthly rate for such space as the same is adjusted from time to time.

8. Services. Sublandlord will not be obligated to provide any services to subtenant. Subtenant's sole source of such services is landlord, pursuant to the master lease. Sublandlord makes no representation about the availability or adequacy of such services.

9. The Master Lease. This sublease is subject to the master lease. The provisions of the master lease are applicable to this sublease as though landlord under the master lease were the sublandlord under this sublease and tenant under the master lease were subtenant under this sublease. Subtenant has received a copy of the master lease. Subtenant will not cause or allow to be caused any default under the master lease. Subtenant will indemnify sublandlord against any loss, liability, and expenses (including reasonable attorneys' fees and costs) arising out of any default under the master lease caused by subtenant, and sublandlord will indemnify subtenant against any loss, liability, and expenses (including reasonable attorneys' fees and costs) arising out of any default under the master lease caused by sublandlord.

Sublandlord and subtenant have executed this sublease on the date first written above.

Sublandlord

[signature]

By: [* * *]

Date: [date], 19[00]

Subtenant

[signature]

By: [* * *]

Date: [date], 19[00]

CONSENT

Landlord consents to the subletting of the subleased premises in accordance with the terms and conditions of the sublease so long as:

1. Tenant continues to remain primarily liable for the payment of all rent and other sums and the performance of all covenants required of tenant under the master lease in accordance with the terms of the master lease.

2. No further subletting or assignment of all or any portion of the subleased premises will be made without the prior written consent of landlord.

3. If any default under the master lease occurs, landlord will have the right to collect the rent attributable to the subleased premises directly from subtenant without waiving any of landlord's rights against sublandlord as a result of such default. If the master lease is terminated as a result of sublandlord's default under the master lease, in addition to all other rights and remedies of landlord, this sublease will automatically terminate.

4. The sublease constitutes the entire agreement between sublessor and sublessee, and there are no other oral or written agreements of the sublease

between them. No modification or amendment of the sublease will be made without the prior written consent of landlord.

5.   Any rights and remedies of subtenant, if any, will be solely against sub-landlord. Neither this consent nor the sublease will give subtenant any rights under the master lease except those expressly granted by the sublease.

6.   If any conflict between the master lease and the sublease occurs, the master lease will control.

Landlord

[signature]

By: [* * *]

Date: [date], 19[00]

[See Commercial Real Estate Leases: Preparation and Negotiation § 12.15.]

§ 2.6   Sublease (Another Form)

FORM 2.6
SUBLEASE
(Another Form)

THIS SUBLEASE is made the [* * *] day of [* * *], 19[00], between [name], a [* * *] corporation ("landlord") and [name], a [* * *] corporation ("tenant").

RECITALS

Landlord, as tenant, entered into a lease with [name], as landlord (the "prime landlord"), dated [date], 19[00], leasing Suite [* * *], [* * *] Building, [address], [city] (the "prime lease"). Landlord wishes to sublet approximately [number] square feet of that space (as more particularly shown on Exhibit A to this sublease) (the "premises") to tenant, and tenant wishes to sublet the premises from landlord.

Accordingly, landlord and tenant agree:

1.   Agreement. Landlord subleases the premises to tenant and tenant subleases the premises from landlord according to this sublease.

2.   Term. The term will begin on [date], 19[00], and end on [date], 19[* *], unless sooner terminated in accordance with this sublease.

3.   Rent. Tenant will pay $[* * *] each month and the additional rent mentioned in paragraph 6.

4.   Use. The premises will be used for executive offices and for no other purpose.

5.   No Assignment. Tenant will not assign this sublease nor sublet the premises in whole or in part, and will not permit tenant's interest in this sublease to be vested in any third party by operation of law or otherwise.

6.   Additional Rent. If landlord is charged for additional rent or other sums pursuant to the provisions of the prime lease, tenant will be liable for [* * *]% of such additional rent or sums. If such rent or sums are due to additional use by tenant of utilities in excess of tenant's proportionate part of additional use in the premises subject to the prime lease, the excess will be paid by tenant. If tenant procures any additional services from the building, such as alterations or after-hours air conditioning, tenant will pay for them at the rates charged by the prime landlord and will make payment to the landlord or prime landlord, as landlord directs. Any rent or other sums payable by tenant under this paragraph 6 will be collectible as additional rent. If landlord receives any refund pursuant to the prime lease, tenant will be entitled to the return of so much of it as is attributable to prior payments by tenant.

7.   The Prime Lease. This sublease is subject and subordinate to the prime lease. Except as may be inconsistent with the terms of this sublease, all the terms, covenants, and conditions in the prime lease apply to this sublease as if landlord were the landlord under the prime lease and tenant were the tenant under it. In case of any breach of this sublease by tenant, landlord will have all the rights against tenant that would be available to the landlord against the tenant under the prime lease if the breach were by the tenant under the prime lease. Tenant will not do or permit anything to be done that is a default under the prime lease. Tenant will indemnify and hold landlord harmless from and against all claims by reason of any breach or default on the part of tenant under the prime lease. Tenant represents that it has read and is familiar with the terms of the prime lease.

8.   Services. The only services or rights to which tenant is entitled are those to which landlord is entitled under the prime lease, and for all those services and rights, tenant will look to the prime landlord.

9.   Security Deposit. Tenant has paid landlord on the execution and delivery of this sublease $[* * *] as security for the full and faithful performance of the terms, covenants, and conditions of this sublease to be performed or observed by tenant, including but not limited to payment of rent and additional rent or for any other sum that landlord may expend by reason of tenant's default, including any damages or deficiency in reletting the premises, in whole or in part, whether such damages accrue before or after summary proceedings or other reentry by landlord. If tenant fully and faithfully complies with all the terms, covenants, and conditions of this sublease to be performed or observed by tenant, the security deposit, or any unapplied balance of it, will be returned to tenant after surrender of possession of the premises to landlord.

10. Delay in Delivery of Possession. If actual possession of the premises will not be available by [date], 19[* *], tenant may elect, within 30 days after that date, to cancel this sublease. If this sublease is cancelled, landlord will refund to tenant any rent or security deposit paid or delivered to landlord, and upon such refund, this sublease will have no force or effect.

11. Entireties; Amendment. All prior understandings and agreements between landlord and tenant are merged within this sublease, which fully and completely sets forth their understanding. This sublease may not be changed or terminated orally or in any manner other than by an agreement in writing and signed by the party against whom enforcement of the change or termination is sought.

12. Notices. Any notice or demand which either landlord or tenant may or must give to the other will be in writing and delivered personally or sent by United States first-class registered mail, addressed, if to landlord:

[name]
[address]

and, if to tenant:

[name]
[address]

Either landlord or tenant may, by notice in writing, direct that future notices or demands be sent to a different address. Notices will be effective upon receipt.

13. Binding Effect. The covenants and agreements in this sublease will bind and inure to the benefit of landlord, tenant, and their successors and assigns.

Landlord and tenant have executed this sublease as of the date first written above.

[signature]
Landlord

[signature]
Tenant

Exhibit A—The Premises

§ 2.7   Rules and Regulations for a Shopping Center

FORM 2.7
RULES AND REGULATIONS FOR A SHOPPING CENTER

1. The sidewalks, halls, passages, exits, entrances, stairways, and elevators (if any) of the shopping center will not be obstructed by tenant or used by tenant for any purpose other than ingress to and egress from the premises. The halls, passages, exits, entrances, elevators, and stairways are not for the general public, and landlord will in all cases retain the right to control and prevent access to them by all persons whose presence, in the judgment of

landlord, would be prejudicial to the safety, character, reputation, and interests of the shopping center and its tenants; however, such access will be permitted to persons with whom any tenant normally deals in the ordinary course of its business, unless such persons are engaged in illegal activities. No tenant and no employee or invitee of any tenant will go upon the roof of the shopping center.

2.   No sign, placard, picture, name, advertisement, or notice visible from the exterior of the premises will be inscribed, painted, affixed, or otherwise displayed by tenant on any part of the shopping center without the prior written consent of landlord. Landlord will adopt and furnish to tenant general guidelines relating to signs inside the shopping center and the sales floor. Tenant agrees to comply with those guidelines. All approved signs or lettering on doors will be printed, painted, affixed, or inscribed at the expense of the tenant by a person approved in writing by landlord. Material visible outside the shopping center will not be permitted.

3.   The premises will not be used for lodging or the storage of merchandise held for sale to the public, and unless ancillary to a restaurant or other food service use specifically authorized in the lease of a particular tenant, no cooking will be done or permitted by tenant on the premises. The preparation of coffee, tea, hot chocolate, and similar items for tenants and their employees and invitees will be permitted.

4.   Landlord will furnish tenant with two keys free of charge. Landlord may make reasonable charge for any additional keys. Tenant will not have any keys made. Tenant will not alter any lock or install a new or additional lock or any bolt on any door of the premises without the prior written consent of landlord; tenant will furnish landlord with a key for each of those locks. Tenant, upon the termination of its tenancy, will deliver to landlord all keys to doors in the shopping center that have been furnished to tenant.

5.   Tenant will not use or keep in the premises or the shopping center any kerosene, gasoline, or inflammable or combustible fluid or material, or use any method of heating or air conditioning other than that supplied by landlord. Tenant will not use, keep, or permit to be used or kept any foreign or noxious gas or substance in the premises, or permit or suffer the premises to be occupied or used in a manner offensive or objectionable to landlord or other occupants of the shopping center by reason of noise, odors, or vibrations, or interfere in any way with other tenants or those having business in the shopping center.

6.   In the case of invasion, mob, riot, public excitement, or other circumstances rendering such action advisable in landlord's opinion, landlord may prevent access to the shopping center by such action as landlord may deem appropriate, including closing entrances to the shopping center.

7.   The toilet rooms, toilets, urinals, wash bowls, and other apparatus will not be used for any purpose other than that for which they were constructed, and no foreign substance of any kind whatsoever will be thrown in them. The expense of any breakage, stoppage, or damage resulting from the violation of

this rule will be borne by the tenant who, or whose employees or invitees, caused it.

8.   Except with prior written consent of landlord, tenant will not sell, or permit the sale in the premises, or use or permit the use of any common area for the sale of newspapers, magazines, periodicals, or theatre tickets. Tenant will not carry on, or permit or allow any employee or other person to carry on the business of stenography, typewriting, or any similar business in or from the premises for the service or accommodation of occupants of any other portion of the shopping center. The premises will not be used for manufacturing of any kind or for any business or activity other than that specifically provided in the lease.

9.   Tenant will not use any advertising media within the shopping center that may be heard outside of the premises and tenant will not place or permit the placement of any radio or television antenna, loudspeaker, sound amplifier, phonograph, searchlight, flashing light, or other device of any nature on the roof or outside of the boundaries of the premises (except for tenant's approved identification sign or signs) or at any place within the shopping center where they may be seen or heard outside of the premises.

10.   All loading and unloading of merchandise, supplies, materials, garbage, and refuse will be made only through such entryways and elevators (if any) and at such times as landlord may designate. In its use of the loading areas, tenant will not obstruct or permit the obstruction of the loading area and at no time will park or allow its officers, agents, or employees to park vehicles in the loading areas except for loading and unloading.

11.   Landlord will have the right, exercisable without notice and without liability to any tenant, to change the name and street address of the shopping center.

12.   The freight elevator, if any, will be available for use by all tenants in the shopping center, subject to reasonable scheduling that landlord in its discretion may deem appropriate. The persons employed to move such equipment in or out of the shopping center must be acceptable to landlord. Landlord will have the right to prescribe the weight, size, and position of all equipment, materials, furniture, or other property brought into the shopping center. Heavy objects will, if considered necessary by landlord, stand on wood strips of such thickness as is necessary to distribute the weight properly. Landlord will not be responsible for loss of or damage to that property from any cause, and all damage done to the shopping center by moving or maintaining that property will be repaired at the expense of tenant.

13.   The directory of the shopping center, if any, will be provided for the display of the name and location of tenants, and landlord reserves the right to exclude any other names from the directory. Any additional name that tenant desires to place upon the directory must first be approved by landlord, and, if so approved, a charge will be made for the additional name.

14.   No curtains, draperies, blinds, shutters, shades, screens, or other coverings, hangings, or decorations will be attached to, hung, or placed in, or

used in connection with any window of the shopping center without the prior written consent of landlord.

15.   Tenant will assure that the doors of the premises are closed and locked and that all water faucets, water apparatus, and utilities are shut off before tenant or tenant's employees leave the premises, so as to prevent waste or damage, and for any default or carelessness in this regard tenant will pay for all injuries sustained by other tenants or occupants of the shopping center or landlord.

16.   Landlord may waive any one or more of these rules and regulations for the benefit of any particular tenant or tenants, but no waiver by landlord will be construed as a waiver of those rules and regulations in favor of any other tenant or tenants, nor prevent landlord from enforcing any those rules and regulations against any or all of the tenants of the shopping center.

17.   These rules and regulations are in addition to and will not be construed to modify, alter, or amend the lease, in whole or in part.

18.   Landlord reserves the right to make such other and reasonable rules and regulations as in its judgment may from time to time be needed for the safety, care, and cleanliness of the shopping center, and for the preservation of good order in it.

[See Commercial Real Estate Leases: Preparation and Negotiation § 14.2.]

§ 2.8   Rules and Regulations for an Office Building

FORM 2.8
RULES AND REGULATIONS FOR AN OFFICE BUILDING

1.   Landlord may from time to time adopt appropriate systems and procedures for the security or safety of the building, any persons occupying, using, or entering the building, or any equipment, finishings, or contents of the building, and tenant will comply with landlord's reasonable requirements relative to such systems and procedures.

2.   The sidewalks, halls, passages, exits, entrances, elevators, and stairways of the building will not be obstructed by any tenants or used by any of them for any purpose other than for ingress to and egress from their respective premises. The halls, passages, exits, entrances, elevators, escalators, and stairways are not for the general public, and landlord will in all cases retain the right to control and prevent access to such halls, passages, exits, entrances, elevators, and stairways of all persons whose presence in the judgment of landlord would be prejudicial to the safety, character, reputation, and interests of the building and its tenants, provided that nothing contained in these rules and regulations will be construed to prevent such access to persons with whom any tenant normally deals in the ordinary course of its business, unless such persons are engaged in illegal activities. No tenant and no employee or

invitee of any tenant will go upon the roof of the building, except such roof or portion of such roof as may be contiguous to the premises of a particular tenant and may be designated in writing by landlord as a roof deck or roof garden area. No tenant will be permitted to place or install any object (including without limitation radio and television antenna, loud speakers, sound amplifiers, microwave dishes, solar devices, or similar devices) on the exterior of the building or on the roof of the building.

3.   No sign, placard, picture, name, advertisement, or notice visible from the exterior of tenant's premises will be inscribed, painted, affixed, or otherwise displayed by tenant on any part of the building or the premises without the prior written consent of landlord. Landlord will adopt and furnish to tenant general guidelines relating to signs inside the building on the office floors. Tenant agrees to conform to such guidelines. All approved signs or lettering on doors will be printed, painted, affixed or inscribed at the expense of the tenant by a person approved by landlord. Other than draperies expressly permitted by landlord and building standard mini-blinds, material visible from outside the building will not be permitted. In the event of the violation of this rule by tenant, landlord may remove the violating items without any liability, and may charge the expense incurred by such removal to the tenant or tenants violating this rule.

4.   Other than draperies expressly permitted by landlord and building standard mini-blinds, no curtains, draperies, blinds, shutters, shades, screens or other coverings, hangings or decorations will be attached to, hung or placed in, or used in connection with any window of the building or the premises.

5.   The sashes, sash doors, skylights, windows, heating, ventilating and air conditioning vents, and doors that reflect or admit light and air into the halls, passageways, or other public places in the building will not be covered or obstructed by any tenant, nor will any bottles, parcels, or other articles be placed on any window sills.

6.   No showcases or other articles will be put in front of or affixed to any part of the exterior of the building, nor placed in the public halls, corridors, or vestibules without the prior written consent of landlord.

7.   No tenant will occupy or permit any portion of the premises to be occupied as an office for a public stenographer or typist, or for the possession, storage, manufacture, or sale of liquor or narcotics, in any form, or as a barber or manicure shop or as a public employment bureau or agency, or for a public finance (personal loan) business. No tenant will permit the premises to be used for lodging or sleeping or for any immoral or illegal purpose. No tenant will use or permit the use of the premises in any manner that involves an unusual risk of injury to any person. No tenant will engage or pay any nonsalaried employees on the premises except those actually working for tenant on the premises. No tenant will advertise for laborers giving an address at the building. No cooking will be done or permitted by any tenant on the premises, except in areas of the premises that are specially constructed for cooking and except that use by the tenant of

Underwriters' Laboratory approved equipment for brewing coffee, tea, hot chocolate and similar beverages will be permitted, provided that such use is in accordance with all applicable federal, state, and city laws, codes, ordinances, rules, and regulations.

8.   No tenant will employ any person or persons other than the cleaning service of landlord for the purpose of cleaning the premises, unless otherwise agreed to by landlord in writing. Except with the written consent of landlord, no person or persons other than those approved by landlord will be permitted to enter the building for the purpose of cleaning it. No tenant will cause any unnecessary labor by reason of such tenant's carelessness or indifference in the preservation of good order and cleanliness. If tenant's actions result in any increased expense for any required cleaning, landlord reserves the right to assess tenant for such expenses. Janitorial service will not be furnished on nights to offices that are occupied after business hours on those nights unless, by prior written agreement of landlord and tenant, service is extended to a later hour for specifically designated offices.

9.   The toilet rooms, toilets, urinals, wash bowls, and other plumbing fixtures will not be used for any purposes other than those for which they are constructed, and no sweepings, rubbish, rags, or other foreign substances will be thrown in such plumbing fixtures. All damages resulting from any misuse of the fixtures will be borne by the tenant who, or whose servants, employees, agents, visitors, or licensees, caused the same.

10.   No tenant will in any way deface any part of the premises or the building of which they form a part. Without the prior written consent of landlord, no tenant will lay linoleum, or other similar floor covering, so that the same will come in direct contact with the floor of the premises, and, if linoleum or other similar floor covering is desired to be used, an interlining of builder's deadening felt will be first affixed to the floor, by a paste or other material, soluble in water, the use of cement or other similar adhesive material being expressly prohibited. In those portions of the premises in which carpet has been provided directly or indirectly by landlord, tenant will at its own expense install and maintain pads to protect the carpet under all furniture having casters other than carpet casters.

11.   No tenant will alter, change, replace, or rekey any lock or install a new lock or a knocker on any door of the premises. Landlord, its agents, or employees will retain a pass (master) key to all door locks on the premises. Any new door locks required by tenant or any change in keying of existing locks will be installed or changed by landlord following tenant's written request to landlord and will be at tenant's expense. All new locks and rekeyed locks will remain operable by landlord's pass (master) key. Landlord will furnish each tenant, free of charge, with two (2) keys to each door lock on the premises and two (2) building/area access cards. Landlord will have the right to collect a reasonable charge for additional keys and cards requested by any tenant. Each tenant, upon termination of its tenancy, will deliver to landlord all keys and access cards for the premises and building that have been furnished to such tenant.

12. The elevator designated for freight by landlord will be available for use by all tenants in the building during the hours and pursuant to such procedures as landlord may determine from time to time. The persons employed to move tenant's equipment, material, furniture, or other property in or out of the building must be acceptable to landlord. The moving company must be a locally recognized professional mover, whose primary business is the performing of relocation services, and must be bonded and fully insured. A certificate or other verification of such insurance must be received and approved by landlord prior to the start of any moving operations. Insurance must be sufficient in landlord's sole opinion to cover all personal liability, theft, or damage to the project, including, but not limited to, floor coverings, doors, walls, elevators, stairs, foliage, and landscaping. Special care must be taken to prevent damage to foliage and landscaping during adverse weather. All moving operations will be conducted at such times and in such a manner as landlord will direct, and all moving will take place during nonbusiness hours unless landlord agrees in writing otherwise. Tenant will be responsible for the provision of building security during all moving operations, and will be liable for all losses and damages sustained by any party as a result of the failure to supply adequate security. Landlord will have the right to prescribe the weight, size, and position of all equipment, materials, furniture, or other property brought into the building. Landlord will not be responsible for loss of or damage to any such property from any cause, and all damage done to the building by moving or maintaining such property will be repaired at the expense of tenant. Landlord reserves the right to inspect all such property to be brought into the building and to exclude from the building all such property that violates any of these rules and regulations or the lease of which these rules and regulations are a part. Heavy objects will, if considered necessary by landlord, stand on wood strips of such thickness as is necessary to properly distribute the weight. Supplies, goods, materials, packages, furniture, and all other items of every kind delivered to or taken from the premises will be delivered or removed through the entrance and route designated by landlord, and landlord will not be responsible for the loss or damage of any such property unless such loss or damage results from the negligence of landlord, its agents, or employees.

13. No tenant will use or keep in the premises or the building any kerosene, gasoline, or inflammable or combustible or explosive fluid or material or chemical substance other than limited quantities of such materials or substances reasonably necessary for the operation or maintenance of office equipment or limited quantities of cleaning fluids and solvents required in tenant's normal operations in the premises. Without landlord's prior written approval, no tenant will use any method of heating or air conditioning other than that supplied by landlord. No tenant will use or keep or permit to be used or kept any foul or noxious gas or substance in the premises, or permit or suffer the premises to be occupied or used in a manner offensive or objectionable to landlord or other occupants of the building by reason of noise, odors, or vibrations, or interfere in any way with other tenants or those having business in the building.

14. Landlord will have the right, exercisable upon notice and without liability to any tenant, to change the name and street address of the building.

15. Landlord will have the right to prohibit any advertising by tenant mentioning the building that, in landlord's reasonable opinion, tends to impair the reputation of the building or its desirability as a building for offices, and upon written notice from landlord, tenant will refrain from or discontinue such advertising.

16. Tenant will not bring any animals (except "seeing eye" dogs) or birds into the building, and will not permit bicycles or other vehicles inside or on the sidewalks outside the building except in areas designated from time to time by landlord for such purposes.

17. All persons entering or leaving the building between the hours of 6 p.m. and 7 a.m. Monday through Friday, and at all hours on Saturdays, Sundays and holidays, will comply with such off-hour regulations as landlord may establish and modify from time to time. Landlord reserves the right to limit reasonably or restrict access to the building during such time periods.

18. Each tenant will store all its trash and garbage within its premises. No material will be placed in the trash boxes or receptacles if such material is of such nature that it may not be disposed of in the ordinary and customary manner of removing and disposing of trash and garbage without being in violation of any law or ordinance governing such disposal. All garbage and refuse disposal will be made only through entryways and elevators provided for such purposes and at such times as landlord designates. Removal of any furniture or furnishings, large equipment, packing crates, packing materials, and boxes will be the responsibility of each tenant and such items may not be disposed of in the building's trash receptacles, nor will they be removed by the building's janitorial service, except at landlord's sole option and at the tenant's expense. No furniture, appliances, equipment, or flammable products of any type may be disposed of in the building trash receptacles.

19. Canvassing, peddling, soliciting, and distribution of handbills or any other written materials in the building are prohibited, and each tenant will cooperate to prevent the same.

20. The requirements of the tenants will be attended to only upon application by written, personal, or telephone notice at the office of the building. Employees of landlord will not perform any work or do anything outside of their regular duties unless under special instructions from landlord.

21. A directory of the building will be provided for the display of the name and location of tenants only and such reasonable number of the principal officers and employees of tenants as landlord in its sole discretion approves, but landlord will not in any event be obligated to furnish more than one (1) directory strip for each 2,500 square feet of rentable area in the premises. Any additional name(s) tenant desires to place in such directory must first be approved by landlord, and if so approved, tenant will pay to landlord a charge, set by landlord, for each such additional name. All entries on the building

directory display will conform to standards and style set by landlord in its sole discretion. Space on any exterior signage will be provided in landlord's sole discretion. No tenant will have any right to the use of any exterior sign.

22. Tenant will see that the doors of the premises are closed and locked and that all water faucets, water apparatus, and utilities are shut off before tenant or tenant's employees leave the premises, so as to prevent waste or damage, and for any default or carelessness in this regard tenant will make good all injuries sustained by other tenants or occupants of the building or landlord. On multiple-tenancy floors, all tenants will keep the doors to the building corridors closed at all times except for ingress and egress.

23. Tenant will not conduct itself in any manner which is inconsistent with the character of the building as a first quality building or which will impair the comfort and convenience of other tenants in the building.

24. Neither landlord nor any operator of the parking areas within the project, as the same are designated and modified by landlord, in its sole discretion, from time to time (the "parking areas") will be liable for loss of or damage to any vehicle or any contents of such vehicle or accessories to any such vehicle, or any property left in any of the parking areas, resulting from fire, theft, vandalism, accident, conduct of other users of the parking areas and other persons, or any other casualty or cause. Further, tenant understands and agrees that: (a) landlord will not be obligated to provide any traffic control, security protection, or operator for the parking areas; (b) tenant uses the parking areas at its own risk; and (c) landlord will not be liable for personal injury or death, or theft, loss of, or damage to property. Tenant indemnifies and agrees to hold landlord, any operator of the parking areas, and their respective employees and agents harmless from and against any and all claims, demands, and actions arising out of the use of the parking areas by tenant, its employees, agents, invitees, and visitors, whether brought by any of such persons or any other person.

25. Tenant (including tenant's employees, agents, invitees, and visitors) will use the parking spaces solely for the purpose of parking passenger model cars, small vans, and small trucks and will comply in all respects with any rules and regulations that may be promulgated by landlord from time to time with respect to the parking areas. The parking areas may be used by tenant, its agents, or employees for occasional overnight parking of vehicles. Tenant will ensure that any vehicle parked in any of the parking spaces will be kept in proper repair and will not leak excessive amounts of oil or grease or any amount of gasoline. If any of the parking spaces are at any time used (a) for any purpose other than parking as provided above, (b) in any way or manner reasonably objectionable to landlord, or (c) by tenant after default by tenant under the lease, landlord, in addition to any other rights otherwise available to landlord, may consider such violation an event of default under the lease.

26. Tenant's right to use the parking areas will be in common with other tenants of the project and with other parties permitted by landlord to use the parking areas. Landlord reserves the right to assign and reassign, from time to time, particular parking spaces for use by persons selected by landlord

provided that tenant's rights under the lease are preserved. Landlord will not be liable to tenant for any unavailability of tenant's designated spaces, if any, nor will any unavailability entitle tenant to any refund, deduction, or allowance. Tenant will not park in any numbered space or any space designated as: RESERVED, HANDICAPPED, VISITORS ONLY, or LIMITED TIME PARKING (or similar designation).

27. If the parking areas are damaged or destroyed, or if the use of the parking areas is limited or prohibited by any governmental authority, or the use or operation of the parking areas is limited or prevented by strikes or other labor difficulties or other causes beyond landlord's control, tenant's inability to use the parking spaces will not subject landlord or any operator of the parking areas to any liability to tenant and will not relieve tenant of any of its obligations under the lease and the lease will remain in full force and effect. Tenant will pay to landlord upon demand, and tenant indemnifies landlord against, any and all loss or damage to the parking areas or any equipment, fixtures, or signs used in connection with the parking areas and any adjoining buildings or structures caused by tenant or any of its employees, agents, invitees, or visitors.

28. Tenant has no right to assign or sublicense any of its rights in the parking spaces, except as part of a permitted assignment or sublease of the lease; however, tenant may allocate the parking spaces among its employees.

29. No act or thing done or omitted to be done by landlord or landlord's agent during the term of the lease in connection with the enforcement of these rules and regulations will constitute an eviction by landlord of any tenant, nor will it be deemed an acceptance of surrender of the premises by any tenant, and no agreement to accept such termination or surrender will be valid unless in a writing signed by landlord. The delivery of keys to any employee or agent of landlord will not operate as a termination of the lease or a surrender of the premises unless such delivery of keys is done in connection with a written instrument executed by landlord approving the termination or surrender.

30. In these rules and regulations, "tenant" includes the employees, agents, invitees, and licensees of tenant and others permitted by tenant to use or occupy the premises.

31. Landlord may waive any one or more of these rules and regulations for the benefit of any particular tenant or tenants, but no such waiver by landlord will be construed as a waiver of such rules and regulations in favor of any other tenant or tenants, nor prevent landlord from enforcing any such rules and regulations against any or all of the tenants of the building after such waiver.

32. These rules and regulations are in addition to, and will not be construed to modify or amend, in whole or in part, the terms, covenants, agreements, and conditions of the lease.

[See Commercial Real Estate Leases: Preparation and Negotiation § 14.3.]

§ 2.9   Subordination—Nondisturbance, Attornment, Estoppel, and Subordination Agreement

FORM 2.9
SUBORDINATION—NONDISTURBANCE, ATTORNMENT, ESTOPPEL, AND SUBORDINATION AGREEMENT

THIS NONDISTURBANCE, ATTORNMENT, ESTOPPEL, AND SUBORDINATION AGREEMENT is made on [date], 19[00], by landlord, tenant, and lender.

RECITALS

Landlord and tenant have entered into the lease with respect to the premises. The premises are part of the property. Lender has agreed to make the loan to landlord and to accept the mortgage as security for repayment of the loan and performance of landlord's obligations related to the loan. However, as a condition to making the loan, lender has required a subordination of the lease to the mortgage. Tenant is willing to subordinate the lease to the mortgage so long as tenant is assured that its possession of the premises will not be disturbed. Accordingly, landlord, tenant, and lender agree that:

1.   Definitions.

   (a)   date: [date], 19[00].

   (b)   landlord: [name].

   (c)   lease: the lease agreement dated [date], 19[00], between landlord and tenant.

   (d)   lender: [name], its successors, and assigns, and anyone else who succeeds to landlord's interest in the lease through foreclosure (both judicial and power-of-sale), or deed in lieu of foreclosure.

   (e)   loan: a loan of $* * * by lender to landlord.

   (f)   premises: the subject matter of the lease.

   (g)   property: the real property described in Exhibit A to this agreement.

   (h)   tenant: [name].

   (i)   mortgage: the loan agreement, mortgage, security agreement, and assignment of rents, all dated [date], 19* *, between landlord and lender, and any extensions, modifications, renewals, substitutions, replacements, or consolidations of any of them.

2.   Nondisturbance. So long as no event of default under the lease has occurred, lender will not disturb tenant's possession of the premises.

3.   Attornment. If lender succeeds to landlord's interest in the lease, tenant will be bound to lender according to the lease for the balance of the term of the lease and any extension of the lease as if lender were the landlord under the lease, and tenant will attorn to lender as its landlord, immediately upon lender's succeeding to the interest of landlord under the lease; however, tenant will not be obligated to pay rent to lender until tenant receives written

notice from lender that it has succeeded to the interest of landlord in the lease. Subject to paragraph 4, upon such attornment the rights and obligations of tenant and lender will be the same as they would have been if lender had been landlord under the lease.

4.   Limitation on Lender's Obligations. If lender succeeds to the interest of landlord in the lease, lender will not be:

(a)   liable for any act or omission of landlord or any predecessor of landlord (including landlord);

(b)   subject to any offsets or defenses that tenant may have against landlord or any predecessor of landlord;

(c)   bound by any rent or additional rent or advance rent that tenant may have paid for more than the current month to any prior landlord (including landlord) and all such rent will remain due and owing without regard to such advance payment;

(d)   bound by any amendment or modification of the lease made without its consent and written approval;

(e)   required to complete the building of which the premises are a part;

(f)   bound by any promise by landlord or any predecessor of landlord not to compete with tenant; or

(g)   responsible to return tenant's security deposit pursuant to the lease.

5.   Subordination. Subject to the terms of this agreement, the lease now is, and will be, subject and subordinate to the mortgage. This agreement will not limit lender's rights under the mortgage.

6.   Estoppel. Landlord and tenant certify to lender that:

(a)   the lease is in effect and unmodified;

(b)   the term of the lease will commence or did commence on [date], 19[00], or within sixty (60) days after tenant's receipt of a written notice from landlord advising that the premises have been substantially completed, whichever occurs later, and full rental will then accrue or is now accruing under the lease;

(c)   all conditions required under the lease that could have been satisfied as of the date have been met;

(d)   no rent under the lease has been paid more than thirty (30) days in advance of its due date;

(e)   no default exists under the lease;

(f)   tenant, as of the date, has no charge, lien, or claim of offset, under the lease or otherwise, against rents or other charges due to become due under the lease;

(g)   the lease constitutes the entire agreement between them;

(h)   lender will have no liability or responsibility with respect to tenant's security deposit;

(i)   the only persons, firms, or corporations in possession of the premises or having any right to the possession or use of the premises (other than the record owner) are those holding under the lease; and

(j)   tenant has no right or interest in or under any contract, option, or agreement involving the sale or transfer of the premises.

7.   Limitation on Tenant's Rights. In the absence of lender's prior written consent, tenant will not:

(a)   prepay the rent under the lease for more than one (1) month;

(b)   enter into any agreement with landlord to amend or modify the lease; or

(c)   voluntarily surrender the premises or terminate the lease without cause.

8.   Curing Defaults; Landlord's Termination. If landlord fails to perform any of its obligations under the lease, tenant will give written notice of the failure to lender and lender will have the right (but not the obligation) to cure such failure. Tenant will not take any action with respect to such failure under the lease, including without limitation any action to terminate, rescind, or avoid the lease or to withhold any rent under the lease, for a period of thirty (30) days after receipt of such written notice by lender; however, in the case of any default which cannot with diligence be cured within said thirty-day period, if lender proceeds promptly to cure such failure and prosecutes the curing of such failure with diligence and continuity, the time within which such failure may be cured will be extended for such period as may be necessary to complete the curing of such failure with diligence and continuity. If landlord exercises its right to terminate the lease pursuant to paragraph [damage and destruction] or paragraph [condemnation] of the lease, lender will have the right (but not the obligation) to elect to repair or restore the premises. Lender will give tenant notice of its election (if at all) within [* * *] [(* *)] days after landlord terminates the lease. If lender so elects to repair or restore the premises, landlord's termination of the lease will be ineffective and lender will have the right to repair or restore the premises within the periods set forth in relevant paragraphs of the lease.

9.   Amendments and Binding Effect. This agreement may be modified only by an agreement in writing signed by landlord, tenant, and lender. Subject to paragraph [transfer of the premises] of the lease, this agreement will inure to the benefit of and will be binding upon landlord, tenant, and lender, their successors and assigns.

10.   Counterparts. This agreement may be executed in several counterparts, and, when executed by landlord, tenant, and lender, will constitute one agreement, binding upon them, even though they are not signatories to the original or the same counterpart.

11.   Notices. All notices under this agreement will be in writing and will be considered properly given if mailed by first class United States mail, postage prepaid, registered or certified with return receipt requested, or if personally delivered to the intended addressee, or by prepaid telegram. Notice by mail will be effective two (2) days after deposit in the United States mail. Notice given in any other manner will be effective when received by the addressee. For purposes of notices, the addresses of landlord, tenant, and lender are:

Any of them may change its address for notice to any other location within the continental United States by the giving of thirty (30) days' notice in the manner set forth in this paragraph.

Landlord, tenant and lender have executed this agreement as of [date], 19[00].

LANDLORD: TENANT: LENDER:
[signature]   [signature]   [signature]

[See Commercial Real Estate Leases: Preparation and Negotiation § 24.3.]

§ 2.10   Estoppel, Subordination, Nondisturbance, and Attornment Agreement

FORM 2.10
ESTOPPEL, SUBORDINATION, NONDISTURBANCE, AND ATTORNMENT AGREEMENT

THIS ESTOPPEL, SUBORDINATION, NONDISTURBANCE, AND ATTORN-MENT AGREEMENT is made as of [date], 19[00], by and between [name] ("lender"), whose address is [* * * Street, City, State], and [name] ("tenant") whose address is [* * * Street, City, State].

RECITALS

Pursuant to the terms of a loan agreement dated as of [date], 19[00] (the "loan agreement"), the lender has agreed to make a loan (the "loan") to [name] ("landlord"). Landlord is the owner of the building on the parcel of land legally described on Exhibit A (the "property"). Tenant has entered into a lease dated [date], 19[00], covering certain premises (the "premises") within the property (as the lease may be amended, modified, or supplemented from time to time, the "lease"). The loan will be secured by a first deed of trust, assignment of leases and rents, and security agreement encumbering the property (as it may be amended, increased, renewed, modified, consolidated, replaced, combined, substituted, severed, split, spread, or extended, the "mortgage"), and a first assignment of the rents due under the lease, in each case in favor of lender.

In consideration of the mutual agreements in this agreement and other good and valuable consideration, the receipt and sufficiency of which are acknowledged, and understanding that lender will rely on tenant's covenants and certifications in making the loan, lender and tenant agree:

1.   Tenant covenants and certifies that:

(a)   The lease is dated [date], 19[* *]. The lease has been amended by the following: amendment to office lease dated [date], 19[00], and lease commencement certificate dated [date], 19[00].

(b)   Tenant's security deposit is $[amount].

(c)   Tenant is the original tenant under the lease.

(d)   The premises leased to tenant are [* * *] rentable square feet of office space on the [* * *] floor of the property.

(e)   The term of the lease began (or is scheduled to begin) on [date], 19[00].

(f)   The term of the lease (excluding unexercised options) will expire (or, if the term has not yet begun, it is scheduled to expire) on [date], 19[00], unless sooner terminated as prescribed in the lease. No notice to terminate has been given or received by tenant.

(g)   Tenant has the option to extend or renew the term of the lease for [* * *] successive terms of [* * *] years each. Tenant has no option or right of refusal to purchase all or any portion of the property. Except as set forth in the lease, tenant is not entitled to any right of first refusal to expand, option to expand, option to terminate, free or partial rent period, rental rebate, credit, offset or deduction in rent, lease support payments, lease buyout, or any other rent concessions.

(h)   The current monthly fixed minimum rent for the premises is $[amount] and has been paid through and including [date], 19[00].

(i)   Tenant is required to pay its pro rata share, being [* *]%, of all real estate taxes and operating expenses above the base amount of $[amount] per rentable square foot.

(j)   The lease is in full force and effect and constitutes the entire agreement between tenant and landlord with respect to the premises; has not been modified, changed, altered, or amended in any respect, except for the amendments described in subparagraph 1(a); and is the only lease between tenant and landlord affecting the premises. There are no agreements, formal or informal, in writing or oral, between tenant and landlord that purport to settle or reserve rights with respect to any dispute under the lease or otherwise with respect to the premises.

(k)   Except as may be set forth in this agreement or in the lease, tenant has not sublet the premises to any subtenant and has not assigned or encumbered any of its rights under the lease, and tenant is the sole occupant of the premises.

(l)   Tenant has accepted possession of the premises, and any and all work and improvements required by the terms of the lease to be made or done by landlord as of the date of this agreement have been completed. Except as set forth in this agreement, all contributions required to be paid or credited by landlord to tenant on account of tenant's tenant improvements as of the date of this agreement have been paid or credited.

(m)   No defaults by tenant, and to the best of tenant's knowledge, no defaults by landlord of any kind exist under the lease, nor, to the best of tenant's knowledge, has there occurred any event or state of facts that, by the giving of notice, the lapse of time, or both, would constitute a default by tenant or landlord under the lease; no rent payable under the lease has been paid more than one month in advance of its due date; and to the best of tenant's knowledge, tenant has no existing defense, charge, lien, claim, or offset (and no claim for any credit or deduction) under the lease or otherwise against rents or other charges due or to become due under the lease or on account of any prepayment of rent or otherwise.

(n)   Since the date of the lease, there have been no actions, voluntary or otherwise, pending against tenant (or any general partner, if any, of tenant) or any guarantor of tenant's obligations under the lease under the bankruptcy, reorganization, arrangement, moratorium, or other debtor relief laws of the United States, any state, or any other jurisdiction.

(o)   Tenant has not received notice of any other assignment, hypothecation, mortgage, or pledge of landlord's interest in the lease or the rents or other amounts payable under the lease.

2.   Tenant agrees that the lease now is and at all times will continue to be subject and subordinate in each and every respect to the mortgage, to the full extent of the principal, interest, and other sums secured by the mortgage. Tenant, upon request, will execute and deliver any certificate or other instrument, whether or not in recordable form, that lender may reasonably request to confirm such subordination.

3.   As long as tenant is in compliance with the terms of this agreement and is not in default in the performance of its obligations under the lease, lender will not name tenant as a party defendant in any action for foreclosure or other enforcement of the mortgage (unless required by law), nor will the lease be terminated by lender in connection with, or by reason of, foreclosure or other proceedings for the enforcement of the mortgage, or by reason of a transfer of the landlord's interest under the lease pursuant to the taking of a deed or assignment (or similar device), nor will tenant's use or possession of the premises be interfered with by lender, except that the person acquiring or succeeding to the interest of landlord as the result of any such action or proceeding and such person's successor and assigns (any of the foregoing being hereinafter referred to as the "successor") will not be:

(a)   subject to any credits, offsets, defenses, or claims that tenant might have against any prior landlord;

(b)   bound by any prepayment of more than one month's rent;

(c)   liable for any act or omission of any prior landlord;

(d)   bound by any amendment or modification of the lease, other than those described in paragraph 1(a), made without the consent of such successor or any of its predecessors-in-interest that reduces the rent due, shortens the term, or otherwise materially increases landlord's obligations or materially decreases tenant's obligations under the lease;

(e)   bound by any covenant to undertake or complete any improvement in the premises or the building or buildings forming a part of the property, except as expressly required pursuant to the lease;

(f)   required to account for any security deposit other than any security deposit actually delivered to the successor;

(g)   liable for any payment to tenant of any sums, or the granting to tenant of any credit, in the nature of a contribution towards the cost of preparing, furnishing, or moving into the premises or any portion of the premises, except pursuant to the lease.

4. If the interest of the landlord under the lease is transferred by reason of foreclosure or other proceedings for enforcement of the mortgage or the obligations that it secured or pursuant to a taking of a deed or assignment in lieu of foreclosure (or similar device), tenant will be bound to the successor and, except as provided in this agreement, the successor will be bound to tenant under all of the terms, covenants, and conditions of the lease for the unexpired balance of its remaining term (and any extensions, if exercised), with the same force and effect as if the successor were the landlord, and tenant agrees to attorn to the successor, including lender if it is the successor, as its landlord; affirms its obligations under the lease; and agrees to make payments of all sums due under the lease to the successor. The attornment, affirmation, and agreement will be effective and self-operative without the execution of any further instruments, upon the successor's succeeding to the interest of the landlord under the lease. To the extent permitted by applicable law, tenant waives the provisions of any statute or rule of law now or after this date in effect that may give or purport to give it any right or obligation to terminate or otherwise adversely affect the lease or the obligations of tenant under the lease by reason of any foreclosure or other proceedings for enforcement of the mortgage or the taking of a deed of assignment in lieu of foreclosure (or similar device).

5. Tenant will not change the terms, covenants, conditions, and agreements of the lease in a manner that would reduce the rent due, shorten the term, or otherwise materially increase landlord's obligations or materially decrease tenant's obligations under the lease without the express written consent of lender in each such instance.

6. Tenant will provide lender with a copy of any cancellation or termination notice or notice of default (including notices of abatement, setoff, or counterclaim) served upon the landlord by tenant under the lease. The copies will be delivered to lender in accordance with the provisions of paragraph 13. No such notice of cancellation or termination (if tenant's right to cancel or terminate arose by virtue of a default by the landlord under the lease) and no such notice of default, abatement, setoff, or counterclaim will be effective unless lender has failed within 30 days of its receipt of such notice to cure the default or, if the default cannot be cured within 30 days, has failed to commence and diligently prosecute the curing of the default (which may include, but not be limited to, commencement of foreclosure proceedings, if necessary to effect such cure) that gave rise to such right of cancellation, termination, or abatement.

7. If a successor succeeds to the interests of the landlord under the lease, successor will have no obligation, nor incur any liability, beyond its then interest, if any, in the property, and tenant will look exclusively to such interest of the successor, if any, in the property for the payment and discharge of any obligations imposed upon the successor under the lease. The successor is released or relieved of any other liability under the lease. Tenant agrees that with respect to any judgment that may be obtained or secured by tenant

against the successor, tenant will look solely to the estate or interest owned by the successor in the property, and tenant will not collect or attempt to collect any such judgment out of any other assets of the successor.

8. Tenant understands that the interests of landlord in the lease have been collaterally assigned to lender, and tenant understands and agrees that lender assumes no duty, liability, or obligation under the lease or any extension or renewal of the lease unless and until lender becomes a successor.

9. Tenant acknowledges that it has notice that landlord's interest under the lease and in the rent and all other sums due under the lease have been assigned to lender as part of the security for the indebtedness secured by the mortgage. If lender notifies tenant of any default under the mortgage and demands that tenant pay rent and all other sums due under the lease to lender, tenant agrees that (waiving any proof of the occurrence of such event of default other than receipt of lender's notice), it will pay rent and all other sums due under the lease directly to lender. Any payments made to lender by tenant will not affect or impair the other rights and remedies of lender under the mortgage or otherwise against landlord.

10. This agreement may not be modified except by an agreement in writing signed by tenant and lender or their respective successors-in-interest. This agreement will inure to the benefit of and be binding upon the tenant and lender and their respective successors and assigns.

11. Nothing contained in this agreement impairs or affects the lien created by the mortgage, except as specifically set forth in this agreement.

12. Tenant agrees that this agreement satisfies any condition or requirement in the lease relating to the granting of a nondisturbance agreement with respect to the mortgage. Tenant further agrees that if there is any inconsistency between the terms and provisions of this agreement and the terms and provisions of the lease dealing with nondisturbance, the terms and provisions of this agreement will control.

13. All notices, demands, or requests made pursuant to, under, or by virtue of this agreement must be in writing and delivered by hand, sent by an overnight courier service providing dated evidence of delivery, or mailed by United States certified or registered mail, return receipt requested, to the person to whom the notice, demand, or request is being made at its address set forth in this agreement. Notices will be deemed to have been properly given and received for all purposes:

(a) if hand delivered, effective upon delivery;

(b) if mailed, by United States registered or certified mail, postage prepaid return receipt requested, effective three business days after mailing; or

(c) if sent by Federal Express or other reliable express courier, effective on the next business day after delivery to such express courier service.

Any person may change the place that notices and demands are to be sent by written notice delivered in accordance with this agreement. "Business day" means any day, except Saturday, Sunday, and any day that is in New York City a legal holiday or a day on which banking institutions are authorized or re-quired by law or other government action to close.

14. This agreement will be governed by the laws of the state of [state]. If any of the terms of this agreement or the application of it to any person or circumstances are invalid or unenforceable, the remainder of this agreement or the application of any of those terms to any person or circumstances other than those as to which it is invalid or unenforceable will not be affected, and each term of this agreement will be valid and enforceable to the fullest extent permitted by law.

Lender and tenant have executed this agreement as of its date.

[signature]   [signature]

Tenant   Lender

[acknowledgments]

§ 2.11   Estoppel Certificate Form

FORM 2.11
MISCELLANEOUS—ESTOPPEL CERTIFICATE FORM

Landlord: [name]

Tenant: [name]

Lease Dated: [date], 19[00]

Premises: [* * *]

Security Deposit: $[amount]

Purchaser: [name]

Purchaser's Address: [* * *] Street
                     [city], [state]

Lender: [name]

Lender's Address: [* * *] Street
                  [city], [state]

Effective Date: [date], 19[00]

Tenant certifies to purchaser and to lender, their successors and assigns, that as of the date of tenant's execution of this instrument:

(a)   The lease is unmodified and in full force and effect, and there are no other agreements between landlord and tenant with respect to the lease, the premises, or the building of which the premises are a part;

(b)   Tenant has accepted possession of the premises, and any improvements required by the terms of the lease to be made by landlord have been completed to the satisfaction of tenant;

(c)   Rental and other amounts payable under the lease have been paid to the date of tenant's execution of this instrument and will be paid through the effective date;

(d)   Landlord is not in default under any of the terms of the lease;

(e)   No notice has been received by tenant or given by tenant of any default under the lease that has not been cured and there are no circumstances that with the passage of time or giving of notice would be a default by landlord or tenant under the lease;

(f)   The address for notices to be sent to tenant is set forth in the lease;

(g)   Tenant has no charge, lien, or claim of offset under the lease or against rent or other charges due or to become due under the lease, and tenant has no outstanding claim for credit or reimbursement on account of tenant's improvements to the premises;

(h)   The amount of any security or other deposit returnable to the tenant pursuant to the lease is set forth above and the amount of any rental and other amounts paid more than thirty (30) days prior to the date on which they are due under the lease are set forth in the lease;

(i)   A correct copy of the lease and all amendments and side agreements to it are attached to this instrument as Exhibit [* *]; and

(j)   Tenant has no right or option to purchase the premises or any part or all of the building of which they are a part, or to renew or extend the lease, or to expand the premises, except as set forth in Exhibit [* *].

Tenant further warrants to purchaser, its successors and assigns, and lender that tenant (except as set forth in the lease): has not paid and will not pay any rent under the lease more than thirty (30) days in advance of its due date; prior to the effective date, will not surrender or consent to the modification of any of the terms of the lease or to the termination of the lease by landlord, and will not seek to terminate the lease by reason of any act or omission of landlord until tenant will have given written notice of such act or omission to purchaser and lender at their addresses above and until a reasonable period of time has elapsed following the giving of such notice, during which period purchaser and lender will have the right, but will not be obligated, to remedy such act or omission; will notify purchaser in writing at purchaser's address above prior to the effective date if any of the statements made by tenant in this instrument are materially false or misleading, or omit to state a material fact, as a result of any circumstances occurring or becoming known to tenant after the date of tenant's execution of this instrument; understands it may be prevented from taking a position after the effective date that is inconsistent with the statements made by it in this instrument.

Date of execution: [date]

Tenant's signature [name]

[See Commercial Real Estate Leases: Preparation and Negotiation § 32.15.]

§ 2.12   Tenant Estoppel Certificate

FORM 2.12
TENANT ESTOPPEL CERTIFICATE

Tenant certifies to [name] ("lender") and [name] ("landlord"):

1.   A correct and complete copy of the lease dated [date], 19[00], between landlord and tenant (the "lease"), with regard to premises located at [address] is attached as Exhibit A. The lease is now in full force and effect and has not been amended, modified or supplemented, except as set forth in paragraph 4.

2.   The term of the lease commenced on [date], 19[* *].

3.   The term of the lease will expire on [date], 19[00].

4.   The lease has:

( ) not been amended, modified, supplemented, extended, renewed, or assigned.

( ) been amended, modified, supplemented, extended, renewed, or assigned by these agreements, copies of which are attached:

    [list]

5.   Tenant has accepted and is now in possession of the premises.

6.   Tenant and landlord acknowledge that the lease will be assigned to lender; that no modification, adjustment, revision, or cancellation of the lease or amendments will be effective unless the written consent of lender and landlord is obtained; and that, until further notice, payments under the lease will continue.

7.   The amount of base monthly rent is $[amount].

8.   The amount of security deposits (if any) is $[amount]. No other security deposits have been made.

9.   Tenant is paying the full lease rental, which has been paid in full as of this date. No rent under the lease has been paid for more than 30 days in advance of its due date.

10. All work required to be performed by landlord under the lease has been completed.

11. There are no defaults on the part of the landlord or tenant under the lease.

12. Tenant has no defense as to its obligations under the lease and claims no setoff or counterclaim against landlord.

13. Tenant has no right to any concession (rental or otherwise) or similar compensation in connection with renting the premises, except as provided in the lease.

14. There are no actions, voluntary or involuntary, pending by or against tenant under the bankruptcy laws of the United States or the insolvency laws of any state.

Tenant ratifies and confirms the lease and the amendments to it (if any).

This certification is made with the knowledge that lender is about to lend money to landlord and that lender and landlord are relying upon tenant's representations in making the loan.

This certificate has been duly executed and delivered by the authorized officers of tenant as of [date], 19[* *].

TENANT:

[name],

a [* * *] corporation

By [signature]

Its [title]

By [signature]

Its [title]

§ 2.13 Memorandum of Lease

FORM 2.13
MISCELLANEOUS—MEMORANDUM OF LEASE

Landlord, whose address is [* * *], [* * *], [* * *], leases to tenant, whose address is [* * *], [* * *], [* * *], for a term beginning the [* * *] day of [date], 19[00], and continuing for a maximum period of [* * *], including extensions and renewals, if any, the property commonly known as [* * *], [* * *], [* * *], more particularly described as:

Lot [* * *]

Block [* * *]

[* * *] Subdivision
City of [city]
County of [county]
State of [state]

(If applicable: There exists an option to purchase with respect to this leased property, in favor of tenant that expires the [* * *] day of [* * *], 19[00], and that is set forth at large in the lease agreement between the landlord and tenant.)

The provisions set forth in the lease agreement between landlord and tenant dated the [* * *] day of [* * *], 19[00], are incorporated in this memorandum.

[signature]

("landlord")

[signature]

("tenant")

(Acknowledgments)

[See Commercial Real Estate Leases: Preparation and Negotiation § 32.6.]

§ 2.14   Short Form Lease

FORM 2.14
MISCELLANEOUS—SHORT FORM LEASE

THIS SHORT-FORM LEASE is made as of [date], 19[00] by [name] ("land-lord"), and [name] ("tenant").

RECITALS

Landlord and tenant have entered into a lease dated [date], 19[00] (the "lease") with respect to certain premises commonly known as [street] Street, City of [city], County of [county], State of [state] (the "premises"). Landlord and tenant wish to give notice of the lease. Accordingly they agree:

1.   Agreement. Landlord leases to tenant, and tenant leases from landlord, the real property commonly known as:

[street] Street
City of [city]
County of [county]
State of [state]

(the "premises"), and more particularly described as

Lot [* *],

Block [* *],

[* * *] SUBDIVISION,

City of [city],

County of [county],

State of [state].

2.   Term. The term of the lease begins [date], 19[00] and ends [date], 19[00], inclusive. The lease gives tenant the following rights:

[RENEWAL OR EXTENSION PROVISION]

3.   Option to Purchase. The lease gives tenant the following rights:

[OPTION TO PURCHASE]

4.   Exclusive Use. The lease provides:

[EXCLUSIVE USE]

5.   The Lease. The terms of this short-form lease are subject to the lease, and any amendments, renewals, or extensions of the lease. The lease (except for the provisions relating to the rent) may be examined at the premises.

LANDLORD:

[signature]

By: [* * *]

Title: [* * *]

TENANT:

[signature]

By: [* * *]

Title: [* * *]

(Acknowledgments)

[See Commercial Real Estate Leases: Preparation and Negotiation § 32.6.]

§ 2.15   Commencement Date Certificate

FORM 2.15
COMMENCEMENT DATE CERTIFICATE

This commencement date certificate is entered into by landlord and tenant pursuant to Section [* *] of the lease.

1.   Definitions. In this certificate the following terms have the meanings given to them:

(a)   Landlord: [name]

(b)   Tenant: [name]

(c)   Lease: office lease dated [date] between landlord and tenant

(d)   Premises: Suite [* * *]

(e)   Building Address: [* * *]
                        [city]
                        [state]

2.   Confirmation of Term: Landlord and tenant confirm that the commencement date of the lease is [date], 19[00], and the expiration date is [date], 19[00], and that Sections [* *] and [* *] are accordingly amended.

3.   Acceptance of the Premises. Tenant accepted the premises on [date], 19[00], and first occupied the premises on [date], 19[00].

Landlord and tenant have executed this commencement date certificate as of the dates set forth below.

TENANT: LANDLORD:

[Signature]   [Signature]

By [name]   By [name]
Its [title]   Its [title]
Date [date], 19[00]   Date [date], 19[00]

§ 2.16   Lease Commencement Memorandum

FORM 2.16
LEASE COMMENCEMENT MEMORANDUM

1.   Definitions:

(a)   Landlord: [name]

(b)   Tenant: [name]

(c)   Lease: Office Lease dated [date], 19[00], between landlord and tenant.

(d)   Premises: Suite [* * *]

(e)   Building Address: [* * *] Street
                        [city]
                        [state]

2.   Confirmation of Lease Commencement: Landlord and tenant confirm that the commencement date of the lease is [date], 19[00], and the expiration date is [date], 19[00].

Landlord and tenant have executed this lease commencement memorandum as of the dates set forth below.

TENANT: LANDLORD:

[signature]   [signature]

By [name]   By [name]

Its [title]   Its [title]

Date [date], 19[00]   Date [date], 19[00]

§ 2.17   Basic Lease Information—Office Building

This form presents basic lease information for an office building lease. For this form, the lease is one in which the tenant pays its share of costs—both operating costs and real estate taxes—to the extent that those costs exceed a base year's costs. Some office building leases identify the rentable area of the building. This form does not because it tries to avoid any controversy in the measurement of the building and premises; of course, the tenant can compute the rentable area of the building by dividing its rentable area by its pro rata share. For this reason, some leases omit the area of the premises and provide only the tenant's pro rata share. Often, no fixed term is stated because it can vary with the delivery of possession. The terms in the basic lease information are often defined terms that are capitalized and used throughout the lease.

FORM 2.17
BASIC LEASE INFORMATION—OFFICE BUILDING

[Name and Address of the Office Building]

Date of the Lease: [date], 19[00]

Landlord: [name]

Tenant: [name]

Premises: Suite [* * *]

Lease Commencement Date: [date], 19[00]

Lease Expiration Date: [date], 19[00]

Base Monthly Rent: $[amount]

Base Year for Taxes: 19[00]

Base Year for Operating Expenses: 19[00]

Rentable Area of the Premises: Approximately [number] square feet

Tenant's Pro Rata Share: [* * *] percent ([* *]%)

Landlord's Address for Notices: [name]
                                 [* * *] Street
                                 [city], [state]

Tenant's Address for Notices: [name]
                                 [* * *] Street
                                 [city], [state]

Security Deposit: [* * *] dollars ($[* * *])

Broker: [name]

Exhibits: A—Legal Description of the Building
             B—The Premises
             C—Workletter
             D—Rules and Regulations

The basic lease information is part of the lease; however, if any of the basic lease information contradicts any provision of the lease, the provisions of the lease will prevail.

§ 2.18   Basic Lease Information—Shopping Center

In this basic lease information for a shopping center, an unusual variation has been added: stepped up rent.

FORM 2.18
BASIC LEASE INFORMATION—SHOPPING CENTER

[Name and Address of Shopping Center]

Date of the Lease: [date], 19[00]

Landlord: [name]

Tenant: [name]

Premises: Suite or Unit No. [* * *]

Lease Commencement Date: [date], 19[00]

Lease Expiration Date: [date], 19[00]

Minimum Monthly Rent:

[* * *] dollars per month ($[* * *] per month) commencing on [date], 19[00], and continuing to [date], 19[00], inclusive.

[* * *] dollars per month ($[* * *] per month) commencing on [date], 19[00], and continuing to [date], 19[00], inclusive.

[* * *] dollars per month ($[* * *] per month) commencing on [date], 19[00], and continuing to [date], 19[00], inclusive.

[* * *] dollars per month ($[* * *] per month) commencing on [date], 19[00], and continuing to [date], 19[00], inclusive.

[* * *] dollars per month ($[* * *] per month) commencing on [date], 19[00], and continuing to [date], 19[00], inclusive.

Percentage Rent: [* * *] percent ([* *]%)

Leasable Area of Premises: approximately [number] square feet

Leasable Area of Shopping Center: approximately [number] square feet

Tenant's Pro Rata Share: [* * *] percent ([* *]%)

Use: [* * *]

Trade Name: [* * *]

Radius: [* * *]

Landlord's Address for Notices: [name]
                                 [* * *] Street
                                 [city], [state]

Tenant's Address for Notices: [name]
                                 [* * *] Street
                                 [city], [state]

Business Hours: Monday-Friday: [* *] a.m. to [* *] p.m.
                   Saturday: [* *] a.m. to [* *] p.m.
                   Sunday: [* *] a.m. to [* *] p.m.

Security Deposit: [* * *] dollars ($[* * *])

Broker: [name]
         [* * *] Street
         [city], [state]

Guarantor: [name]
[* * *] Street
[city], [state]

Exhibits: A—Legal Description of the Shopping Center
B—Site Plan of the Shopping Center
C—Rules and Regulations
D—Guaranty of Lease
E—Sign Criteria

The basic lease information is part of the lease; however, if any of the basic lease information contradicts any provision of the lease, the provisions of the lease will prevail.

§ 2.19 Basic Lease Information—Single Tenant Building

FORM 2.19
BASIC LEASE INFORMATION—SINGLE TENANT BUILDING

[Name and Address of Building]

Date: [date], 19[00]

Landlord: [name]

Tenant: [name]

Trade Name: [name]

Premises: [* * *] Street
[city]
[county]
[state]

Length of Term: [* * *] ([* *]) years

Lease Commencement Date: [date], 19[00]

Lease Expiration Date: [date], 19[00]

Monthly Rent: $[amount]

Landlord's Address for Notices: [name]
[* * *] Street
[city], [state]

Tenant's Address for Notices: [name]
                                   [* * *] Street
                                   [city], [state]

Security Deposit: $[amount]

The basic lease information is part of the lease; however, if any of the basic lease information contradicts any provision of the lease, the provisions of the lease will prevail.

§ 2.20   Amendment to Office Lease

FORM 2.20
[* * *] AMENDMENT TO OFFICE LEASE

For valuable consideration, the receipt and adequacy of which are expressly acknowledged, landlord and tenant agree that:

1.   Definitions:

   (a)   Landlord: [name]
   (b)   Tenant: [name]
   (c)   Lease: [type] dated [date], 19[00], between landlord and tenant.
   (d)   Premises: Suite [* * *]
   (e)   Building Address: [* * *] Street
                            [city]
                            [state]
   (f)   Date: [date], 19[00]
   (g)   Effective Date: [date], 19[00]

Any defined term used in this [* * *] Amendment that is not defined in this amendment has the meaning set forth for such term in the lease.

2.   Amendment to Section [* *]: [Example: Amendment to Article 1.00(1): As of the effective date, Article 1.00(1) is amended to read in its entirety:

   (1)   RENTABLE AREA OF THE PREMISES: [new number] square feet.]

3.   Confirmation of Lease: As amended by this [* * *] amendment, landlord and tenant confirm the lease.

Landlord and tenant have executed this amendment as of the date.

LANDLORD: TENANT:

[signature]   [signature]

By [name]   By [name]
Its [title]   Its [title]

§ 2.21   Lease Summary

FORM 2.21
LEASE SUMMARY

Date [date]

Prepared by [name]

Tenant [name]   Building [* * *]

Tenant's Address [* * *]   Address [* * *]

Documents Reviewed: Metro Area [* * *]

(a) the lease dated [date]   Area of the building:

(b) Exhibits [* * *]   [* * *] n.r.s.f.

(c) Addendums dated [date]   Broker [name]

The Premises:

(a) Suite [* * *]   (b) Type of space [* * *]

(c) [number] rentable square feet; [number] usable square feet

(d) Tenant's share: [* * *]%

Term: (a)   [number] years [number] months
       (b)   Commencement date [date]   Termination date [date]

Rent:

Current annual base rent per rentable square foot $[amount]

Current base monthly rent $[amount]

Abatement of rent $[amount]

Escalations:

Type: CPI [* * *]   Fixed step [* * *]

Rent [* * *]   Date [* * *]

Operating expense [* * *]   Date [* * *]

Rent Payment:

Rent payable on [date]

Commencing on [date]

Late charge $[amount]

Expense stop per rentable square foot [* * *]

Current monthly operating expenses [* * *] includes:
　Additional costs [* * *]

Services (T/LL):
　[* *] Property Taxes
　[* *] Janitorial
　[* *] Insurance
　[* *] Utilities [* * *]
　　(a)　[* *] Electrical [* * *]
　　(b)　[* *] Water [* * *]
　　(c)　[* *] Other [* * *]

Security Deposit:　$[amount]

Guarantor:　[* * *]

Leasehold Improvements:　[* * *]

T.I. Costs:
　Allowance $[amount]
　Completed date [date]
　Excess $[amount]　　　　Paid $[amount]　　　　By Whom [* * *]

Are excess T.I. costs to be amortized over the lease term: [* * *]
If so,
　　(a)　Interest rate [* * *]
　　(b)　Amortization period [* * *]
　　(c)　Other terms [* * *]

Lease Acquisition Costs:
　(a)　Moving expenses $[amount]
　(b)　Lease assumption $[amount]
　(c)　Broker commissions $[amount]
　(d)　Other lease acquisition costs $[amount]

Parking:
　(a)　[number] covered spaces; $[amount] per mo.　Abatement? [* * *]
　(b)　[number] surface spaces; $[amount] per mo.　Abatement? [* * *]
　(c)　Any reserved or other special parking rights? [* * *]

Tenant Options:

	Article
Renewal:	[* *]

Rate: [* * *]   Commencing on [* * *]
Notification date: [date]
Term: [* * *]

Expansion space: [* *]
When: [* * *]
Sq. ft.: [number]
Rate: [* * *]
Notification date: [date]

Deletions: [* *]
On what floor: [* * *]
When: [* * *]
Sq. ft.: [number]

First refusal: [* *]
When: [* * *]
What space: [* * *]

Termination by tenant: [* * *]   [* *]

Comments: [* * *]

Other Rights and Obligations:

	Article
Tenant estoppel: [* * *]	[* *]
Signage rights: [* * *]	[* *]
Holding over clause: [* * *]	[* *]
Alterations by tenant: [* * *]	[* *]
Landlord remodel approval: [* * *]	[* *]
Restoration request: [* * *]	[* *]
Subordination to mort: [* * *]	[* *]
Assignment: [* * *]	[* *]
Subletting: [* * *]	[* *]
Insurance:	[* *]

Casualty: [* *]
Liability: [* * *]

Unusual or Burdensome Provisions: [* * *]

PART II

THE ESSENTIAL LEASE PROVISIONS

CHAPTER 3

INTRODUCTORY PROVISIONS

§ 3.1   Presenting Basic Lease Information (Reserved)

§ 3.2   Identifying the Lease

§ 3.3   Date of the Lease (Reserved)

§ 3.4   Tradenames and Service Marks (Reserved)

§ 3.5   Individuals

§ 3.6   Co-Owners and Co-Tenants (Reserved)

§ 3.7   Corporations

§ 3.8   Partnerships

§ 3.9   Agents, Representatives, and Guardians

§ 3.10   Charitable Associations, Campaign Committees, and Government Entities (Reserved)

§ 3.11   Tax-Exempt Organizations (Reserved)

§ 3.12   Tenants with Sovereign Immunity (Reserved)

§ 3.13   Franchisors and Franchisees (Reserved)

§ 3.14   Guarantors (Reserved)

§ 3.15   Guaranty of Lease (Reserved)

§ 3.16   Contesting Guaranties (Reserved)

§ 3.17   "and/or Assigns" (Reserved)

§ 3.18   Grant or Agreement of Lease

§ 3.1   Presenting Basic Lease Information (Reserved)

§ 3.2 Identifying the Lease

FORM 3.2(1)
INTRODUCTION

THIS LEASE is made on [date], 19[00], by [name] ("landlord") and [name] ("tenant").

FORM 3.2(2)
INTRODUCTION—AN ALTERNATIVE
(For Use with Basic Lease Information)

THIS LEASE is entered into by landlord and tenant described in the basic lease information on the date set forth for reference only in the basic lease information.

§ 3.3 Date of the Lease (Reserved)

§ 3.4 Tradenames and Service Marks (Reserved)

§ 3.5 Individuals

FORM 3.5(1)
SOLE PROPRIETOR TENANT—TERMINATION OF LEASE AFTER DEATH

If tenant dies or becomes disabled (as defined in this paragraph), tenant or tenant's personal representative may cancel this lease by notice given to landlord within [* *] days after the date on which tenant dies or becomes disabled. The lease will terminate without further liability to tenant on the [* * *] day after landlord's receipt of the notice. The term "disabled" means that tenant is unable to conduct its business at the premises because of tenant's physical or mental illness or injury.

§ 3.6 Co-Owners and Co-Tenants (Reserved)

§ 3.7   Corporations

FORM 3.7(1)
CORPORATE TENANT—CORPORATE RESOLUTION

RESOLVED, that the lease dated [date], 19[00], between [name], as landlord, and the company, as tenant, in the form attached to these minutes, with respect to certain real property, known as [* * *] Street, City of [* * *], County of [* * *], State of [* * *] is approved and that [* * *], as president of the company, and [* * *], as secretary of the company, are authorized and directed to execute and deliver the lease to the landlord on behalf of the company.

§ 3.8   Partnerships

FORM 3.8(1)
PARTNERSHIP TENANT—LIMITING LIABILITY OF
RETIRING OR DECEASED PARTNERS

So long as tenant's new partners assume tenant's obligations under this lease accruing after the date of their assumption and agree to be bound by this lease after that date, any partner in tenant who retires or dies will be released from any liability under this lease that accrues after the date of retirement or death. This paragraph applies to present and future partners in tenant and to any successor partnership that becomes tenant under this lease.

§ 3.9   Agents, Representatives, and Guardians

FORM 3.9(1)
EXCULPATION OF LANDLORD ACTING IN REPRESENTATIVE CAPACITY

Landlord is acting solely in its representative capacity as [trustee under the John Jones Irrevocable Trust dated [date], 19[00] (the "trust")], in entering into this lease. Landlord has no personal liability under this lease. Landlord's liability under this lease will be limited to the trust's assets as they may exist from time to time.

§ 3.10   Charitable Associations, Campaign Committees, and Government Entities (Reserved)

§ 3.11   Tax-Exempt Organizations (Reserved)

§ 3.12   Tenants with Sovereign Immunity (Reserved)

§ 3.13   Franchisors and Franchisees (Reserved)

§ 3.14   Guarantors (Reserved)

§ 3.15   Guaranty of Lease (Reserved)

§ 3.16   Contesting Guaranties (Reserved)

§ 3.17   "and/or Assigns" (Reserved)

§ 3.18   Grant or Agreement of Lease

FORM 3.18(1)
AGREEMENT OF LEASE

Landlord leases the premises to tenant, and tenant leases the premises from landlord, according to this lease.

CHAPTER 4

THE PREMISES

§ 4.1   An Approach to Description of Premises (Reserved)

§ 4.2   Description of Single Tenant Building

§ 4.3   Description of Shopping Center Premises

§ 4.4   Measurement of Shopping Center Premises

§ 4.5   Appurtenances in a Shopping Center (Reserved)

§ 4.6   Designating Certain Areas (Reserved)

§ 4.7   Preserving Flexibility in Shopping Center Development (Reserved)

§ 4.8   Description of Office Building Premises

§ 4.9   An Approach to Measurement of Office Building Premises (Reserved)

§ 4.10   Introduction to BOMA Measurement (Reserved)

§ 4.11   Usable Area (Reserved)

§ 4.12   Rentable Area (Reserved)

§ 4.13   Importance of Measurement (Reserved)

§ 4.14   An Illustration of Office Building Measurement (Reserved)

§ 4.15   Appurtenances in an Office Building (Reserved)

§ 4.16   Personal Property (Reserved)

§ 4.17   Storage Space (Reserved)

§ 4.18   Lenders' Concerns about Premises (Reserved)

§ 4.19   Options (Reserved)

§ 4.20   Options to Expand Premises

§ 4.21   "Build-Out" Expansion Option

§ 4.22   Right of First Refusal to Lease Additional Space

§ 4.23   Options to Purchase

§ 4.24   Lenders' Concerns about Options to Purchase (Reserved)

§ 4.25   Right of First Refusal to Purchase Premises

§ 4.26   Lenders' Concerns about Right of First Refusal to Purchase Premises (Reserved)

§ 4.27   Landlord's Right to Relocate Premises

§ 4.1   An Approach to Description of Premises (Reserved)

§ 4.2   Description of Single Tenant Building

FORM 4.2(1)
PREMISES—SINGLE TENANT BUILDING LEASE

The premises are the land and building commonly known as [name] Street, City of [city], County of [county], State of [state], and more particularly described as:

Lot [* *],

Block [* *],

LANDLORD'S SUBDIVISION,

according to the plat recorded [date],

19[00], in book [* * *], page [* * *] of maps,

City of [* * *]

County of [* * *]

State of [* * *]

The land consists of approximately [number] square feet. The building consists of approximately [number] square feet on the ground floor, a basement, and a mezzanine and includes without limitation all heating, ventilating, air conditioning, mechanical, electrical, elevator, and plumbing systems, roof, walls, and foundations, and fixtures within it. The premises include all appurtenances, easements, and rights of way related to them.

§ 4.3   Description of Shopping Center Premises

FORM 4.3(1)
PREMISES—SHOPPING CENTER LEASE

The premises are:

Store [* *]

[* * *] Shopping Center

City of [city]

County of [county]

State of [state]

The premises are depicted on Exhibit A to this lease. The premises do not include and landlord reserves the exterior walls and roof of the premises, the land beneath the premises, and the pipes, ducts, conduits, wires, fixtures, and equipment above the suspended ceiling, and structural elements that serve the premises or the shopping center. Landlord's reservation includes the rights to install, inspect, maintain, use, repair, and replace those areas and items and to enter the premises in order to do so.

§ 4.4   Measurement of Shopping Center Premises

FORM 4.4(1)
PREMISES—DEFINITION OF "FLOOR AREA" IN
A SHOPPING CENTER LEASE

The term "floor area" means, with respect to each store area separately leased, the number of square feet of floor space on all floor levels in the premises, including any mezzanine area, measured from the exterior faces of exterior walls, store fronts, walls fronting on the enclosed malls or interior common areas, corridors, and service areas, and the center lines of party walls or common partitions. No deduction or exclusion from floor area will be made by reason of columns, stairs, elevators, escalators, shafts, or other interior construction.

§ 4.5   Appurtenances in a Shopping Center (Reserved)

§ 4.6   Designating Certain Areas (Reserved)

§ 4.7   Preserving Flexibility in Shopping Center Development (Reserved)

§ 4.8   Description of Office Building Premises

FORM 4.8(1)
PREMISES—OFFICE BUILDING LEASE

The premises are Suite [* * *], [* * *] Building, [name] Street, [city], [state], as shown on the floor plan attached as Exhibit A, consisting of [number] rentable square feet.

§ 4.9   An Approach to Measurement of Office Building Premises (Reserved)

§ 4.10   Introduction to BOMA Measurement (Reserved)

§ 4.11   Usable Area (Reserved)

§ 4.12   Rentable Area (Reserved)

§ 4.13   Importance of Measurement (Reserved)

§ 4.14   An Illustration of Office Building Measurement (Reserved)

§ 4.15   Appurtenances in an Office Building (Reserved)

§ 4.16   Personal Property (Reserved)

§ 4.17   Storage Space (Reserved)

§ 4.18   Lenders' Concerns about Premises (Reserved)

§ 4.19   Options (Reserved)

§ 4.20   Options to Expand Premises

FORM 4.20(1)
PREMISES—EXPANSION OPTION
(Office Building)

(a)   Tenant has the right, but not the obligation, to add to the premises any or all of the spaces shown on Exhibit [* *] (each an "expansion space") on the respective anniversaries of the commencement date of this lease according to the further provisions of this paragraph. Tenant must exercise its right to add any expansion space (if at all) by written notice to landlord given at least [* * *] ([* *]) days before the anniversary on which the relevant expansion space may be added to the premises. If tenant does not exercise its right in a timely manner, tenant will have irretrievably lost its right to the relevant expansion space.

(b)   Any expansion space with respect to which tenant exercises its rights will be delivered by landlord to tenant either (1) in its condition on the date on which the expansion premises are added to the premises if the expansion space has been previously occupied or (2) with the building standard tenant finish allowance available on the date on which the expansion premises are added to the premises if the expansion space has not been previously occupied; however, if the relevant expansion space has been occupied, landlord will use so much of the occupant's security deposit as it lawfully can use to repair and restore the expansion space. Any expansion space will become part of the premises on the relevant anniversary of the commencement date, and the premises will then be deemed to include any such expansion space. All of the provisions of this lease will apply to any expansion space. Landlord will not be obligated to grant any concessions or allowances with respect to any expansion space except as set forth in this paragraph.

(c)   The base monthly rent for any expansion space will be the base monthly rent per rentable square foot of the premises in effect on the date on which the expansion space becomes part of the premises. The base monthly rent will be increased as of the day on which the expansion space becomes part of the premises by an amount equal to the product of (1) the number of rentable square feet of the expansion space multiplied by (2) the base monthly rent per rentable square foot of the premises in effect on the day on which the expansion space becomes part of the premises. Tenant's share [of operating expenses] will be increased as of the day on which any expansion space becomes part of the premises by a fraction whose numerator is the sum of the rentable square feet of the premises and the new expansion space, and whose denominator is the rentable square feet of the premises. The base monthly rent and tenant's share [of operating expenses] will be increased in a similar manner whenever expansion space is added to the premises. The landlords' share [of operating expenses] with respect to the expansion space will be the landlord's share then prevailing for new leases in the building.

(d)   Tenant will have not have any rights according to this paragraph if, at the time tenant is obligated to give any notice, or at the time landlord delivers possession of the expansion premises, either (1) an event of default then exists, or (2) tenant has assigned the lease with respect to, or sublet, more than [number] rentable square feet of the premises.

§ 4.21   "Build-Out" Expansion Option

FORM 4.21(1)
PREMISES—CREDIT VERIFICATION AS A CONDITION TO EXPANSION
(Landlord's Form)

(a)   Tenant's Rights. Subject to paragraph (c), tenant has the right, but not the obligation, to add to the premises the space shown on Exhibit [* *] (the "expansion space") on the [* * *] anniversary of the commencement date of this lease according to the further provisions of this paragraph. Tenant must exercise its right to add the expansion space by written notice to landlord given at least [number] days prior to the anniversary on which the expansion space may be added to the premises. If tenant does not exercise its right in a timely manner, tenant will have irretrievably lost its right to the expansion space.

(b)   Documents Tenant Must Submit. The notice given by tenant to landlord pursuant to paragraph (a) will be accompanied by:

(i)   The current quarterly financial statement (which may be unaudited but must be certified by the president or chief financial officer) and last annual financial statement (which must be audited) of tenant and any guarantor ("guarantor") that has furnished a guaranty ("guaranty") of this lease. The financial statements (the "financial statements") required by this paragraph include income statements, balance sheets, statements of cash flow, and footnotes; and

(ii)   tenant's and guarantor's written authorization to all credit-rating agencies of the release of their credit reports.

(c)   When Option May Be Invalid. Tenant will not have any rights under paragraph (a) if tenant does not give landlord notice strictly according to this paragraph, or if at the time either that tenant gives landlord notice under paragraph (a) or that the expansion space is delivered to tenant:

(i)   An event of default exists;

(ii)   The original occupant of the premises occupies less than [* *]% of the rentable square feet of the premises;

(iii)   Any lender whose deed of trust, mortgage, or other security interest affects either the premises or the landlord does not approve tenant's creditworthiness;

(iv)   Landlord does not approve tenant's or guarantor's creditworthiness (in determining tenant's creditworthiness, landlord may consider the financial statements of tenant and guarantor and may compare them to financial statements submitted by tenant and guarantor in connection with the entry into this lease);

(v) Guarantor has endeavored to rescind or terminate the guaranty.

(d) Security Deposit. At landlord's request, tenant will deliver an amount sufficient to make the security deposit equal to one month's rent for the premises and the expansion space, and tenant will deliver guarantor's ratification of its guaranty of the lease as amended by the addition of the expansion space.

§ 4.22 Right of First Refusal to Lease Additional Space

FORM 4.22(1)
PREMISES—RIGHT OF FIRST OFFER TO LEASE
(Landlord's Form)

(a) Notice. Before entering into a lease for all or any portion of the space adjacent to the premises, consisting of approximately [* * *] ([* * *]) square feet, as more particularly shown on Exhibit [* *] (the "additional space"), during the first forty-eight (48) months of the term, and so long as tenant is not then in default under this lease, landlord will notify tenant of the monthly rent and rental increases ("rental terms") on which it would be willing to lease the additional space to tenant.

If within five (5) days after receipt of landlord's notice, tenant agrees in writing to lease the additional space for a term not to exceed the remaining initial term of this lease at the rental terms, landlord and tenant will execute a lease for the additional space within ten (10) days after landlord's receipt of tenant's notice of intent to lease on all the same terms as this lease except for the rental terms, and other matters dependent upon the size of the premises, such as tenant's share of the common area expenses, insurance premium payments, and security deposit. If tenant does not deliver its notice of intent to lease the additional space or portion of the additional space offered in landlord's notice within such five (5) day period, or if landlord and tenant do not enter into a fully executed lease for the additional space or such portion within such ten (10) day period, then this right of first offer to lease the additional space or portion of the additional space will lapse and be of no further effect and landlord will have the right to lease the additional space or such portion of the additional space to a third party on the same or any other terms and conditions, whether or not such terms and conditions are more or less favorable than those offered to tenant. This right of first offer to lease the additional space is personal to [name of tenant] and is not transferable.

(b) Time of Essence. Time is of the essence of the provisions of this paragraph.

FORM 4.22(2)
PREMISES—RIGHT OF FIRST REFUSAL TO LEASE
(Another Form)

If landlord receives a bona fide offer for the lease of all or any portion of the (the "space") of the building not then leased by tenant, landlord will give tenant the right of first refusal to lease the space, at the rent and on the terms and conditions of the offer. The right of first refusal will be extended by landlord giving tenant written notice of the particular offer received by landlord, together with a summary of the offer, requiring tenant to accept the offer and to sign an appropriate amendment to this lease subjecting the space to this lease at the rent and for the term set forth in the offer, within 30 days after the mailing of such notice. If the lease with tenant is not signed within the 30-day period, landlord will have the right to accept the offer free of the rights of tenant under this paragraph. Tenant's right of first refusal to lease the space will continue throughout the term and the renewal term with respect to any space available for lease from time to time. Any space leased by tenant will be added to the premises as of the date provided in the offer, and the rent will be adjusted to reflect the rent provided to be paid in accordance with the offer. Tenant agrees to execute amendments to this lease to reflect additions to the premises resulting from the exercise of the right of first refusal to lease. Tenant's lease of any space pursuant to this right of first refusal will be on all the terms and conditions set forth in this lease except as to rent, which will be that set forth in the offer. Landlord is under no obligation to offer for lease all or any portion of the space to tenant or any other person.

FORM 4.22(3)
PREMISES—RIGHT OF FIRST REFUSAL TO LEASE
(Another Form)

So long as this lease is in full force and effect without default by tenant, tenant may lease the space outlined on Exhibit [* *] to this lease on the terms and conditions of this paragraph. If landlord desires to offer the space for lease, landlord will deliver to tenant a written notice specifying the terms of the offer. Tenant will then have 30 days from the delivery of such notice to accept the offer and lease the space in accordance with the offer. If tenant fails to accept or rejects the offer within the 30-day period, landlord will be entitled for a period of 180 days to lease the space on the same terms stated in the notice to tenant. If landlord does lease the space during the 180-day period, the right granted tenant under this paragraph will automatically terminate. However, if landlord does not lease the space during the 180-day period, the space will not subsequently be leased without landlord's compliance with this paragraph.

FORM 4.22(4)
PREMISES—RIGHT OF FIRST OFFER FOR DESIGNATED SPACE

During the term, tenant will have a right of first offer to lease the space shown on the floor plan attached as Schedule [* *], and known as suite [* * *], containing approximately [number] square feet of rentable area (the "expansion space"), prior to the expansion space being offered to any person or entity not then occupying the expansion space, in its "then as is" condition, when it becomes legally available to lease, on the same terms and provisions then in effect under the lease, except that the monthly base rent for the expansion space will be the prevailing rental rate. The "prevailing rental rate" means the average per square foot rental rate per month for all leases for comparable space and approximately the same number of months, executed by existing tenants in the building for office space expansions during the 6 months immediately prior to the date upon which the prevailing rental rate is to become effective and payable under the terms of this lease, when the rates for such expansions were not set in the leases, subject to reasonable adjustments for comparable space on more desirable or less desirable floors or areas of the building. If no comparable space has been leased during the 6-month period, the rental rates used for purposes of this provision will be adjusted to the amounts landlord would have used had leases for comparable space been entered. In all cases, the rates will be determined without regard to any free rent periods, improvement allowances, takeover lease obligations, or other economic incentives; however, any economic incentives generally provided by landlord in comparable expansion leases will also be provided to tenant. In addition, if comparable expansion leases include base years, tax or expense stops, or other provisions respecting taxes or operating expenses, or include any other economic provisions, including but not limited to consumer price index provision, utility reimbursements, or fixed rent increases, they will be included in the expansion terms to tenant.

If tenant has given written notice to landlord at least once every 6 months of its continued desire to be notified of the availability of the expansion space, landlord will notify tenant in writing within 30 days after the expansion space becomes legally available to lease or, at landlord's option, any earlier time as landlord is in a position to project when the expansion space will be legally available to lease, advising tenant of such projected date. Tenant will then have 10 days in which to notify landlord in writing exercising tenant's right to lease the expansion space. If tenant exercises the right to lease the expansion space, the lease will commence on the later of 30 days after tenant's notice exercising the right, or the date the expansion space is available for occupancy, and will continue for the duration of the term. Landlord and tenant will execute an amendment to the lease adding the expansion space, or a new lease for the expansion space, or such other documentation as landlord may require in order to confirm the leasing of the expansion space to tenant.

If landlord and tenant are unable to agree on the prevailing rental rate within 60 days after the commencement of the lease for the expansion space, either may request that the prevailing rental rate be determined by arbitration, under the Commercial Arbitration Rules of the American Arbitration Association then in effect. Since the prevailing rental rate may not be determined until after the commencement of the lease for the expansion space, tenant will pay, as monthly base rent for the expansion space, until the prevailing rental monthly base rate is determined, the amount of monthly base rent then in effect under the lease on a per rentable square foot basis (including monthly base rent and all other charges). Under no circumstances will the monthly base rent under the lease ever be less than the monthly base rent then in effect under the lease, on a per rentable square foot basis, regardless of the prevailing rental rate as determined in accordance with the preceding provisions. If the prevailing rental rate is determined to be greater than that estimated amount, tenant will pay landlord, within 30 days after written request, the difference between the amount required by the determination of the prevailing rental rate and the amount previously paid by tenant for the expansion space.

This expansion right will apply only to the entire expansion space, and may not be exercised with respect to only a portion of it, unless only a portion first becomes available (in which case, the expansion right will also apply to the remaining portions as they become available). If tenant fails to exercise such expansion right, after notice by landlord of the availability of the expansion space, the right will be deemed to have lapsed and expired, and will be of no further effect. Landlord may freely lease all or a portion of the expansion space to any other party, at any time, on any terms, in landlord's sole discretion. If the expansion space is currently legally available to lease, landlord and tenant will be deemed to have agreed that this right of first offer will only apply after the expansion space has been leased, and subsequently becomes available to lease. If the expansion space is currently not legally available to lease, this right of first offer will be subject to the existing tenants or occupants renewing their existing leases or exercising any options to extend, and in all events is subject and subordinate to any other rights of any other person or entity to lease the expansion space, if such rights have already been granted prior to the date of this lease.

If tenant exercises the right of first offer, landlord does not guarantee that the expansion space will be available on the commencement date for the lease, if the then existing occupants of the expansion space hold over, or for any other reason beyond landlord's reasonable control. In those events, rent with respect to the expansion space will be abated until landlord legally delivers the expansion space to tenant, as tenant's sole recourse. Tenant's exercise of its expansion right will not cure any default by tenant of any of the terms or provisions in the lease, nor extinguish or impair any rights or remedies of landlord arising by virtue of any default. The expansion right herein will, at landlord's election, be null and void if tenant is in default under the lease on the date tenant exercises its rights or at any time prior to commencement of the lease for the expansion space. If the lease or tenant's right to possession of the premises terminates in any manner before tenant exercises the expansion right, or if tenant has subleased or assigned all or any portion of the premises, then immediately upon such termination, sublease, or assignment, the right to lease the expansion space will simultaneously terminate. The expansion right is personal to tenant. Under no circumstances will the assignee under a complete or partial assignment of the lease, or a subtenant under a sublease of the premises, have any right to exercise the expansion right. Tenant agrees that time is of the essence of this right.

FORM 4.22(5)
FIRST RIGHT TO LEASE
(Tenant's Right to "Call" Any Available Space)

(1)   Tenant's Rights. Tenant may send notice to landlord from time to time whenever tenant determines that it is in need of additional space ("tenant's notice"). For 180 days after landlord's receipt of tenant's notice, landlord will not lease any of the space in the building not consisting of the premises which is presently vacant and not leased, or which becomes vacant and not leased after the expiration, surrender, or termination of any lease and any applicable renewal term ("space") until 10 business days after tenant's receipt of landlord's notice setting forth landlord's desire to lease all or a portion of the space and the terms on which it wishes to do so, including with respect to the space all of the information set forth on the basic lease information for this lease.

Tenant may, upon notice delivered by tenant within the 10-day period, elect to lease all of the space described in the landlord's notice. If tenant does not elect to lease the space, then, for a period of 180 days following the expiration of the 10-day period, landlord may lease all of the space substantially as described in the landlord's notice to anyone else on the terms set forth in the landlord's notice or on terms more beneficial to the landlord than the terms set forth in the landlord's notice. If landlord does not lease the space to anyone else during the 180-day period, then landlord will, after the expiration of the period, if landlord has received a tenant's notice, be required to send tenant another landlord's notice, and the preceding procedures will be repeated.

(2)   Documentation. Landlord and tenant will execute and deliver appropriate documentation to evidence any exercise of the tenant's right.

(3)   Effect of Default on Tenant's Rights. Tenant will have no rights under this paragraph (i) if, at the time permitted for the exercise of its rights, an event of default by tenant has occurred, or (ii) during the time commencing from the date landlord gives tenant a notice of default pursuant to paragraph [default] and continuing until the event of default alleged in said notice is cured.

§ 4.23   Options to Purchase

FORM 4.23(1)
PREMISES—OPTION TO PURCHASE THE PREMISES

(a)   Grant. Landlord grants tenant the option to purchase the premises at any time during the term of this lease. Tenant must exercise this option, if at all, by written notice. The notice must state a closing date no more than one hundred twenty (120) days after the date of tenant's notice.

(b)   Assignment. This option may be assigned apart from this lease.

(c)   Conditions. This option is conditioned upon tenant not being in default at either the time of its exercise of this option or the time of closing of this option.

(d)   Purchase Price. The purchase price will be payable in cash, or certified funds as directed by landlord, and is: $[amount].

(e)   Closing. At closing landlord will convey the premises to tenant by general warranty deed, subject only to those exceptions or matters of record stated on the form of deed attached as Exhibit [* *]. At closing landlord will also supply tenant with a pinned survey of the premises. The surveyor will certify the survey to tenant and tenant's title insurance company. Landlord and tenant will each pay fifty percent (50%) of the cost of the survey, title insurance policy, and any documentary, transfer, and recording fees and charges. At closing, landlord will deliver the general warranty deed, tenant will pay the purchase price to landlord, and tenant will assume all obligations for real estate taxes and assessments applicable to the premises without adjustment or proration.

(f)   Insurance. Landlord will provide a title insurance policy on an ALTA Form B with standard printed exceptions 1 through 4 deleted and with Form [* * *] (mineral protection) if minerals are severed. As soon as practicable after tenant's election to purchase the premises, landlord will cause the title insurance company to issue a commitment for title insurance and will deliver a copy of it to tenant for tenant's review. Tenant will notify landlord of its objections to exceptions to title, except that tenant may not object to any exceptions to title described in Exhibit [* *], and landlord will exercise reasonable efforts to cause such objections to be deleted within thirty (30) days after the date on which landlord receives notification from tenant. If landlord is unable to secure deletion of those exceptions or secure, at its expense, title insurance against them, then tenant will have the option to rescind its agreement to purchase or to proceed with the purchase and waive any such exception.

FORM 4.23(2)
PREMISES—FIRST RIGHT TO NEGOTIATE PURCHASE

If landlord desires to sell the premises, before entering into an agreement to sell them to anyone else, landlord will notify tenant of its desire to sell the premises and the price and basic terms landlord is asking. If, within 5 days after receipt of the notice, tenant gives landlord written notice of its interest in purchasing the premises at the price and upon the terms contained in landlord's notice to tenant, landlord and tenant agree to attempt to negotiate a legally binding agreement to carry out their previously expressed intent promptly and in good faith. If tenant fails to respond to the notice within said 5 day period, or if landlord and tenant fail to enter into a written agreement for such a purchase and sale within 7 business days after tenant's notice expressing its interest in purchasing the premises, landlord will be free to sell the premises to anyone else upon the same or any other terms and without any further obligation to tenant, whether or not the terms of sale are more or less favorable than those offered to tenant.

§ 4.24   Lenders' Concerns about Options to Purchase (Reserved)

§ 4.25   Right of First Refusal to Purchase Premises

FORM 4.25(1)
PREMISES—RIGHT OF FIRST REFUSAL TO PURCHASE THE PREMISES

(a) Grant. Landlord grants tenant a right of first refusal to purchase the premises pursuant to this section.

(b) Applicable Transactions. If landlord receives an offer to sell the premises and it intends to accept the offer, or if landlord decides to make an offer to sell the premises, landlord will give a written copy of the offer to tenant. Tenant will have the right to accept the offer by written notice to landlord given within fifteen (15) days after tenant's receipt of the offer. If tenant accepts the offer, tenant will be bound to purchase the premises strictly in accordance with the terms of the offer. So long as landlord's rights are not affected, tenant has the right to bid at any foreclosure sale of the premises.

(c) Excluded Transactions. Tenant does not have any right of first refusal to purchase the premises in any of the following transactions: (i) sales of the premises to a related entity (as that term is defined in this paragraph); (ii) encumbrances of the premises; and (iii) any offer after the first one that landlord gives to tenant. The term "related entity" means any corporation (A) that owns eighty percent (80%) or more of the voting stock of landlord; (B) eighty percent (80%) or more of whose voting stock is owned by landlord; or (C) eighty percent (80%) or more of whose voting stock is owned by a corporation that also owns fifty percent (50%) or more of the voting stock of landlord.

(d) Conditions. Tenant does not have any right of first refusal to purchase the premises if, at the time landlord receives the offer or decides to make the offer, (i) tenant is in default under this lease, or (ii) an event has occurred that would be a default under this lease after either notice or the passage of time, or (iii) tenant has assigned all or part of this lease or has sublet all or part of the premises.

(e) No Assignment. The rights granted to tenant in this section are personal and may not be assigned by tenant in connection with an assignment of this lease or otherwise, and tenant's rights in this paragraph may not be exercised by anyone other than tenant. Any attempted assignment of tenant's rights in this paragraph will be of no effect, and will terminate these rights as of the date of the purported assignment.

(f) Apportionment of Rent. If tenant purchases the premises, prepaid rent will be credited against the purchase price.

(g) No Recording. Tenant must not allow its rights in this section to be placed of record. If it does, its rights under this section will terminate as of the time of recording. No recording of tenant's rights in this paragraph will be of any effect.

(h) Time of the Essence. Time is of the essence of each and every agreement and condition in this paragraph.

§ 4.26 Lenders' Concerns about Right of First Refusal to Purchase Premises (Reserved)

§ 4.27 Landlord's Right to Relocate Premises

FORM 4.27(1)
PREMISES—RELOCATION

Landlord reserves the right to relocate the premises to substantially comparable space within the building. Landlord will give tenant written notice of its intention to relocate the premises, and tenant will complete its relocation within thirty (30) days after landlord's notice. The base monthly rent of the new space will not exceed the base monthly rent for the former premises. If tenant does not wish to relocate its premises, tenant may terminate this lease effective as of thirty (30) days after landlord's initial notice. Upon tenant's vacation and abandonment of the premises, landlord will pay to tenant a sum equal to one monthly installment of the base monthly rent payable under this lease, and will return the unused portion of the security deposit, and landlord's and tenant's obligations to each other will then end. If tenant does relocate within the building, then effective on the date of such relocation this lease will be amended by deleting the description of the former premises and substituting for it a description of the new space. Landlord agrees to pay the reasonable costs of moving tenant to the new space.

FORM 4.27(2)
RIGHT TO RELOCATE TENANT
(Another Form)

At any time after the execution of this lease, but prior to the date on which tenant first occupies the premises, landlord may substitute for the premises other premises in the building (the "new premises") in which event the new premises will be deemed to be the premises for all purposes so long as:

(a) The new premises are substantially similar in area and in appropriateness for tenant's purposes;

(b) The base rent and other amounts payable under this lease remain the same;

(c) The new premises are not located on any floor that is below the floor on which the premises are located; and

(d) All costs and expenses of relocating to the new premises, including without limitation all reasonable costs incurred by tenant with respect to the premises, are paid or reimbursed by landlord.

If landlord exercises its rights under this paragraph, landlord and tenant will promptly execute an appropriate amendment to this lease.

CHAPTER 5

THE TERM

§ 5.1   Defining the Term (Reserved)

§ 5.2   Landlord's Failure to Deliver Possession

§ 5.3   Existing Premises

§ 5.4   Completion of New Office Premises

§ 5.5   Workletters (Reserved)

§ 5.6   —Checklist for Reviewing Workletters (Reserved)

§ 5.7   Building Standard Specifications (Reserved)

§ 5.8   Completion and Acceptance of New Shopping Center Premises

§ 5.9   Requiring Completion of Other Parts of the Shopping Center
        and Occupancy by Other Tenants (Reserved)

§ 5.10 Allowing Early Occupancy

§ 5.11 Implied Warranty of Fitness (Reserved)

§ 5.12 Lenders' Concerns about Term (Reserved)

§ 5.13 Option to Extend or Renew a Lease

§ 5.14 —Notice (Reserved)

§ 5.15 —Terms of Renewal

§ 5.16 Tenant's Option to Terminate Lease

§ 5.1   Defining the Term (Reserved)

§ 5.2   Landlord's Failure to Deliver Possession

FORM 5.2(1)
TERM—FAILURE TO DELIVER PREMISES

If for any reason landlord cannot deliver possession of the premises to tenant on the commencement date, (a) this lease will not be void or voidable, (b) landlord will not be liable to tenant for any resultant loss or damage, and (c) unless landlord is unable to deliver possession of the premises to tenant on the commencement date because of tenant's delays, rent will be waived for the period between the commencement date and the date on which landlord delivers possession of the premises to tenant. No delay in delivery of possession of the premises will extend the term.

§ 5.3 Existing Premises

FORM 5.3(1)
TERM—EXISTING PREMISES

The term of this lease will begin on January 1, 19[00], and expire on December 31, 19[00].

§ 5.4 Completion of New Office Premises

FORM 5.4(1)
TERM—OFFICE BUILDING

The term of this lease will commence on [date], 19[00], and will expire on [date], 19[00]. Prior to the commencement date landlord will improve the premises according to its obligations in the workletter. Landlord will be deemed to have delivered possession of the premises to tenant when landlord has given tenant ten (10) days' notice that landlord has substantially completed (or will complete within ten (10) days) these improvements, subject only to the completion of landlord's architect's "punch-list" items that do not materially interfere with tenant's use and enjoyment of the premises. Neither landlord nor its agents or employees have made any representations or warranties as to the suitability or fitness of the premises for the conduct of tenant's business or for any other purpose, nor has landlord or its agents or employees agreed to undertake any alterations or construct any tenant improvements to the premises except as expressly provided in this lease and the workletter. If landlord cannot deliver possession of the premises to tenant on the commencement date, (a) this lease will not be void or voidable, (b) landlord will not be liable to tenant for any resultant loss or damage, and (c) unless landlord is unable to deliver possession of the premises to tenant on the commencement date because of tenant's delays, rent will be waived for the period between the commencement date and the date on which landlord delivers possession of the premises to tenant. No delay in delivery of possession of the premises will extend the term. Tenant will execute the commencement date certificate attached to this lease as Exhibit [* *] within 15 days after landlord's request.

FORM 5.4(2)
TERM—FORCE MAJEURE

If landlord is delayed or prevented from completing its work according to [the workletter] by reason of acts of God, strikes, lockouts, labor troubles, inability to procure labor or materials, fire, accident, riot, civil commotion, laws or regulations of general applicability, acts of tenant, or other cause without its fault and beyond its control (financial inability excepted), completion will be excused for the period of the delay and the period for completion will be extended for a period equal to the period of such delay.

§ 5.5   Workletters (Reserved)

§ 5.6   —Checklist for Reviewing Workletters (Reserved)

§ 5.7   Building Standard Specifications (Reserved)

§ 5.8   Completion and Acceptance of New Shopping Center Premises

FORM 5.8(1)
TERM—SHOPPING CENTER

The term will commence on the earlier of:

(a)   the date on which tenant opens the premises for business to the public, or

(b)   [* * *] ([* *]) days after the delivery of the premises to tenant by landlord. Delivery will be established by a written notice by landlord to tenant specifying the date upon which the premises will be delivered to tenant.

FORM 5.8(2)
TERM—LATE OPENING

If tenant fails to open its store for business upon the commencement date of the term, then, in order to compensate landlord for its loss, tenant will pay to landlord $[amount] as additional base monthly rent for each full or partial calendar month after the commencement date of the term that tenant fails to open its store for business. This remedy is in addition to any and all other remedies provided in this lease or by law to landlord in the event of default by tenant. Such additional base monthly rent will be deemed to be in lieu of any percentage rent that might have been earned during the period of tenant's failure to open.

§ 5.9   Requiring Completion of Other Parts of the Shopping Center and Occupancy by Other Tenants (Reserved)

§ 5.10   Allowing Early Occupancy

FORM 5.10(1)
TERM—EARLY OCCUPANCY

At tenant's request, made at any time after a temporary certificate of occupancy has been issued for the premises, landlord may permit tenant to occupy so much of the premises as tenant wishes to occupy prior to the commencement date. Landlord will cooperate with tenant in order to facilitate tenant's moving into the premises. If tenant occupies the premises prior to the commencement date with landlord's permission, all of the provisions of this lease will be in effect from the beginning of the occupancy; however, rent otherwise due under this lease will be abated up to the commencement date, and tenant will pay as rent landlord's actual costs (but in no event more than the base monthly rent that would have been due in the absence of any applicable abatements) incurred by reason of tenant's early occupancy.

§ 5.11   Implied Warranty of Fitness (Reserved)

§ 5.12   Lenders' Concerns about Term (Reserved)

§ 5.13   Option to Extend or Renew a Lease

FORM 5.13(1)
TERM—OPTION TO EXTEND AT NEW BASE MONTHLY RENT

Tenant may extend the term until the fifth anniversary of the expiration date by written notice of its election to do so given to landlord at leasy one year prior to the expiration date. The extended term will be on all of the terms and conditions of the lease applicable at the expiration date; however, tenant will have no further right to extend the term and the base monthly rent will be $[amount]. Tenant will not have any rights under this paragraph if (a) an event of default exists on the expiration date or on the date on which tenant gives its notice, or (b) tenant occupies less than [number] rentable square feet of the premises on the expiration date, or (c) tenant exercises its rights less than one year before the expiration date.

§ 5.14   —Notice (Reserved)

§ 5.15   —Terms of Renewal

FORM 5.15(1)
TERM—OPTION TO EXTEND AT MARKET RENT

(a)   Option Period. So long as tenant is not in default under this lease, either at the time of exercise or at the time the extended term commences, tenant will have the option to extend the initial five (5) year term of this lease for an additional period of five (5) years (the "option period") on the same terms, covenants, and conditions of this lease, except that the monthly rent during the option period will be determined pursuant to paragraph (b). Tenant will exercise its option by giving landlord written notice ("option notice") at least one hundred eighty (180) days but not more than two hundred seventy (270) days prior to the expiration of the initial term of this lease.

(b)   Option Period Monthly Rent. The initial monthly rent for the option period will be determined as follows:

(1)   Landlord and tenant will have fifteen (15) days after landlord receives the option notice within which to agree on the then-fair market rental value of the premises as defined in paragraph (b)(3), and rental increases to the monthly rent for the option period. If they agree on the initial monthly rent and rental increases for the option period within fifteen (15) days, they will amend this lease by stating the initial monthly rent and rental increases for the option period.

(2)   If they are unable to agree on the initial monthly rent and rental increases for the option period within fifteen (15) days, then, the initial monthly rent for the option period will be the then-fair market rental value of the premises as determined in accordance with paragraph (b)(4) and the periodic rental increases will be consistent with current market standards for rent increases at that time, in amounts and at frequencies determined by the appraisers pursuant to paragraph (b)(4).

(3)   The "then-fair market rental value of the premises" means what a landlord under no compulsion to lease the premises and a tenant under no

compulsion to lease the premises would determine as rents (including initial monthly rent and rental increases) for the option period, as of the commencement of the option period, taking into consideration the uses permitted under this lease, the quality, size, design, and location of the premises, and the rent for comparable buildings located in the vicinity of [* * *]. The then-fair market rental value of the premises and the rental increases in the monthly rent for the option period will not be less than that provided during the initial term.

(4)   Within seven (7) days after the expiration of the fifteen (15) day period set forth in paragraph (b)(2), landlord and tenant will each appoint a real estate appraiser with at least five (5) years' full-time commercial appraisal experience in the area in which the premises are located to appraise the then-fair market rental value of the premises. If either landlord or tenant does not appoint an appraiser within ten (10) days after the other has given notice of the name of its appraiser, the single appraiser appointed will be the sole appraiser and will set the then-fair market rental value of the premises. If two appraisers are appointed pursuant to this paragraph, they will meet promptly and attempt to set the then-fair market rental value of the premises. If they are unable to agree within thirty (30) days after the second appraiser has been appointed, they will attempt to elect a third appraiser meeting the qualifications stated in this paragraph within ten (10) days after the last day the two appraisers are given to set the then fair market rental value of the premises. If they are unable to agree on the third appraiser, either landlord or tenant, by giving ten (10) days' prior notice to the other, can apply to the then presiding judge of the [* * *] County Court for the selection of a third appraiser who meets the qualifications stated in this paragraph. Landlord and tenant will bear one-half ($\frac{1}{2}$) of the cost of appointing the third appraiser and of paying the third appraiser's fee. The third appraiser, however selected, must be a person who has not previously acted in any capacity for either landlord or tenant.

Within thirty (30) days after the selection of the third appraiser, a majority of the appraisers will set the then-fair market rental value of the premises. If a majority of the appraisers are unable to set the then-fair market rental value of the premises within thirty (30) days after selection of the third appraiser, the three appraisals will be averaged and the average will be the then-fair market rental value of the premises.

§ 5.16   Tenant's Option to Terminate Lease

FORM 5.16(1)
TERM—TENANT'S OPTION TO CANCEL THE LEASE

Tenant may cancel this lease according to this paragraph.

(a)   Tenant will give landlord at least thirty (30) days' prior written notice of tenant's election to cancel this lease.

(b)   Tenant may cancel this lease only as of the last day of a month (the "cancellation date"). The cancellation date will be stated in tenant's notice and will be no less than [* * *] ([* *]) days after the date of tenant's notice. At least ten (10) days before the cancellation date, as a condition of tenant's election, tenant will pay landlord in bank funds of (1) the unamortized portion of the commission paid by landlord to [* * *] in connection with this lease, and (2) the unamortized cost of the improvements (without consideration of any salvage value) made by landlord pursuant to [* * *], both as of the cancellation date, and (3) $[amount], as those amounts are determined and certified to tenant by landlord. The amortizations will be on a straight-line basis over the initial term of the lease.

(c)   Landlord may reject tenant's election to cancel this lease if an event of default has occurred at the time of its election.

(d)   If landlord does not reject tenant's election to cancel this lease, tenant will cure any event of default under this lease that exists on the cancellation date, and tenant's obligation to cure any such default within the period of time specified in this lease will survive the cancellation date.

(e)   On or prior to the cancellation date, tenant will surrender possession of the premises to landlord in accordance with the provisions of this lease, as if the cancellation date were the expiration date of this lease.

(f)   Upon cancellation, landlord and tenant will be relieved of their obligations under this lease, except for those accruing prior to the cancellation date.

CHAPTER 6

RENT

§ 6.1   **Fixed Rent**

§ 6.2   **"Free Rent" Arrangements (Reserved)**

§ 6.3   **Stepped Up Rent**

§ 6.4   **An Approach to Cost of Living Adjustments (Reserved)**

§ 6.5   **Preparing the Cost of Living Adjustment Provision**

§ 6.6   **Refining the Cost of Living Adjustment**

§ 6.7   **Common Mistakes in Cost of Living Adjustments (Reserved)**

§ 6.8   **Porters' Wage Escalations (Reserved)**

§ 6.9   **Operating Expense Escalations (Reserved)**

§ 6.10   **Operating Costs in Office Building Leases (Reserved)**

§ 6.11   **Preparing an Office Building Operating Expenses Provision**

§ 6.12   **"Grossing Up" Operating Expenses**

§ 6.13   **Comparing Several Office Leases (Reserved)**

§ 6.14   **Operating Expenses in Shopping Centers (Reserved)**

§ 6.15   **Operating Expenses in Single Tenant Leases**

§ 6.16   **An Approach to Percentage Rent (Reserved)**

§ 6.17   **Definition of Gross Sales**

§ 6.18   **Deductions and Exclusions from Gross Sales (Reserved)**

§ 6.19   **How to Choose an Appropriate Percentage Rate (Reserved)**

§ 6.20   **Computation and Payment Period**

§ 6.21   **Recordkeeping**

§ 6.22   **Verification**

§ 6.23   **Controlling Percentage Rent (Reserved)**

§ 6.24   **Lenders' Concerns about Rent (Reserved)**

§ 6.1 Fixed Rent

FORM 6.1(1)
RENT—BASIC PROVISION

Tenant will pay landlord $[* * *] (the "monthly rent") in equal consecutive monthly installments on or before the first day of each month during the term of this lease. The monthly rent will be paid in advance at the address specified for landlord in paragraph [notices], or at such other place as landlord designates, without prior demand and without any abatement, deduction, or setoff. If the commencement date occurs on a day other than the first day of a calendar month, or if the expiration date occurs on a day other than the last day of a calendar month, then the monthly rent for the fractional month will be prorated on a daily basis.

FORM 6.1(2)
RENT—BASIC PROVISION
(For Use with Basic Lease Information)

Tenant will pay landlord the monthly rent in equal consecutive monthly installments on or before the first day of each month during the term of this lease. The monthly rent will be paid in advance at the address specified for landlord in the basic lease information, or at such other place as landlord designates, without prior demand and without any abatement, deduction, or setoff. If the commencement date occurs on a day other than the first day of a calendar month, or if the expiration date occurs on a day other than the last day of a calendar month, then the monthly rent for the fractional month will be prorated on a daily basis.

FORM 6.1(3)
RENT—ADDITIONAL RENT

Tenant will pay landlord as additional rent without deduction or offset all amounts that this lease requires tenant to pay (the "additional rent"), including without limitation any increase in the monthly rent resulting from the provisions of [cost of living adjustment paragraph], at the place where the monthly rent is payable. Landlord will have the same remedies for a default in the payment of additional rent as it has for a default in the payment of monthly rent.

FORM 6.1(4)
RENT—LATE PAYMENT CHARGE

If tenant fails to pay any monthly rent or additional rent on the date they are due and payable, the unpaid amounts will be subject to a late payment charge equal to two percent (2%) of the unpaid amounts. This late payment charge is intended to compensate landlord for its additional administrative costs resulting from tenant's failure, and has been agreed upon by landlord and tenant, after negotiation, as a reasonable estimate of the additional administrative costs that will be incurred by landlord as a result of tenant's failure. The actual cost in each instance is extremely difficult, if not impossible, to determine. This late payment charge will constitute liquidated damages and will be paid to landlord together with such unpaid amounts. The payment of this late payment charge will not constitute a waiver by landlord of any default by tenant under this lease.

§ 6.2   "Free Rent" Arrangements (Reserved)

§ 6.3   Stepped Up Rent

FORM 6.3(1)
RENT—STEPPED UP RENT

Tenant will pay landlord as rent ("the rent"): $[amount] per month commencing on [date] 1, 19[00], and continuing up to and including [date] 1, 19[00]; $[amount] per month commencing on [date] 1, 19[00], and continuing up to and including [date] 1, 19[00]; $[amount] per month commencing on [date] 1, 19[00], and continuing up to and including [date] 1, 19[00]; $[amount] per month commencing on [date] 1, 19[00] and continuing up to and including [date] 1, 19[00]. The rent will be paid on or before the first day of each month during the term of this lease. The rent will be paid in advance at the address specified for landlord in the basic lease information, or at such other place as landlord designates, without prior demand and without any abatement, deduction, or setoff. If the commencement date occurs on a day other than the first day of a calendar month, or if the expiration date occurs on a day other than the last day of a calendar month, then the rent for such fractional month will be prorated on a daily basis.

FORM 6.3(2)
RENT—FIXED PERCENTAGE INCREASES

Tenant will pay landlord during the term, at landlord's office at the address set forth in the basic lease information or to such other persons or at such other places as directed from time to time by written notice to tenant from landlord, a monthly rental (the "base rent") in the amount set forth in the basic lease information due and payable without demand or offset or deduction, in advance on the first day of each calendar month. If the commencement date occurs on a day other than the first day of a calendar month, then the base rent for the fraction of the month starting with the commencement date will be paid on the commencement date, prorated on the basis of a 30-day month. The base rent will be increased every 12 months after the commence-ment date by 10% of the base rent payable during the prior 12 months.

§ 6.4 An Approach to Cost of Living Adjustments (Reserved)

§ 6.5 Preparing the Cost of Living Adjustment Provision

FORM 6.5(1)
RENT—CPI RENT ADJUSTMENT

The rent in paragraph [* *] will be adjusted according to this paragraph on each January 1 and July 1 during the term of this lease.

(a) In this paragraph,

(1) "base year" means the full calendar year during which the term of this lease commences.

(2) "price index" means the consumer price index published by the Bureau of Labor Statistics of the United States Department of Labor, U.S. City Average, All Items and Major Group Figures for Urban Wage Earners and Clerical Workers (1982–84 = 100).

(3) "price index for the base year" means the average of the monthly price indexes for each of the twelve (12) months of the base year.

(b) The January 1 adjustment will be based on the percentage difference between the price index for the preceding month of December and the price index for the the base year. The July 1 adjustment will be based on the percentage difference between the price index for the preceding month of June and the price index for the base year.

(1) If the price index for June in any calendar year during the term of this lease is greater than the price index for the base year, then the rent in paragraph [* *] payable on the next July 1 (without regard to any adjustments under this paragraph) will be multiplied by the percentage difference between the price index for June and the price index for the base year, and the product will be added to the rent in paragraph [* *] effective as of July 1. The adjusted annual rent will be payable until it is readjusted pursuant to the terms of this lease.

(2) If the price index for December in any calendar year during the term of this lease is greater than the price index for the base year, then the rent in paragraph [* *] payable on the next January 1 (without regard to any adjustments under this paragraph) will be multiplied by the percentage difference between the price index for December and the price index for the base year, and the product will be added to the rent in paragraph [* *] effective as of

January 1. The adjusted annual rent will be payable until it is readjusted pursuant to the terms of this lease.

If a substantial change is made in the price index, then the price index will be adjusted to the figure that would have been used had the manner of computing the price index in effect at the date of this lease not been altered. If the price index (or a successor or substitute index) is not available, a reliable governmental or other nonpartisan publication evaluating the information used in determining the price index will be used.

No adjustments will be made due to any revision that may be made in the price index for any month.

(c)   The statements of the adjustment to be furnished by landlord as provided in subparagraph (b) will consist of data prepared for the landlord by a firm of certified public accountants (which may be the firm now or then currently employed by landlord for the audit of its accounts). The statements thus furnished to tenant will constitute a final determination as between landlord and tenant of the relevant adjustment.

(d)   The rent in paragraph [* *] (exclusive of the adjustments under this paragraph) will not be reduced.

(e)   The landlord's delay or failure of landlord, beyond July 1 or January 1 of any year, in computing or billing for these adjustments will not impair the continuing obligation of tenant to pay rent adjustments.

(f)   Tenant's obligation to pay rent as adjusted by this paragraph will continue up to the expiration of this lease and will survive any earlier termination of this lease.

§ 6.6   Refining the Cost of Living Adjustment

FORM 6.6(1)
RENT—COST OF LIVING ADJUSTMENTS
(Tenant's Right to Terminate)

If rent is increased pursuant to (the cost of living paragraph) by more than [* *] % over the rent applicable during the prior twelve-month period, tenant may cancel this lease. This rental adjustment limitation will be applied on a twelve-month basis and will not be cumulative. Tenant will have 30 days after written notice from landlord of any such rent increase exceeding [* *] % in which to cancel this lease by written notice of cancellation to landlord. If tenant timely gives to landlord such a notice of cancellation, tenant will have an additional 30 days in which to give written notice to landlord of the effective date of cancellation, which cannot be later than [* * *] months after the written notice from landlord. If tenant fails to give landlord such notice, then the effective date of cancellation will be [* * *] months after the written notice from landlord. Tenant will be responsible for the increased rent until the effective date of cancellation even if the premises are vacated earlier.

FORM 6.6(2)
RENT—BIANNUAL ADJUSTMENT TO "MARKET"

Tenant will pay landlord during the term, at landlord's office at the address set forth in the basic lease information or to such other persons or at such other places as directed from time to time by written notice to tenant from landlord, a monthly rental (the "base rent") in the amount set forth in the basic lease information (subject to adjustment) due and payable without demand in advance on the first day of each calendar month. If the commencement date occurs on a day other than the first day of a calendar month, then the base rent for the fraction of the month starting with the commencement date will be paid on such commencement date, prorated on the basis of a 30-day month.

On every even numbered anniversary of the commencement date during the term, base rent will be adjusted upwards (but not downwards) to the then fair market base rent for the premises (the "fair market rent"). If landlord and tenant fail to agree on the fair market rent, the determination of the fair market rent will be submitted to an arbitrator in [city], who will be selected in accordance with the rules of the American Arbitration Association. If the arbitrator has not determined the fair market rent as of the anniversary date in question, tenant will temporarily pay landlord as base rent $[* * *] per square foot of rentable area per month until the arbitrator determines the fair market rent.

If the arbitrator's determination of the fair market rent exceeds $[amount] per square foot of rentable area, within 10 days after written notice of such determination tenant will pay landlord the total amount of the deficiency with interest at the same rate as landlord is then paying for its permanent financing on the building. If the arbitrator determines the fair market rent is less than $[amount] per square foot of rentable area, the excess base rent paid by tenant to landlord will be credited against the next rental payments coming due from tenant. The arbitrator will be paid by landlord if the decision is that the fair market rent is less than 95% of the amount demanded by landlord; by tenant if the decision is that the fair market rent is 105% or more of the amount demanded by landlord; and equally by landlord and tenant if the decision is other than those alternatives.

§ 6.7   Common Mistakes in Cost of Living Adjustments (Reserved)

§ 6.8   Porters' Wage Escalations (Reserved)

§ 6.9   Operating Expense Escalations (Reserved)

§ 6.10   Operating Costs in Office Building Leases (Reserved)

§ 6.11   Preparing an Office Building Operating Expenses Provision

FORM 6.11(1)
OPERATING EXPENSES (SHORT FORM)

In addition to the monthly rent payable during the term, tenant will pay tenant's share of the amount by which operating expenses paid or incurred by landlord in each calendar year or partial calendar year during the term exceed landlord's share for such period. If operating expenses are calculated for a partial calendar year, landlord's share will be appropriately prorated. If landlord's share exceeds operating expenses for any full year or partial year, then tenant will have no obligation to pay any part of the operating expenses for such period, and tenant will not be entitled to any adjustment of monthly rent. As used in this lease, the term "operating expenses" means:

(a)   all reasonable costs of management, operation, and maintenance of the project, including without limitation real property taxes (and any tax levied in whole or in part in lieu of real property taxes), wages, salaries and compensation of employees, janitorial, maintenance, guard and other services, reasonable reserves for operating expenses, that part of office rent or rental value of space in the project used by landlord to operate the project, power, water, waste disposal, and other utilities, materials and supplies, maintenance and repairs, insurance, and depreciation on personal property, and

(b)   the cost (amortized over such reasonable period as landlord determines, together with interest on the unamortized balance at the prime rate from time to time prevailing) of any capital improvements (i) that are made to the project by landlord during the term and that reduce other operating expenses, or (ii) that are made to the project by landlord after the date of this lease and that are required under any governmental law or regulation that was not applicable to the project at the time it was constructed.

Operating expenses will not include depreciation on the project (other than depreciation on exterior window coverings provided by landlord and carpeting in public corridors and common areas), costs of improvements made for other tenants of the project, real estate brokers' commissions, mortgage interest, and capital items other than those referred to in clause (b) above.

FORM 6.11(2)
OPERATING EXPENSES (LONG FORM)

The term "operating expenses" means all operating expenses of any kind or nature with respect to the building complex and includes without limitation:

(a)   the cost of building supplies;

(b)   costs incurred in connection with all energy sources for the building, such as propane, butane, natural gas, steam, electricity, solar energy, and fuel oil;

(c)   the costs of water and sewer service, janitorial services, general maintenance and repair of the building complex, including the heating and air conditioning systems and structural components of the building;

(d)   landscaping, maintenance, repair, and striping of all parking areas used by tenants of the building;

(e)   insurance, including fire and extended coverage and public liability insurance and any rental insurance and all risk insurance (if landlord decides to carry any of them), but tenant will have no interest in such insurance or the proceeds of such insurance, and any deductible paid by landlord.

(f)   labor costs incurred in the operation and maintenance of the building complex (including any health club, cafeteria, or other special facilities available to tenants of the building complex), including wages and other payments;

(g)   costs to landlord for workmen's compensation and disability insurance;

(h)   payroll taxes and welfare fringe benefits, including professional building management fees, architectural, engineering, and space planning costs, legal, accounting, inspection, and consultation fees incurred in connection with the building complex;

(i)   a general overhead and administrative charge equal to two percent (2%) of all other operating expenses incurred by landlord;

(j)   any expense attributable to costs incurred by landlord for any capital improvements or structural repairs to the building complex required by any change in the laws, ordinances, rules, regulations or otherwise that were not in effect on the date landlord obtained its building permit to construct the building complex or required by any governmental or quasi-governmental authority having jurisdiction over the building complex, which costs will be amortized over the useful life of the capital improvement or structural repair; and

(k)   any costs incurred by landlord in making capital improvements or other modifications to the building complex or any part of the building complex that reduce the operating expenses. These costs will be amortized over the useful life of such improvement or modification; however, the annual amortization amount will not exceed the reduction in operating expenses as projected by landlord's accountant for the relevant year, and the amortization schedule will be extended accordingly, if necessary.

FORM 6.11(3)
OPERATING EXPENSES—EXCLUSIONS

Operating expenses shall not include:

(a)   Costs of decorating, redecorating, special cleaning, or other services not provided on a regular basis to tenants of the building;

(b)   Wages, salaries, fees, and fringe benefits paid to administrative or executive personnel or officers or partners of landlord unless employed at competitive rates as independent contractors;

(c)   Any charge for depreciation of the building or equipment and any interest or other financing charge;

(d)   Any charge for landlord's income taxes, excess profit taxes, franchise taxes, or similar taxes on landlord's business;

(e)   All costs relating to activities for the solicitation and execution of leases of space in the building;

(f)   All costs and expenses of operating the garage space and commercial space in the building;

(g)   All costs for which tenant or any other tenant in the building is being charged other than pursuant to [the operating expense] clause;

(h)   The cost of any electric current furnished to the premises or any rentable area of the building for purposes other than the operation of building equipment and machinery and the lighting of public toilets, stairways, shaftways, and building machinery or fan rooms;

(i)   The cost of correcting defects in the construction of the building or in the building equipment, except that conditions (not occasioned by construction defects) resulting from ordinary wear and tear will not be deemed defects for the purpose of this category;

(j)   The cost of any repair made by landlord because of the total or partial destruction of the building or the condemnation of a portion of the building;

(k)   Any insurance premium to the extent that landlord is entitled to be reimbursed for it by tenant pursuant to this lease or by any tenant of the building pursuant to a similar lease other than pursuant to clauses comparable to this [paragraph];

(l)   The cost of any items for which landlord is reimbursed by insurance or otherwise compensated by parties other than tenants of the building pursuant to clauses similar to this [paragraph];

(m)   The cost of any additions or capital improvements to the building subsequent to the date of original construction;

(n)   The cost of any repairs, alterations, additions, changes, replacements, and other items that under generally accepted accounting principles are properly classified as capital expenditures to the extent they upgrade or improve the building as opposed to replace existing items that have worn out;

(o)   Any operating expense representing an amount paid to a related corporation, entity, or person that is in excess of the amount that would be paid in the absence of such relationship;

(p)   The cost of tools and equipment used initially in the construction, operation, repair, and maintenance of the building;

(q)   The cost of any work or service performed for or facilities furnished to any tenant of the building to a greater extent or in a manner more favorable to such tenant than that performed for or furnished to tenant;

(r)   The cost of alterations of space in the building leased to other tenants; and

(s)   The cost of overtime or other expense to landlord in curing its defaults or performing work expressly provided in this lease to be borne at landlord's expense;

(t)   Amounts paid (including interest) on account of or to cure statutes, laws, notes, or ordinances by landlord or any part of the building.

FORM 6.11(4)
OPERATING EXPENSES—EXCLUSIONS
(Another Form)

Operating expenses will exclude any costs or expenses not specifically authorized in this (operating expense paragraph), including:

(a)   any and all capital costs, except as permitted under (specific list of permitted capital expenses);

(b)   any and all depreciation or amortization of the building or any portion or component of the building or any equipment or other property, except as permitted under (specific list of permitted capital expenses);

(c)   any and all loan payments, principal or interest, or ground lease, or similar payments;

(d)   any and all leasing costs, including brokerage commissions, legal fees, vacancy costs, and refurbishment or improvement expenses;

(e)   any and all collection costs, including legal fees and bad debt losses or reserves;

(f)   any otherwise permissible fees or costs, to the extent in excess of prevailing and competitive rates;

(g)   any costs or expenses resulting from landlord's violation of any agreement to which it is a party or any applicable laws or ordinances or governmental rules, regulations, or orders;

(h)   any documentary transfer taxes imposed in connection with the lease or any other lease; and

(i)   any increase in property taxes attributable to or as a result of any sale, refinancing, transfer, or change of ownership in the building, or any portion of or interest in the building, whether directly or otherwise.

FORM 6.11(5)
OPERATING EXPENSES—TENANT'S VERIFICATION RIGHT

Tenant will be entitled from time to time to audit and verify the operations of the building and the related books and records of landlord to assure that the operating expenses from time to time reported by landlord are in keeping with the provisions of this (operating expense paragraph). As to any calendar year, any undertaking by tenant must be initiated before the end of the following calendar year; and absent fraud or gross negligence on landlord's part, the operating expenses as timely reported by landlord for the calendar year will be deemed controlling upon the expiration of tenant's audit and verification rights for such calendar year. In the event of any errors, the appropriate party will make a correcting payment in full to the other party within 30 days after the determination and communication to all parties of the amount of such error. In the event of any errors on the part of landlord in excess of 3% of tenant's actual operating expenses liability for that calendar year, landlord will also reimburse tenant for all costs of the audit and verification reasonably incurred by tenant within the 30-day period. Within 3 months of the commencement date, tenant will be entitled to verify the rentable building area, the rental premises, the usable premises area, and the tenant share. In the event of any errors, these terms will be restated to eliminate the errors. In the event of any errors in excess of 3% of the actual amounts, landlord will also reimburse tenant for all costs of the verification reasonably incurred by tenant within 30 days after the determination and communication to all parties of the amount of the error. In the event of any dispute or difference between the parties under this paragraph, such dispute or difference will be resolved pursuant to the provisions of (arbitration paragraph).

§ 6.12   "Grossing Up" Operating Expenses

FORM 6.12(1)
OPERATING EXPENSES—"GROSSING UP"

The operating expenses that vary with occupancy and that are attributable to any part of the term in which less than 95% of the rentable area of the building is occupied by tenants will be adjusted by landlord to the amount landlord reasonably believes such expenses would have been if 95% of the rentable area of the building had been occupied.

§ 6.13   Comparing Several Office Leases (Reserved)

§ 6.14   Operating Expenses in Shopping Centers (Reserved)

§ 6.15   Operating Expenses in Single Tenant Leases

FORM 6.15(1)
OPERATING EXPENSES—"NET" RENT PAYMENTS

The rent will be a net rental payment. All costs of maintenance, repairs, utilities, taxes, insurance, and any and all other expenses necessary in connection with the operation or maintenance of the premises will be paid solely by tenant during this lease.

§ 6.16   An Approach to Percentage Rent (Reserved)

§ 6.17   Definition of Gross Sales

FORM 6.17(1)
PERCENTAGE RENT—DEFINITION OF GROSS SALES

"Gross sales" means the actual sales or rental price of all goods, wares, and merchandise sold, leased, licensed, or delivered, and the actual charges for all services performed by the tenant or by any subtenant, licensee, or concessionaire in, at, from, or arising out of the use of the premises, wholesale and retail, whether for cash, credit, exchange, or otherwise, without reserve or deduction for inability or failure to collect. Gross sales will include without limitation, sales, rentals, and services:

(a)   when the orders for them originate in, at, from, or arising out of the use of the premises, whether delivery or performance is made from the premises or from some other place;

(b)   made or performed by mail, telephone, or telegraph orders;

(c)   made or performed by means of mechanical or other vending devices in the premises; or

(d)   that tenant or any subtenant, licensee, concessionaire, or other person in the normal and customary course of its business would credit or attribute to its operations in any part of the premises.

Any deposit that is not refunded will be included in gross sales. Each installment sale or credit sale will be treated as a sale for the full price in the month during which the sale is made, regardless of whether or when tenant receives payment for it. Gross sales will not be reduced by any franchise, occupancy, capital stock, income, or similar tax based on income or profits.

FORM 6.17(2)
PERCENTAGE RENT—GROSS SALES
(Another Definition)

"Gross sales" means the aggregate selling price of all merchandise and services sold in, upon, or from the premises by tenant, its subtenants, licensees, and concessionaires, personally or from salesmen operating out of the premises when sales are not made in, upon, or from the premises, or from any vending or coin-operated or token-operated device, whether for cash or on credit, excluding only:

(a)   Goods returned to suppliers or which are delivered to another store of tenant or to a warehouse of tenant or to other retailers without profit to tenant, when such deliveries are made solely for the convenient operation of the business of tenant and not for the purpose of consummating a sale made in, upon, or from the premises;

(b)   Monies and credits received by tenant in the settlement of claims for loss of or damage to tenant's merchandise;

(c)   The amount of cash refunded or credit allowed on merchandise returned by customers and accepted by tenant, or the amount of cash refunded or credit allowed in lieu of tenant's acceptance of the merchandise, but only to the extent that the sales relating to such merchandise were made in, upon, or from the premises; however, the cost or value of any trading stamps, premiums, advertising, or other promotional devices will not be deducted or excluded from gross sales or be otherwise construed as a discount, refund, allowance, or credit;

(d)   Sales taxes, so-called luxury taxes, consumer excise taxes, gross receipts taxes, and other similar taxes imposed upon the sale of merchandise or services, or both, whether such taxes are added separately to the selling price and collected from customers or are paid by tenant and included in the retail selling price;

(e)   Sales cancelled, but only to the extent of the purchase price not retained by tenant;

(f)   Interest, service, or sales carrying charges paid by customers for extension of credit on sales and not included in the merchandise sales price;

(g)   Receipts from public telephones, stamp machines, and vending machines installed solely for the use of tenant's employees;

(h)   Bad debts and bad checks, to the extent the same do not exceed 1% of gross sales annually; and

(i)   Employee discount sales, to the extent the same do not exceed 1% of gross sales annually.

All sales originating at, upon, or from the premises will be considered as made and completed at the premises and will be included in gross sales, even though bookkeeping and payment of the account may be transferred to another place for collection, and even though actual filling of the sale or order or actual delivery of the merchandise may be made from a place other than the premises.

FORM 6.17(3)
PERCENTAGE RENT—GROSS SALES, EXCLUSIONS AND DEDUCTIONS
(Another Form)

Gross Sales. "Gross sales" means all revenues received by tenant for all goods sold and services rendered from the premises, whether by mail, telephone, or otherwise, for cash or credit, excluding:

(a) all credits for or in lieu of "trade-ins", and all refunds made to tenant's customers;

(b) returns to suppliers or manufacturers;

(c) amounts received at the premises for convenience only, for sales made or services rendered at other premises of tenant;

(d) sales, excise, and gross receipt taxes on such goods;

(e) transfers to other premises of tenant for convenience only;

(f) amounts received by tenant for settlement of any claim of tenant;

(g) charges for customer service, including deliveries, repairs, installations, alterations and costs for use of credit cards;

(h) interest, service, carrying charges or charges for layaway (in excess of the sale price of any such goods);

(i) the cost of any premium plans, promotional give-aways (such as trading stamps and games);

(j) receipts from pay telephones, stamp machines, public toilets, lockers, vending machines, coin or token operated games and amusement devices;

(k) discount sales to employees;

(l) sale price of any inventory sold in bulk;

(m) sales price of fixtures, equipment or property sold not in the ordinary course of business;

(n) gift certificates until redeemed;

(o) receipts from sale of hunting and fishing licenses, money orders, and government-run lottery tickets;

(p) the amounts of accounts receivable charged off as bad debts.

§ 6.18   Deductions and Exclusions from Gross Sales
(Reserved)

§ 6.19   How to Choose an Appropriate Percentage
Rate (Reserved)

§ 6.20   Computation and Payment Period

FORM 6.20(1)
PERCENTAGE RENT—COMPUTATION AND PAYMENT PERIOD

Tenant will pay landlord percentage rent in the amount by which [* * *] percent ([* *]%) of tenant's gross sales during each year exceeds the minimum rent paid by tenant for such year. Beginning within ten (10) days after the month in which the term commences and continuing within (10) days after each month during the term, tenant will furnish landlord a statement of gross sales during the preceding month and tenant will pay landlord the amount by which [* * *] percent ([* *]%) of gross sales during the preceding month exceeds the minimum rent paid for such month.

FORM 6.20(2)
PERCENTAGE RENT—COMPUTATION AND PAYMENT PERIOD
(Tenant's Form)

For each lease year, tenant will first pay percentage rent for the month in which the aggregate of gross sales for the lease year multiplied by 6% exceeds the minimum rent for the lease year, and tenant will continue to pay percentage rent monthly on all additional gross sales made during the remainder of the lease year concurrently with the submission by tenant to landlord of the written statement of monthly gross sales.

§ 6.21   Recordkeeping

FORM 6.21(1)
PERCENTAGE RENT—RECORDKEEPING

(a)   Each statement of gross sales furnished by tenant will be certified as correct by tenant or an employee of tenant authorized to so certify and will show the computations of gross sales for tenant and each of its subtenants, licensees, and concessionaires separately.

(b)   For the purpose of ascertaining the amount of gross sales, tenant will record each and every sale at the time of the transaction on either a cash register having a sealed, continuous cash register tape with cumulative totals that numbers, records, and duplicates each transaction entered into the register, or on serially prenumbered sales slips. If tenant chooses to record each sale by using a cash register, the continuous cash register tape will be sealed or locked in such a manner that it is not accessible to the person operating the cash register. If tenant chooses to record each sale on individual sales slips, the sales slips (including those canceled, voided, or not used) will be retained in numerical sequence for three (3) years.

(c)   Tenant will prepare, preserve, and maintain, each lease year for a period of not less than three (3) years these books, accounts and records:

(1)   daily cash register summary tapes (normally referred to as "Z tapes") and sealed, continuous cash register tapes or prenumbered sales slips;

(2)   a single, separate bank account into which all receipts of business or other revenue from operations on or from the premises are deposited;

(3)   all bank statements detailing transactions in or through any business bank account;

(4)   daily or weekly sales recapitulations;

(5)   a sales journal;

(6)   a general ledger or a summary record of all cash receipts and disbursements from operations on or from the premises;

(7)   copies of all tax returns filed with any governmental authority that reflect in any manner sales, income, or revenue generated in or from the premises, including, but not limited to, federal income tax returns and state sales or use tax returns;

(8)   other records or accounts that landlord may reasonably require in order to ascertain, document, or substantiate gross sales.

FORM 6.21(2)
PERCENTAGE RENT—RECORDKEEPING
(Tenant's Suggestion)

Landlord will not audit tenant's records more than once each lease year. Only tenant's records pertaining to operations from the premises may be reviewed or inspected. Landlord will not have the right to inspect or audit any of tenant's books or records that reflect any of tenant's operations at any other location or with which records of tenant's operations at the premises have been consolidated or combined with records of the operations are of tenant or any affiliate of any other locations of tenant or affiliates. All information pertaining to tenant's gross sales, books, and records will be held in strict confidence by landlord, its agents, and employees, except as may be required for prospective purchasers or lenders.

§ 6.22   Verification

FORM 6.22(1)
PERCENTAGE RENT—LANDLORD'S RIGHT TO
AUDIT TENANT'S REPORTS

All of the books, records, and other documents will be maintained at the premises and in the manner recited in this paragraph, and will be open to inspection, examination, or audit by landlord or landlord's designated representative upon giving tenant five (5) days' prior notice of landlord's intention to exercise its rights under this paragraph. In connection with an examination or audit, landlord will have the right to inspect the records of sales from any other store operated by tenant, but only if the examination is reasonably necessary to ascertain gross sales from the premises. If upon inspection or examination of tenant's available books and records of account, landlord determines that tenant has failed to maintain, preserve, or retain the documents, books, and records that this lease requires tenant to maintain in the manner set forth in this paragraph, landlord will give the tenant sixty (60) days to cure the deficiencies. Further, if tenant is found to be deficient in maintaining any of documents, books, or records, tenant will reimburse landlord for all reasonable expenses incurred by landlord in determining the deficiencies, including without limitation any audit or examination fees.

§ 6.23   Controlling Percentage Rent (Reserved)

§ 6.24   Lenders' Concerns about Rent (Reserved)

PART III

ADDITIONAL EXPENSES FOR THE TENANT

CHAPTER 7

TAXES AND ASSESSMENTS

§ 7.1   Introduction (Reserved)

§ 7.2   Definition of Taxes

§ 7.3   Taxes and the Single Tenant Building

§ 7.4   Net Tax Provision in a Multitenant Development

§ 7.5   Base Amount Tax Provision in a Multitenant Development

§ 7.6   Base Year Tax Provision in a Multitenant Development

§ 7.1   Introduction (Reserved)

§ 7.2   Definition of Taxes

FORM 7.2(1)
TAXES—DEFINITION

"Taxes" means the aggregate amount of real estate taxes, water and sewer rents, and any general or special assessments (exclusive of penalties and interest) imposed upon the property, including without limitation:

(1) assessments made upon or with respect to any air and development rights at any time appurtenant to the property;

(2) any fee, tax, or charge imposed by any governmental authority for any vaults, vault space, or other space within or outside the boundaries of the property, except that if the vault fee, tax, or charge is payable by any tenant (including tenant) directly to the governmental authority, the vault fee, tax, or charge will not be considered as part of taxes for the tax year in which the vault fee, tax, or charge is so paid; and

(3) any assessments levied after the date of this lease for public benefits to the property (excluding an amount equal to the assessments payable in whole or in part during or for the first tax year, which assessments, if payable in installments, will be deemed payable in the maximum number of permissible installments) in the manner in which taxes and assessments are imposed as of the date of this lease.

If, because of any change in the taxation of real estate, any other tax or assessment (including without limitation any franchise, income, profit, sales, use, occupancy, gross receipts, or rental tax) is imposed upon landlord as the owner of the property or the building, or the occupancy, rents, or income from either of them, in substitution for any taxes, such other tax or assessment, computed as if the property were landlord's sole asset, will be deemed part of taxes. All expenses, including attorneys' fees and disbursements, experts' and other witnesses' fees, incurred in contesting the validity or amount of any taxes or in obtaining a refund of taxes will be considered as part of the taxes for the tax year in which the expenses are incurred.

§ 7.3   Taxes and the Single Tenant Building

FORM 7.3(1)
TAXES—SINGLE TENANT BUILDING

(a)   Obligation for Payment. Tenant will pay all taxes (collectively the "tax"), including without limitation real estate and personal property taxes and assessments assessed, levied, confirmed, or imposed during the term of this lease (other than net income taxes) whether or not now customary or within the contemplation of landlord and tenant:

(1)   upon, measured by, or reasonably attributable to the cost or value of tenant's equipment, furniture, fixtures, and other personal property located in the premises or by the cost or value of any leasehold improvements made in or to the premises by or for tenant, regardless of whether title to such improvements is in tenant or landlord;

(2)   upon or measured by the monthly rent, including without limitation any gross receipts tax or excise tax levied by the federal government or any other governmental body with respect to the receipt of monthly rent;

(3)   upon or with respect to the possession, leasing, operation, management, maintenance, alteration, repair, use, or occupancy by tenant of the premises or any portion of the premises;

(4)   upon this transaction or any document to which tenant is a party creating or transferring an interest or an estate in the premises;

(5)   upon the premises and all personal property, furniture, fixtures, and equipment, and all replacements, improvements, or additions to them, whether owned by landlord or tenant; and

(6)   impositions based in whole or in part on monthly rent, whether made in addition to or in substitution for any other tax.

(b)   Taxes Payable in Installments. Unless landlord has exercised its rights under subparagraph (f), and if, by law, any tax may at the option of the taxpayer be paid in installments (whether or not interest accrues on the unpaid balance of such tax), tenant may exercise the option to pay the tax (and any accrued interest on the unpaid balance of such tax) in installments and in that event tenant will pay the installments as they become due during the term of this lease and before any fine, penalty, further interest, or cost may be added to them.

(c)   Taxes for Period Other than Term. Any tax, including taxes that have been converted into installment payments, relating to a fiscal period of the taxing authority, a part of which is included within the term and a part of which is included in a period of time prior to the commencement or after the end of the term, will, whether or not such tax or installments are assessed, levied, confirmed, imposed upon, in respect of, or become a lien upon the premises, or become payable, during the term, be adjusted between landlord and tenant as of the commencement or end of the term, so that tenant will pay the portion of the tax or installment that the part of the fiscal period included in the term bears to the entire fiscal period, and landlord will pay the remainder.

(d)   Other Impositions. Tenant will not be obligated to pay local, state, or federal net income taxes assessed against landlord; local, state, or federal capital levy of landlord; or sales, excise, franchise, gift, estate, succession, inheritance, or transfer taxes of landlord.

(e)   Right to Contest Taxes. Tenant will have the right to contest the amount or validity, in whole or in part, of any tax by appropriate proceedings diligently conducted in good faith, only after paying such tax or posting security that landlord reasonably requires in order to protect the premises against loss or forfeiture. Upon the termination of any proceedings, tenant will pay the amount of the tax or part of the tax as finally determined, the payment of which may have been deferred during the prosecution of the proceedings, together with any costs, fees, interest, penalties, or other related liabilities. Landlord will not be required to join in any contest or proceedings unless the provisions of any law or regulations then in effect require that the proceedings be brought by or in the name of landlord. In that event landlord will join in the proceedings or permit them to be brought in its name; however, landlord will not be subjected to any liability for the payment of any costs or expenses in connection with any contest or proceedings, and tenant will indemnify landlord against and save landlord harmless from any costs and expenses.

(f)   Estimated Payments. If any lender requires landlord to do so, then, in each December during the term or as soon after December as practicable, landlord will give tenant written notice of its estimate of amounts payable under subparagraph (a) for the ensuing calendar year. On or before the first day of each month during the ensuing calendar year, tenant will pay to landlord one-twelfth ($^1/_{12}$th) of the estimated amounts; however, if notice is not given in December, tenant will continue to pay on the basis of the prior year's estimate until the month after notice is given. If at any time or times it appears to landlord that the amounts payable under subparagraph (a) for the current calendar year will vary from its estimate by more than ten percent (10%), landlord will, by written notice to tenant, revise its estimate for the year, and subsequent payments by tenant for the year will be based upon the revised estimate.

(g)   Final Settlement. Within ninety (90) days after the close of each calendar year or as soon after such ninety-day period as practicable, landlord will deliver to tenant a statement of amounts payable under subparagraph (a) for the calendar year prepared by certified public accountants designated by landlord, or prepared by landlord and certified by one of its officers, and the certified statement will be final and binding upon landlord and tenant. If the statement shows an amount owing by tenant that is less than the estimated payments previously made by tenant for the calendar year, the statement will be accompanied by a refund of the excess by landlord to tenant. If the statement shows an amount owing by tenant that is more than the estimated payments previously made by tenant for the calendar year, tenant will pay the deficiency to landlord within thirty (30) days after the delivery of the statement.

§ 7.4   Net Tax Provision in a Multitenant Development

FORM 7.4(1)
TAXES—NET TAX PROVISION IN A MULTITENANT DEVELOPMENT

(a)   In addition to the base monthly rental payable during the term of this lease, tenant will pay as additional rental tenant's percentage share of the amount of property taxes levied against the building for each calendar year of the term of this lease.

(b)   On or before the first day of the term of this lease, or as soon after that day as practicable, landlord will give tenant written notice of landlord's estimate of the additional rental payable under subparagraph (a) for the remainder of that calendar year. During December of each calendar year or as soon after December as practicable, landlord will give tenant notice of its estimate of the payments to be made pursuant to subparagraph (a) for the ensuing calendar year. On or before the first day of each month during the ensuing calendar year, tenant will pay to landlord one-twelfth ($^{1}/_{12}$th) of the estimated amount; however, if the notice is not given in December, tenant will continue to pay on the basis of the prior year's estimate until the month after the notice is given. If at any time or times it appears to landlord that the payments to be made under subparagraph (a) for the current calendar year will vary from its estimate by more than five percent (5%), landlord will, by notice to tenant, revise its estimate for the year, and subsequent payments by tenant for the year will be based upon the revised estimate.

(c)   Within ninety (90) days after the close of each calendar year or as soon after the ninety-day period as practicable, landlord will deliver to tenant (i) a statement of property taxes for the calendar year certified by certified public accountants designated by landlord, which certified statement will be final and binding upon landlord and tenant, and (ii) a statement of the payments made or to be made under subparagraph (a) for the calendar year that has been prepared on the basis of the certified statement. If on the basis of those statements tenant owes an amount that is less than the estimated payments for the calendar year previously made by tenant, landlord will credit the excess to the next succeeding monthly installment of rent. If on the basis of those statements tenant owes an amount that is more than the estimated payments for such calendar year previously made by tenant, tenant will pay the deficiency to landlord within thirty (30) days after delivery of those statements.

(d)   If this lease commences on a day other than the first day of the calendar year or ends on a day other than the last day of a calendar year, the amount of the payments pursuant to this paragraph payable by tenant with respect to the year in which such commencement or end occur will be prorated on the basis that the number of days of the term included in the year bears to 365. The end of this lease will not affect the obligations of landlord and tenant pursuant to subparagraph (c).

(e)   The term "property taxes" means any form of real or personal property taxes, assessments, special assessments, fees, charges, levies, penalties, service payments in lieu of taxes, excises, assessments, and charges for transit, housing, or any other purposes, impositions or taxes of every kind and nature whatsoever, assessed or levied or imposed by any authority having the direct or indirect power to tax, including without limitation any city, county, state, or federal government, or any improvement or assessment district of any kind, whether or not consented to or joined in by tenant, against the building or any legal or equitable interest of landlord in the building or any personal property of landlord used in the operation of the building, whether now imposed or imposed in the future, whether or not now customary or in the contemplation of landlord and tenant on the date of this lease, excepting only taxes measured by the net income of landlord from all sources.

§ 7.5   Base Amount Tax Provision in a Multitenant Development

FORM 7.5(1)
TAXES—BASE AMOUNT TAX PROVISION
(Base Is Stated As A Dollar Amount)

(a)   Tenant will pay all real estate taxes assessed against the building, building complex, or premises during the term of this lease; however, landlord agrees to expend as its share of real estate taxes during any calendar year $[amount] (the "base real estate taxes").

"Real estate taxes" will include:

(1)   any form of tax or assessment (including any so-called "special" assessment), license fee, license tax, business license fee, business license tax, commercial rental tax, levy, charge, penalty, or tax, imposed by any authority having the direct power to tax, including any city, county, state, or federal government, or any school, agricultural, lighting, water, drainage, or other improvement or special district, against the premises, the building, or building complex, or any legal or equitable interest of landlord in any of them;

(2)   any tax on landlord's right to rent the premises or against landlord's business of leasing the premises; and

(3)   any assessment, tax, fee, levy, or charge in substitution, partially or totally, of or in addition to any assessment, tax, fee, levy, or charge previously

included within the definition of real estate taxes that may be imposed by governmental agencies for services such as fire protection, street, sidewalk and road maintenance, refuse removal, and for other governmental services formerly provided without charge to property owners or occupants. All new and increased assessments, taxes, fees, levies, and charges will be included within the definition of real estate taxes for purposes of this lease. Tenant will pay landlord the entire amount of:

(i)   any tax allocable to or measured by the area of the premises or the rental payable under this lease, including without limitation any gross income, privilege, sales, or excise tax levied by the state, any political subdivision of the premises, city, municipal, or federal government, with respect to the receipt of such rental, or upon or with respect to the possession, leasing, operating, management, maintenance, alteration, repair, use, or occupancy by tenant of the premises or any portion of the premises; and

(ii)   any tax upon this transaction, or upon any document to which tenant is a party, creating or transferring an interest or an estate in the premises.

"Real estate taxes" will not include landlord's federal or state income, franchise, inheritance, or estate taxes.

(b)   Within ninety (90) days after the end of each calendar year, landlord will furnish tenant a written comparative statement showing the calculations described in this paragraph and state the increases, if any, for the then-current year. Commencing with the next month following such statement, tenant will pay landlord a lump sum equal to one-twelfth ($1/12$th) of the annual increase for each month of the immediate preceding calendar year and for each month of the current calendar year that has passed since the commencement date of this lease. With the same payment, tenant will commence payment to the landlord of one-twelfth ($1/12$th) of the annual increase by adding that amount to the regular monthly rent installments. The increased monthly rent installments will continue until landlord gives tenant the next written notice calculating any additional rent increases for future calendar years, to which the same procedures for payment will apply. If the total additional rent payments by tenant to landlord for any future calendar years are found at year end to vary from the actual additional rents due for that year, tenant will pay landlord any deficiency as additional rent upon notice of the actual amount, and landlord will credit any excess to the next succeeding additional rent installments becoming due. Any such excess in the last year of this lease will be refunded by landlord to tenant within sixty (60) days after the expiration of the lease, but only if tenant is not in default and has vacated the premises.

Even though the term of this lease has ended and tenant has vacated the premises, when the final determination is made of tenant's share of real estate taxes for the year in which this lease ends, tenant will pay any increase due over the estimated real estate taxes within sixty (60) days after delivery of a statement for them, and, conversely, within sixty (60) days after the end of the term, landlord will rebate any overpayment due of estimated real estate taxes. Tenant will not be relieved of its obligation to pay to landlord any amount due pursuant to this paragraph if landlord fails, for any reason, to provide its comparative statement within the time provided.

§ 7.6 Base Year Tax Provision in a Multitenant Development

FORM 7.6(1)
TAXES—BASE YEAR TAX PROVISION
(Base Is Stated as a Particular Year)

The rental payable during each calendar year in the term of this lease subsequent to the tax year ending [date], 19[00] (the "base tax year") will be increased by tenant's percentage share of the total dollar increase, if any, in real property taxes (and any tax levied wholly or partly in lieu of real property taxes) levied against the building for the tax year, over the taxes for the base tax year. Taxes for the base tax year will be determined by multiplying the assessed valuation of the building for the base tax year by the tax rate actually in effect for the tax year ending [date], 19[00].

During December of each calendar year, or as soon after each December as practicable, landlord will give tenant written notice of its estimate of amounts payable under the preceding paragraph for the ensuing calendar year. On or before the first day of each month during the ensuing calendar year, tenant will pay to landlord one-twelfth ($1/12$th) of the estimated amounts; however, if notice is not given in December, tenant will continue to pay on the basis of the prior year's estimate until the month after notice is given. If at any time the amounts payable under the preceding paragraph for the current calendar year will vary from the estimate by more than five percent (5%), landlord will, by written notice to tenant, revise its estimate for the year, and subsequent payments by tenant for the year will be based upon such revised estimate.

Within ninety (90) days after the end of each calendar year or as soon after the ninety-day period as practicable, landlord will deliver to tenant a statement of amounts payable under this section for the calendar year. The statement will be certified by certified public accountants designated by landlord, and the certified statement will be final and binding upon landlord and tenant. If the statement shows an amount owing by tenant that is less than the estimated payments for the calendar year previously made by tenant, the statement will be accompanied by a refund of the excess by landlord to tenant. If the statement shows an amount owing by tenant that is more than the estimated payments for the calendar year previously made by tenant, tenant will pay the deficiency to landlord within thirty (30) days after delivery of the statement.

If, for any reason other than the default of tenant, this lease ends on a day other than the last day of a calendar year, the amount of increase (if any) in rental payable by tenant applicable to the calendar year in which the end occurs will be prorated on the basis that the number of days from the commencement of such calendar year to and including the end date bears to 365.

FORM 7.6(2)
TAXES—BASE YEAR

(a)　For the purposes of this section:

(1)　"Tax year" means each successive real estate fiscal year commencing on [date] and expiring on [date]. If the present use of the tax year changes, the changed tax year will be used with appropriate adjustment for the transition.

(2)　"Taxes" means the total of all real estate taxes, assessments, special and extraordinary assessments, and government levies imposed upon or with respect to the land and building of which the premises are a part, and any franchise, income, profit, value added, use, or other tax imposed in addition to, in whole or partial substitution for, or in lieu of an increase (in whole or part) in such taxes, whether due to a change in the method of taxation or otherwise.

(3)　"Base tax" means the taxes for the tax year [date], 19[* *], to [date], 19[* *].

(b)　The annual rent will be increased for each tax year during the term of this lease by [* *]% of the amount by which the taxes landlord is required to pay in each such tax year exceed the base tax. Landlord will advise tenant, in a written statement by landlord's accountant or by landlord or its agent, of any change in taxes and the effective date of the change. The statement will show tenant's new annual rent caused by each change, and the manner in which the adjustment is computed, including any adjustments in real estate tax assessments affecting the taxes for any tax year. The monthly installments will be $1/12$ of that amount. The increase will be due and payable with monthly installments of minimum rent. If taxes are required to be paid prior to the expiration of any tax year to avoid a penalty or late charge, then landlord may immediately elect to bill tenant for its share of any increase in taxes in excess of the base tax with respect to such calendar quarter or tax year, as the case may be, and tenant will pay its share within 5 days. To the extent that the change is relevant to a period for which tenant has paid its monthly installments of minimum rent, a lump sum payment will be made by tenant when billed by landlord. Any decrease in annual rent under this paragraph can be applied only to reduce prior increases under this paragraph.

(c)　Landlord's failure to render a statement with respect to any increases in the taxes will not prejudice landlord's right to render a statement retroactively with respect to any increase in the taxes or with respect to any subsequent tax year. The obligations of tenant under the provisions of this section with respect to any increase in the rent will survive the expiration or termination of the term. All sums payable by tenant to landlord pursuant to the provisions of this section will be collectible by landlord in the same manner as any installment of minimum rent.

CHAPTER 8

UTILITIES

§ 8.1 Utilities in Single Tenant Building Lease

§ 8.2 Utilities in Shopping Center Lease

§ 8.3 Utilities in Office Building Lease

§ 8.4 Direct Metering, Submetering, and Electric Rent Inclusion (Reserved)

§ 8.1   Utilities in Single Tenant Building Lease

FORM 8.1(1)
UTILITIES—SINGLE TENANT BUILDING

Tenant will pay the appropriate suppliers for all water, gas, electricity, light, heat, telephone, power, and other utilities and communications services used by tenant on the premises during the term, whether or not such services are billed directly to tenant. Tenant will also procure, or cause to be procured, without cost to landlord, any and all necessary permits, licenses, or other authorizations required for the lawful and proper installation and maintenance upon the premises of wires, pipes, conduits, tubes, and other equipment and appliances for use in supplying any such service to and upon the premises. Landlord, upon request of tenant, and at the sole expense and liability of tenant, will join with tenant in any application required for obtaining or continuing any such services.

FORM 8.1(2)
UTILITIES—TENANT'S ASSURANCE OF UTILITIES

Landlord warrants to tenant that electricity, water, sanitary and drainage sewers, telephone, and natural gas will be available at the outside wall of the building throughout the term of this lease. If any such utility service becomes unavailable or is interrupted for more than [* * *] ([* *]) consecutive days (without default by tenant), tenant may terminate this lease by notice to landlord given within [* * *] ([* *]) days after such services become unavailable, or within [* * *] ([* *]) days after the ninetieth (90th) day of interruption, as the case may be. The notice will specify a termination date no more than thirty

(30) days after the date of such notice. This lease will end on the termination date, and rent and other charges will be appropriately prorated between landlord and tenant as of the termination date.

§ 8.2   Utilities in Shopping Center Lease

FORM 8.2(1)
UTILITIES—SHOPPING CENTER LEASE

Tenant will pay all initial utility deposits and fees, and all monthly service charges for water, electricity, sewage, gas, telephone, and any other utility services furnished to the premises and the improvements on the premises during the entire term of this lease. If any such services are not separately metered or billed to tenant but rather are billed to and paid by landlord, tenant will pay to landlord its pro rata share of the cost of such services, as determined by landlord, together with its pro rata share of the cost of making such determination. Landlord will not be liable for any reason for any loss or damage resulting from an interruption of any of these services.

FORM 8.2(2)
UTILITIES—SHOPPING CENTER LEASE
(Tenant's Form)

(a)   Landlord agrees, at landlord's cost, to provide to the premises at all times during which tenant is lawfully occupying them such sewer facilities and utilities as tenant may require, and to supply and maintain adequate separate meters for the purpose of measuring all such utilities consumed by tenant in the premises. Landlord warrants that at all times during which tenant is lawfully occupying the premises, the building of which the premises are a part will be connected to electric, water, and gas lines of an adequate source of supply, and to storm and sanitary sewer systems of adequate capacity. Landlord will be liable for any interruption of such services if it fails to comply with this provision.

(b)   Tenant agrees to pay during the term of this lease all charges for such utilities (including without limitation light, power, gas, water and, sewer charges) used by tenant in connection with the operation of the premises.

§ 8.3   Utilities in Office Building Lease

FORM 8.3(1)
UTILITIES—OFFICE BUILDING ENERGY ESCALATION

For purposes of this paragraph "building energy costs" means the costs and expenses incurred or borne by landlord for steam, oil, electricity, or any other fuel or energy source purchased or used for the building (other than electricity that is redistributed to tenants on a rent inclusion or a submetering basis). Forty percent (40%) of the building's payment to the public utility for the purchase of electricity will be deemed to be payment for electricity purchased or used for the building. The term "proportionate share" means a fraction whose numerator is the rentable area of the premises and whose denominator is the total rentable area of the building (excluding garage space). The total rentable area of the premises is [number] square feet, and the rentable area of the building is [number] square feet. The term "base year" means the full calendar year prior to the year in which the term of this lease commences. The term "comparison year" means the calendar year in which the term of this lease commences and each subsequent calendar year.

If the building energy costs for any comparison year are greater than those for the base year, tenant will pay to landlord, as additional rent, a sum equal to tenant's proportionate share of the excess (the "energy payment") of the building energy costs and for such comparison year over those for the base year.

(1) After the end of each comparison year, landlord will submit to tenant a statement, certified by landlord, setting forth the building energy costs for the preceding comparison year and the energy payment, if any, due to landlord from tenant for the comparison year. The rendition of the statement to tenant will constitute prima facie proof of the accuracy of the statement. If the statement shows an energy payment due from tenant to landlord with respect to the comparison year then tenant will pay landlord:

(a) any unpaid portion of the energy payment within ten (10) days after receipt of such statement;

(b) within ten (10) days after receipt of such statement, an amount equal to the product obtained by multiplying the total energy payment for the preceding comparison year by a fraction whose denominator is twelve (12) and whose numerator is the number of months of the current comparison year that have elapsed prior to the first day of the month immediately following the rendition of the statement; and

(c) commencing as of the first day of the month immediately following the rendition of the statement and on the first day of each succeeding month until a new statement is rendered, one-twelfth ($\frac{1}{12}$th) of the total energy payment for the comparison year.

These monthly payments based on the total energy payment for the preceding comparison year will be adjusted to reflect known increases in rates for the current comparison year applicable to the categories involved in computing building energy costs whenever the increases become known prior to or during the current comparison year. The payments required to be made under (b) and (c) will be credited toward the energy payment due from tenant for the then-current comparison year, subject to adjustment as and when the statement for the current comparison year is rendered by landlord.

Tenant will make energy payments due for the first comparison year on the basis of reasonable estimates prepared by landlord. Payments will be made monthly on the first day of each month during the first comparison year. The payments based on the estimates will then be adjusted by landlord and tenant after the end of the first comparison year on the basis of landlord's actual costs for that year.

Landlord's certified public accountant may rely on landlord's allocations and estimates wherever allocations or estimates are needed for building energy costs. The statements of the building energy costs thus furnished by landlord to tenant will constitute a final determination as between landlord and tenant of the building energy costs for the periods represented by the statements, unless, within sixty (60) days after they are furnished, tenant gives notice to landlord that it disputes their accuracy. The notice will specify the particular respects in which the statements are inaccurate. Pending the resolution of the dispute, tenant will pay the additional rent to landlord in accordance with the statements furnished by landlord. After payment of the additional rent, tenant will have the right, during reasonable business hours and upon not less than five (5) business days' prior written notice to landlord, to examine landlord's books and records with respect to the statements, so long as such examination is commenced within thirty (30) days and concluded within sixty (60) days after the rendition of the statement in question.

(2)   Any dispute will be resolved by arbitration in accordance with the provisions of paragraph [arbitration provision].

(3)   The base monthly rent will not be reduced by virtue of this paragraph.

(4)   If the commencement date of the term of this lease is not the first day of the first comparison year, then the additional rent due under this paragraph for the first comparison year will be a proportionate share of the additional rent for the entire comparison year. At the end of this lease, the unpaid proportionate share of the additional rent for the comparison year during which the end occurs will immediately become due and payable by tenant to landlord. Landlord will as soon as practicable cause statements of the building energy costs for that comparison year to be prepared and furnished to tenant. Landlord and tenant will make appropriate adjustments of amounts then owing.

(5)   Landlord's and tenant's obligation to make the adjustments referred to in subparagraph (4) will survive this lease.

(6)   Any delay or failure of landlord in billing any energy payment will not impair the continuing obligation of tenant to make the energy payment.

§ 8.4   Direct Metering, Submetering, and Electric Rent Inclusion (Reserved)

CHAPTER 9

INSURANCE

§ 9.1   A Method of Management (Reserved)

§ 9.2   Finding Risk Management Provisions (Reserved)

§ 9.3   The Law and Basic Terms (Reserved)

§ 9.4   Liability Insurance (Reserved)

§ 9.5   Property Insurance (Reserved)

§ 9.6   Actual Cash Value and Replacement Cost (Reserved)

§ 9.7   Co-Insurance (Reserved)

§ 9.8   Contributing Policies (Reserved)

§ 9.9   Insuring the Rent Stream (Reserved)

§ 9.10 Tenant's Insurance (Reserved)

§ 9.11 Waiver of Subrogation

§ 9.12 Blanket Insurance, Excess Insurance, Umbrella Coverage, and Self-Insurance

§ 9.13 Insurance Provision for Office Building Leases

§ 9.14 Insurance Provision for Shopping Center Leases

§ 9.15 Insurance Provision for Single Tenant Building Leases

§ 9.16 Conclusion (Reserved)

§ 9.1 A Method of Management (Reserved)

§ 9.2 Finding Risk Management Provisions (Reserved)

§ 9.3 The Law and Basic Terms (Reserved)

§ 9.4 Liability Insurance (Reserved)

§ 9.5   Property Insurance (Reserved)

§ 9.6   Actual Cash Value and Replacement Cost (Reserved)

§ 9.7   Co-Insurance (Reserved)

§ 9.8   Contributing Policies (Reserved)

§ 9.9   Insuring the Rent Stream (Reserved)

§ 9.10   Tenant's Insurance (Reserved)

§ 9.11   Waiver of Subrogation

FORM 9.11(1)
INSURANCE—MUTUAL WAIVER OF SUBROGATION

Landlord and tenant waive all rights to recover against each other or against any other tenant or occupant of the building, or against the officers, directors, shareholders, partners, joint venturers, employees, agents, customers, invitees, or business visitors of each other or of any other tenant or occupant of the building, for any loss or damage arising from any cause covered by any insurance required to be carried by each of them pursuant to this paragraph or any other insurance actually carried by each of them. Landlord and tenant will cause their respective insurers to issue appropriate waiver of subrogation rights endorsements to all policies of insurance carried in connection with the building or the premises or the contents of either of them. Tenant will cause all other occupants of the premises claiming by, under, or through tenant to execute and deliver to landlord a waiver of claims similar to the waiver in this paragraph and to obtain such waiver of subrogation rights endorsements.

§ 9.12   Blanket Insurance, Excess Insurance, Umbrella Coverage, and Self-Insurance

FORM 9.12(1)
INSURANCE—BLANKET INSURANCE

Tenant may provide the insurance required by this paragraph under a blanket insurance policy covering other properties as well as the premises. Any insurance policy will specify, or tenant will furnish landlord with a written statement from the insurers under the policy specifying, the amount of the total insurance allocated to the premises, which will not be less than the amounts required by (the insurance paragraph), and those amounts will be sufficient to prevent any one of the assureds from becoming a co-insurer within the terms of the applicable policy. Any blanket insurance policy will, as to the premises, comply with the other provisions of (the insurance paragraph).

§ 9.13   Insurance Provision for Office Building Leases

FORM 9.13(1)
INSURANCE—OFFICE BUILDING

(a)   Landlord's Insurance. At all times during the term, landlord will carry and maintain:

(1)   Fire and extended coverage insurance covering the project, its equipment and common area furnishings, and leasehold improvements in the premises to the extent of the tenant finish allowance (as that term is defined in the workletter);

(2)   Bodily injury and property damage insurance; and

(3)   Such other insurance a landlord reasonably determines from time to time.

The insurance coverages and amounts in this Section (a) will be reasonably determined by landlord, based on coverages carried by prudent owners of comparable buildings in the vicinity of the project.

(b)   Tenant's Insurance. At all times during the term, tenant will carry and maintain, at tenant's expense, the following insurance, in the amounts specified or such other amounts as landlord may from time to time reasonably request, with insurance companies and on forms satisfactory to landlord:

(1)   Bodily injury and property damage liability insurance, with a combined single occurrence limit of not less than [* * * dollars ($ amount)]. All such insurance will be equivalent to coverage offered by a commercial general liability form, including without limitation personal injury and contractual

liability coverage for the performance by tenant of the indemnity agreements set forth in this lease;

(2)   Insurance covering all of tenant's furniture and fixtures, machinery, equipment, stock, and any other personal property owned and used in tenant's business and found in, on, or about the project, and any leasehold improvements to the premises in excess of the allowance, if any, provided pursuant to the workletter in an amount not less than the full replacement cost. Property forms will provide coverage on a broad form basis insuring against "all risks of direct physical loss." All policy proceeds will be used for the repair or replacement of the property damaged or destroyed; however, if this lease ceases under the provisions of [casualty damage], tenant will be entitled to any proceeds resulting from damage to tenant's furniture and fixtures, machinery and equipment, stock, and any other personal property;

(3)   Worker's compensation insurance insuring against and satisfying tenant's obligations and liabilities under the worker's compensation laws of the state in which the premises are located, including employer's liability insurance in the limits required by the laws of the state in which the project is located; and

(4)   If tenant operates owned, hired, or nonowned vehicles on the project, comprehensive automobile liability will be carried at a limit of liability not less than [* * * ($ amount)] combined bodily injury and property damage.

(c)   Forms of the Policies. Certificates of insurance, together with copies of the endorsements, when applicable, naming landlord and any others specified by landlord as additional insureds, will be delivered to landlord prior to tenant's occupancy of the premises and from time to time at least 10 days prior to the expiration of the term of each such policy. All commercial general liability or comparable policies maintained by tenant will name landlord and such other persons or firms as landlord specifies from time to time as additional insureds, entitling them to recover under such policies for any loss sustained by them, their agents, and employees as a result of the negligent acts or omissions of tenant. All such policies maintained by tenant will provide that they may not be terminated nor may coverage be reduced except after 30 days' prior written notice to landlord. All commercial general liability and property policies maintained by tenant will be written as primary policies, not contributing with and not supplemental to the coverage that landlord may carry.

(d)   Waiver of Subrogation. Landlord and tenant each waive any and all rights to recover against the other or against any other tenant or occupant of the project, or against the officers, directors, shareholders, partners, joint venturers, employees, agents, customers, invitees, or business visitors of each other or of the other tenants or occupants of the project, for any loss or damage to the waiving party arising from any cause covered by any property insurance required to be carried by the party pursuant to this Article [* *] or any other property insurance actually carried by the party to the extent of the limits of the policy. Landlord and tenant from time to time will cause their respective insurers to issue appropriate waiver of subrogation rights endorsements to all property insurance policies carried in connection with the project or the premises or the contents of the project or the premises. Tenant agrees to cause all other occupants of the premises claiming by, under, or through tenant to execute and deliver to landlord a waiver of claims and to obtain waiver of subrogation rights endorsements.

(e)   Adequacy of Coverage. Landlord, its agents, and employees make no representation that the limits of liability specified to be carried by tenant pursuant to this Article [* *] are adequate to protect tenant. If tenant believes that any insurance coverage is inadequate, tenant will obtain additional insurance coverage as tenant deems adequate, at tenant's sole expense.

§ 9.14   Insurance Provision for Shopping Center Leases

FORM 9.14(1)
INSURANCE—SHOPPING CENTER

(a)   Tenant will maintain in full force and effect during the entire term of this lease, at its own expense and in companies acceptable to landlord, the following policy or policies of insurance:

(1)   Commercial general liability insurance, including property damage, insuring landlord and tenant (and any mortgagee, ground landlord, or other person or persons whom landlord may designate, called "additional insured" in this lease) from and against all claims, demands, actions, or liability for injury to or death of any persons, and for damage to property arising from or related to the use or occupancy of the premises or the operation of tenant's business. No deductible will be carried under this coverage without the prior written consent of landlord. This policy must contain, but not be limited to, coverage for premises and operations, products and completed operations, blanket contractual, personal injury, operations, ownership, maintenance and use of owned, non-owned, or hired automobiles, bodily injury, and property damage. The policy must have limits in amounts not less than $[amount] per occurrence and $[amount] in the aggregate. This insurance will include a contractual coverage endorsement specifically insuring the performance by tenant of its indemnity agreement contained in [indemnity paragraph]. If landlord's insurance advisor reasonably concludes that these amounts of coverage or coverages are no longer adequate, then such amount or coverage will be appropriately increased, or obtained, as the case may be.

(2)   Worker's compensation insurance with a limit of no less than that amount required by law.

(3)   "All-risk" fire insurance, including without limitation vandalism and malicious mischief, to the extent of ninety percent (90%) of the replacement value of all furnishings, trade fixtures, leasehold improvements, equipment, merchandise, and other personal property from time to time situated in, on, or upon the premises. The proceeds from any such insurance will be payable

to landlord and held in trust by the landlord to be used only for the repair or replacement of the improvements, fixtures, and other property so insured.

(b)   Landlord may elect to procure and maintain insurance covering fire and such other risks of direct or indirect loss or damage as it deems appropriate, including extended and broad form coverage risks, mudslide, land subsidence, volcanic eruption, flood, and earthquake, on improvements in the shopping center. Tenant will reimburse landlord for the costs of all such insurance as part of operating expense reimbursable pursuant to [common area paragraph]. Any such insurance coverage will be for the benefit of landlord, tenant, and any additional insured or loss payee, as their interests may appear. Tenant will not adjust losses or execute proofs of loss under such policies without landlord's prior written approval.

(c)   If this lease is canceled by reason of damage or destruction and tenant is relieved of its obligation to restore or rebuild the improvements on the premises, any insurance proceeds for damage to the premises, including all fixtures and leasehold improvements, will belong to landlord, free and clear of any claims by tenant.

(d)   All policies of insurance described in this paragraph that tenant is to procure and maintain will be issued by responsible companies, reasonably acceptable to landlord and qualified to do business in the state in which the shopping center is situated. Executed copies of such policies of insurance or, at landlord's election, certificates of such insurance, will be delivered to landlord and any additional insureds or loss payee within ten (10) days after delivery of possession of the premises to tenant and within thirty (30) days prior to the termination or expiration of the term of each existing policy. All public liability and property damage policies will contain the following provisions:

(1)   Landlord, and any additional designated insureds, although named as insured, will nevertheless be entitled to recovery under said policies for any loss occasioned to them, their servants, agents, and employees by reason of the negligence of tenant, its officers, agents, or employees;

(2)   The company writing the policy will agree to give landlord and any additional insured or loss payee not less than thirty (30) days' notice in writing prior to any cancellation, reduction, or modification of such insurance; and

(3)   At the election of landlord's mortagee, the proceeds of any insurance will be paid to a trustee or depository designated by landlord's mortagee.

All public liability, property damage, and other casualty policies will be written as primary policies, not entitled to contribution from, nor contributing with, any coverage that landlord may carry.

(e)   Tenant's obligations to carry the insurance required by this lease may be brought within the coverage of a so-called blanket policy or policies of insurance carried and maintained by tenant, so long as:

(1)   Landlord and such other persons will be named as additional insureds under such policies as their interests may appear;

(2)   The coverage afforded to landlord and such other persons will not be reduced or diminished by reason of the use of such blanket policy of insurance; and

(3)   All other requirements set forth in this paragraph are otherwise satisfied.

(f)   If tenant fails either to acquire the insurance required pursuant to this paragraph or to pay the premiums for such insurance or to deliver required certificates or policies, landlord may, in addition to any other rights and remedies available to landlord, acquire such insurance and pay the requisite premiums for them. Those premiums will be payable by tenant to landlord immediately upon demand.

(g)   Landlord and tenant waive any rights each may have against the other for loss or damage to its property or property in which it may have an interest if the loss is caused by a peril of the type generally covered by property insurance with extended coverage or arising from any cause that the claiming party was obligated to insure against under this lease. Landlord and tenant on behalf of their insurer waive any right of subrogation that the insurer might otherwise have against the other. Landlord and tenant agree to cause their respective insurance companies insuring the premises or insuring their property on or in the premises to execute a waiver of any such rights of subrogation.

§ 9.15   Insurance Provision for Single Tenant Building Leases

FORM 9.15(1)
INSURANCE—SINGLE TENANT BUILDING

(a)   "All-Risk" Coverage. Tenant will, at its sole expense, obtain and keep in force from the commencement of construction of the improvements to the premises and during the term of this lease, "all-risk" coverage insurance (including earthquake and flood insurance) naming landlord and tenant as their interests may appear and such other parties as landlord or tenant may designate as additional insureds, in the customary form in the City of [city] for buildings and improvements of similar character, on all buildings and improvements now or after this date located on the premises. The amount of insurance will be designated by landlord no more frequently than once every twelve (12) months; will be set forth on an "agreed amount endorsement" to the policy of insurance; will not be less than the agreed value of the buildings and improvements; and will be subject to arbitration pursuant to [arbitration paragraph] if landlord and tenant do not agree with regard to the value. Landlord and tenant agree that the value of the existing building on the premises is [* * * dollars ($ amount)].

(b)   Commercial General Liability. Tenant will, at its sole expense, obtain and keep in force during the term of this lease commercial general liability insurance with a combined single limit of not less than [* * * dollars ($ amount)] for injury to or death of any one person, for injury to or death of any number of persons in one occurrence, and for damage to property, insuring against any and all liability of landlord and tenant, including without limitation coverage for contractual liability, broad form property damage, host liquor liability, and non-owned automobile liability, with respect to the premises or arising out of the maintenance, use, or occupancy of the premises. Such insurance will insure the performance by tenant of the indemnity agreement as to liability for injury to or death of persons and damage to property set forth in [indemnity paragraph]. Such insurance will be noncontributing with any insurance that may be carried by landlord and will contain a provision that landlord, although named as an insured, will nevertheless be entitled to recover under the policy for any loss, injury, or damage to landlord, its agents, and employees, or the property of such persons. The limits and coverage of all such insurance will be adjusted by agreement of landlord and tenant during every third lease year during the term of this lease in conformity with the then prevailing custom of insuring liability in the City of [city], and any disagreement regarding such adjustment will be submitted to arbitration in the manner provided in [arbitration paragraph].

(c)   Other Matters. All insurance required in this paragraph and all renewals of it will be issued by companies authorized to transact business in the State of [state] and rated at least A Class X by Best's Insurance Reports (property liability) or approved by landlord. The builder's "all-risk" coverage insurance will be payable to landlord, tenant, and any lender as their interests may appear. The "all-risk" coverage insurance and the general liability insurance will be carried in the joint names of tenant, landlord, and such other parties having an interest in the premises as landlord and tenant may designate. All insurance policies will be subject to approval by landlord and any lender as to form and substance; will expressly provide that such policies will not be canceled or altered without thirty (30) days' prior written notice to landlord and any lender, in the case of "all-risk" coverage insurance, and to landlord, in the case of general liability insurance; will, to the extent obtainable, provide that no act or omission of tenant that would otherwise result in forfeiture or reduction of the insurance will affect or limit the obligation of the insurance company to pay the amount of any loss sustained; and will, to the extent obtainable, contain a waiver by the insurer of its rights of subrogation against landlord. Upon issuance, each insurance policy or a duplicate or certificate of such policy will be delivered to landlord and any lender whom landlord designates. Tenant may satisfy its obligation under this paragraph by appropriate endorsements of its blanket insurance policies.

§ 9.16   Conclusion (Reserved)

PART IV

CONTROLLING THE TENANT'S CONDUCT

CHAPTER 10

USE

§ 10.1   The Law

§ 10.2   Use Provisions in Leases of Office Buildings and Single Tenant Buildings

§ 10.3   Lenders' Concerns about General Use Provisions (Reserved)

§ 10.4   Use Provisions in Shopping Center Leases

§ 10.5   Drafting an Exclusive Use Provision (Reserved)

§ 10.6   Tenant's Remedies (Reserved)

§ 10.7   Antitrust Implications of Exclusive Uses (Reserved)

§ 10.8   Federal Trade Commission's Response to Exclusive Uses (Reserved)

§ 10.9   Lenders' Concerns about Exclusive Uses (Reserved)

§ 10.10   Express Covenant of Continuous Operation

§ 10.11   Implied Covenant of Continuous Operation (Reserved)

§ 10.12   Manner of Conducting Business

§ 10.13   Radius Restriction

§ 10.14   Use Provisions in a Bankruptcy Not Involving a Shopping Center Lease (Reserved)

§ 10.15   Use Provisions in a Shopping Center Bankruptcy (Reserved)

§ 10.1   The Law

FORM 10.1(1)
USE—LANDLORD'S WARRANTY OF LEGALITY OF TENANT'S USE

Landlord warrants that tenant's use of the premises according to this paragraph is lawful and that it does not breach any restriction of record, zoning ordinance, or other agreement that affects the premises.

§ 10.2   Use Provisions in Leases of Office Buildings and Single Tenant Buildings

FORM 10.2(1)
USE—LIBERAL SINGLE TENANT BUILDING

Tenant may use the premises only for lawful purposes.

FORM 10.2(2)
USE—OFFICE BUILDING

The premises will be used for business offices and for no other purpose. The premises will be used in a careful, safe, and proper manner. The premises will not be used for any activity or in any manner that would tend to lower the first-class character of the building. Tenant will not use or occupy or permit the premises to be used or occupied for any purpose or in any manner prohibited by the laws of the United States, or the State of [state], or the ordinances of the City of [city]. Tenant will not commit waste nor suffer or permit waste to be committed in, on, or about the premises. Tenant will conduct its business and control its employees, agents, invitees, and visitors in such manner as not to create any nuisance, interfere with, annoy, or disturb any other tenant or occupant of the building or landlord in its operation of the building. Tenant will not do anything that is prohibited by the standard form of extended coverage fire policy, or that will increase the existing rate of such insurance or otherwise affect any other insurance related to the building or cause a cancellation of landlord's insurance.

§ 10.3   Lenders' Concerns about General Use Provisions (Reserved)

§ 10.4   Use Provisions in Shopping Center Leases

FORM 10.4(1)
PROHIBITED USES—SHOPPING CENTER (TENANT'S FORM)

Landlord will not lease or sublease or permit the use of any portion of the shopping center, or any future expansion of it, to any tenant whose business creates strong, unusual, or offensive odors, fumes, dust, or vapors; is a public or private nuisance; emits noise or sounds that are objectionable due to intermittence, beat, frequency, shrillness, or loudness; creates unusual fire, explosive, or other hazards; or is used, in whole or in part, as or for warehousing, the dumping or disposing of garbage or refuse, the sale of indecent or pornographic literature, catering halls, theaters, movie theaters, off-track betting parlors, bars, night clubs, discotheques, bowling alleys, so-called "head shops," car washes, auto body shops, unsupervised amusement arcade or game room, amusement centers, billiard parlor, funeral parlor, automobile (used or new) dealership, skating rink, health spa, adult book store, or massage parlor.

FORM 10.4(2)
USE—SUPERMARKET
(True Exclusive)

(a)   The premises may be used by tenant for the purpose of conducting a general retail grocery supermarket for the sale of all foods, liquor, wine and beer, tobacco, drugs, sundries, candy, hardware, clothing, home and building supplies, garden supplies, nursery stock, seeds, flowers, Christmas trees, barbecue and patio furniture and supplies, and all other types of merchandise and services offered or sold by public supermarkets, including a fountain, coffee shop, or restaurant, any or all of which may be sold or offered at the election of tenant through the use of separate departments, and for any other legal use.

(b)   Landlord covenants that tenant's market will be the only grocery supermarket or convenience market located in the shopping center, and that tenant will have the exclusive right to the sale of meat, bakery products, delicatessen items, liquor, wine, and beer.

§ 10.5   Drafting an Exclusive Use Provision
(Reserved)

§ 10.6   Tenant's Remedies (Reserved)

§ 10.7   Antitrust Implications of Exclusive Uses
(Reserved)

§ 10.8   Federal Trade Commission's Response to Exclusive Uses (Reserved)

§ 10.9   Lenders' Concerns about Exclusive Uses
(Reserved)

§ 10.10   Express Covenant of Continuous Operation

FORM 10.10(1)
USE—EXPRESS COVENANT OF CONTINUOUS OPERATION

Tenant will operate tenant's business in the premises so as to maximize the gross sales produced by such operation, and will carry in the premises at all times a stock of merchandise of such size, character, and quality as is reasonably designed to produce the greatest gross sales and the greatest possible amount of percentage rent. Tenant will carry on its business diligently and continuously at the premises through the term of this lease and will keep the premises open for business on all business days in accordance with the schedule of minimum hours specified in the basic lease information. If landlord from time to time establishes different standard retail hours for the shopping center, tenant will remain open during those hours. If tenant fails to carry on its business each business day as required pursuant to this paragraph, tenant will, at landlord's option, pay, in addition to the minimum rental due pursuant to this lease, for each day during which the premises are not open or during which the required hours are not maintained, an amount equal to twenty-five percent (25%) of the per diem minimum rental then in effect. That additional rental will be deemed to be in lieu of any percentage rent that may have been earned during the period of tenant's breach.

FORM 10.10(2)
USE—TENANT'S LIMITATION ON THE COVENANT
OF CONTINUOUS OPERATION

Unless it wishes to do so, tenant will not operate in the premises:

(a)   unless [number] square feet of the shopping center are open for business to the general public by tenants in their premises;

(b)   unless the anchor tenant(s) are open for business to the general public;

(c)   if it is prevented from doing so by strikes, labor disputes, the elements, fire or other casualty, unavailability of its stock in trade, or other matters beyond its control;

(d)   while alterations are being made to the premises;

(e)   for two weeks each calendar year when tenant will be on vacation, on national legal holidays, on religious holidays, and on days when inventory is taken;

(f)   during the last two months of the term of the lease when tenant will be moving out; and

(g)   in any hours or on any days when tenant demonstrates that its operations are not profitable.

§ 10.11   Implied Covenant of Continuous Operation (Reserved)

§ 10.12   Manner of Conducting Business

FORM 10.12(1)
MANNER OF CONDUCTING BUSINESS
(Shopping Center Lease)

The premises will be used solely for the purpose specified in the basic lease information. Tenant's business in the premises will be conducted under the trade name specified in the basic lease information during the business hours specified in the basic lease information. Tenant will not use or permit the premises to be used for any other purpose or under any other trade name without landlord's prior consent. Tenant will maintain an adequate number of capable employees and sufficient inventory in order to achieve the greatest possible gross sales. Tenant's advertising in the [* * *], [* * *] area will refer to the business conducted at the premises and will mention the name of the shopping center. The identity of tenant, the specific character of tenant's business, the anticipated use of the premises, and the relationship between that use and other uses within the shopping center have been material considerations to landlord's entry into this lease. Any material change in the character of tenant's business or use will constitute a default under this lease.

Tenant will not, without the consent of landlord, use the name of the shopping center for any purpose other than as the address of the business to be conducted by tenant in the premises, nor will tenant do or permit the doing of anything in connection with tenant's business or advertising that in the reasonable judgment of landlord may reflect unfavorably on landlord or the shopping center, or confuse or mislead the public as to any relationship between landlord and tenant.

Tenant will not:

(a)   use or permit the use of any portion of the premises for the conduct in or on the premises of what is commonly known in the retail trade as an outlet store or second-hand store, or army, navy, or government surplus store;

(b)   advertise any distress, fire, bankruptcy, liquidation, relocation or closing, or going out of business sale unless such advertisements are true and landlord gives its prior written consent;

(c)   warehouse and stock within the premises any goods, wares, or merchandise other than that which tenant intends to offer for sale in the premises; or

(d)   use or permit the use on the premises of any pinball machines, video games, or other devices or equipment for amusement or recreation, or any vending machines, newspaper racks, pay telephones, or other coin-operated devices.

§ 10.13   Radius Restriction

FORM 10.13(1)
USE—RADIUS RESTRICTION

Tenant will not engage in any business that is both (a) competitive with the business or any part of it that the use provision requires tenant to operate in the premises and (b) located within [number] miles of any point on the perimeter of the premises. For purpose of this paragraph, tenant will be deemed to be engaged in a business if it or any of its present or future employees, shareholders, or partners (while any of them is also an employee, shareholder, or partner of tenant) or any of the guarantors of tenant's obligations under this lease, is an owner, shareholder, principal, partner, employee, agent, or independent contractor of any such business or is a lender to any such business, or is a guarantor of the debts of any such business, or is entitled to compensation, dividends, profits, or any other payments or other things of value from any such business.

§ 10.14   Use Provisions in a Bankruptcy Not Involving a Shopping Center Lease (Reserved)

§ 10.15   Use Provisions in a Shopping Center Bankruptcy (Reserved)

CHAPTER 11

COMPLIANCE WITH LAWS

§ 11.1 General Compliance Provisions

§ 11.2 Right to Contest

§ 11.3 Landlord's Warranty of Compliance

§ 11.4 Compliance with Environmental Laws

§ 11.5 Negotiating the Environmental Compliance Provisions

§ 11.1 General Compliance Provisions

FORM 11.1(1)
COMPLIANCE WITH LAWS

Tenant will not use or occupy the premises, or permit any portion of the premises to be used or occupied:

(a) in violation of any law, ordinance, order, rule, regulation, certificate of occupancy, or other governmental requirement;

(b) for any disreputable business or purpose; or

(c) in any manner or for any business or purpose that creates risks of fire or other hazards, or that would in any way violate, suspend, void, or increase the rate of fire or liability or any other insurance of any kind at any time carried by landlord upon all or any part of the building in which the premises are located or its contents.

Tenant will comply with all laws, ordinances, orders, rules, regulations, and other governmental requirements relating to the use, condition, or occupancy of the premises, and all rules, orders, regulations, and requirements of the board of fire underwriters or insurance service office, or any other similar body, having jurisdiction over the building in which the premises are located. The cost of such compliance (including without limitation capital expenditures) will be borne by tenant.

§ 11.2   Right to Contest

FORM 11.2(1)
COMPLIANCE WITH LAWS—RIGHT TO CONTEST

Tenant will have the right to contest by appropriate proceedings diligently conducted in good faith in the name of tenant, or, with the prior consent of the landlord (which will not be unreasonably withheld or delayed), in the name of landlord, or both, without cost or expense to landlord, the validity or application of any law, ordinance, order, rule, regulation, or legal requirement of any nature. If compliance with any law, ordinance, order, rule, regulation, or requirement may legally be delayed pending the prosecution of any proceeding without incurring any lien, charge, or liability of any kind against the premises, or tenant's interest in the premises, and without subjecting tenant or landlord to any liability, civil or criminal, for failure to comply, tenant may delay compliance until the final determination of the proceeding. Even if a lien, charge, or liability may be incurred by reason of any delay, tenant may contest and delay, so long as (a) the contest or delay does not subject landlord to criminal liability and (b) tenant furnishes to landlord security, reasonably satisfactory to landlord, against any loss or injury by reason of any contest or delay. Landlord will not be required to join any proceedings pursuant to this paragraph unless the provision of any applicable law, rule, or regulation at the time in effect requires that the proceedings be brought by or in the name of landlord or both landlord and tenant. In that event landlord will join the proceedings or permit them to be brought in its name if tenant pays all related expenses.

§ 11.3   Landlord's Warranty of Compliance

FORM 11.3(1)
COMPLIANCE WITH LAWS—LANDLORD'S WARRANTY

Landlord represents and warrants to tenant that on the date of delivery of possession of the premises to tenant, the premises will be in compliance with all laws, ordinances, orders, rules, regulations, and other governmental requirements relating to the use, condition, and occupancy of the premises, and all rules, orders, regulations, and requirements of the board of fire underwriters or insurance service office, or any similar body having jurisdiction over the premises and the building of which the premises are a part.

§ 11.4   Compliance with Environmental Laws

FORM 11.4(1)
COMPLIANCE WITH ENVIRONMENTAL LAWS
(Landlord's Form)

Tenant represents, warrants, and covenants to landlord that:

(a)   Tenant and the premises will remain in compliance with all applicable laws, ordinances, and regulations (including consent decrees and administrative orders) relating to public health and safety and protection of the environment, including those statutes, laws, regulations, and ordinances identified in subparagraph (g), all as amended and modified from time to time (collectively, "environmental laws"). All governmental permits relating to the use or operation of the premises required by applicable environmental laws are and will remain in effect, and tenant will comply with them.

(b)   Tenant will not permit to occur any release, generation, manufacture, storage, treatment, transportation, or disposal of hazardous material, as that term is defined in subparagraph (g), on, in, under, or from the premises. Tenant will promptly notify landlord, in writing, if tenant has or acquires notice or knowledge that any hazardous material has been or is threatened to be released, generated, manufactured, stored, treated, transported, or disposed of, on, in, under, or from the premises; and if any hazardous material is found on the premises, tenant, at its own cost and expense, will immediately take such action as is necessary to detain the spread of and remove the hazardous material to the complete satisfaction of landlord and the appropriate governmental authorities.

(c)   Tenant will immediately notify landlord and provide copies upon receipt of all written complaints, claims, citations, demands, inquiries, reports, or notices relating to the condition of the premises or compliance with environmental laws. Tenant will promptly cure and have dismissed with prejudice any of those actions and proceedings to the satisfaction of landlord. Tenant will keep the premises free of any lien imposed pursuant to any environmental laws.

(d)   Landlord will have the right at all reasonable times and from time to time to conduct environmental audits of the premises, and tenant will cooperate in the conduct of those audits. The audits will be conducted by a consultant of landlord's choosing, and if any hazardous material is detected or if a violation of any of the warranties, representations, or covenants contained in this paragraph is discovered, the fees and expenses of such consultant will be borne by tenant and will be paid as additional rent under this lease on demand by landlord.

(e)   If tenant fails to comply with any of the foregoing warranties, representations, and covenants, landlord may cause the removal (or other cleanup acceptable to landlord) of any hazardous material from the premises. The costs of hazardous material removal and any other cleanup (including transportation and storage costs) will be additional rent under this lease, whether or not a court has ordered the cleanup, and those costs will become due and payable on demand by landlord. Tenant will give landlord, its agents, and employees access to the premises to remove or otherwise clean up any hazardous material. Landlord, however, has no affirmative obligation to remove or otherwise clean up any hazardous material, and this lease will not be construed as creating any such obligation.

(f) Tenant agrees to indemnify, defend (with counsel reasonably acceptable to landlord and at tenant's sole cost), and hold landlord and landlord's affiliates, shareholders, directors, officers, employees, and agents free and harmless from and against all losses, liabilities, obligations, penalties, claims, litigation, demands, defenses, costs, judgments, suits, proceedings, damages (including consequential damages), disbursements, or expenses of any kind (including attorneys' and experts' fees and expenses and fees and expenses incurred in investigating, defending, or prosecuting any litigation, claim, or proceeding) that may at any time be imposed upon, incurred by, asserted, or awarded against landlord or any of them in connection with or arising from or out of:

(1) any hazardous material on, in, under, or affecting all or any portion of the premises;

(2) any misrepresentation, inaccuracy, or breach of any warranty, covenant, or agreement contained or referred to in this paragraph;

(3) any violation or claim of violation by tenant of any environmental law; or

(4) the imposition of any lien for the recovery of any costs for environmental cleanup or other response costs relating to the release or threatened release of hazardous material.

This indemnification is the personal obligation of tenant and will survive termination of this lease. Tenant, its successors, and assigns waive, release, and agree not to make any claim or bring any cost recovery action against landlord under CERCLA, as that term is defined in subparagraph (g), or any state equivalent or any similar law now existing or enacted after this date. To the extent that landlord is strictly liable under any such law, regulation, ordinance, or requirement, tenant's obligation to landlord under this indemnity will also be without regard to fault on the part of tenant with respect to the violation or condition that results in liability to landlord.

(g) For purposes of this lease, "hazardous material" means:

(1) "hazardous substances" or "toxic substances" as those terms are defined by the Comprehensive Environmental Response, Compensation, and Liability Act (CERCLA), 42 U.S.C. § 9601, et seq., or the Hazardous Materials Transportation Act, 49 U.S.C. § 1801, et seq., both as amended to and after this date;

(2) "hazardous wastes," as that term is defined by the Resource Conservation and Recovery Act ("RCRA"), 42 U.S.C. § 6901, et seq., as amended to and after this date;

(3) any pollutant or contaminant or hazardous, dangerous, or toxic chemicals, materials, or substances within the meaning of any other applicable federal, state, or local law, regulation, ordinance, or requirement (including consent

decrees and administrative orders) relating to or imposing liability or standards of conduct concerning any hazardous, toxic, or dangerous waste substance or material, all as amended to and after this date;

(4)   crude oil or any fraction of it that is liquid at standard conditions of temperature and pressure (60 degrees Fahrenheit and 14.7 pounds per square inch absolute);

(5)   any radioactive material, including any source, special nuclear, or by-product material as defined at 42 U.S.C. § 2011, et seq., as amended to and after this date;

(6)   asbestos in any form or condition; and

(7)   polychlorinated biphenyls (PCB's) or substances or compounds containing PCB's.

FORM 11.4(2)
COMPLIANCE WITH LAWS—TENANT'S
ENVIRONMENTAL RESPONSIBILITIES

Tenant, at its sole cost and expense, will comply with:

(a)   all federal, state, and municipal laws, ordinances, notices, orders, rules, regulations, and requirements;

(b)   any requirements of the National Board of Fire Underwriters or any other body exercising similar functions; and

(c)   the requirements of all public liability, fire, and other policies of insurance covering the premises relating to the treatment, production, storage, handling, transfer, processing, transporting, use, disposal, and release of hazardous substances, toxic, or radioactive matter.

In addition, tenant will take similar precautions with any other material or substance that, even if not regulated by those laws or requirements, may or could pose a hazard to the health and safety of the current or future occupants of the premises or the owners or occupants of property adjacent to or in the vicinity of the premises. All of the above activities are called "restricted activities" in this paragraph. Tenant will be solely responsible for and will defend, indemnify, and hold landlord, and its agents, successors, and assigns harmless from and against all claims, actions, damages, liabilities, and expenses (including without limitation fees of attorneys, investigators, and experts) arising out of or in connection with the (1) restricted activities by tenant, its agents, contractors, employees, licensees, or invitees and (2) the removal, cleanup, and restoration work and materials necessary to return the premises and any other property of whatever nature (including, but not limited to, property adjacent to or in the vicinity of the premises and the building) to their condition prior to the restricted activities. Tenant's obligations will survive the expiration or termination of this lease. If at any time during or after the term and any extended term of this lease tenant becomes aware of any inquiry, investigation, administrative proceeding, or judicial proceeding regarding the restricted activities, tenant will within 5 days after first learning of such inquiry, investigation, or proceeding give landlord written notice providing all available information regarding such inquiry, investigation, or proceeding.

§ 11.5 Negotiating the Environmental Compliance Provisions

FORM 11.5(1)
COMPLIANCE WITH ENVIRONMENTAL LAWS
(Tenant's Form)

With respect to both the premises and the project, landlord represents and warrants to tenant:

(a)   Landlord has no knowledge and has received no notice of any pollution, health, safety, fire, environmental, sewerage or building code violation, asbestos, PCB's, PCB articles, PCB containers, PCB article containers, PCB equipment, PCB transformers or PCB-contaminated electrical equipment, as those terms are defined in any hazardous substance laws as that term is defined in this subparagraph;

(b)   Neither the premises, the project nor the ground under or about the project is contaminated with or contains any hazardous or toxic substance, pollutant, contaminants, or petroleum, including crude oil or any fraction of it, or contains any underground storage tank;

(c)   The project has never been nor is it currently used for the generation, transportation, treatment, storage, or disposal of hazardous or toxic substances, pollutants, contaminants, or petroleum, including crude oil or any fraction thereof;

(d)   The project does not contain any conditions that could result in recovery by any governmental or private party of remedial or removal costs, natural resource damages, property damages, damages for personal injuries or other costs, expenses, or damages or could result in injunctive relief of any kind arising from any alleged injury or threat of injury;

(e)   The project is not subject to investigation or is currently in administrative or judicial litigation regarding any environmental condition, such as alleged noncompliance or alleged contamination.

(f)   Landlord has undertaken all appropriate inquiry into the previous ownership and uses of the project consistent with good commercial or customary practice, in light of any specialized knowledge or experience on the part of landlord, and reasonably ascertainable information about the project.

(g)   No part of the project has been used in connection with hazardous or toxic substances, pollutants, contaminants, or petroleum, including crude oil or any fraction of them, as defined in any of the hazardous substance laws. No releases of hazardous or toxic substances, pollutants, contaminants, or petroleum, including crude oil or any fraction of them, as such terms are defined under the hazardous substance laws, has occurred from the project into the environment, and no threat of such release exists.

(h)   Landlord will indemnify and hold harmless tenant, its directors, officers, employees, and agents, and any assignees, subtenants, or successors to tenant's interest in the premises, their directors, officers, employees, and agents, from and against any and all losses, claims, damages, penalties, and liability, including all out-of-pocket litigation costs and the reasonable fees and expenses of counsel, including without limitation all consequential damages directly or indirectly arising out of the use, generation, storage, release, or disposal of hazardous materials by landlord, its agents, or contractors prior to execution of this lease or at any time after execution, or by any prior owner or operator of the premises or the project, and also from and against the cost of any required repair, cleanup, or detoxification and any closure or other required plans to the full extent that such action is attributable, directly or indirectly, to the presence or use, generation, storage, release, threatened release, or disposal of hazardous materials by any person on, under, or in the project prior to execution of this lease.

(i)   The provisions of this lease relating to hazardous substances will survive the expiration or termination of this lease.

(j)   If any cleanup, repair, detoxification, or other similar action is required by any governmental or quasi-governmental agency as a result of the storage, release, or disposal of hazardous materials by landlord, its agents or contractors, at any time, or by any prior owner, possessor, or operator of any part of the project, and such action requires that tenant be closed for business or that access be denied for greater than a 24-hour period, then the rent will be abated entirely during the period beyond 24 hours. If the closure or denial of access persists in excess of 30 days then, at tenant's election by written notice to landlord given within 10 days after the end of the 30-day period, this lease will end as of the commencement of such closure.

(k)   In this paragraph, "hazardous materials" includes but is not limited to substances defined as "hazardous substances," "hazardous materials," or "toxic substances" in the Comprehensive Environmental Response, Compensation and Liability Act of 1980, as amended, 42 U.S.C. § 9601, et seq.; the Hazardous Materials Transportation Act, 49 U.S.C. § 1801, et seq.; the Resource Conservation and Recovery Act, 42 U.S.C. § 6901, et seq.; and those substances defined as hazardous, toxic, hazardous wastes, toxic wastes, or as hazardous or toxic substances by any law or statute now or after this date in effect in the state in which the premises are located; and in the regulations adopted and publications promulgated pursuant to those laws (all collectively "hazardous substance laws").

CHAPTER 12

ASSIGNMENTS AND SUBLEASES

§ 12.1   An Approach to Provisions for Assignments and Subleases (Reserved)

§ 12.2   Assignment and Sublease Defined (Reserved)

§ 12.3   Privity (Reserved)

§ 12.4   Promises Running with the Land (Reserved)

§ 12.5   An Absolute Prohibition

§ 12.6   Requirement of Landlord's Consent

§ 12.7   Requirement of Consent Not to Be Unreasonably Withheld (Reserved)

§ 12.8   Limiting the Tenant's Remedies (Reserved)

§ 12.9   Redefining the Assignment and Sublease

§ 12.10   Imposing Further Conditions to Consent (Reserved)

§ 12.11   Relationship of Prohibitions of Assignment and Sublease to Default Provisions (Reserved)

§ 12.12   Recapture and Profit Sharing (Reserved)

§ 12.13   Lenders' Concerns about Assignments and Subleases

§ 12.14   Preparing a Form of Assignment (Reserved)

§ 12.15   Preparing a Form of Sublease

§ 12.1   An Approach to Provisions for Assignments and Subleases (Reserved)

§ 12.2   Assignment and Sublease Defined (Reserved)

§ 12.3   Privity (Reserved)

§ 12.4   Promises Running with the Land (Reserved)

§ 12.5   An Absolute Prohibition

FORM 12.5(1)
ASSIGNMENT—AN ABSOLUTE PROHIBITION

Tenant will not assign this lease in part or in full and tenant will not sublease all or part of the premises.

§ 12.6   Requirement of Landlord's Consent

FORM 12.6(1)
ASSIGNMENT—REQUIRING LANDLORD'S CONSENT

Without landlord's prior written consent, tenant will neither assign this lease in part or in full nor sublease all or part of the premises.

FORM 12.6(2)
ASSIGNMENT—LANDLORD'S RIGHT TO BE ARBITRARY
AND CAPRICIOUS

Tenant will not assign this lease in whole or in part and will not sublease the premises in whole or in part without landlord's prior written consent. Landlord may withhold its consent arbitrarily and capriciously. Landlord and tenant have fully bargained for this provision with the intention that landlord has absolutely no obligation to consider a proposed assignment or sublease.

FORM 12.6(3)
ASSIGNMENT—REQUIRING LANDLORD'S CONSENT, WHICH
WILL NOT BE UNREASONABLY WITHHELD OR DELAYED
(General)

(a)   Without landlord's prior written consent, which landlord agrees will not be unreasonably withheld or delayed, tenant will neither assign this lease in whole or in part nor sublease all or part of the premises.

(b)   These transactions will also require landlord's prior written consent:

(1)   an assignment by operation of law;

(2)   an imposition (whether or not consensual) of a lien, mortgage, or encumbrance upon tenant's interest in this lease;

(3)   an arrangement (including without limitation management agreements, concessions, and licensees) that allows the use and occupancy of all or part of the premises by anyone other than tenant;

(4)   a transfer of voting control of tenant (if tenant is a corporation);

(5)   a transfer of more than fifty percent (50%) of the interest in the capital of tenant (if tenant is a partnership).

(c)   If tenant requests landlord's consent to a specific assignment or sublease, tenant will give landlord:

(1)   the name and address of the proposed assignee or subtenant;

(2)   a copy of the proposed assignment or sublease;

(3)   reasonably satisfactory information about the nature, business and business history of the proposed assignee or subtenant, and its proposed use of the premises; and

(4)   banking, financial, or other credit information and references about the proposed assignee or subtenant sufficient to enable landlord to determine the financial responsibility and character of the proposed assignee or subtenant.

(d)   Landlord's consent to an assignment or sublease will not be effective until: a fully executed copy of the instrument of assignment or sublease has been delivered to landlord; in the case of an assignment, landlord has received a written instrument in which the assignee has assumed and agreed to perform all of tenant's obligations in the lease; and landlord has been reimbursed for its attorneys' fees and costs incurred in connection with both determining whether to give its consent and giving its consent.

(e)   Landlord's consent to an assignment or sublease will not release tenant from the payment and performance of its obligations in the lease, but rather tenant and its assignee will be jointly and severally primarily liable for such payment and performance. An assignment or sublease without landlord's prior written consent will be void at landlord's option.

(f)   Landlord's consent to one assignment or sublease will not waive the requirement of its consent to any subsequent assignment or sublease.

(g)   If tenant intends to assign all or part of this lease or to sublease all or any portion of the premises, it will first submit to landlord the documents described in paragraph (c), and will offer in writing:

(1)   with respect to a prospective assignment, to assign this lease to landlord without cost; or,

(2)   with respect to a prospective sublease, to sublease to landlord the portion of the premises involved (the "leaseback area")

(A)   for the term specified by tenant in its offer,

(B)   at the lower of tenant's proposed subrent or the rate of base monthly rent and additional rent then in effect according to this lease, and

(C)   on the same terms, covenants, and conditions contained in this lease and applicable to the leaseback area.

The offer will specify the date on which the leaseback area will be made available to landlord; however, that date will not be earlier than 30 days nor later than 180 days after landlord's acceptance of the offer. Tenant may withdraw the offer at any time before it is accepted. If the prospective sublease results in all or substantially all of the premises being subleased, then, if landlord accepts the offer, landlord will have the option to extend the term of its sublease for the balance of the term of this lease less one day.

(h) Without affecting any of its other obligations under this lease, tenant will pay landlord as additional rent one-half of any sums or other economic consideration that:

(1)   are received by tenant as a result of an assignment or subletting (other than the rental or other payments that are attributable to the amortization over the term of this lease of the cost of nonbuilding standard leasehold improvements that are part of the assigned or sublet portion of the premises and have been paid for by tenant), whether or not denominated rentals under the assignment or sublease, and

(2)   exceed in total the sums tenant is obligated to pay landlord under this lease (prorated to reflect obligations allocable to that portion of the premises subject to such assignment or sublease).

The failure or inability of the assignee or subtenant to pay tenant pursuant to the assignment or sublease will not relieve tenant from its obligations to landlord under this paragraph. Tenant will not amend the assignment or sublease in such a way as to reduce or delay payment of amounts that are provided in the assignment or sublease approved by landlord.

(i)   If tenant believes that landlord has unreasonably withheld its consent, tenant's sole remedy will be to seek a declaratory judgment that landlord has unreasonably withheld its consent or an order of specific performance or mandatory injunction of landlord's agreement to give its consent. Tenant will not have any right to recover damages or to terminate this lease.

§ 12.7   Requirement of Consent Not to Be Unreasonably Withheld (Reserved)

§ 12.8   Limiting the Tenant's Remedies (Reserved)

§ 12.9   Redefining the Assignment and Sublease

FORM 12.9(1)
ASSIGNMENT—MODIFICATION OF ASSIGNMENT PROVISION TO PERMIT CERTAIN CORPORATE TRANSFERS

Tenant may assign all or part of this lease, or sublease all or a part of the premises, to:

(a)   any corporation that has the power to direct tenant's management and operation, or any corporation whose management and operation is controlled by tenant;

(b)   any corporation a majority of whose voting stock is owned by tenant;

(c)   any corporation in which or with which tenant, its corporate successors, or assigns, is merged or consolidated, in accordance with applicable statutory provisions for merger or consolidation of corporations, so long as the liabilities of the corporations participating in such merger or consolidation are assumed by the corporation surviving such merger or created by such consolidation;

(d)   any corporation acquiring this lease and a substantial portion of tenant's assets; or

(e)   any corporate successor to a successor corporation becoming such by either of the methods described in (c) or (d), so long as on the completion of such merger, consolidation, acquisition, or assumption, the successor has a net worth no less than tenant's net worth immediately prior to such merger, consolidation, acquisition, or assumption.

§ 12.10   Imposing Further Conditions to Consent (Reserved)

§ 12.11   Relationship of Prohibitions of Assignment and Sublease to Default Provisions (Reserved)

§ 12.12   Recapture and Profit Sharing (Reserved)

§ 12.13   Lenders' Concerns about Assignments and Subleases

FORM 12.13(1)
ASSIGNMENT—OFFICE

(a)   Tenant will not transfer, assign, sublet, enter into license or concession agreements, or hypothecate this lease or tenant's interest in and to the premises without first procuring the written consent of landlord. Landlord may base its consent upon such terms, provisions, and conditions as landlord, in its sole discretion, determines are appropriate. Any attempted transfer, assignment, subletting, licensing or concession agreement, or hypothecation without landlord's consent will be void and will, at the option of landlord, terminate this lease. This lease will not, nor will any interest herein, be assignable as to the interest of tenant by operation of law without the consent of landlord. Tenant agrees to reimburse landlord for landlord's reasonable attorneys' fees incurred in conjunction with the processing and documentation of any such requested transfer, assignment, subletting, licensing or concession agreement, or hypothecation of this lease or tenant's interest in and to the premises.

(b)   Before entering into any assignment of this lease or into a sublease of all or part of the premises, tenant will give written notice to landlord identifying the intended assignee or subtenant by name and address and specifying the terms of the intended assignment or sublease. For a period of 30 days after notice is given, landlord will have the right by written notice to tenant to:

(1)   in the case of a proposed sublease, either

(A)   sublet from tenant any portion of the premises proposed to be sublet for the term for which such portion is proposed to be sublet but at the same rent as tenant is required to pay to landlord under this lease for the same space, computed on a pro rata square footage basis, or

(B)   if the proposed subletting is for substantially the remaining period of the term of this lease, terminate this lease, or terminate this lease as it pertains to the portion of the premises so proposed by tenant to be sublet; or

(2)   in the case of a proposed assignment, terminate this lease.

If landlord terminates this lease, such termination will be as of the date specified in the notice. If landlord terminates this lease, landlord may, if it elects, enter into a new lease covering the premises or a portion thereof with the intended assignee or subtenant, on such terms as landlord and such person may agree, or enter into a new lease covering the premises or a portion of the premises with any other person. In such event, tenant will not be entitled to any portion of the profit, if any, which landlord may realize on account of such termination and reletting. Landlord's exercise of its aforesaid option will not be construed to impose any liability upon landlord with respect to any real estate brokerage commission(s) or any other costs or expenses incurred by tenant in connection with its proposed subletting or assignment.

(c)   If tenant complies with the provisions of this section and landlord does not exercise an option provided to landlord under (b), landlord's consent to a proposed assignment or subletting will not be unreasonably withheld. Without limiting the other instances in which it may be reasonable for landlord to withhold its consent to an assignment or subletting, landlord and tenant acknowledge that it will be reasonable for landlord to withhold its consent in any of the following instances:

(1)   the proposed assignee or sublessee is a governmental agency;

(2)   in landlord's reasonable judgment the use of the premises by the proposed assignee or sublessee would entail alterations that would lessen the value of the leasehold improvements in the premises or would require increased services by landlord;

(3) in landlord's reasonable judgment, the financial worth of the proposed assignee or sublessee does not meet the credit standards applied by landlord for other tenants under leases with comparable terms;

(4) in landlord's reasonable judgment, the character, reputation, or business of tenant is inconsistent with the desired tenant mix or the quality of other tenancies in the building;

(5) landlord has received from any prior lessor to the proposed assignee or subtenant a negative report concerning such prior lessor's experience with the proposed assignee or subtenant;

(6) landlord has experienced previous defaults by or is in litigation with the proposed assignee or subtenant;

(7) (i) the proposed assignee's or subtenant's anticipated use of the premises involves the generation, storage, use, treatment, or disposal of hazardous material; (ii) the proposed assignee or subtenant has been required by any prior landlord, lender, or governmental authority to take remedial action in connection with hazardous material contaminating a property if the contamination resulted from such assignee's or subtenant's actions or use of the property in question; or (iii) the proposed assignee or subtenant is subject to an enforcement order issued by any governmental authority in connection with the use, disposal, or storage of a hazardous material;

(8) the use of the premises by the proposed assignee or subtenant will violate any applicable law, ordinance, or regulation;

(9) the proposed assignment or sublease will create a vacancy elsewhere in the building;

(10) the proposed assignee or subtenant, or any person that, directly or indirectly, controls, is controlled by, or is under common control with the proposed assignee or subtenant, is then an occupant of the building;

(11) the proposed assignee or subtenant is a person with whom landlord is negotiating to lease space in the building;

(12) the proposed assignment or sublease fails to include all of the terms and provisions required to be included pursuant to this paragraph;

(13) tenant is in default of any obligation of tenant under this lease, or tenant has defaulted under this lease on three or more occasions during the 12 months preceding the date that tenant requests consent; or

(14) in the case of a subletting of less than the entire premises, if the subletting would result in the division of the premises into more than two subparcels or would require access to be provided through space leased or held for lease to another tenant or improvements to be made outside the premises.

(d) In the case of an assignment, 100% of any sums or other economic consideration received by tenant as a result of such assignment will be paid to landlord, after first deducting the unamortized cost of leasehold improvements paid by tenant and the cost of any real estate commissions incurred in connection with such assignment. In the case of a subletting, 100% of any sum or economic consideration received by tenant as a result of such subletting will be paid to landlord, after first deducting the rental due under this lease, prorated to reflect only rental allocable to the sublet portion of the premises, and the cost of any real estate commissions incurred in connection with such subletting, amortized over the term of the sublease. Upon landlord's request, tenant will assign to landlord all amounts to be paid to tenant by any such subtenant or assignee and will direct such subtenant or assignee to pay the same directly to landlord.

(e) Tenant may assign this lease or sublet the premises or any portion of the premises without landlord's consent to any corporation which controls, is controlled by, or is under common control with tenant or to any corporation resulting from merger or consolidation with tenant, so long as there is no change in control of tenant, provided that said assignee assumes, in full, the obligations of tenant under this lease.

(f) Regardless of landlord's consent, no subletting, assignment, hypothecation, license, or concession will release tenant from tenant's obligation or alter the primary liability of tenant to pay the rental and to perform all other obligations under the lease to be performed by tenant. The acceptance of rental by landlord from any other person will not be deemed to be a waiver by landlord of any provision of this lease. Consent to one assignment, subletting, hypothecation, license, or concession agreement will not be deemed consent to any subsequent assignment, subletting, hypothecation, license, or concession agreement. In the event of default by any assignee of tenant or any successor of tenant in the performance of any of the terms of this lease, landlord may proceed directly against tenant without the necessity of exhausting remedies against such assignee or successor. Landlord may consent to subsequent assignments, subletting, hypothecations, licenses, or concession agreements and to amendments or modifications to this lease with assignees of tenant without notifying tenant or any successor of tenant and without obtaining its or their consent, and such action shall not relieve tenant of liability under this lease.

(g) Each transfer, assignment, subletting, license, concession agreement, and hypothecation to which there has been consent will be by an instrument in form satisfactory to landlord and will be executed by the transferor, assignor, sublessor, licensor, concessionaire, hypothecator, or mortgagor and the transferee, assignee, subtenant, licensee, concessionaire, or mortgagee in each instance, as the case may be; and each transferee, assignee, or subtenant will agree in writing for the benefit of landlord to assume, to be bound by, and to perform the terms, covenants, and conditions of this lease to be done, kept, and performed by tenant. One executed copy of such instrument will be delivered to landlord.

(h) If tenant assigns or sublets the premises or requests landlord's consent to a proposed assignment, subletting, or other act, then tenant will pay to landlord an administrative fee in the sum of $[amount] and also landlord's reasonable attorneys' fees.

(i) For the purposes of this lease, a transfer of more than 50% of the partnership interest in tenant, if tenant is a partnership, or 50% of the outstanding voting stock, if tenant is a corporation, shall constitute an assignment of this lease.

FORM 12.13(2)
ASSIGNMENT—SHOPPING CENTER

(a)   Tenant will not transfer, assign, sublet, enter into license or concession agreements, or hypothecate this lease or tenant's interest in and to the premises without first procuring the written consent of landlord. Landlord may base its consent upon such terms, provisions, and conditions as landlord, in its sole discretion, determines are appropriate. Any attempted transfer, assignment, subletting, license or concession agreement, or hypothecation without landlord's consent will be void and will, at the option of landlord, terminate this lease. This lease will not, nor will any interest herein, be assignable as to the interest of tenant by operation of law without the consent of landlord. Tenant agrees to reimburse landlord for landlord's reasonable attorneys' fees incurred in conjunction with the processing and documentation of any such requested transfer, assignment, subletting, licensing or concession agreement, or hypothecation of this lease or tenant's interest in and to the premises.

(b)   Any sums or other economic consideration received by tenant as a result of any subletting, assignment, license, or concession agreement (other than the rental or other payments received that are attributable to the amortization over the terms of this lease of the cost of nonbuilding standard leasehold improvements to the sublet portion of the premises at the cost of tenant), whether denominated rentals under the sublease or otherwise, which exceed in the aggregate the total sums which tenant is obligated to pay landlord under this lease (prorated to reflect obligations allocable to that portion of the premises subject to such sublease), will be payable to landlord as additional rent under this lease without affecting or reducing any other obligation of tenant under this lease.

(c)   Before entering into any assignment of this lease or into a sublease of all or part of the premises, tenant will give written notice to landlord identifying the intended assignee or subtenant by name and address and specifying the terms of the intended assignment or sublease. For a period of 30 days after notice is given, landlord will have the right by written notice to tenant to:

(1)   in the case of a proposed sublease, either

(A)   sublet from tenant any portion of the premises proposed to be sublet for the term for which such portion is proposed to be sublet but at the same rent as tenant is required to pay to landlord under this lease for the same space, computed on a pro rata square footage basis, or

(B)   if the proposed subletting is for substantially the remaining period of the term of this lease, terminate this lease, or terminate this lease as it pertains to the portion of the premises so proposed by tenant to be sublet; or

(2)   in the case of a proposed assignment, terminate this lease.

If landlord terminates this lease, such termination will be as of the date specified in the notice. If landlord terminates this lease, landlord may, if it elects, enter into a new lease covering the premises or a portion thereof with the intended assignee or subtenant, on such terms as landlord and such person may agree, or enter into a new lease covering the premises or a portion of the premises with any other person. In such event, tenant will not be entitled to any portion of the profit, if any, which landlord may realize on account of such termination and reletting. Landlord's exercise of its aforesaid option will not be construed to impose any liability upon landlord with respect to any real estate brokerage commission(s) or any other costs or expenses incurred by tenant in connection with its proposed subletting or assignment.

(d) Tenant may assign this lease or sublet the premises or any portion of the premises without landlord's consent to any corporation which controls, is controlled by, or is under common control with tenant or to any corporation resulting from merger or consolidation with tenant, so long as there is no change in control of tenant, provided that said assignee assumes, in full, the obligations of tenant under this lease.

(e) Regardless of landlord's consent, no subletting, assignment, hypothecation, license or concession will release tenant from tenant's obligation or alter the primary liability of tenant to pay the rental and to perform all other obligations to be performed by tenant. The acceptance of rental by landlord from any other person will not be deemed to be a waiver by landlord of any provision of this lease. Consent to one assignment, subletting, hypothecation, license, or concession agreement will not be deemed consent to any subsequent assignment, subletting, hypothecation, license, or concession agreement. In the event of default by any assignee of tenant or any successor of tenant in the performance of any of the terms of this lease, landlord may proceed directly against tenant without the necessity of exhausting remedies against such assignee or successor. Landlord may consent to subsequent assignments, subletting, hypothecations, licenses, or concession agreements and to amendments or modifications to this lease with assignees of tenant without notifying tenant or any successor of tenant and without obtaining its or their consent, and such action shall not relieve tenant of liability under this lease.

(f) Each transfer, assignment, subletting, license, concession agreement, and hypothecation to which there has been consent will be by an instrument in form satisfactory to landlord and will be executed by the transferor, assignor, sublessor, licensor, concessionaire, hypothecator, or mortgagor and the transferee, assignee, subtenant, licensee, concessionaire, or mortgagee in each instance, as the case may be; and each transferee, assignee, or subtenant will agree in writing for the benefit of landlord to assume, to be bound by, and to perform the terms, covenants, and conditions of this lease to be done, kept, and performed by tenant. One executed copy of such instrument will be delivered to landlord.

(g) If tenant assigns or sublets the premises or requests landlord's consent to a proposed assignment, subletting, or other act, then tenant will pay to landlord an administrative fee in the sum of $[amount] and also landlord's reasonable attorneys' fees.

§ 12.14   Preparing a Form of Assignment (Reserved)

§ 12.15   Preparing a Form of Sublease

FORM 12.15(1)
ASSIGNMENT AND SUBLETTING—SHOPPING CENTER
(Tenant's Form)

Tenant may sublet the premises or any part of them, but tenant will continue liable for the performance of the terms, conditions, and covenants of this lease. Tenant may assign this lease at any time, subject to the prior written consent of landlord, which will not unreasonably be withheld or delayed. If landlord declines to consent to the assignment, or if landlord does not act on tenant's request within a 15-day period after receipt of a written request for consent, without waiving any other remedy to which tenant may be entitled, tenant may cancel this lease by giving landlord written notice. If tenant exercises its option to cancel, the term of this lease will end as of the date specified in tenant's notice, but not sooner than the date on which the notice of cancellation is served upon landlord, and both landlord and tenant will be released from any and all obligations subsequently accruing under this lease.

At any time during the term of this lease, tenant may assign this lease to any legal entity that takes over all of the stores of tenant in the state in which the premises are located, or to any corporation that may, as the result of a reorganization, merger, consolidation, or sale of stock or assets, succeed to the business now carried on by tenant in the state, or to any subsidiary corporation of tenant, parent corporation of tenant, or subsidiary of a parent corporation of tenant, and the occupancy of the premises by any such assignee will be considered to be the continued occupancy of the premises by tenant. If tenant does so assign this lease, tenant will remain liable under it; however, tenant will be released from further liability under it if such assignment is to a corporation that acquires all or substantially all of the assets of tenant, and that, by written instrument, duly executed and acknowledged and delivered to landlord, assumes and agrees to pay the rent to be paid by tenant and to perform all the terms, covenants, and conditions of this lease that are to be performed by tenant.

CHAPTER 13

SIGNS

§ 13.1 Introduction (Reserved)

§ 13.2 Signs in Single Tenant Leases

§ 13.3 Signs in Office Building Leases

§ 13.4 Signs in Shopping Center Leases

§ 13.1 Introduction (Reserved)

§ 13.2 Signs in Single Tenant Leases

FORM 13.2(1)
SIGNS—SINGLE TENANT BUILDING
(Landlord's Form)

Except for signs that are located inside the building and are not visible outside the building, no signs will be placed at any place on the premises without the prior written consent of landlord as to their size, design, color, location, content, illumination, composition, material, and mobility. All signs will be maintained by tenant in good condition during the term of this lease. Tenant will remove all signs at the end of this lease and repair and restore any damage caused by their installation or removal.

FORM 13.2(2)
SIGNS—SINGLE TENANT BUILDING
(Tenant's Form)

Tenant may install signs on the premises in accordance with federal, state, and local statutes, laws, ordinances, and codes.

§ 13.3   Signs in Office Building Leases

FORM 13.3(1)
SIGNS—OFFICE BUILDING

Without landlord's prior written permission, tenant will not attach any sign on any part of the outside of the premises or the building, or on any part of the inside of the premises that is visible outside the premises, or in the halls, lobbies, windows, or elevator banks of the building. Permitted signs will comply with the requirements of the governmental authorities having jurisdiction over the building. At its expense, tenant will maintain all permitted signs and will, at the end of this lease and at its expense, remove all permitted signs and repair any damage caused by their removal. If tenant fails to do so, landlord may remove all unpermitted signs without notice to tenant and at tenant's expense. Landlord may name the building and change the name, number, or designation of the building. Tenant will not use the name of the building for any purpose other than the address of the building. Landlord will provide a directory in a conspicuous place in the building with names of tenants of the building. Tenant will be given one line on the building directory. Landlord will also provide one suite identification sign adjacent to the main entry door of the premises in landlord's standard form. Tenant will pay landlord's reasonable charges for changing the directory listing and identification sign at tenant's request.

§ 13.4   Signs in Shopping Center Leases

FORM 13.4(1)
SIGNS—SHOPPING CENTER

(a)   Tenant will purchase and erect one sign on the front of the premises not later than the date on which tenant opens for business or within thirty (30) days after the date of commencement of this lease, whichever is sooner, in accordance with landlord's sign criteria attached to this lease as Exhibit [* *]. Tenant will maintain, repair, and replace the sign as required by landlord during this lease. At the end of this lease, the sign will immediately become the property of landlord.

(b)   Tenant will keep the display windows and signs of the premises well lighted during business hours and until 12:00 midnight each night or such earlier time as may be prescribed by any applicable policies or regulations adopted by any utility or governmental agency, and will maintain adequate night lights after that hour or period.

(c)   Without the prior written consent of landlord, tenant will not place or permit to be placed (1) any sign, advertising material, or lettering upon the exterior of the premises or (2) any sign, advertising material, or lettering upon the exterior or interior surface of any door or show window or at any point inside the premises from which the same may be visible from outside the premises. Upon request of landlord, tenant will immediately remove any sign, advertising material, or lettering that tenant has placed or permitted to be placed in violation of the provisions of the preceding sentence, and if tenant fails so to do, landlord may enter the premises and remove such sign, advertising material, or lettering at tenant's expense. Tenant will comply with such regulations as may from time to time be promulgated by landlord governing signs, advertising material, or lettering of all tenants in the retail area; however, tenant will not be required to change any sign or lettering that was in compliance with applicable regulations at the time it was installed or placed in, on, or about the premises.

CHAPTER 14

RULES AND REGULATIONS

§ 14.1 Introduction
§ 14.2 Rules and Regulations for Shopping Centers (Reserved)
§ 14.3 Rules and Regulations for Office Buildings (Reserved)
§ 14.4 Rules and Regulations for Single Tenant Buildings (Reserved)

§ 14.1 Introduction

FORM 14.1(1)
RULES AND REGULATIONS—LEASE PROVISION

Tenant will faithfully observe and comply with the rules and regulations attached to this lease, and all modifications and additions from time to time promulgated by landlord. Landlord will not be responsible to tenant for the nonperformance of any such rules and regulations by any other tenant or occupant of the building.

§ 14.2 Rules and Regulations for Shopping Centers (Reserved)

§ 14.3 Rules and Regulations for Office Buildings (Reserved)

§ 14.4 Rules and Regulations for Single Tenant Buildings (Reserved)

CHAPTER 15

MERCHANTS' ASSOCIATIONS, PROMOTION FUNDS, AND ADVERTISING FUNDS

§ 15.1 Introduction to Merchants' Associations (Reserved)

§ 15.2 Purposes of Merchants' Associations (Reserved)

§ 15.3 Requirements of Merchants' Associations (Reserved)

§ 15.4 Payments to Merchants' Associations (Reserved)

§ 15.5 Voting in Merchants' Associations (Reserved)

§ 15.6 Concluding Thoughts about Merchants' Associations

§ 15.7 Promotion Funds and Advertising Funds (Reserved)

§ 15.1 Introduction to Merchants' Associations (Reserved)

§ 15.2 Purposes of Merchants' Associations (Reserved)

§ 15.3 Requirements of Merchants' Associations (Reserved)

§ 15.4 Payments to Merchants' Associations (Reserved)

§ 15.5 Voting in Merchants' Associations (Reserved)

§ 15.6   Concluding Thoughts about Merchants' Associations

FORM 15.6(1)
MERCHANTS' ASSOCIATION

Tenant will become a member of, participate fully in, and remain in good standing in the merchants' association (as soon as the same has been formed) limited to tenants occupying premises in the shopping center, and will abide by the regulations of such association. Each member tenant will have one vote and the owner will also have one vote in the operation of the association. The objects of the association will be to encourage its members to deal fairly and courteously with their customers, to sell their merchandise or services at fair prices, to follow ethical business practices, to assist the business of the tenants by sales promotions and center-wide advertising, and in particular to help the interests of members of the association. Tenant agrees to pay minimum dues to the merchants' association in the amount of $[amount] per month (calculated on the basis of 15 cents per square foot per year of area of the premises), subject, however, to annual adjustments, approved by a majority vote of the members of the association, increasing said dues to the extent required by increases in the costs of promotional, public relations, and advertising services. In any event, the continuing monthly contributions to the association will be adjusted annually by a percentage equal to the percentage increase or decrease from the base period of the United States Department of Labor, Bureau of Labor Statistics Cost of Living Index, provided that index has increased or decreased by ten percent or more from the base period. The term "base period" will refer to the date on which that index is published that is closest to the date of the formation of the merchants' association. Tenant also agrees to pay to the merchants' association an initial assessment, in addition to the foregoing dues, in the amount of $[amount] (calculated on the basis of [* *] per square foot of the area of the leased premises) for the purposes of defraying the promotional and public relations expenses to be incurred by the merchants' association in connection with the joint opening of the shopping center. Owner will pay to the merchants' association for the purpose of promotion of such joint opening an amount equal to one-third of the aggregate assessments payable by all members of the association for such promotion, and will pay to the merchants' association for the continuing promotion of the shopping center an amount equal to one-fourth of the aggregate monthly dues payable by the members of the association. Nothing in the by-laws or regulations of the said association will be in conflict with the provisions of this lease, including without limiting the generality of the foregoing any reasonable rules and regulations adopted pursuant to the provisions of Section [* *] of this lease, or in any wise shall affect the rights of the owner.

FORM 15.6(2)
MERCHANTS' ASSOCIATION
(Another Form)

(a)   Landlord reserves the right at any time to cause a merchants' association to be formed. Upon formation of the association, tenant will become a member, will maintain membership in good standing, and will abide by the regulations and cooperate in the activities of the association throughout the term of this lease and any extensions or renewals. The purpose of the association will be to encourage its members to deal fairly and courteously with their customers, to follow ethical business practices, and to assist the business of its members by sales promotions and center-wide advertising. If landlord elects to provide promotional services and personnel to formulate and effect an advertising, promotional, and public relations program for the shopping center, landlord will be reimbursed by the association for landlords' cost of providing such promotional services and personnel, in an amount equal to 25% of the annual dues payable to the association. Any promotional services and personnel provided under the paragraph will be under the exclusive control and supervision of landlord, who will have the sole authority to employ and discharge such personnel. Tenant's dues to the association will be $[* * *] per month, subject to annual adjustments approved by the board of directors of the association increasing the dues to the extent required by increases in the cost of promotional, public relations, and advertising services.

(b)   Landlord reserves the right, at any time, to dissolve any merchants' association that may exist and to provide, or cause to be provided, a program of advertising and promotional events that, in landlord's sole judgment, will serve to promote the shopping center.

(c)   All payments, charges, dues, and assessments payable under this section will be due in monthly installments on the first day of each month during the term of this lease and will be paid without deduction or offset. Failure by tenant to pay all amounts when due will carry the same consequences as tenant's failure to pay rent.

§ 15.7   Promotion Funds and Advertising Funds
(Reserved)

PART V

GIVING THE TENANT RIGHTS

CHAPTER 16

LANDLORD'S SERVICES

§ 16.1 Introduction (Reserved)

§ 16.2 Short Provision for Landlord's Services

§ 16.3 Long Provision for Landlord's Services

§ 16.1 Introduction (Reserved)

§ 16.2 Short Provision for Landlord's Services

FORM 16.2(1)
LANDLORD'S SERVICES (SHORT PROVISION)

So long as tenant is not in breach of this lease, landlord agrees to furnish to the premises during reasonable hours of generally recognized business days, to be determined by landlord at its sole discretion, and subject to the rules and regulations of the building of which the premises are part, electricity for normal lighting and fractional horsepower office machines, heat and air conditioning required in landlord's judgment for the comfortable use and occupation of the premises, and janitorial service, all in a manner comparable to that of similar buildings.

§ 16.3 Long Provision for Landlord's Services

FORM 16.3(1)
LANDLORD'S SERVICES (LONG PROVISION)

(a) Landlord's Maintenance. Landlord will maintain the common areas of the project, including lobbies, stairs, elevators, corridors, and restrooms, the windows in the building, the mechanical, plumbing and electrical equipment serving the building, and the structure of the building in reasonably good

331

order and condition except for damage occasioned by the act of tenant, which will be repaired by landlord at tenant's expense.

(b)   Landlord's Services. Landlord will furnish the premises with:

(1)   electricity for lighting and the operation of low-wattage office machines (such as desktop calculators and typewriters) during business hours, as that term is defined in this section, but landlord will not be obligated to furnish more than 1.3 watts per rentable square foot for nonlighting power and 1.5 watts per rentable square foot for building standard fluorescent lighting;

(2)   heat and air conditioning reasonably required for the comfortable occupation of the premises during business hours;

(3)   access and elevator service during business hours;

(4)   lighting replacement (for building standard lights), during business hours;

(5)   restroom supplies;

(6)   window washing with reasonable frequency, as determined by landlord in its sole discretion; and

(7)   cleaning service during the times and in the manner that those services are customarily furnished in comparable office buildings in the area.

Tenant will have the right to purchase for use during business hours the services described in clauses (1) and (2) in excess of the amounts that landlord has agreed to furnish so long as tenant gives landlord reasonable prior notice of its desire to do so, the excess services are reasonably available to landlord and to the premises, and tenant pays as additional rent (at the time the next payment of base monthly rent is due) the cost of such excess services from time to time charged by landlord. Tenant will have the right to purchase for use during nonbusiness hours the services described in clauses (1) through (7), inclusive, in excess of the amounts that landlord has agreed to furnish, so long as tenant gives landlord reasonable prior notice of its desire to do so, the excess services are reasonably available to landlord and the premises, landlord agrees in its sole discretion to furnish the excess services, and tenant pays as additional rent (at the time the next payment of base monthly rent is due) the cost of the excess services from time to time charged by landlord. Landlord will not be in default under this section or be liable for any damages directly or indirectly resulting from, nor will the rental reserved in this section be abated by reason of, the installation, use, or interruption of use of any equipment in connection with the furnishing of any of those services, failure to furnish or delay in furnishing any such services when the failure or delay is caused by accident or any condition beyond the reasonable control of landlord or by the making of necessary repairs or improvements to the premises or to the building, or the limitation, curtailment, rationing, or restrictions on use of water, electricity, gas, or any other form of utility serving the premises or the building. Landlord will use reasonable efforts diligently to remedy any interruption in the services. The term "business hours" means 7:00 a.m. to 6:00 p.m. on Monday through Friday, except holidays (as that term is defined in this paragraph), and 8:00 a.m. to 12:00 noon on Saturdays, except holidays. The term "holidays" means New Year's Day, Presidents' Day, Memorial Day, Independence Day, Labor Day,

Thanksgiving Day, Christmas Day, and such other national holidays as may be established by the United States government.

(c)   Tenant's Costs. Whenever equipment or lighting (other than building standard lighting) is used in the premises by tenant and it affects the temperature otherwise maintained by the air conditioning system, landlord will have the right, after notice to tenant, to install supplementary air conditioning facilities in the premises or otherwise modify the ventilating and air conditioning system serving the premises, and the cost of those facilities and modifications will be borne by tenant. Tenant will also pay as additional rent the cost of providing all cooling energy to the premises in excess of that required for normal office use or during hours requested by tenant when air conditioning is not otherwise furnished by landlord. If tenant installs lighting or equipment requiring power in excess of that furnished by landlord pursuant to paragraph (b)(1), tenant will pay for the cost of the excess power as additional rent, together with the cost of installing any additional risers, meters, or other facilities that may be necessary to furnish or measure such excess power to the premises.

FORM 16.3(2)
LANDLORD'S SERVICES—BREAKDOWN PROVISION

Landlord will not be liable to tenant or any other person or entity for direct or consequential damage, or otherwise, for any failure to supply any heat, air conditioning, elevator, cleaning, lighting, security, or other service that landlord has agreed to supply during any period when landlord uses reasonable diligence to supply such services. Landlord reserves the right to discontinue such services, or any of them, temporarily at such times as may be necessary by reason of accident, unavailability of employees, repairs, alterations or improvements, strikes, lockouts, riots, acts of God, governmental preemption in connection with a national or local emergency, any rule, order, or regulation of any governmental agency, conditions of supply and demand that make any product unavailable, landlord's compliance with any mandatory governmental energy conservation or environmental protection program or any voluntary governmental energy conservation program, the request, consent, or acquiescence of tenant, or any other happening beyond the control of landlord. Landlord will not be liable to tenant or any other person or entity for direct or consequential damages resulting from the admission to or exclusion from the building or project of any person. In the event of invasion, riot, public excitement, or other circumstances rendering such action advisable in landlord's sole opinion, landlord will have the right to prevent access to or from the building by such means as landlord in its sole discretion may deem appropriate, including without limitation locking doors and closing parking areas and other common areas. Landlord will not be liable for damages to person or property or for injury to, or interruption of, business for any discontinuance permitted under this paragraph, nor will that discontinuance in any way be construed as an eviction of tenant or cause an abatement of rent or operate to release tenant from any of tenant's obligations under this lease.

FORM 16.3(3)
SERVICES—BUILDING SECURITY

(a)   Landlord will have the right, but not the obligation, from time to time to adopt such policies, procedures, and programs as it deems necessary or appropriate for the security of the building, and tenant will cooperate with landlord in the enforcement of the policies, procedures, and programs adopted by landlord.

(b)   Without limiting the generality of subparagraph (a), landlord reserves the right to exclude from the building between the hours of 6:00 p.m. and 7:00 a.m. and at all hours on Saturdays, Sundays, and holidays all persons who do not present a valid pass to the building. If landlord does elect to adopt such a pass system, landlord will furnish passes to persons for whom tenant requests the same in writing, and tenant will be responsible for all persons for whom it requests passes and will be liable to landlord for all acts of such persons. Landlord will in no case be liable for damages for any error with regard to the admission to or exclusion from the building of any person. In case of invasion, mob, riot, public demonstration, or other circumstances rendering such action advisable in landlord's opinion, landlord reserves the right to prevent access to the building by such action as landlord may deem appropriate, including closing doors.

(c)   In the event of any picketing, public demonstration, or other threat to the security of the building that is directly attributable to tenant, tenant will reimburse landlord for any costs incurred by landlord in connection with such picketing, demonstration, or other threat in order to protect the security of the building.

CHAPTER 17

COMMON AREAS

§ 17.1 Introduction (Reserved)

§ 17.2 Common Areas in Office Buildings

§ 17.3 Common Areas in Shopping Centers—Grant

§ 17.4 —Definition (Reserved)

§ 17.5 —Landlord's Reserved Rights

§ 17.6 —Expenses (Reserved)

§ 17.7 —Allocation of Expenses (Reserved)

§ 17.8 —Payment of Expenses (Reserved)

§ 17.9 —Landlord's Obligations

§ 17.1 Introduction (Reserved)

§ 17.2 Common Areas in Office Buildings

FORM 17.2(1)
COMMON AREAS—OFFICE BUILDING

The term "common areas" means all areas and facilities in the project that are provided and designated from time to time by landlord for the general nonexclusive use and convenience of tenant with other tenants of the project and their respective employees, invitees, licensees, or other visitors, and may include without limitation the hallways, entryways, stairs, elevators, driveways, walkways, terraces, docks, loading areas, restrooms, and trash facilities. Landlord grants tenant, its employees, invitees, licensees, and other visitors a nonexclusive license for the term to use the common areas in common with others entitled to use the common areas, including without limitation landlord and other tenants of the building and their respective employees and invitees and other persons authorized by landlord, subject to the terms and conditions of this lease. Without advance notice to tenant, except with respect to matters covered by subsection (a) of this paragraph, and without any liability to tenant in any respect, landlord may:

(a) establish and enforce reasonable rules and regulations concerning the maintenance, management, use, and operation of the common areas;

(b) close off any of the common areas to any extent required in the opinion of landlord and its counsel to prevent a dedication of any of the common areas or the accrual of any rights by any person or the public to the common areas, so long as such closure does not deprive tenant of the substantial benefit and enjoyment of the premises;

(c) temporarily close any of the common areas for maintenance, alteration, or improvement purposes;

(d) select, appoint, or contract with any person for the purpose of operating and maintaining the common areas, subject to such terms and at such rates as landlord deems reasonable and proper;

(e) change the size, use, shape, or nature of any such common areas, so long as such change does not deprive tenant of the substantial benefit and enjoyment of the premises. So long as tenant is not thus deprived of the substantial use and benefit of the premises, landlord may change the arrangement or location of, or both, or regulate or eliminate the use of any concourse, garage, elevators, stairs, toilets, or other public conveniences in the project, without incurring any liability to tenant or entitling tenant to abatement of rent, and such action will not constitute an actual or constructive eviction of tenant;

(f) erect one or more additional buildings on the common areas, expand the building to cover a portion of the common areas, convert common areas to a portion of the building, or convert any portion of the building to common areas, so long as any such change does not deprive tenant of the substantial benefit and enjoyment of the premises. Upon erection or change of location of the buildings, the portion of the project on which buildings or structures have been erected will no longer be deemed to be a part of the common areas, except to the extent the building contains common areas. If any changes in the size or use of the building or common areas are made, landlord will make an appropriate adjustment in the rentable area of the building and in tenant's share of the operating expenses payable pursuant to paragraph [operating expense paragraph] of this lease.

§ 17.3   Common Areas in Shopping Centers—Grant

FORM 17.3(1)
COMMON AREAS—SHOPPING CENTER

Landlord grants tenant and tenant's customers and invitees the nonexclusive right to use the common areas, in common with others to whom the landlord has granted or will grant a similar right.

The term "common areas" means the parking areas, roadways, pedestrian sidewalks, driveways, sidewalks, mall, whether open or closed, delivery areas, trash removal areas, landscaped areas, security areas, public washrooms, and all other areas or improvements that may be provided by landlord for the common use of the tenants in the shopping center.

Landlord reserves the following rights with respect to the common areas:

(a)   to establish reasonable rules and regulations for the use of the common areas (including without limitation the delivery of goods and the disposal of trash);

(b)   to use or permit the use of such common areas by others to whom landlord may grant or may have granted such rights in such manner as landlord may from time to time designate, including without limitation truck and trailer sales and special promotional events;

(c)   to close all or any portion of the common areas to make repairs or changes, to prevent a dedication of the common areas or the accrual of any rights to any person or the public, or to discourage noncustomer use or parking;

(d)   to construct additional buildings in the common areas and to change the layout of such common areas, including the right to add to or subtract from their shape and size, whether by the addition of building improvements or otherwise;

(e)   to enter into operating agreements with respect to the common areas; and

(f)   to do such other acts in and to the common areas as in landlord's judgment may be desirable.

Tenant will pay landlord as a common area charge tenant's proportionate share of all costs paid or incurred by landlord in operating and maintaining the common areas, including without limitation: cleaning, window washing, landscaping, lighting, heating, air conditioning, maintaining, painting, repairing, and replacing (except to the extent proceeds of insurance or condemnation awards are available) the enclosed malls and other enclosed common areas; maintaining, repairing, replacing, cleaning, lighting, removing snow and ice from, painting, and landscaping all vehicle parking areas and other outdoor common areas, including any shopping center pylon and sign; providing security; seasonal holiday decorations; removing trash from the common areas; providing public liability, property damage, fire, extended coverage, and such other insurance as landlord deems appropriate; total compensation and benefits (including premiums for workmen's compensation and other insurance) paid to or on behalf of employees; personal property taxes; supplies; fire protection and fire hydrant charges; steam, water, and sewer charges; gas, electricity, and telephone utility charges; licenses and permit fees; supplying music to the common areas; reasonable depreciation of equipment used in operating and maintaining the common areas and rent paid for leasing such equipment; administrative costs equal to [* * *] percent ([* *]%) of all common area costs and expenses.

Tenant's common area charge will be determined by multiplying the total cost incurred by landlord by a fraction, the numerator of which is the number of square feet of floor area within the premises and the denominator of which is the total number of square feet of floor area leased and occupied within all the buildings in the shopping center.

Tenant's common area maintenance charge will be paid in monthly installments on the first day of each month in an amount estimated by landlord.

Within ninety (90) days after the end of the period used by landlord in estimating landlord's cost, landlord will furnish to tenant a statement of the actual amount of tenant's proportionate share of such common area maintenance charge for such period. Within fifteen (15) days after its receipt of such statement, tenant will pay to landlord any excess of the actual amount of tenant's common area maintenance charge over the estimated amounts paid by tenant. If the estimated amounts paid by tenant exceed the actual amount of tenant's common area maintenance charge for the period as shown by the statement, the excess will be credited against the next monthly installment due from tenant.

§ 17.4   —Definition (Reserved)

§ 17.5   —Landlord's Reserved Rights

FORM 17.5(1)
LANDLORD'S RIGHT TO CHANGE COMMON AREAS

Landlord reserves the right at any time and from time to time to add to, change, relocate, improve, or demolish all or any portion of the complex, buildings, common areas, and parking areas (including without limitation the right to add additional floors to the buildings, to build new improvements adjoining the buildings, and to change, relocate, remove, or designate those parties who may use the lobbies, corridors, elevators, escalators, and loading docks). Landlord's exercise of these rights will not require landlord to compensate tenant in any way, nor will it result in any liability to landlord or in any way affect tenant's obligations under the lease.

§ 17.6   —Expenses (Reserved)

§ 17.7   —Allocation of Expenses (Reserved)

§ 17.8   —Payment of Expenses (Reserved)

§ 17.9   —Landlord's Obligations

FORM 17.9(1)
COMMON AREAS—TENANT'S FORM

During the term of the lease, landlord will make all necessary repairs:

(a)   to the sidewalks, driveways, service areas, curbs, and parking areas;

(b)   to the exterior and to the structure of the building;

(c)   to the exterior water, sewerage, gas, and electrical services up to the point of entry to the building;

(d)   to the interior walls, ceilings, floors, and floor coverings when such repairs are made necessary because of faulty construction or landlord's failure to keep the structure in proper repair;

(e)   to the heating and air conditioning systems, except ordinary maintenance; and

(f)   all repairs or restoration made necessary by fire or other peril covered by the standard extended coverage endorsement on fire insurance policies or by reason of war, windstorm, or acts of God.

FORM 17.9(2)
COMMON AREAS
(Tenant's Form)

(a)   Landlord agrees that the parking and common areas shown on Exhibit [* *] will remain as shown on Exhibit [* *] throughout the term and that no building, fence, wall, sign, or other obstruction will be erected or maintained upon any portion without prior written consent of tenant and except pursuant to subparagraph (f). Landlord grants tenant a nonexclusive easement appurtenant to the premises, over and upon the parking and common areas shown on Exhibit [* *], for the purpose of foot and vehicular ingress and egress, and the parking of motor vehicles of the customers, patrons, suppliers, licensees, agents, and employees of tenant, its subtenants, and concessionaires. Landlord acknowledges that the parking and common areas consist of all areas shown on Exhibit [* *] not delineated as leaseable space for the exclusive use of tenant or other tenants of the shopping center.

(b)   Landlord will maintain and repair the entire parking and common areas and keep them in good condition. Landlord's obligation will (without limitation) include:

(1)   resurfacing, including keeping the surfaces in a level, smooth, and evenly covered condition with the type of surfacing material originally installed or a substitute material in all respects equal in quality, use, and durability;

(2)   cleaning, striping, lighting, and all other tasks necessary to maintain the parking and common areas in a clean, safe, and orderly condition, including removal of trash, rubbish, garbage, and other refuse;

(3)   maintaining any perimeter wall in good condition and repair;

(4)   placing, keeping in repair, and replacing any necessary appropriate directional signs, markers, and lines and operating, keeping in repair, and replacing when necessary such artificial lighting facilities as are required to keep the areas adequately lit;

(5)   maintaining all landscaped areas, making such replacements of shrubs and other landscaping as is necessary, and keeping those areas at all times adequately weeded, fertilized, and watered;

(6)   maintaining comprehensive public liability and property damage insurance (naming tenant as an additional insured).

(c)   Tenant agrees to reimburse landlord for tenant's proportionate share of the expense of maintaining and repairing the parking and common areas ("CAM charges"). Tenant's proportionate share of such CAM charges will be the fraction of CAM charges, the numerator of which is the total number of square feet of ground floor space within the premises, and the denominator of which is the number of total square feet of leaseable space within the shopping center, whether such space is leased or occupied or not. If additional buildings are at any time constructed within the shopping center for any reason, tenant's proportionate share will be appropriately adjusted as of the day the additional buildings are substantially completed. Landlord will pay or cause to be paid all taxes and assessments which are levied against the parking and common areas. Provision for tenant to pay its pro rata share of taxes and assessments has been made in [the tax paragraph], and no portion of real property taxes and assessments are to be included in tenant's pro rata share of CAM charges.

The following items are specifically excluded from tenant's pro rata share: administrative expenses of landlord, including landlord's personnel salaries such as secretarial and executive salaries (other than personnel used in direct common area maintenance), landlord's general overhead, costs of major resurfacing (except for annual amounts attributable to such period if such costs are amortized over its estimated useful life on a straight line basis), initial construction and landscaping, and other capital improvements, all in accordance with generally accepted accounting principles consistently applied, and landlord's legal fees attributable to any matters concerning tenant or any other tenant of the shopping center and the common areas.

(d)   Landlord will keep accurate records showing in detail all expenses incurred for maintenance and showing the ground floor area of each building and similar structure in the shopping center. These records will, upon demand, be made available during business hours at the office of landlord for inspection by tenant. Within sixty (60) days after the end of each lease year, landlord will provide tenant with a written statement ("yearly statement") itemizing (1) income and expenses for the period covered, (2) the total ground floor area within the shopping center, (3) the ground floor area occupied by each tenant, and (4) tenant's pro rata share of CAM charges.

(e)   Upon receipt of the yearly statements, tenant will pay to landlord tenant's pro rata share of CAM charges. In no event will such charges exceed $[amount] for each square foot within the premises (exclusive of taxes with respect to the premises).

(f)   Except in the case of emergency, in which event tenant may perform such maintenance immediately, if landlord fails or refuses to fulfill adequately any of its obligations under this paragraph with 15 days after written demand by tenant to do so, tenant may so perform and landlord will pay to tenant on demand the cost (less tenant's pro rata share of appropriate CAM charges as set forth in this paragraph) plus interest on such costs at the highest legal rate until paid; or tenant may at its option deduct the cost (as so adjusted) plus interest from the rent reserved to landlord until said amount has been paid in full.

(g)   Landlord agrees that the shopping center (including the parking and common areas) will be operated as a single mercantile unit, and that no buildings, structures, improvements, fences, barriers, or other obstructions, except improvements incidental to the operation and maintenance of the common facilities, will be placed, constructed, or maintained in the shopping center except as shown on Exhibit [* *], and in no event will (1) the ratio of the number of parking spaces available for standard size American cars to the amount of square footage of ground floor space within the buildings comprising the shopping center be reduced below 3 parking spaces for each 1,000 square feet of gross leaseable area, (2) there be any interference in the access to the premises from the abutting public thoroughfares and the parking and common areas, or (3) the visibility of the premises from the parking and common areas and from the abutting public thoroughfares be obstructed in any way.

PART VI

PRESERVING THE PREMISES

CHAPTER 18

REPAIRS AND MAINTENANCE

§ 18.1 Common Law Rules (Reserved)

§ 18.2 Practical Overview (Reserved)

§ 18.3 Repairs Provisions in Shopping Center Leases

§ 18.4 Repairs Provisions in Office Building Leases

§ 18.5 Comments on the Typical Multitenant Provision (Reserved)

§ 18.6 Repairs Provisions in Single Tenant Leases

§ 18.1   Common Law Rules (Reserved)

§ 18.2   Practical Overview (Reserved)

§ 18.3   Repairs Provisions in Shopping Center Leases

FORM 18.3(1)
REPAIRS—SHOPPING CENTER

(a)   Tenant will at all times during the term of this lease keep and maintain the premises (including without limitation all improvements, fixtures, and equipment on the premises) at its own cost and expense, in good order, condition, and repair, and will make all repairs and replacements, interior and exterior, above or below ground, and ordinary or extraordinary. Landlord will keep in good order, condition, and repair the foundations and exterior walls (excluding the interior of all walls and the exterior and interior of all doors, plate glass, display, and other windows excluding interior ceiling) of the premises, except for (1) any damage caused by any act, negligence, or omission of tenant or tenant's employees, agents, contractors, or customers, (2) reasonable wear and tear, and (3) any structural alterations or improvements required by any governmental agency by reason of tenant's use and occupancy of the premises. Tenant will reimburse landlord for tenant's pro rata share of the costs that landlord incurs in performing its repair and maintenance obligations with respect to the shopping center. Tenant's pro rata share will be in the same proportion as the area of the premises bears to the total area of the shopping center. Reimbursement by tenant to landlord for its share of such costs will be made in the manner set forth in paragraph [* *]. As a condition precedent to all obligations of landlord to repair the shopping center, tenant will notify landlord in writing of the need for such repair. If landlord fails to commence the making of repairs within thirty (30) days after such notice, and the failure to repair has materially interfered with tenant's use of the premises, tenant's sole right and remedy for such failure on the part of the landlord will be to cause such repairs to be made and to charge landlord the reasonable cost of such repairs. If the repair is necessary to end or avert an emergency and if landlord after receiving notice from tenant of such necessity fails to commence repair as soon as reasonably possible, tenant may do so at landlord's cost, without waiting thirty (30) days.

(b) Tenant's obligation to keep and maintain the premises in good order, condition, and repair includes without limitation all plumbing and sewage facilities in the premises, floors (including floor coverings), doors, locks, and closing devices, window casements and frames, glass and plate glass, grilles, all electrical facilities and equipment, HVAC systems and equipment, and all other appliances and equipment of every kind and nature, and all landscaping upon, within, or attached to the premises. In addition, tenant will at its sole cost and expense install or construct any improvements, equipment, or fixtures required by any governmental authority or agency as a consequence of tenant's use and occupancy of the premises. Tenant will replace any damaged plate glass within forty-eight (48) hours after the occurrence of such damage.

(c) Landlord will assign to tenant, and tenant will have the benefit of, any guarantee or warranty to which landlord is entitled under any purchase, construction, or installation contract relating to a component of the premises that tenant is obligated to repair and maintain. Tenant will have the right to call upon the contractor to make such adjustments, replacements, or repairs that are required to be made by the contractor under such contract.

(d) Landlord may at landlord's option employ and pay a firm satisfactory to landlord, engaged in the business of maintaining systems, to perform periodic inspections of the HVAC systems serving the premises and to perform any necessary work, maintenance, or repair of it. In that event, tenant will reimburse landlord for all reasonable amounts paid by landlord in connection with such employment. Reimbursement will be made in the manner set forth in paragraph [* *].

(e) Upon the expiration or termination of this lease, tenant will surrender the premises to landlord in good order, condition, and repair, ordinary wear and tear excepted. To the extent allowed by law, tenant waives the right to make repairs at landlord's expense under the provisions of any laws permitting repairs by a tenant at the expense of a landlord.

FORM 18.3(2)
REPAIRS—SHOPPING CENTER
(Tenant's Form)

If any alteration, addition, or change is required by law, regulation, rule, or the requirements of any insurance company (as a condition to the issuance or continuation of insurance coverage) to be made to the premises, or any portion of the premises, then:

(a)   If the alteration, addition, or change is required by reason of the omission or lack of care or maintenance of portions of the premises that tenant is required to care for and maintain, or is required by reason of a change in the manner or mode of use of the premises by tenant, then the alteration, addition, or change will be made and paid for by tenant;

(b)   If the alteration, addition, or change is required by reason of the existence or nonexistence of anything a part of the premises at the time of the execution of this lease, or by reason of any defect in the structural portions of the building or a part of the premises, if the defect is not caused by the manner of use of any portion of the premises, or if it is required as to any portion of the premises landlord has expressly agreed to care for or maintain, then said alteration, addition, or change will be made and paid for by landlord.

§ 18.4   Repairs Provisions in Office Building Leases

FORM 18.4(1)
REPAIRS—OFFICE BUILDING

Tenant will, at its sole cost and expense, maintain the premises and the fixtures and appurtenances in the premises as and when needed to preserve them in good working order and condition. Tenant will immediately advise landlord of any material damage to the premises or any damage to the building. All damage or injury to the premises and to its fixtures, appurtenances, and equipment or to the building or to its fixtures, appurtenances, and equipment that is caused by tenant, its agents, employees, or invitees will be repaired, restored, or replaced promptly by tenant at its sole cost and expense. Such repairs, restorations, and replacements will be in quality and class equal to the original work or installations. Landlord will have the right to supervise the making of repairs, restorations, and replacements by tenant and to charge tenant for its reasonable cost of doing so, and all those repairs, restorations, and replacements will be performed by a contractor approved in advance by landlord. If tenant fails to maintain the premises or to make those repairs, restorations, or replacements, they may be made by landlord at the expense of tenant and the expense, including fifteen percent (15%) for landlord's overhead, will be collectible as additional rent and will be paid by tenant within fifteen (15) days after delivery of a statement for the expense.

FORM 18.4(2)
REPAIRS—OFFICE BUILDING
(Tenant's Form)

Tenant will take good care of the premises and will make all repairs necessitated by its misuse of the premises. Landlord will maintain and keep in repair (and will put into repair where necessary) the common areas, walls, foundation, and roof of the building of which the premises are a part, the plumbing, heating, and electrical system, and other installations serving more than one tenant of the building, and will make all other repairs except those required to be made by tenant.

§ 18.5   Comments on the Typical Multitenant Provision (Reserved)

§ 18.6   Repairs Provisions in Single Tenant Leases

FORM 18.6(1)
REPAIRS—SINGLE TENANT BUILDING

Tenant will, at its sole cost and expense, maintain the premises and make repairs, restorations, and replacements to the premises, including without limitation the heating, ventilating, air conditioning, mechanical, electrical, elevator, and plumbing systems, structural roof, walls, and foundations, and the fixtures and appurtenances to the premises as and when needed to preserve them in good working order and condition, and regardless of whether the repairs, restorations, and replacements are ordinary or extraordinary, foreseeable or unforeseeable, capital or noncapital, or the fault or not the fault of tenant, its agents, employees, invitees, visitors, and contractors. All such repairs, restorations, and replacements will be in quality and class equal to the original work or installations. If tenant fails to make those repairs, restorations, or replacements, landlord may make them at the expense of tenant and the expense will be collectible as additional rent due and payable by tenant within fifteen (15) days after delivery of a statement for the expense.

FORM 18.6(2)
REPAIRS—TENANT'S FORM

Tenant will take good care of the premises and will make all repairs necessitated by its misuse of the premises. Landlord will maintain and repair the walls, foundation, and roof of the building of which the premises are a part, the plumbing, heating, and electrical system, and other installations serving more than one tenant of the building, and will make all other repairs except those required to be made by tenant.

CHAPTER 19

ALTERATIONS

§ 19.1 The Law (Reserved)

§ 19.2 Further Considerations (Reserved)

§ 19.3 Alterations Provisions in Office Building Leases

§ 19.4 Alterations Provisions in Shopping Center Leases

§ 19.5 Alterations Provisions in Single Tenant Leases

§ 19.6 Lenders' Concerns about Alterations (Reserved)

§ 19.1 The Law (Reserved)

§ 19.2 Further Considerations (Reserved)

§ 19.3 Alterations Provisions in Office Building Leases

FORM 19.3(1)
ALTERATIONS—OFFICE BUILDING

(a) General.

(1) During the term, tenant will not make or allow to be made any alterations, additions, or improvements to any part of the premises, or attach any fixtures or equipment to the premises, without first obtaining landlord's written consent. All alterations, additions, and improvements consented to by landlord, and capital improvements that are required to be made to the building as a result of the nature of tenant's use of the premises:

(A) will be performed by contractors approved by landlord and subject to conditions specified by landlord (which may include requiring the posting of a mechanics' or materialmens' lien bond); and

(B) at landlord's option, will be made by landlord for tenant's account, in which event tenant will reimburse landlord for their cost (including 15% of their cost for landlord's overhead) within 10 days after receipt of a statement of their cost.

(2)   Subject to tenant's rights in paragraph [end of term], all alterations, additions, fixtures, and improvements, whether temporary or permanent in character, made in the premises by tenant or landlord, will immediately become landlord's property and at the end of the term will remain on the premises without compensation to tenant, unless when consenting to alterations, additions, fixtures, or improvements, landlord has advised tenant in writing that the alterations, additions, fixtures, or improvements must be removed at the end of this lease.

(b)   Free-Standing Partitions. Tenant will have the right to install at its sole expense free-standing work station partitions, without landlord's prior written consent, so long as no building or other governmental permit is required for their installation or relocation; however, if a permit is required, landlord will not unreasonably withhold its consent to the relocation or installation. The free-standing work station partitions will be part of tenant's trade fixtures for all purposes of this lease. All other partitions that are installed in the premises will be landlord's property for all purposes of this lease.

(c)   Removal. If landlord has required tenant to remove any or all alterations, additions, fixtures, and improvements that are made in the premises pursuant to this paragraph, prior to the expiration of this lease or within 10 days after its termination, tenant will remove the alterations, additions, fixtures, and improvements at tenant's sole cost and will restore the premises to the condition in which they were before the alterations, additions, fixtures, and improvements were made, reasonable wear and tear excepted.

§ 19.4   Alterations Provisions in Shopping Center Leases

FORM 19.4(1)
ALTERATIONS—SHOPPING CENTER

Tenant will not make or cause to be made any alterations, additions, or improvements to or of the premises or any part of the premises, or attach any fixture or equipment to the premises, without first obtaining landlord's written consent. Any alterations, additions, or improvements to the premises consented to by landlord will be made by tenant at tenant's sole cost and expense according to plans and specifications approved by landlord, and any contractor or person selected by tenant to make them must first be approved by landlord. Landlord may require, at its option, that tenant provide landlord at tenant's sole cost a lien and completion bond or payment and performance bond in an amount equal to twice the estimated cost of any contemplated alterations, fixtures, and improvements to insure landlord against any liability for mechanics' or materialmen's liens and to insure the completion of such

work. All alterations, additions, fixtures, and improvements, whether temporary or permanent in character, made in or upon the premises either by tenant or landlord (other than furnishings, trade fixtures, and equipment installed
by tenant), will be landlord's property and, at the end of the term of this
lease, will remain on the premises without compensation to tenant. If landlord requests, tenant will remove all such alterations, fixtures, and improvements from the premises and return the premises to the condition in which
they were delivered to tenant. Tenant will immediately and fully repair any
damage to the premises occasioned by the removal.

FORM 19.4(2)
ALTERATIONS—SHOPPING CENTER
(Tenant's Form)

Tenant may in its discretion and at its own expense make alterations and
additions to the interior of the building. No alterations or additions will diminish the value of the building. All work with respect to any alterations or
additions will be done in a good and workmanlike manner, and diligently
prosecuted to completion to the end that the building will at all times be a
complete unit, except during the period necessarily required for such work.
Tenant will not be obligated to remove alterations or additions upon termination of this lease, but tenant may do so, and if it does, it will repair any damage caused by such removal.

FORM 19.4(3)
ALTERATIONS—SHOPPING CENTER
(Landlord's Form)

Except for alterations that are not structural, mechanical, or electrical, and
for which the costs do not exceed $[* * *] during any 12 month period, tenant
shall not make any changes, alterations, or additions to the premises or any
part of them without the written consent of landlord. Tenant will present
landlord plans and specifications for such work at the time approval is sought.
If tenant is permitted to make alterations, tenant will furnish to landlord a certified statement showing the total cost of alterations. Tenant's leasehold improvements (excluding tenant's trade fixtures, equipment, and furnishings) will
upon the expiration or sooner termination of the term become the sole property of landlord, and, unless landlord requests their removal, will remain upon
and be surrendered with the premises, without damage or injury. If, during
the term, any change, alteration, addition, or correction (other than structural
or major system changes not required as a consequence of the nature of tenant's particular use of the premises) is required by any law, rule, or regulation
of any governmental authority to be made in or to the premises or any portion
of them, and if landlord requests, the change, alteration, addition, or correction will then be made by tenant at its sole cost and expense.

§ 19.5   Alterations Provisions in Single Tenant Leases

FORM 19.5(1)
ALTERATIONS—SINGLE TENANT PREMISES

Tenant will not make any alterations, additions, or improvements to the premises without landlord's prior written consent; however, landlord's prior written consent will not be necessary for any alteration, addition, or improvement that:

(a)   costs less than $[amount] including labor and materials;

(b)   does not change the general character of the premises, or reduce the fair market value of the premises below its fair market value prior to the alteration, addition, or improvement;

(c)   is made with due diligence, in a good and workmanlike manner, and in compliance with all laws as that term is defined in paragraph [compliance with laws paragraph];

(d)   is promptly and fully paid for by tenant; and

(e)   is made under the supervision of an architect or engineer reasonably satisfactory to landlord and in accordance with plans and specifications and cost estimates approved by landlord.

Landlord may designate a supervising architect to assure compliance with the provisions of this paragraph, and if it does, tenant will pay the supervising architect's charges. Promptly after the computation of any alteration, addition, or improvement, tenant will give landlord a copy of "as built" drawings of the alteration, addition, or improvement. Subject to tenant's rights in paragraph [surrender paragraph], all alterations, additions, fixtures, and improvements, whether temporary or permanent in character, made in or upon the premises by tenant will immediately become landlord's property and at the end of the term of this lease will remain on the premises without compensation to tenant. By notice given to tenant no less than ninety (90) days prior to the end of this lease, landlord may require that any alterations, additions, fixtures, and improvements made in or upon the premises be removed by tenant. In that event, tenant will remove the alterations, additions, fixtures, and improvements at tenant's sole cost and will restore the premises to the condition in which they were before the alterations, additions, improvements, and fixtures were made, reasonable wear and tear excepted.

§ 19.6   Lenders' Concerns about Alterations (Reserved)

CHAPTER 20
MECHANICS' LIENS

§ 20.1 Introduction (Reserved)

§ 20.2 Mechanics' Lien Provision

§ 20.1 Introduction (Reserved)

§ 20.2 Mechanics' Lien Provision

FORM 20.2(1)
MECHANICS' LIENS

Tenant will pay or cause to be paid all costs and charges for work done by it or caused to be done by it, in or to the premises, and for all materials furnished for or in connection with the work. Tenant will indemnify landlord against and hold landlord harmless from all liabilities, liens, claims, costs, and demands on account of the work. If any lien is filed against the premises, tenant will cause the lien to be discharged of record within ten (10) days after it is filed. If tenant desires to contest the lien, it will furnish landlord, within the ten-day period, security reasonably satisfactory to landlord of at least one hundred fifty percent (150%) of the amount of the lien, plus estimated costs and interest. If a final, nonappealable judgment establishing the validity or existence of the lien for any amount is entered, tenant will satisfy it at once. If tenant fails to pay any charge for which a lien has been filed, and does not give landlord such security, landlord may, at its option, pay the charge and related costs and interest, and the amount so paid, together with reasonable attorneys' fees incurred in connection with it, will be immediately due from tenant to landlord as additional rent. Nothing contained in this lease is the consent or agreement of landlord to subject landlord's interest in the premises to liability under any lien law. If either landlord or tenant receives notice that a lien has been or is about to be filed against the premises, or that any action affecting title to the premises has been commenced on account of work done by or for tenant or labor or materials furnished to or for tenant, it will immediately give the other written notice of the notice. At least fifteen (15) days prior to the commencement of any work (including without limitation any maintenance, repairs, alterations, additions, improvements, or installations) in or to the premises, by or for tenant, tenant will give landlord written notice of the proposed work and the names and addresses of the persons supplying labor and materials for the proposed work. Landlord will have the right to post notices of nonresponsibility or similar notices on the premises in order to protect the premises against liens.

CHAPTER 21

SURRENDER

§ 21.1 **Early Termination of Lease (Reserved)**

§ 21.2 **Redelivery at End of Term**

§ 21.3 **Fixtures (Reserved)**

§ 21.1 Early Termination of Lease (Reserved)

§ 21.2 Redelivery at End of Term

FORM 21.2(1)
END OF TERM

At the end of this lease, tenant will surrender the premises in good order and condition, ordinary wear and tear excepted. If tenant is not then in default, tenant may remove from the premises any trade fixtures, equipment, and movable furniture placed in the premises by tenant, whether or not the trade fixtures or equipment are fastened to the building. Tenant will not remove any trade fixtures or equipment without landlord's prior written consent if the trade fixtures or equipment are used in the operation of the building or if the removal of the fixtures or equipment will impair the structure of the building. Whether or not tenant is then in default, tenant will remove the alterations, additions, improvements, trade fixtures, equipment, and furniture as landlord has requested in accordance with paragraph [alterations and improvements paragraph]. Tenant will fully repair any damage occasioned by the removal of any trade fixtures, equipment, furniture, alterations, additions, and improvements. All trade fixtures, equipment, furniture, alterations, additions, and improvements not removed will conclusively be deemed to have been abandoned by tenant and may be appropriated, sold, stored, destroyed, or otherwise disposed of by landlord without notice to tenant or to any other person and without obligation to account for them. Tenant will pay landlord all expenses incurred in connection with landlord's disposition of such property, including without limitation the cost of repairing any damage to the building or the premises caused by removal of such property. Tenant's obligation to observe and perform this covenant will survive the end of this lease.

§ 21.3 Fixtures (Reserved)

CHAPTER 22

DAMAGE AND DESTRUCTION

§ 22.1   The Law (Reserved)

§ 22.2   Landlord's and Tenant's Concerns (Reserved)

§ 22.3   —Is the Lease Affected? (Reserved)

§ 22.4   —Is the Rent Affected? (Reserved)

§ 22.5   —How Are the Premises Affected? (Reserved)

§ 22.6   —How Is the Lease Affected? (Reserved)

§ 22.7   Damage and Destruction in Office Building Premises

§ 22.8   Damage and Destruction in Shopping Center Premises

§ 22.9   Damage and Destruction in Single Tenant Premises

§ 22.10 Lenders' Concerns about Damage and Destruction (Reserved)

§ 22.1   The Law (Reserved)

§ 22.2   Landlord's and Tenant's Concerns (Reserved)

§ 22.3   —Is the Lease Affected? (Reserved)

§ 22.4   —Is the Rent Affected? (Reserved)

§ 22.5   —How Are the Premises Affected? (Reserved)

§ 22.6   —How Is the Lease Affected? (Reserved)

§ 22.7   Damage and Destruction in Office Building Premises

FORM 22.7(1)
DAMAGE AND DESTRUCTION—OFFICE BUILDING

(a)   If the premises or the building are damaged by fire or other insured casualty, landlord will give tenant written notice of the time that landlord has determined in its reasonable discretion will be needed to repair the damage and the election (if any) that landlord has made according to this section. The notice will be given before the 30th day (the "notice date") after the fire or other insured casualty.

(b)   If the premises or the building are damaged by fire or other insured casualty to an extent landlord has determined in its reasonable discretion can be repaired within 120 days after the notice date, landlord will promptly begin to repair the damage after the notice date and will diligently pursue the completion of such repair. In that event this lease will continue in full force and effect, except that monthly rent will be abated on a pro rata basis from the date of the damage until the date of the completion of such repairs (the "repair period"), based on the proportion of the rentable area of the premises that tenant is unable to use during the repair period.

(c)   If the premises or the building are damaged by fire or other insured casualty to an extent landlord has determined in its reasonable discretion cannot be repaired within 120 days after the notice date, then (1) landlord may cancel this lease as of the date of the damage by written notice given to tenant on or before the notice date or (2) tenant may cancel this lease as of the date of the damage by written notice given to landlord within 10 days after landlord's delivery of a written notice that the repairs cannot be made within a 120-day period. If neither landlord nor tenant so elects to cancel this lease, landlord will diligently proceed to repair the building and premises and monthly rent will be abated on a pro rata basis during the repair period, based on the proportion of the rentable area of the premises that tenant is unable to use during the repair period.

(d)   If the premises or the building are damaged by uninsured casualty, or if the proceeds of insurance are insufficient to pay for the repair of any damage to the premises or the building, landlord will have the option either to elect to repair the damage or to cancel this lease as of the date of the casualty by written notice to tenant on or before the notice date.

(e)   If any damage by fire or other casualty is the result of the willful conduct or negligence or failure to act of tenant, its agents, contractors, employees, or invitees, monthly rent will not be abated. Tenant will have no right to terminate this lease on account of any damage to the premises, the building, or the project, except as set forth in this lease.

FORM 22.7(2)
DAMAGE AND DESTRUCTION—OFFICE BUILDING
(Tenant's Form)

In the event of any damage or destruction to the building, or any portion of the building, at any time during the term, landlord will promptly repair, replace, restore, and renew the good condition, order, and repair of the building. Landlord or tenant may, in writing delivered to the other party within 30 days after the damage or destruction, terminate the lease as of the date of the damage or destruction if the repair, replacement, restoration, or renewal would likely require more than 6 months to complete or if the damage or destruction occurs within the final 18 months of the term. During the period of any such repair, replacement, restoration, or renewal, the obligation of tenant to pay rent will be abated to the extent the premises are effectively rendered unfit for their intended use by tenant as a result of such damage or destruction.

§ 22.8   Damage and Destruction in Shopping Center Premises

FORM 22.8(1)
DAMAGE AND DESTRUCTION—SHOPPING CENTER

(a)   If the premises or the portion of the shopping center necessary for tenant's occupancy is damaged or destroyed during the term of this lease by any casualty insurable under standard fire and extended coverage insurance policies, landlord will repair or rebuild the premises to substantially the condition in which the premises were immediately prior to such destruction.

(b)   Landlord's obligation under this paragraph will not exceed the lesser of (1) with respect to the premises, the scope of building standard improvements installed by landlord in the original construction of the premises, or (2) the extent of proceeds received by landlord from any insurance policy maintained by landlord.

(c)   The minimum rent will be abated proportionately during any period in which, by reason of any damage or destruction not occasioned by the negligence or willful misconduct of tenant or tenant's employees or invitees, there is a substantial interference with the operation of the business of tenant. The abatement will be proportional to the area of the premises that tenant may be required to discontinue for the conduct of its business. The abatement will continue for the period commencing with the destruction or damage and ending with the completion of the work, repair, or reconstruction that landlord is obligated to do.

(d)   If the premises, or the portion of the shopping center necessary for tenant's occupancy, is damaged or destroyed (1) to the extent of ten percent (10%) or more of the then-replacement value of either, (2) in the last three years of the term of this lease, (3) by a cause or casualty other than those covered by fire and extended coverage insurance, or (4) to the extent that it would take, in landlord's opinion, in excess of ninety (90) days to complete the requisite repairs, then landlord may either terminate this lease or elect to repair or restore the damage or destruction. If this lease is not terminated pursuant to the preceding sentence, it will remain in full force and effect. Landlord and tenant waive the provisions of any law that would dictate automatic termination or grant either of them an option to terminate in the event of damage or destruction. Landlord's election to terminate under this paragraph will be exercised by written notice to tenant given within sixty (60) days after the damage or destruction. The notice will set forth the effective date of the termination of this lease.

(e)   Upon the completion of any of the work, repair, or restoration by landlord, tenant will repair and restore all other parts of the premises, including without limitation nonbuilding standard leasehold improvements and all trade fixtures, equipment, furnishings, signs, and other improvements originally installed by tenant. Tenant's work will be subject to the requirements of [alterations paragraph].

(f)   During any period of reconstruction or repair of the premises, tenant will continue the operation of its business in the premises to the extent reasonably practicable.

§ 22.9   Damage and Destruction in Single Tenant Premises

FORM 22.9(1)
DAMAGE AND DESTRUCTION—SINGLE TENANT BUILDING

(a)   General. If the premises are damaged or destroyed by reason of fire or any other cause, tenant will immediately notify landlord. If the building is damaged or destroyed by fire or any other cause, tenant will promptly repair or rebuild the building at tenant's expense, so as to make the building at least equal in value to the building existing immediately prior to the occurrence and as nearly similar to it in character as is practicable and reasonable. Landlord will apply and make available to pay to tenant the net proceeds of any fire or other casualty insurance paid to landlord, after deduction of any costs of collection, including attorneys' fees, for repairing or rebuilding as the same progresses. Payments will be made against properly certified vouchers of a competent architect in charge of the work and approved by landlord. Landlord will contribute out of the insurance proceeds towards each payment to be made by or on behalf of tenant, for the repairing or rebuilding of the building, under a schedule of payments to be made by tenant and not unreasonably objected to by landlord, an amount in such proportion to the payment by tenant as the total net amount received by landlord from insurers bears to the total estimated cost of the rebuilding or repairing. Landlord, however, may withhold from each amount so to be paid by landlord fifteen percent (15%) of the amount until the work of repairing or rebuilding is completed and proof has been furnished to landlord that no lien or liability has attached or will attach to the premises or to landlord in connection with the repairing or rebuilding. Upon the completion of rebuilding and the furnishing of the proof, the balance of the net proceeds of the insurance will be paid to tenant. If the proceeds of insurance are paid to the holder of any mortgage on landlord's interest in the premises, landlord will make available net proceeds of the insurance in accordance with the provisions of this paragraph. Before beginning the repairs or rebuilding, or letting any contracts in connection with the repairs or rebuilding, tenant will submit for landlord's approval, which landlord will not unreasonably withhold or delay, complete and detailed plans and specifications for the repairs or rebuilding. Promptly after receiving landlord's approval of those plans and specifications, tenant will begin the repairs or rebuilding and will prosecute the repairs and rebuilding to completion with diligence, subject, however, to strikes, lockouts, acts of God, embargoes, governmental restrictions, and other causes beyond tenant's reasonable control. Tenant will obtain and deliver to landlord a temporary or final certificate of occupancy before the premises are reoccupied for any purpose. The repairs or rebuilding will be completed free and clear of mechanics' or other liens, and in accordance with the building codes and all applicable laws, ordinances, regulations, or orders of any state, municipal, or other public authority affecting the repairs or rebuilding, and also in accordance with all requirements of the insurance rating organization, or similar body, and of any liability insurance company insuring landlord against liability for accidents related to the premises. Any remaining proceeds of insurance after the restoration will be tenant's property.

(b)   Landlord's Inspection. During the progress of the repairs or rebuilding, landlord and its architects and engineers may, from time to time, inspect the building and will be furnished, if required by them, with copies of all plans, shop drawings, and specifications relating to the repairs or rebuilding. Tenant will keep all plans, shop drawings, and specifications at the building, and landlord and its architects and engineers may examine them at all reasonable times. If, during the repairs or rebuilding, landlord and its architects and engineers determine that the repairs or rebuilding are not being done in accordance with the approved plans and specifications, landlord will give prompt notice in writing to tenant, specifying in detail the particular deficiency, omission, or other respect in which landlord claims the repairs or rebuilding do not accord with the approved plans and specifications. Upon the receipt of that notice, tenant will cause corrections to be made to any deficiencies, omissions, or other respect. Tenant's obligations to supply insurance, according to [insurance paragraph] will be applicable to any repairs or building under this paragraph.

(c)   Landlord's Costs. The charges of any architect or engineer of landlord employed to pass upon any plans and specifications and to supervise and approve any construction, or for any services rendered by the architect or engineer to landlord as contemplated by any of the provisions of this lease, will be paid by tenant as a cost of the repair or rebuilding. The fees of the architect or engineer will be those that are customarily paid for comparable services.

(d)   No Rent Abatement. Monthly rent and additional rent will not abate pending the repairs or rebuilding except to the extent to which landlord receives a net sum as proceeds of any rent insurance.

(e) Damage During Last Three Years. If at any time during the last three years of the term, as extended according to [term paragraph], the building is so damaged by fire or otherwise that the cost of restoration exceeds fifty percent (50%) of the replacement value of the building (exclusive of foundations) immediately prior to the damage, either landlord or tenant may, within thirty (30) days after the damage, give notice of its election to terminate this lease and, subject to the further provisions of this paragraph, this lease will cease on the tenth (10th) day after the delivery of the notice. Monthly rent will be apportioned and paid to the time of termination. If this lease is so terminated, tenant will have no obligation to repair or rebuild, and the entire insurance proceeds will belong to landlord.

§ 22.10   Lenders' Concerns about Damage and Destruction (Reserved)

CHAPTER 23

CONDEMNATION

§ 23.1 Condemnation and Eminent Domain (Reserved)

§ 23.2 Total Taking (Reserved)

§ 23.3 Partial Taking (Reserved)

§ 23.4 Temporary Taking (Reserved)

§ 23.5 Condemnation of Office Buildings

§ 23.6 Condemnation of Shopping Centers

§ 23.7 Condemnation of Areas of a Shopping Center Other than Premises (Reserved)

§ 23.8 Consequences of Condemnation (Reserved)

§ 23.9 Landlord's Restoration of Premises (Reserved)

§ 23.10 Allocation of Condemnation Award (Reserved)

§ 23.11 Condemnation of Single Tenant Premises

§ 23.12 Lenders' Concerns about Condemnation (Reserved)

§ 23.13 Deceptive Role of Some Mortgages (Reserved)

§ 23.1 Condemnation and Eminent Domain (Reserved)

§ 23.2 Total Taking (Reserved)

§ 23.3 Partial Taking (Reserved)

§ 23.4 Temporary Taking (Reserved)

§ 23.5 Condemnation of Office Buildings

FORM 23.5(1)
CONDEMNATION—OFFICE BUILDING

If all of the premises are taken by exercise of the power of eminent domain (or conveyed by landlord in lieu of that exercise), this lease will terminate on a date (the "termination date") that is the earlier of the date on which the condemning authority takes possession of the premises or the date on which title to the premises is vested in the condemning authority. If more than 25% of the rentable area of the premises is taken, tenant will have the right to cancel this lease by written notice to landlord given within twenty (20) days after the termination date. If less than 25% of the rentable area of the premises is taken, or if the tenant does not cancel this lease according to the preceding sentence, the monthly rent will be abated in the proportion of the rentable area of the premises taken to the rentable area of the premises immediately before the taking, and tenant's share will be appropriately recalculated. If all or substantially all of the building or the project is taken, landlord may cancel this lease by written notice to tenant given within thirty (30) days after the termination date. In the event of any taking, the entire award will be paid to landlord and tenant will have no right or claim to any part of it; however, tenant will have the right to assert a claim against the condemning authority in a separate action and so long as landlord's award is not reduced by the claim, for tenant's moving expenses, leasehold improvements owned by tenant, and tenant's leasehold estate.

FORM 23.5(2)
CONDEMNATION—OFFICE BUILDING
(Tenant's Form)

In the event of any taking or sale of the building, or any portion of the building or any interest in the building, under the power or threat of eminent domain, the lease will terminate to the extent of such taking and landlord will promptly repair, replace, restore, and renew the good condition, order, and repair of the remainder of the building. Either landlord or tenant may, in writing delivered to the other within 30 days after the taking, terminate the lease as of the date of the taking if the repair, replacement, restoration, or renewal of the building is reasonably likely to require more than 6 months, if the taking occurs within the final 18 months of the term, or if the taking includes any portion of the premises and tenant concludes that the remainder of the premises is not sufficient for tenant's intended use of the premises. In the event that any taking of a portion of the premises does not result in a complete termination of the lease, the obligation of tenant to pay rent will be abated during the period of the taking proportionately as the usable square footage of the premises so taken or sold bears to the total usable square footage of the premises. All consideration, compensation, damages, income, rent, awards, and interest that may be paid or made in connection with any taking will be divided between the parties as their respective interests may appear as determined by the condemning authority.

§ 23.6   Condemnation of Shopping Centers

FORM 23.6(1)
CONDEMNATION—SHOPPING CENTER

(a)   The term "total taking" means the taking of the fee title or landlord's master leasehold estate to so much of the premises or a portion of the shopping center as is necessary for tenant's occupancy by right of eminent domain or other authority of law, or a voluntary transfer under the threat of the exercise of the right of eminent domain or other authority, that the premises are not suitable for tenant's intended use. The term "partial taking" means the taking of only a portion of the premises or the shopping center that does not constitute a total taking.

(b)   If a total taking occurs this lease will terminate as of the date of the taking. The phrase "date of the taking" means the date of taking actual physical possession by the condemning authority or an earlier date on which the condemning authority gives notice that it is deemed to have taken possession.

(c)   If a partial taking of more than [number]% of the leasable area of the premises occurs during the term of this lease, either landlord or tenant may cancel this lease by written notice given within thirty (30) days after the date of the taking, and this lease will terminate as to the portion of the premises taken on the date of the taking. If the lease is not terminated, this lease will continue in full force and effect as to the remainder of the premises. The minimum rent payable by tenant for the balance of the term will be abated in the proportion that the leasable area of the premises taken bears to the leasable area of the premises immediately prior to the taking, and landlord will make all necessary repairs or alterations to make the remaining premises a complete architectural unit. Tenant will have no right to cancel this lease if [number]% of the leasable area of the premises or less is taken.

(d)   All compensation and damages awarded for the taking of the premises, any portion of the premises, or the whole or any portion of the common areas or shopping center will belong to landlord. Tenant will not have any claim or be entitled to any award for diminution in value of its rights under this lease or for the value of any unexpired term of this lease; however, tenant may make its own claim for any separate award that may be made by the condemnor for tenant's loss of business or for the taking of or injury to tenant's improvements, or on account of any cost or loss tenant may sustain in the removal of tenant's trade fixtures, equipment, and furnishing, or as a result of any alterations, modifications, or repairs that may be reasonably required by tenant in order to place the remaining portion of the premises not taken in a suitable condition for the continuance of tenant's occupancy.

(e)   If this lease is terminated pursuant to the provisions of this paragraph, then all rentals and other charges payable by tenant to landlord under this lease will be paid to the date of the taking, and any rentals and other charges paid in advance and allocable to the period after the date of the taking will be repaid to tenant by landlord. Landlord and tenant will then be released from all further liability under this lease.

FORM 23.6(2)
CONDEMNATION—SHOPPING CENTER
(Tenant's Right to Terminate)

Tenant may terminate this lease if there is any substantial impairment of ingress or egress from or to [* * *] Street through condemnation or if the following property, or any interest in it, is condemned for public or quasi-public use:

(a)   Any part of the premises; or

(b)   More than [* * *] percent [(* * %)] of the common area as shown on Exhibit [* *].

Tenant will be entitled to a share, measured by its interest in the premises, of any award for the condemnation of the premises or any interest in them.

§ 23.7   Condemnation of Areas of a Shopping Center Other than Premises (Reserved)

§ 23.8   Consequences of Condemnation (Reserved)

§ 23.9   Landlord's Restoration of Premises (Reserved)

§ 23.10   Allocation of Condemnation Award (Reserved)

§ 23.11   Condemnation of Single Tenant Buildings

FORM 23.11(1)
CONDEMNATION—SINGLE TENANT BUILDING

(a)   Termination. If all of the premises are taken in a condemnation, or if a portion of the premises are taken in condemnation and tenant determines in good faith that it will be economically unfeasible to operate its business in any facility that could be reconstructed on the remaining portion of the premises, this lease will terminate and all obligations under it will cease as of the date upon which possession is taken by the condemnor, and the rent will be apportioned and paid in full by tenant to landlord to that date and all rent prepaid beyond that date will be repaid by landlord to tenant, and tenant will comply with paragraph (e). If, after a partial condemnation of the premises, tenant remains in possession of the remaining portion of the premises after the date on which the condemnor takes possession of the portion of the premises taken in condemnation, then the remaining portion will be deemed sufficient for the reasonable operation of tenant's business and this lease will terminate only with respect to the portion of the premises possessed by the condemnor.

(b)   Partial Condemnation. If there is a partial condemnation and this lease has not been terminated pursuant to paragraph (a), landlord will promptly restore the building and other improvements on the land to a condition and size as nearly comparable as reasonably possible to their condition and size immediately prior to the taking; the time of restoration will be extended for time lost due to causes beyond landlord's reasonable control. Tenant will pay the costs of restoration as the work progresses within fifteen (15) days after delivery of an invoice to it. Landlord agrees to pay to tenant, when received, the proceeds of any condemnation award recovered in excess of counsel and appraiser's fees and other costs incurred in collecting the proceeds (the "net condemnation proceeds") up to the total amount paid by tenant for the cost of restoration. In that event, there will be an equitable abatement of the minimum annual rent according to the value of the premises before and after the taking, commencing from and after the date on which the condemnor takes possession; however, the minimum annual rent will be at lease equal to the percentage of the minimum annual rent payable prior to the condemnation produced by multiplying the amount of any first mortgage encumbering the premises by a fraction whose numerator is the sum equal to its original principal amount less the net condemnation proceeds retained by landlord or the holder after the payment of all costs of restoration and whose denominator is the original principal amount of the mortgage.

(c)   Award. If a condemnation affecting tenant occurs, tenant will have the right to make a claim against the condemnor for removal expenses, business dislocation damages, and moving expenses to the extent that such claims or payments do not reduce the sums payable by the condemnor to landlord. Tenant waives all claims against landlord and all other claims against the condemnor, and tenant assigns to landlord all claims against the condemnor, including without limitation all claims for leasehold damages and diminution in value of tenant's leasehold.

(d) Temporary Taking. If the condemnor takes possession for a fixed period of time or for the duration of an emergency or other temporary condition, then this lease will continue in full force and effect without any abatement of rent, but the amounts payable by the condemnor with respect to any period of time prior to the expiration or sooner termination of this lease will be paid by the condemnor to landlord and the condemnor will be considered a subtenant of tenant. Landlord will apply the amount received from the condemnor applicable to the rent due, net of the costs to landlord for its collection, or as much of it as may be necessary for that purpose, toward the amount due from tenant as rent for that period. Tenant will pay landlord any deficiency between the amount paid by the condemnor and the amount of the rent, or landlord will pay tenant any excess of the amount of the award over the amount of the rent.

(e) Effect of Termination of Lease. For the purposes of this paragraph these phrases have the following meanings:

(1) "Subject property" means the premises, if any portion remains after a condemnation, all outstanding rights and claims against the condemnor at the time of settlement, and that portion of the proceeds of condemnation, if any, received by landlord equal to or less than the purchase price;

(2) "Purchase price" means the unpaid principal balance secured by the first mortgage encumbering the premises at the time when landlord is no longer entitled to possession together with accrued interest to the date of settlement and other sums secured by the mortgage.

If this lease terminates in accordance with the provision of paragraph (a), then tenant will be deemed irrevocably to have offered to purchase the subject property from landlord upon the terms and conditions of this paragraph (e), and landlord will be deemed to have accepted the offer unless landlord rejects the offer in writing within ninety (90) days after the termination of this lease. Tenant will pay the purchase price to landlord; settlement will occur at a location determined by landlord that is reasonably convenient for tenant within forty-five (45) days after expiration of the ninety (90) day period; the subject property shall be conveyed free and clear of the first mortgage, but subject to all other encumbrances and restrictions existing at the execution of this lease, utility and public road rights-of-way hereafter created, all encumbrances and restrictions that are created or suffered by tenant, and all encumbrances and restrictions to which tenant has consented; and tenant will pay all realty transfer taxes, if any.

FORM 23.11(2)
CONDEMNATION—SINGLE TENANT BUILDING

(a) Total Taking. If, by exercise of the right of eminent domain or by conveyance made in response to the threat of the exercise of that right (in either case a "taking"), all of the premises are taken or so much of the premises that they cannot be used by tenant for the purposes for which they were used immediately before the taking, even if the restorations described in subparagraph (b) were to be made, this lease will end on the earlier of the vesting of title to the premises in the condemning authority, or the taking of possession of the premises by the condemning authority (in either case the "ending date"). If this lease ends according to this subparagraph (a), prepaid rent will be appropriately prorated to the ending date. The award in a taking subject to this subparagraph (a) will be allocated according to subparagraph (d).

(b)   Partial Taking. If, after a taking, so much of the premises remains that they can be used for substantially the same purposes for which they were used immediately before the taking:

(1)   This lease will end on the ending date as to the part of the premises that is taken;

(2)   Prepaid rent will be appropriately allocated to the part of the premises that is taken and prorated to the ending date;

(3)   Beginning on the day after the ending date, rent for so much of the premises as remains will be reduced in the proportion of the floor area of the building remaining after the taking to the floor area of the building before the taking;

(4)   At its cost, tenant will restore so much of the premises as remains to a sound architectural unit substantially suitable for the purposes for which they were used immediately before the taking, using good workmanship and new first class materials, all according to alterations paragraph;

(5)   Upon the completion of restoration according to clause (4), landlord will pay tenant the lesser of the net award made to landlord on account of the taking (after deducting from the total award attorneys' fees, appraisers' fees, and other costs incurred in connection with obtaining the award, and amounts paid to the holders of mortgages affecting the premises) or tenant's actual out-of-pocket cost of restoring the premises; and

(6)   Landlord will keep the balance of the net award.

(c)   Tenant's Award. In connection with any taking subject to subparagraph (a) or (b), tenant may prosecute its own claim by separate proceedings against the condemning authority for damages legally due to it (such as the loss of fixtures that tenant was entitled to remove and moving expenses) only so long as tenant's award does not diminish or otherwise adversely affect landlord's award.

(d)   Allocation of an Award for a Total Taking. If this lease ends according to subparagraph (a), the condemnation award will be paid in the order in this subparagraph to the extent it is sufficient:

(1)   First, landlord will be reimbursed for its attorneys' fees, appraisal fees, and other costs incurred in prosecuting the claim for the award.

(2)   Second, landlord will be compensated for lost rent and the value of the reversion as of the ending date.

(3)   Third, tenant will be paid its adjusted book value as of the date of the taking of its improvements (excluding trade fixtures) made to the premises. In computing its adjusted book value, improvements will be conclusively presumed to have been depreciated or amortized for federal income tax purposes over their useful lives with a reasonable salvage value.

(4)   Fourth, the balance will be divided equally between landlord and tenant.

§ 23.12   Lenders' Concerns about Condemnation (Reserved)

§ 23.13   Deceptive Role of Some Mortgages

PART VII

PROTECTING THE LANDLORD

CHAPTER 24

SUBORDINATION

§ 24.1   Introduction and General Rules (Reserved)

§ 24.2   Significance to Lender

§ 24.3   Significance to Tenant (Reserved)

§ 24.1   Introduction and General Rules (Reserved)

§ 24.2   Significance to Lender

FORM 24.2(1)
SUBORDINATION AND ATTORNMENT

(a)   This lease and tenant's rights under this lease are subject and subordinate to any ground lease or underlying lease, first mortgage, first deed of trust, or other first lien encumbrance or indenture, together with any renewals, extensions, modifications, consolidations, and replacements of them (each a "superior lien"), that now or at any subsequent time affects the premises or any interest of landlord in the premises or landlord's interest in this lease and the estate created by this lease (except to the extent that the recorded instrument evidencing the superior lien expressly provides that this lease is superior to the superior lien). This provision will be self-operative and no further instrument of subordination will be required in order to effect it. Nevertheless, tenant will execute, acknowledge, and deliver to landlord, at any time and from time to time upon demand by landlord, documents requested by landlord, any ground landlord, underlying lessor, or any mortgagee, or any holder of a deed of trust or other instrument described in this paragraph, to confirm or effect the subordination. If tenant does not execute, acknowledge, and deliver any of those documents within twenty (20) days after written demand, landlord, its successors and assigns will be entitled to execute, acknowledge, and deliver those documents on behalf of tenant as tenant's as attorney-in-fact. Tenant constitutes and irrevocably appoints landlord, its successors and assigns, as tenant's attorney-in-fact to execute, acknowledge, and deliver those documents on behalf of tenant.

(b) If the holder of any mortgage, indenture, deed of trust, or other similar instrument described in paragraph (a) succeeds to landlord's interest in the premises, tenant will pay to it all rents subsequently payable under this lease. Tenant will, upon request of any one succeeding to the interest of landlord, automatically become tenant of, and attorn to, the successor without change in this lease. The successor will not be bound by: (1) any payment of rent for more than one month in advance; (2) any amendment or modification of this lease made without its written consent; (3) any claim against landlord arising prior to the date that the successor succeeded to landlord's interest; or (4) any claim or offset of rent against landlord. Upon request by the successor and without cost to landlord or the successor, tenant will execute, acknowledge, and deliver documents confirming the attornment. The document of attornment will also provide that the successor will not disturb tenant in its use of the premises in accordance with this lease. If tenant fails or refuses to execute, acknowledge, and deliver those documents within twenty (20) days after written demand, the successor will be entitled to execute, acknowledge, and deliver those documents on behalf of tenant as tenant's attorney-in-fact. Tenant constitutes and irrevocably appoints the successor as tenant's attorney-in-fact to execute, acknowledge, and deliver those documents on behalf of tenant.

§ 24.3   Significance to Tenant (Reserved)

CHAPTER 25

LANDLORD'S ACCESS

§ 25.1 General Access Provisions

§ 25.2 Considerations for Shopping Center Tenants (Reserved)

§ 25.1   General Access Provisions

FORM 25.1(1)
LANDLORD'S ACCESS

Landlord, its agents, employees, and contractors may enter the premises at any time in response to an emergency, and at reasonable hours to (a) inspect the premises, (b) exhibit the premises to prospective purchasers, lenders, or tenants, (c) determine whether tenant is complying with its obligations in this lease, (d) supply cleaning service and any other service that this lease requires landlord to provide, (e) post notices of nonresponsibility or similar notices, or (f) make repairs that this lease requires landlord to make, or make repairs to any adjoining space or utility services, or make repairs, alterations, or improvements to any other portion of the building; however, all work will be done as promptly as reasonably possible and so as to cause as little interference to tenant as reasonably possible.

Tenant waives any claim of injury or inconvenience to tenant's business, interference with tenant's business, loss of occupancy or quiet enjoyment of the premises, or any other loss occasioned by such entry. Landlord will at all times have a key to unlock all of the doors in the premises (excluding tenant's vaults, safes, and similar areas designated in writing by tenant in advance). Landlord will have the right to use any means that landlord may deem proper to open doors in the premises and to the premises in an emergency. No entry to the premises by landlord by any means will be a forcible or unlawful entry into the premises or a detainer of the premises or an eviction, actual or constructive, of tenant from the premises, or any part of the premises, nor will the entry entitle tenant to damages or an abatement of rent or other charges that this lease requires tenant to pay.

§ 25.2   Considerations for Shopping Center Tenants (Reserved)

CHAPTER 26

INDEMNIFICATION, WAIVER, AND RELEASE

§ 26.1   Introduction (Reserved)

§ 26.2   Indemnification

§ 26.3   Waiver and Release

§ 26.1   Introduction (Reserved)

§ 26.2   Indemnification

FORM 26.2(1)
INDEMNIFICATION—BY TENANT ONLY

Tenant will indemnify landlord, its agents, and employees against, and hold landlord, its agents, and employees harmless from, any and all demands, claims, causes of action, fines, penalties, damages (including consequential damages), losses, liabilities, judgments, and expenses (including without limitation attorneys' fees and court costs) incurred in connection with or arising from:

(a)   the use or occupancy of the premises by tenant or any person claiming under tenant;

(b)   any activity, work, or thing done or permitted by tenant in or about the premises;

(c)   any acts, omissions, or negligence of tenant or any person claiming under tenant or the employees, agents, contractors, invitees, or visitors of tenant or any such person;

(d)   any breach, violation, or nonperformance by tenant or any person claiming under tenant or the employees, agents, contractors, invitees, or visitors of tenant or any such person of any term, covenant, or provision of this lease or any law, ordinance, or governmental requirement of any kind; or

(e)   (except for loss of use of all or any portion of the premises or tenant's property located within the premises that is proximately caused by or results proximately from the negligence of landlord), any injury or damage to the person, property, or business of tenant, its employees, agents, contractors, invitees, visitors, or any other person entering upon the premises under the express or implied invitation of tenant.

If any action or proceeding is brought against landlord, its employees, or agents by reason of any such claim, tenant, upon notice from landlord, will defend the claim at tenant's expense with counsel reasonably satisfactory to landlord.

FORM 26.2(2)
INDEMNITY BY TENANT—LIMITING TENANT'S LIABILITY

The liability of tenant to indemnify landlord will not extend to any matter against which landlord is protected by insurance; however, if any liability exceeds the amount of the collected insurance, the liability of tenant will apply to the excess.

§ 26.3   Waiver and Release

FORM 26.3(1)
WAIVER AND RELEASE—BY TENANT ONLY

Tenant waives and releases all claims against landlord, its employees, and agents with respect to all matters for which landlord has disclaimed liability pursuant to the provisions of this lease. In addition, tenant agrees that landlord, its agents, and employees will not be liable for any loss, injury, death, or damage (including consequential damages) to persons, property, or tenant's business occasioned by theft, act of God, public enemy, injunction, riot, strike, insurrection, war, court order, requisition, order of governmental body or authority, fire, explosion, falling objects, steam, water, rain or snow, leak or flow of water (including water from the elevator system), rain or snow from the premises or into the premises or from the roof, street, subsurface or from any other place, or by dampness or from the breakage, leakage, obstruction, or other defects of the pipes, sprinklers, wires, appliances, plumbing, air conditioning, or lighting fixtures of the building, or from construction, repair, or alteration of the premises or from any acts or omissions of any other tenant, occupant, or visitor of the premises, or from any cause beyond landlord's control.

CHAPTER 27

SECURITY DEPOSITS

§ 27.1   Preparing and Reviewing a Security Deposit Provision
§ 27.2   Lender's Obligation to Return Security Deposits (Reserved)
§ 27.3   Lenders' Other Concerns about Security Deposits (Reserved)

§ 27.1   Preparing and Reviewing a Security Deposit Provision

FORM 27.1(1)
SECURITY DEPOSIT

Tenant has deposited $[amount] with landlord as security for tenant's payment of rent and performance of its other obligations under this lease and any renewals or extensions of this lease. If tenant defaults in its payment of rent or performance of its other obligations under this lease, landlord may use all or part of the security deposit for the payment of rent or any other amount in default, or for the payment of any other amount that landlord may spend or become obligated to spend by reason of tenant's default, or for the payment to landlord of any other loss or damage that landlord may suffer by reason of tenant's default. If landlord so uses any portion of the security deposit, tenant will restore the security deposit to its original amount within five (5) days after written demand from landlord. Landlord will not be required to keep the security deposit separate from its own funds and tenant will not be entitled to interest on the security deposit. The security deposit will not be a limitation on landlord's damages or other rights under this lease, or a payment of liquidated damages, or an advance payment of the rent. If tenant pays the rent and performs all of its other obligations under this lease, landlord will return the unused portion of the security deposit to tenant within sixty (60) days after the end of the term; however, if landlord has evidence that the security deposit has been assigned to an assignee of the lease, landlord will return the security deposit to the assignee. Landlord may deliver the security deposit to a purchaser of the premises and be discharged from further liability with respect to it.

FORM 27.1(2)
SECURITY DEPOSIT—RIGHT TO SUBSTITUTE ALTERNATE SECURITY
(Addition to Form 27.1(1))

After no less than fifteen (15) days' prior notice to landlord, tenant may substitute alternate security for its security deposit according to this paragraph:

(1) The term "alternate security" means obligations of the United States of America having a market value at all times of at least [* * *] percent ([* *]%) of the security deposit.

(2) As a continuing condition to its right to substitute alternate security, tenant will always maintain on deposit with landlord alternate security whose market value is equal to [* * *] percent ([* *]%) of such security deposit. If the market value of the alternate security falls below [* * *] percent ([* *]%) of the security deposit (whether by reason of a decrease in market value, or by landlord's application of the alternate security according to this paragraph) and tenant fails to deposit sufficient additional alternate security within five (5) days after notice from landlord, then in addition to any other rights that landlord may have under paragraph [default] on account of tenant's failure to restore its security deposit landlord may sell the alternate security and hold the proceeds (less landlord's cost of sale) as a security deposit subject to the provisions of paragraph [security deposit].

(3) So long as tenant is not in default under this lease, the earnings of the alternate security will be paid to tenant by landlord promptly after landlord receives them or, if the earnings are paid directly to tenant, tenant may keep them. At any time after tenant defaults under this lease, the earnings of the alternate security will be kept by landlord or, if the earnings are paid directly to tenant, tenant will remit them to landlord promptly after they are received.

(4) The alternate security may be used by landlord for any purpose for which the security deposit may be used. Tenant authorizes landlord to sell all or part of the alternate security at any time after landlord would be entitled to apply the security deposit. The sale may be conducted at public or private sale, landlord may be the purchaser, and the proceeds of sale (less landlord's cost of sale) will be applied according to the provisions of paragraph [security deposit].

(5) Tenant may exercise its rights under this paragraph more than once. The alternate security will be returned to tenant whenever a cash security deposit replaces alternate security. The cash security deposit will be returned to tenant whenever tenant deposits alternate security.

FORM 27.1(3)
SECURITY DEPOSIT—LETTER OF CREDIT

In lieu of depositing cash pursuant to this paragraph, or after depositing cash, in substitution for the cash deposit, tenant may deliver to landlord an unconditional and irrevocable letter of credit in favor of landlord, in form reasonably satisfactory to landlord's attorney, drawn upon [* * *] Bank, [City], [State], or such other bank as landlord may approve, for the principal sum of $[amount] as security for the faithful performance and observance by tenant of the terms, provisions, and conditions of this lease. So long as tenant is not in default under any of the terms, provisions, and conditions of this lease on the expiration date of the term of this lease, landlord will return the letter of credit to tenant, and it may be cancelled or permitted to expire. If the term of any letter of credit held by landlord will expire prior to the expiration date of the term of this lease, and it is not extended or a new letter of credit for an extended period of time is not substituted within 10 days prior to the expiration date of the letter of credit, then landlord may make demand for the principal amount of the letter of credit and hold such funds in accordance with this paragraph until the expiration date of the term of this lease. At any time that tenant is in default under the terms of this lease, landlord may make demand for the principal amount of the letter of credit, and hold such funds for the balance of the term in accordance with this paragraph.

§ 27.2   Lender's Obligation to Return Security Deposits (Reserved)

§ 27.3   Lenders' Other Concerns about Security Deposits (Reserved)

CHAPTER 28

COVENANT OF QUIET ENJOYMENT

§ 28.1   General Rules

§ 28.2   Limitations of Covenant (Reserved)

§ 28.3   Inappropriate Uses (Reserved)

§ 28.1   General Rules

FORM 28.1(1)
COVENANT OF QUIET ENJOYMENT
(Tenant's Preference)

Landlord covenants that tenant's use and enjoyment of the premises will not be disturbed during the term of this lease.

FORM 28.1(2)
COVENANT OF QUIET ENJOYMENT
(Landlord's Preference)

So long as tenant pays the rent, and performs all of its obligations in this lease, tenant's possession of the premises will not be disturbed by landlord, or anyone claiming by, through, or under landlord.

§ 28.2   Limitations of Covenant (Reserved)

§ 28.3   Inappropriate Uses (Reserved)

CHAPTER 29

LIMITATION ON TENANT'S RECOURSE; SALE OF PREMISES

§ 29.1   Introduction (Reserved)

§ 29.2   Limitation on Tenant's Recourse

§ 29.3   Sale of Premises

§ 29.1   Introduction (Reserved)

§ 29.2   Limitation on Tenant's Recourse

FORM 29.2(1)
LIMITATION ON TENANT'S RECOURSE

Tenant's sole recourse against landlord, and any successor to the interest of landlord in the premises, is to the interest of landlord, and any successor, in the premises and the building of which the premises are a part. Tenant will not have any right to satisfy any judgment that it may have against landlord, or any successor, from any other assets of landlord, or any successor. In this paragraph the terms "landlord" and "successor" include the shareholders, venturers, and partners of "landlord" and "successor" and the officers, directors, and employees of "landlord" and "successor." The provisions of this paragraph are not intended to limit tenant's right to seek injunctive relief or specific performance, or tenant's right to claim the proceeds of insurance (if any) specifically maintained by landlord for tenant's benefit.

§ 29.3   Sale of Premises

FORM 29.3(1)
SALE OF THE PREMISES

If landlord, or any subsequent owner of the premises, sells the premises, its liability for the performance of its agreements in this lease will end on the date of the sale of the premises, and tenant will look solely to the purchaser for the performance of those agreements. For the purposes of this paragraph, any holder of a mortgage or deed of trust that affects the premises at any time, and any landlord in any lease to which this lease is subordinate at any time, will be a subsequent owner of the premises when it succeeds to the interest of the landlord or any subsequent owner of the premises. Tenant will attorn to any subsequent owners of the premises. The provisions of this paragraph are made in addition to, and not in lieu of, the provisions of paragraph [limitation on tenant's recourse paragraph].

PART VIII

DEFAULT AND ARBITRATION

CHAPTER 30

DEFAULT

§ 30.1   Landlord's Default

§ 30.2   Lenders' Concerns about Tenant's Cure Rights (Reserved)

§ 30.3   Introduction to Tenant's Default (Reserved)

§ 30.4   Tenant's Default and Other Parts of the Lease

§ 30.5   Landlord's Right to Cure

§ 30.6   Events of Default

§ 30.7   Remedies

§ 30.8   —Termination (Reserved)

§ 30.9   —Maintaining the Lease (Reserved)

§ 30.10   —Reentry (Reserved)

§ 30.11   —Rent Acceleration (Reserved)

§ 30.12   —Retained Jurisdiction (Reserved)

§ 30.13   —Form (Reserved)

§ 30.14   Special Bankruptcy Provisions (Reserved)

§ 30.15   Duty to Mitigate (Reserved)

§ 30.16   Landlord's Lien

§ 30.1   Landlord's Default

FORM 30.1(1)
DEFAULT—TENANT'S PERFORMANCE OF LANDLORD'S COVENANTS

If (a) landlord fails to discharge fully any of its obligations imposed by a mortgage that is superior to this lease, or (b) landlord fails to pay any real estate taxes and assessments affecting the premises, or (c) landlord fails to make any repairs that this lease or any law requires it to make, then tenant may (but will not be required to) discharge those obligations, or pay those taxes and assessments, or make those repairs, as the case may be. If it does, all amounts paid by tenant in doing so and all costs and expenses incurred by tenant in connection with doing so (together with interest at [* * *] percent ([* *]%) per annum from the date of tenant's payment of the amount or incurring of

389

each the cost or expense until the date of full repayment by landlord) will be payable by landlord to tenant on demand. If landlord fails to make the repayment, in addition to any other rights it may have, tenant will have the right to offset the amount of the repayment against its rent and other charges under this lease; however, tenant will have no lien or claim against the premises or the building.

§ 30.2 Lenders' Concerns about Tenant's Cure Rights (Reserved)

§ 30.3 Introduction to Tenant's Default (Reserved)

§ 30.4 Tenant's Default and Other Parts of the Lease

FORM 30.4(1)
DEFAULTS BY TENANT

If tenant at any time is in default with respect to any rental payments or other charges payable by tenant, and if the default continues for a period of 3 days after written notice from landlord to tenant; or if tenant is in default in the prompt and full performance of any other of its promises, covenants, or agreements contained in this lease, and if the default or breach of performance continues for more than a reasonable time (in no event to exceed 30 days) after written notice from landlord to tenant specifying the particulars of such default or breach of performance; or if tenant vacates or abandons the premises, landlord may treat the occurrence of any one or more of the foregoing events as a breach of this lease, and in addition to any or all other rights or remedies of landlord by law, landlord may, at the option of landlord, without further notice or demand of any kind to tenant or any other person:

(a) Declare the term ended, reenter the premises, take possession of the premises, and remove all persons from the premises; or

(b) Without declaring this lease terminated, reenter the premises, occupy the whole or any part of the premises for and on account of tenant, and collect any unpaid rentals and other charges which have become payable or which may thereafter become payable; or

(c) Even though it may have reentered the premises, elect to terminate this lease and all of the rights of tenant in or to the premises.

If landlord has reentered the premises under the provisions of subparagraph (b), landlord will not be deemed to have terminated this lease, or the liability of tenant to pay any rental or other charges accruing after landlord's entry, or to have terminated tenant's liability for damages under any of the provisions of this lease, by any reentry or by any action, in unlawful detainer or otherwise, to obtain possession of the premises, unless landlord has notified tenant in writing that it has elected to terminate this lease. Tenant further covenants that the service by landlord of any notice pursuant to the unlawful detainer statutes of the state where the shopping center is situated and the surrender of possession pursuant to such notice will not (unless landlord elects to the contrary at the time of or at any time subsequent to the serving of such notices and such election is evidenced by a written notice to tenant) be deemed to be a termination of this lease. In the event of any entry or taking possession of the premises, landlord will have the right, but not the obligation, to remove all or any part of the personal property located in them and may place it in storage at a public warehouse at the expense and risk of tenant.

If landlord elects to terminate this lease pursuant to the provisions of subparagraph (a) or (c), landlord may recover from tenant as damages:

(1)   The worth at the time of award of any unpaid rental that had been earned at the time of termination;

(2)   The worth at the time of award of the amount by which the unpaid rental that would have been earned after termination until the time of award exceeds the amount of such rental loss tenant proves could have been reasonably avoided; plus

(3)   The worth at the time of award of the amount by which the unpaid rental for the balance of the term after the time of award exceeds the amount of such rental loss tenant proves could be reasonably avoided; plus

(4)   Any other amount necessary to compensate landlord for all the detriment proximately caused by tenant's failure to perform its obligations under this lease or which in the ordinary course of things would be likely to result from tenant's failure, including, but not limited to, any costs or expenses incurred by landlord in retaking possession of the premises, including reasonable attorneys' fees; maintaining or preserving the premises after such default; preparing the premises for reletting to a new tenant, including repairs or alterations to the premises for such reletting; leasing commissions; or any other costs necessary or appropriate to relet the premises.

As used in subparagraphs (1) and (2), the "worth at the time of award" is computed by allowing interest at the maximum lawful rate but in no event greater than 18% per annum. As used in subparagraph (3), the "worth at the time of award" is computed by discounting such amount at the discount rate of the Federal Reserve Bank situated nearest to the location of the shopping center at the time of award plus 1%.

The term "rental" will be deemed to be the minimum annual rental and all other sums required to be paid by tenant pursuant to the terms of this lease. All such sums, other than the minimum annual rental, will, for the purpose of calculating any amount due under the provisions of subparagraph (3), be computed on the basis of the average monthly amount accruing during the immediately preceding 60-month period, except that if it becomes necessary to compute the rental before such a 60-month period has elapsed then the rental will be computed on the basis of the average monthly amount accruing during the shorter period.

In the event of default, all of tenant's fixtures, furniture, equipment, improvements, additions, alterations, and other personal property will remain on the premises and landlord will have the right to take the exclusive possession of it and to use it, rent or charge free, until all defaults are cured or, at its option, to require tenant to remove it at any time during the term of this lease.

Notwithstanding any other provisions of this paragraph, landlord agrees that if the default complained of, other than for the payment of monies, is of such a nature that it cannot be cured within the period requiring such curing as specified in the written notice relating to it, then the default will be deemed to be cured if tenant, within such period, has commenced the curing and continues with all due diligence to cause the curing and completes the curing with the use of such diligence.

The rights and remedies given to landlord in this paragraph will be in addition and supplemental to all other rights or remedies that landlord may have under laws then in force.

§ 30.5   Landlord's Right to Cure

FORM 30.5(1)
DEFAULT—LANDLORD'S PERFORMANCE OF TENANT'S COVENANTS

If tenant fails to pay when due amounts payable under this lease or to perform any of its other obligations under this lease within the time permitted for their performance, then landlord, after ten (10) days' prior written notice to tenant (or, in case of any emergency, upon such notice or without notice, as may be reasonable under the circumstances) and without waiving any of its rights under this lease, may (but will not be required to) pay the amount or perform the obligation.

All amounts paid by landlord and all costs and expenses incurred by landlord in connection with the performance of any of those obligations (together with interest at the prime rate from the date of landlord's paying the amount or incurring each cost or expense until the date of full repayment by tenant) will be payable by tenant to landlord on demand. In the proof of any damages that landlord may claim against tenant arising out of tenant's failure to maintain insurance, landlord will not be limited to the amount of the unpaid insurance premium but will also be entitled to recover as damages for the breach the amount of any uninsured loss (to the extent of any deficiency in the insurance required by the provisions of this lease), damages, costs and expenses of suit, including attorneys' fees, arising out of damage to or destruction of the premises occurring during any period for which tenant has failed to provide such insurance.

§ 30.6   Events of Default

FORM 30.6(1)
DEFAULT—EVENTS OF DEFAULT

The following occurrences are "events of default":

(a)   Tenant defaults in the due and punctual payment of rent, and the default continues for five (5) days after notice from landlord; however, tenant will not be entitled to more than one (1) notice for default in payment of rent during any twelve-month period, and if, within twelve (12) months after any such notice, any rent is not paid when due, an event of default will have occurred without further notice;

(b)   Tenant vacates or abandons the premises;

(c)   This lease or the premises or any part of the premises are taken upon execution or by other process of law directed against tenant, or are taken upon or subjected to any attachment by any creditor of tenant or claimant against tenant, and the attachment is not discharged within fifteen (15) days after its levy;

(d)   Tenant files a petition in bankruptcy or insolvency or for reorganization or arrangement under the bankruptcy laws of the United States or under any insolvency act of any state, or is dissolved, or makes an assignment for the benefit of creditors;

(e)   Involuntary proceedings under any bankruptcy laws or insolvency act or for the dissolution of tenant are instituted against tenant, or a receiver or trustee is appointed for all or substantially all of tenant's property, and the proceeding is not dismissed or the receivership or trusteeship is not vacated within sixty (60) days after the institution or appointment;

(f)   Tenant fails to take possession of the premises on the commencement date of the term; or

(g)   Tenant breaches any of the other agreements, terms, covenants, or conditions that this lease requires tenant to perform, and the breach continues for a period of thirty (30) days after notice by landlord to tenant.

§ 30.7   Remedies

FORM 30.7(1)
DEFAULT—LANDLORD'S REMEDIES

If any one or more events of default set forth in paragraph [events of default] occurs, then landlord may, at its election, either:

(a)   Give tenant written notice of its intention to terminate this lease on the date of the notice or on any later date specified in the notice, and, on the date specified in the notice, tenant's right to possession of the premises will cease and the lease will be terminated (except as to tenant's liability set forth in this paragraph (a)), as if the expiration of the term fixed in the notice were the end of the term of this lease. If this lease is terminated pursuant to the provisions of this paragraph (a), tenant will remain liable to landlord for damages in an amount equal to the rent and other sums that would have been owing by tenant under this lease for the balance of the term if this lease had not been terminated, less the net proceeds, if any, of any reletting of the premises by landlord subsequent to the termination, after deducting all of landlord's expenses in connection with the reletting, including without limitation the expenses set forth in paragraph (b)(2). Landlord will be entitled to collect those damages from tenant monthly on the days on which the rent and other amounts would have been payable under this lease if this lease had not been terminated, and landlord will be entitled to receive those damages from tenant on those days. Alternatively, at the option of landlord, if this lease is terminated, landlord will be entitled to recover from tenant:

(1)   The worth at the time of award of the unpaid rent that had been earned at the time of termination;

(2)   The worth at the time of award of the amount by which the unpaid rent that would have been earned after termination until the time of award exceeds the amount of the rent loss that tenant proves could reasonably have been avoided;

(3)   The worth at the time of award of the amount by which the unpaid rent for the balance of the term of this lease after the time of award exceeds the amount of the rent loss that tenant proves could reasonably be avoided; and

(4)   Any other amount necessary to compensate landlord for all the detriment proximately caused by tenant's failure to perform its obligations under this lease or that in the ordinary course of things would be likely to result from that failure. The "worth at the time of award" of the amount referred to in clauses (1) and (2) is computed by allowing interest at the highest rate permitted by law. The worth at the time of award of the amount referred to in clause (3) is computed by discounting the amount at the discount rate of the Federal Reserve Bank of [* * *] at the time of award. For the purpose of determining unpaid rental under clause (3), the monthly rent reserved in this lease will be deemed to be the sum of the rent due under [the minimum rent paragraph] and the amounts last payable by tenant pursuant to [the operating expense paragraph] for the calendar year in which the award is made; or

(b) (1) Without demand or notice, reenter and take possession of the premises or any part of the premises; repossess the premises as of landlord's former estate; expel tenant and those claiming through or under tenant from the premises; and remove the effects of both or either, without being deemed guilty of any manner of trespass and without prejudice to any remedies for arrears of rent or preceding breach of covenants or conditions. If landlord elects to reenter as provided in this paragraph (b) or if landlord takes possession of the premises pursuant to legal proceedings or pursuant to any notice provided by law, landlord may, from time to time, without terminating this lease, relet the premises or any part of the premises, either alone or in conjunction with other portions of the building of which the premises are a part, in landlord's or tenant's name but for the account of tenant, for such term or terms (which may be greater or less than the period that would otherwise have constituted the balance of the term of this lease) and on such terms and conditions (which may include concessions of free rent, and the alteration and repair of the premises) as landlord, in its uncontrolled discretion, may determine. Landlord may collect and receive the rents for the premises. Landlord will not be responsible or liable for any failure to relet the premises, or any part of the premises, or for any failure to collect any rent due upon reletting. No reentry or taking possession of the premises by landlord will be construed as an election on landlord's part to terminate this lease unless a written notice of such intention is given to tenant. No notice from landlord under this lease or under a forcible entry and detainer statute or similar law will constitute an election by landlord to terminate this lease unless the notice specifically says so. Landlord reserves the right following any reentry or reletting, or both, to exercise its right to terminate this lease by giving tenant written notice, and, in that event, the lease will terminate as specified in the notice.

(2) If landlord elects to take possession of the premises according to this paragraph (b) without terminating the lease, tenant will pay landlord the rent and other sums that would have been payable under this lease if such repossession had not occurred, less the net proceeds, if any, of any reletting of the premises after deducting all of landlord's expenses incurred in connection with such reletting, including without limitation all repossession costs, brokerage commissions, legal expenses, attorneys' fees, expenses of employees, alteration, remodeling, repair costs, and expenses of preparation for reletting. If, in connection with any reletting, the new lease term extends beyond the existing term or the premises covered by reletting include areas that are not part of the premises, a fair apportionment of the rent received from such reletting and the expenses incurred in connection with such reletting will be made in determining the net proceeds received from reletting. In addition, in determining the net proceeds from reletting, any rent concessions will be apportioned over the term of the new lease. Tenant will pay such amounts to landlord monthly on the days on which the rent and all other amounts owing under this lease would have been payable if possession had not been retaken, and landlord will be entitled to receive the rent and other amounts from tenant on those days.

(c) Suit or suits for the recovery of the rents and other amounts and damages set forth in this paragraph may be brought by landlord, from time to time, at landlord's election, and nothing in this lease will be deemed to require landlord to await the date on which the term of this lease expires. Each right and remedy in this lease will be cumulative and will be in addition to every other right or remedy in this lease or existing at law or in equity or by statute or otherwise, including without limitation suits for injunctive relief and specific performance. The exercise or beginning of the exercise by landlord of any right or remedy will not preclude the simultaneous or later exercise by landlord of any other rights or remedies. All rights and remedies are cumulative and nonexclusive.

§ 30.8 —Termination (Reserved)

§ 30.9 —Maintaining the Lease (Reserved)

§ 30.10 —Reentry (Reserved)

§ 30.11 —Rent Acceleration (Reserved)

§ 30.12 —Retained Jurisdiction (Reserved)

§ 30.13 —Form (Reserved)

§ 30.14 Special Bankruptcy Provisions (Reserved)

§ 30.15 Duty to Mitigate (Reserved)

§ 30.16 Landlord's Lien

FORM 30.16(1)
DEFAULT—LANDLORD'S LIEN

To secure the payment of all rent and its performance of this lease, tenant grants to landlord an express first and prior contractual lien and security interest on all property (including fixtures, equipment, chattels, and merchandise) that may be placed in the premises, and also upon all proceeds of any insurance that may accrue to tenant by reason of the destruction or damage of that property. Tenant will not remove that property from the premises (except in the ordinary course of business) without the written consent of landlord until all arrearages in rent have been paid. Tenant waives the benefit of all exemption laws in favor of this lien and security interest. This lien and security interest is given in addition to landlord's statutory lien and is cumulative with it. Upon the occurrence of an event of default, these liens may be foreclosed with or without court proceedings by public or private sale, so long as landlord gives tenant at least fifteen (15) days' notice of the time and place of the sale. Landlord will have the right to become the purchaser if it is the highest bidder at the sale. Contemporaneously with its execution of this lease (and if requested after such execution by landlord), tenant will execute and deliver to landlord Uniform Commercial Code financing statements in form and substance sufficient (upon proper filing) to perfect the security interest granted in this paragraph. If requested by landlord, tenant will also execute and deliver to landlord Uniform Commercial Code continuation statements in form and substance sufficient to reflect any proper amendment of, modification in, or extension of the security interest granted in this paragraph.

FORM 30.16(2)
DEFAULT—WAIVER OF LANDLORD'S LIEN

Landlord waives any statutory liens, and any rights of distress, with respect to tenant's property. This lease does not grant a contractual lien or any other express or implied security interest to landlord with respect to tenant's property.

CHAPTER 31

ARBITRATION

§ 31.1   Introduction (Reserved)

§ 31.2   Possible Arbitration Provisions

§ 31.1   Introduction (Reserved)

§ 31.2   Possible Arbitration Provisions

FORM 31.2(1)
ARBITRATION (SHORT FORM)

Any question that this lease requires to be resolved by arbitration will be submitted to the American Arbitration Association and will be decided according to its rules.

FORM 31.2(2)
ARBITRATION—AMERICAN ARBITRATION ASSOCIATION'S
STANDARD ARBITRATION CLAUSE

Any controversy or claim arising out of or relating to this contract, or the breach thereof, shall be settled by arbitration in accordance with the Commercial Arbitration Rules of the American Arbitration Association, and judgment upon the award rendered by the arbitrator(s) may be entered in any court having jurisdiction thereof.

FORM 31.2(3)
ARBITRATION (LONG FORM)

These procedures will govern any arbitration according to this lease:

(a)   Arbitration will be commenced by a written demand made by landlord or tenant upon the other. The written demand will contain a statement of the question to be arbitrated and the name and address of the arbitrator appointed by the demandant. Within ten (10) days after its receipt of the written demand, the other will give the demandant written notice of the name and address of its arbitrator. Within ten (10) days after the date of the appointment of the second arbitrator, the two arbitrators will meet. If the two arbitrators are unable to resolve the question in dispute within ten (10) days after their first meeting, they will select a third arbitrator. The third arbitrator will be designated as chairman and will immediately give landlord and tenant written notice of its appointment. The three arbitrators will meet within ten (10) days after the appointment of the third arbitrator. If they are unable to resolve the question in dispute within ten (10) days after their first meeting, the third arbitrator will select a time, date, and place for a hearing and will give landlord and tenant thirty (30) days' prior written notice of it. The date for the hearing will not be more than sixty (60) days after the date of appointment of the third arbitrator. The first two arbitrators may be partial. The third arbitrator must be neutral. All of the arbitrators must have these qualifications: [qualifications of arbitrators].

(b)   At the hearing, landlord and tenant will each be allowed to present testimony and tangible evidence and to cross-examine each other's witnesses. The arbitrators may make additional rules for the conduct of the hearing or the preparation for it. The arbitrators will render their written decision to landlord and tenant not more than thirty (30) days after the last day of the hearing.

(c)   If the one of whom arbitration is demanded fails to appoint its arbitrator within the time specified or if the two arbitrators appointed are unable to agree on an appointment of the third arbitrator within the time specified, either landlord or tenant may petition a justice of the [* * *] Court of the State of [state] to appoint a third arbitrator. The petitioner will give the other five (5) days' prior written notice before filing its petition.

(d)   The arbitration will be governed by the Arbitration Law of the State of [state], and when not in conflict with that law, by the general procedures in the Commercial Arbitration Rules of the American Arbitration Association.

(e)   The arbitrators will not have power to add to, modify, detract from, or alter in any way the provisions of this lease or any amendments or supplements to this lease. The written decision of at least two arbitrators will be conclusive and binding upon landlord and tenant. No arbitrator is authorized to make an award of punitive or exemplary damages.

(f)   Landlord and tenant will each pay for the services of its appointees, attorneys, and witnesses, plus one-half (1/2) of all other proper costs relating to the arbitration.

(g)   The decision of the arbitrators will be final and nonappealable, and may be enforced according to the laws of the State of [state].

PART IX

MISCELLANEOUS PROVISIONS

CHAPTER 32

MISCELLANEOUS

§ 32.1   Submission of the Lease

§ 32.2   Brokers

§ 32.3   No Recordation

§ 32.4   Notice, Possession, and Recordation (Reserved)

§ 32.5   Importance of Recordation (Reserved)

§ 32.6   Memorandum of Lease and Short-Form Lease (Reserved)

§ 32.7   Leasehold Title Insurance (Reserved)

§ 32.8   Holding Over

§ 32.9   Time of the Essence

§ 32.10   No Light, Air, and View Easements

§ 32.11   No Partnership

§ 32.12   No Merger

§ 32.13   Modification and Financing Conditions

§ 32.14   Consents and Approvals

§ 32.15   Estoppel Certificates

§ 32.16   No Waiver

§ 32.17   Joint and Several Liability

§ 32.18   Authority

§ 32.19   Captions, Exhibits, Gender, and Number

§ 32.20   Entire Agreement

§ 32.21   Amendments

§ 32.22   Severability

§ 32.23   No Construction Against Preparer of Lease

§ 32.24   Notices

§ 32.25   Attorneys' Fees

§ 32.26   Waiver of Jury Trial

§ 32.27   Governing Law and Venue

§ 32.28   Binding Effect

§ 32.1 Submission of the Lease

FORM 32.1(1)
MISCELLANEOUS—NO OFFER

The submission of this lease to tenant is not an offer to lease the premises, or an agreement by landlord to reserve the premises for tenant. Landlord will not be bound to tenant until tenant has duly executed and delivered duplicate original leases to landlord and landlord has duly executed and delivered one of those duplicate original leases to tenant.

§ 32.2 Brokers

FORM 32.2(1)
MISCELLANEOUS—BROKERS
(Landlord's Provision)

Tenant has not dealt with any broker or finder other than [* * *] with regard to the premises or this lease. Tenant will indemnify landlord against any loss, liability, and expense (including attorneys' fees and court costs) arising out of claims for fees or commissions from anyone other than [* * *] with whom tenant has dealt with regard to the premises or this lease. Landlord agrees to pay any commission or fee owing to [* * *].

FORM 32.2(2)
MISCELLANEOUS—BROKERS
(Tenant's Reciprocal Provision)

Landlord and tenant warrant to each other that neither of them has consulted or negotiated with any broker or finder with regard to the premises or this lease other than [* * *]. Tenant agrees to indemnify landlord against any loss, liability, and expense (including attorneys' fees and court costs) arising out of claims for fees or commissions from anyone other than [* * *] with whom tenant has dealt with regard to the premises or this lease. Landlord agrees to indemnify tenant against any loss, liability, and expense (including attorneys' fees and court costs) arising out of claims for fees or commissions from anyone other than [* * *] with whom landlord has dealt with regard to the premises or this lease. Landlord agrees to pay any commission or fee owing to [* * *].

§ 32.3   No Recordation

FORM 32.3(1)
MISCELLANEOUS—NO RECORDATION

Tenant's recordation of this lease or any memorandum or short form of it will be void and, at landlord's option, a default under this lease.

§ 32.4   Notice, Possession, and Recordation (Reserved)

§ 32.5   Importance of Recordation (Reserved)

§ 32.6   Memorandum of Lease and Short-Form Lease (Reserved)

§ 32.7   Leasehold Title Insurance (Reserved)

§ 32.8   Holding Over

FORM 32.8(1)
MISCELLANEOUS—HOLDING OVER
(Tenant's Form Without Penalty)

If tenant remains in possession of the premises after the end of this lease, tenant will occupy the premises as a tenant from month to month, subject to all conditions, provisions, and obligations of this lease in effect on the last day of the term.

FORM 32.8(2)
HOLDING OVER
(Another Form)

If tenant holds possession of the premises after the expiration of the term, tenant will be a tenant from month to month on the terms of this lease except that the monthly minimum rent will be 200% of the monthly minimum rent payable in the month before expiration.

§ 32.9　Time of the Essence

FORM 32.9(1)
MISCELLANEOUS—TIME OF THE ESSENCE

Time is of the essence of each and every provision of this lease.

§ 32.10　No Light, Air, and View Easements

FORM 32.10(1)
MISCELLANEOUS—NO LIGHT AND AIR EASEMENT

The reduction or elimination of tenant's light, air, or view will not affect tenant's liability under this lease, nor will it create any liability of landlord to tenant.

§ 32.11　No Partnership

FORM 32.11(1)
MISCELLANEOUS—NO PARTNERSHIP

This lease is not intended to create a partnership or joint venture between landlord and tenant or to create a principal-and-agent relationship between them. The percentage rent is intended only as a method of computing rent.

§ 32.12　No Merger

FORM 32.12(1)
MISCELLANEOUS—NO MERGER

The surrender of this lease by tenant or the cancellation of this lease by agreement of tenant and landlord or the termination of this lease on account of tenant's default will not work a merger, and will, at landlord's option, terminate any subleases of part or all of the premises or operate as an assignment to landlord of any of those subleases. Landlord's option under this paragraph will be exercised by notice to tenant and all known subtenants in the premises.

§ 32.13   Modification and Financing Conditions

FORM 32.13(1)
MISCELLANEOUS—MODIFICATION AND FINANCING CONDITIONS

Landlord has obtained financing and intends to obtain further financing that is secured by mortgages or deeds of trust encumbering the premises. Landlord may also elect to enter into a ground lease of the premises. If any mortgage lender requires any modification of this lease as a condition to financing or pursuant to rights of approval set forth in the mortgage or deed of trust encumbering the premises, or if any ground lessee requires any modification of this lease as a condition to a ground lease or pursuant to rights of approval set forth in the ground lease, tenant agrees to execute the modification, so long as such modification (a) does not increase the rent or tenant's share of any costs in addition to rent, (b) does not materially interfere with tenant's use or occupancy, and (c) if requested by a mortgage lender with a lien on the premises as of the date of this lease, or a ground lessee in effect as of the date of this lease, has been requested prior to thirty (30) days after the date of this lease. If tenant refuses to execute any such modification within ten (10) days after it is delivered to tenant, landlord will have the right to cancel this lease by notice to tenant. Upon cancellation landlord will refund any unearned rent or security deposit, and neither landlord nor tenant will have any liability under this lease after the date of cancellation.

FORM 32.13(2)
MISCELLANEOUS—LENDER'S APPROVAL

Landlord's obligations under this lease are subject to the approval of the lender furnishing the permanent loan for the building. If that lender disapproves of this lease within [* * *] [(* *)] days after tenant executes this lease, landlord will have the right to cancel this lease, without any liability, by written notice of cancellation given to tenant within ten (10) days after landlord learns of the disapproval. If no written notice of cancellation is given to tenant within thirty (30) days after the date of this lease, this lease will continue in full force and effect.

§ 32.14   Consents and Approvals

FORM 32.14(1)
MISCELLANEOUS—CONSENTS AND APPROVALS
(Tenant's Preference)

Whenever this lease requires landlord's consent or approval, landlord will not withhold its approval or consent unreasonably or in bad faith, and landlord will not unreasonably delay its response to tenant's request for its approval or consent. Landlord will be deemed to have given its consent or approval to any request made by tenant if landlord does not respond to tenant in writing within [* * *] [(* *)] days after landlord's receipt of the request. If landlord withholds its consent or approval, its response will explain its reasons for doing so.

§ 32.15   Estoppel Certificates

FORM 32.15(1)
MISCELLANEOUS—ESTOPPEL CERTIFICATES

Within no more than [* * *] [(* *)] days after written request by landlord, tenant will execute, acknowledge, and deliver to landlord a certificate stating:

(a)   that this lease is unmodified and in full force and effect, or, if the lease is modified, the way in which it is modified accompanied by a copy of the modification agreement;

(b)   the date to which rental and other sums payable under this lease have been paid;

(c)   that no notice has been received by tenant of any default that has not been cured, or, if such a default has not been cured, what tenant intends to do in order to effect the cure, and when it will do so;

(d)   that tenant has accepted and occupied the premises;

(e)   that tenant has no claim or offset against landlord, or, if it does, stating the circumstances that gave rise to the claim or offset;

(f)   that tenant is not aware of any prior assignment of this lease by landlord, or, if it is, stating the date of the assignment and assignee (if known to tenant); and

(g)   such other matters as may be reasonably requested by landlord.

Any certificate may be relied upon by any prospective purchaser of the premises and any prospective mortgagee or beneficiary under any deed of trust or mortgage encumbering the premises. If landlord submits a completed certificate to tenant, and if tenant fails to object to its contents within [* * *] [(* *)] days after its receipt of the completed certificate, the matters stated in the certificate will conclusively be deemed to be correct. Furthermore, tenant irrevocably appoints landlord as tenant's attorney-in-fact to execute and deliver on tenant's behalf any completed certificate to which tenant does not object within [* * *] [(* *)] days after its receipt.

§ 32.16 No Waiver

FORM 32.16(1)
MISCELLANEOUS—NO WAIVER

No waiver of any condition or agreement in this lease by either landlord or tenant will imply or constitute its further waiver of that or any other condition or agreement. No act or thing done by landlord or landlord's agents during the term of this lease will be deemed an acceptance of a surrender of the premises, and no agreement to accept a surrender will be valid unless in writing signed by landlord. The delivery of tenant's keys to any employee or agent of landlord will not constitute a termination of this lease unless landlord has entered into a written agreement to that effect. No payment by tenant, nor receipt from landlord, of a lesser amount than the rent or other charges stipulated in this lease will be deemed to be anything other than a payment on account of the earliest stipulated rent. No endorsement or statement on any check, or any letter accompanying any check or payment as rent, will be deemed an accord and satisfaction. Landlord will accept the check for payment without prejudice to landlord's right to recover the balance of such rent or to pursue any other remedy available to landlord. If this lease is assigned, or if the premises or any part of the premises are sublet or occupied by anyone other than tenant, landlord may collect rent from the assignee, subtenant, or occupant and apply the net amount collected to the rent reserved in this lease. That collection will not be deemed a waiver of the covenant in this lease against assignment and subletting, or the acceptance of the assignee, subtenant, or occupant as tenant, or a release of tenant from the complete performance by tenant of its covenants in this lease.

§ 32.17 Joint and Several Liability

FORM 32.17(1)
MISCELLANEOUS—JOINT AND SEVERAL LIABILITY

If tenant is composed of more than one signatory to this lease, each signatory will be jointly and severally liable with each other signatory for payment and performance according to this lease.

§ 32.18 Authority

FORM 32.18(1)
MISCELLANEOUS—AUTHORITY

If tenant signs this lease as a corporation, each of the persons executing this lease on behalf of tenant warrants to landlord that tenant is a duly authorized and existing corporation, that tenant is qualified to do business in the state in which the premises are located, that tenant has full right and authority to enter into this lease, and that each and every person signing on behalf of tenant is authorized to do so. Upon landlord's request, tenant will provide evidence satisfactory to landlord confirming these representations.

§ 32.19   Captions, Exhibits, Gender, and Number

FORM 32.19(1)
MISCELLANEOUS—CAPTIONS, EXHIBITS, GENDER, AND NUMBER

The captions and table of contents are inserted in this lease only for convenience of reference and do not define, limit, or describe the scope or intent of any provisions of this lease. The exhibits to this lease are incorporated into the lease. Unless the context clearly requires otherwise, the singular includes the plural, and vice versa, and the masculine, feminine, and neuter adjectives include one another.

§ 32.20   Entire Agreement

FORM 32.20(1)
MISCELLANEOUS—ENTIRE AGREEMENT

This lease contains the entire agreement between landlord and tenant with respect to its subject matter and may be amended only by subsequent written agreement between them. Except for those that are set forth in this lease, no representations, warranties, or agreements have been made by landlord or tenant to one another with respect to this lease.

§ 32.21   Amendments

FORM 32.21(1)
MISCELLANEOUS—AMENDMENT

This lease can be amended only by a written document signed by landlord and tenant.

§ 32.22 Severability

FORM 32.22(1)
MISCELLANEOUS—SEVERABILITY

If any provision of this lease is found by a court of competent jurisdiction to be illegal, invalid, or unenforceable, the remainder of this lease will not be affected, and in lieu of each provision that is found to be illegal, invalid, or unenforceable, provision will be added as a part of this lease that is as similar to the illegal, invalid, or unenforceable provision as may be possible and be legal, valid, and enforceable.

§ 32.23   No Construction Against Preparer of Lease

FORM 32.23(1)
MISCELLANEOUS—NO CONSTRUCTION AGAINST THE
PREPARER OF THE LEASE

This lease has been prepared by landlord and its professional advisors and reviewed by tenant and its professional advisors. Landlord, tenant, and their separate advisors believe that this lease is the product of all of their efforts, that it expresses their agreement, and that it should not be interpreted in favor of either landlord or tenant or against either landlord or tenant merely because of their efforts in preparing it.

§ 32.24   Notices

FORM 32.24(1)
MISCELLANEOUS—NOTICES

Any notice, request, demand, consent, approval, or other communication required or permitted under this lease will be written and will be deemed to have been given only (a) when personally delivered, or (b) when served pursuant to the Federal Rules of Civil Procedure, or (c) on the [* * *] day after it is deposited in any depository regularly maintained by the United States Postal Service, postage prepaid, certified or registered mail, return receipt requested, addressed to:

Landlord:

With a copy at the same time to:

Tenant:

With a copy at the same time to:

Notices may be given by an agent on behalf of landlord or tenant. Either landlord or tenant may change its addresses or addressees for purposes of this paragraph by giving ten (10) days' prior notice according to this paragraph. Any notice from landlord to tenant will also be deemed to have been given if delivered to the premises, addressed to tenant, whether or not tenant has vacated or abandoned the premises.

§ 32.25 Attorneys' Fees

FORM 32.25(1)
MISCELLANEOUS—ATTORNEYS' FEES

If landlord and tenant litigate any provision of this lease or the subject matter of this lease, the unsuccessful litigant will pay to the successful litigant all costs and expenses, including reasonable attorneys' fees and court costs, incurred by the successful litigant at trial and on any appeal. If, without fault, either landlord or tenant is made a party to any litigation instituted by or against the other, the other will indemnify the faultless one against all loss, liability, and expense, including reasonable attorneys' fees and court costs, incurred by it in connection with such litigation.

§ 32.26 Waiver of Jury Trial

FORM 32.26(1)
MISCELLANEOUS—WAIVER OF JURY TRIAL

Landlord and tenant waive trial by jury in any action, proceeding, or counterclaim brought by either of them against the other on all matters arising out of this lease or the use and occupancy of the premises (except claims for personal injury or property damage). If landlord commences any summary proceeding for nonpayment of rent, tenant will not interpose (and waives the right to interpose) any counterclaim in any such proceeding.

§ 32.27 Governing Law and Venue

FORM 32.27(1)
MISCELLANEOUS—GOVERNING LAW AND VENUE

This lease will be governed by the law of [* * *] and will be construed and interpreted according to that law. Venue on any action arising out of this lease will be proper only in the District Court of [County] County, State of [State].

§ 32.28 Binding Effect

FORM 32.28(1)
MISCELLANEOUS—BINDING EFFECT (SHORT FORM)

The benefits of this lease and the burdens of this lease will inure to the benefit of and will be binding upon the heirs, successors, personal representatives, and assigns of landlord and tenant.

FORM 32.28(2)
MISCELLANEOUS—BINDING EFFECT
(WITH LIMITATION OF ASSIGNS)

This lease will inure to the benefit of, and will be binding upon, the successors and permitted assigns of landlord and tenant.

FORM 32.28(3)
MISCELLANEOUS—BINDING EFFECT (LONG FORM)

This lease will inure to the benefit of, and will be binding upon, landlord's successors and assigns except as provided in [sale of the premises paragraph]. This lease will inure to the benefit of, and will be binding upon, tenant's successors and assigns so long as the succession or assignment is permitted by [assignments and subleases paragraph].

TABLE OF FORMS

Agreement of Lease, Form 3.18(1)
Alterations—Office Building, Form 19.3(1)
Alterations—Shopping Center (Landlord's Form), Form 19.4(3)
Alterations—Shopping Center (Tenant's Form), Form 19.4(2)
Alterations—Shopping Center, Form 19.4(1)
Alterations—Single Tenant Premises, Form 19.5(1)
Amendment to Office Lease, Form 2.20
Arbitration (Long Form), Form 31.2(3)
Arbitration (Short Form), Form 31.2(1)
Arbitration—American Arbitration Association's Standard Arbitration Clause,
    Form 31.2(2)
Assignment and Subletting—Shopping Center (Tenant's Form), Form 12.15(1)
Assignment—An Absolute Prohibition, Form 12.5(1)
Assignment—Form, Form 2.4
Assignment—Landlord's Right to Be Arbitrary and Capricious, Form 12.6(2)
Assignment—Modification of Assignment Provision to Permit Certain Corporate
    Transfers, Form 12.9(1)
Assignment—Office, Form 12.13(1)
Assignment—Requiring Landlord's Consent, Form 12.6(1)
Assignment—Requiring Landlord's Consent, Which Will Not Be Unreasonably Withheld
    or Delayed (General), Form 12.6(3)
Assignment—Shopping Center, Form 12.13(2)

Basic Lease Information—Office Building, Form 2.17
Basic Lease Information—Shopping Center, Form 2.18
Basic Lease Information—Single Tenant Building, Form 2.19

Commencement Date Certificate, Form 2.15
Common Areas—Office Building, Form 17.2(1)
Common Areas—Shopping Center, Form 17.3(1)
Common Areas—Tenant's Form, Form 17.9(1)
Common Areas—Tenant's Form, Form 17.9(2)
Compliance with Environmental Laws (Landlord's Form), Form 11.4(1)
Compliance with Environmental Laws (Tenant's Form), Form 11.5(1)
Compliance with Laws, Form 11.1(1)
Compliance with Laws—Landlord's Warranty, Form 11.3(1)
Compliance with Laws—Right to Contest, Form 11.2(1)
Compliance with Laws—Tenant's Environmental Responsibilities, Form 11.4(2)
Condemnation—Office Building (Tenant's Form), Form 23.5(2)
Condemnation—Office Building, Form 23.5(1)
Condemnation—Shopping Center (Tenant's Right to Terminate), Form 23.6(2)
Condemnation—Shopping Center, Form 23.6(1)
Condemnation—Single Tenant Building, Form 23.11(1)

Condemnation—Single Tenant Building, Form 23.11(2)
Corporate Tenant—Corporate Resolution, Form 3.7(1)
Covenant of Quiet Enjoyment (Landlord's Preference), Form 28.1(2)
Covenant of Quiet Enjoyment (Tenant's Preference), Form 28.1(1)

Damage and Destruction—Office Building (Tenant's Form), Form 22.7(2)
Damage and Destruction—Office Building, Form 22.7(1)
Damage and Destruction—Shopping Center, Form 22.8(1)
Damage and Destruction—Single Tenant Building, Form 22.9(1)
Defaults by Tenant, Form 30.4(1)
Default—Events of Default, Form 30.6(1)
Default—Landlord's Lien, Form 30.16(1)
Default—Landlord's Performance of Tenant's Covenants, Form 30.5(1)
Default—Landlord's Remedies, Form 30.7(1)
Default—Tenant's Performance of Landlord's Covenants, Form 30.1(1)
Default—Waiver of Landlord's Lien, Form 30.16(2)

End of Term, Form 21.2(1)
Estoppel Certificate, Form 2.11
Estoppel, Subordination, Nondisturbance, and Attornment Agreement, Form 2.10
Exculpation of Landlord Acting in Representative Capacity, Form 3.9(1)

Guaranty of Lease, Form 2.1

Indemnification—By Tenant Only, Form 26.2(1)
Indemnity by Tenant—Limiting Tenant's Liability, Form 26.2(2)
Insurance—Blanket Insurance, Form 9.12(1)
Insurance—Mutual Waiver of Subrogation, Form 9.11(1)
Insurance—Office Building, Form 9.13(1)
Insurance—Shopping Center, Form 9.14(1)
Insurance—Single Tenant Building, Form 9.15(1)
Introduction, Form 3.2(1)
Introduction—An Alternative, Form 3.2(2)

Landlord's Access, Form 25.1(1)
Landlord's Right to Change Common Areas, Form 17.5(1)
Landlord's Services (Long Provision), Form 16.3(1)
Landlord's Services (Short Provision), Form 16.2(1)
Landlord's Services—Breakdown Provision, Form 16.3(2)
Lease Commencement Memorandum, Form 2.16
Lease for Use of Storage Space, Form 2.2
Lease Summary, Form 2.21
Limitation on Tenant's Recourse, Form 29.2(1)

Manner of Conducting Business (Shopping Center Lease), Form 10.12(1)
Mechanics' Liens, Form 20.2(1)
Memorandum of Lease, Form 2.13
Merchants' Association (Another Form), Form 15.6(2)
Merchants' Association, Form 15.6(1)
Miscellaneous—Amendment, Form 32.21(1)
Miscellaneous—Attorneys' Fees, Form 32.25(1)
Miscellaneous—Authority, Form 32.18(1)

Miscellaneous—Binding Effect (Long Form), Form 32.28(3)
Miscellaneous—Binding Effect (Short Form), Form 32.28(1)
Miscellaneous—Binding Effect (With Limitation of Assigns), Form 32.28(2)
Miscellaneous—Brokers (Landlord's Provision), Form 32.2(1)
Miscellaneous—Brokers (Tenant's Reciprocal Provision), Form 32.2(2)
Miscellaneous—Captions, Exhibits, Gender, and Number, Form 32.19(1)
Miscellaneous—Consents and Approvals (Tenant's Preference), Form 32.14(1)
Miscellaneous—Entire Agreement, Form 32.20(1)
Miscellaneous—Estoppel Certificates, Form 32.15(1)
Miscellaneous—Governing Law and Venue, Form 32.27(1)
Miscellaneous—Holding Over (Another Form), Form 32.8(2)
Miscellaneous—Holding Over (Tenant's Form Without Penalty), Form 32.8(1)
Miscellaneous—Joint and Several Liability, Form 32.17(1)
Miscellaneous—Lender's Approval, Form 32.13(2)
Miscellaneous—Modification and Financing Conditions, Form 32.13(1)
Miscellaneous—No Construction Against the Preparer of the Lease, Form 32.23(1)
Miscellaneous—No Light and Air Easement, Form 32.10(1)
Miscellaneous—No Merger, Form 32.12(1)
Miscellaneous—No Offer, Form 32.1(1)
Miscellaneous—No Partnership, Form 32.11(1)
Miscellaneous—No Recordation, Form 32.3(1)
Miscellaneous—No Waiver, Form 32.16(1)
Miscellaneous—Notices, Form 32.24(1)
Miscellaneous—Severability, Form 32.22(1)
Miscellaneous—Time of the Essence, Form 32.9(1)
Miscellaneous—Waiver of Jury Trial, Form 32.26(1)

Office Lease, Form 1.1
Office Lease (Space Users Network Office Building Lease), Form 1.5
Office Lease (A Tenant's Response to Landlord's Form), Form 1.4
Operating Expenses (Long Form), Form 6.11(2)
Operating Expenses (Short Form), Form 6.11(1)
Operating Expenses—Exclusions (Another Form), Form 6.11(4)
Operating Expenses—Exclusions, Form 6.11(3)
Operating Expenses—"Grossing Up," Form 6.12(1)
Operating Expenses—"Net" Rent Payments, Form 6.15(1)
Operating Expenses—Tenant's Verification Right, Form 6.11(5)

Partnership Tenant—Limiting Liability of Retiring or Deceased Partners, Form 3.8(1)
Percentage Rent—Computation and Payment Period (Tenant's Form), Form 6.20(2)
Percentage Rent—Computation and Payment Period, Form 6.20(1)
Percentage Rent—Definition of Gross Sales, Form 6.17(1)
Percentage Rent—Gross Sales (Another Definition), Form 6.17(2)
Percentage Rent—Gross Sales, Exclusions and Deductions (Another Form), Form 6.17(3)
Percentage Rent—Landlord's Right to Audit Tenant's Reports, Form 6.22(1)
Percentage Rent—Recordkeeping (Tenant's Suggestion), Form 6.21(2)
Percentage Rent—Recordkeeping, Form 6.21(1)
Premises—Credit Verification as a Condition to Expansion (Landlord's Form), Form 4.21(1)
Premises—Definition of "Floor Area" in a Shopping Center Lease, Form 4.4(1)
Premises—Expansion Option (Office Building), Form 4.20(1)

Premises—First Right to Lease (Tenant's Right to "Call" Any Available Space), Form 4.22(5)

Premises—First Right to Negotiate Purchase, Form 4.23(2)

Premises—Office Building Lease, Form 4.8(1)

Premises—Option to Purchase the Premises, Form 4.23(1)

Premises—Relocation, Form 4.27(1)

Premises—Right of First Offer for Designated Space, Form 4.22(4)

Premises—Right of First Offer to Lease (Landlord's Form), Form 4.22(1)

Premises—Right of First Refusal to Lease (Another Form), Form 4.22(2)

Premises—Right of First Refusal to Lease (Another Form), Form 4.22(3)

Premises—Right of First Refusal to Purchase the Premises, Form 4.25(1)

Premises—Right to Relocate Tenant (Another Form), Form 4.27(2)

Premises—Shopping Center Lease, Form 4.3(1)

Premises—Single Tenant Lease, Form 4.2(1)

Prohibited Uses—Shopping Center (Tenant's Form), Form 10.4(1)

Rent—Additional Rent, Form 6.1(3)

Rent—Basic Provision (For Use with Basic Lease Information), Form 6.1(2)

Rent—Basic Provision, Form 6.1(1)

Rent—Biannual Adjustments to "Market," Form 6.6(2)

Rent—Cost of Living Adjustments (Tenant's Right to Terminate), Form 6.6(1)

Rent—CPI Rent Adjustment, Form 6.5(1)

Rent—Fixed Percentage Increases, Form 6.3(2)

Rent—Late Payment Charge, Form 6.1(4)

Rent—Stepped Up Rent, Form 6.3(1)

Repairs—Office Building (Tenant's Form), Form 18.4(2)

Repairs—Office Building, Form 18.4(1)

Repairs—Shopping Center (Tenant's Form), Form 18.3(2)

Repairs—Shopping Center, Form 18.3(1)

Repairs—Single Tenant Building, Form 18.6(1)

Repairs—Tenant's Form, Form 18.6(2)

Rules and Regulations for a Shopping Center, Form 2.7

Rules and Regulations for an Office Building, Form 2.8

Rules and Regulations—Lease Provisions, Form 14.1(1)

Sale of the Premises, Form 29.3(1)

Security Deposit, Form 27.1(1)

Security Deposit—Letter of Credit, Form 27.1(3)

Security Deposit—Right to Substitute Alternate Security (Addition to Form 27.1(1)), Form 27.1(2)

Services—Building Security, Form 16.3(3)

Shopping Center Lease, Form 1.2

Short Form Lease, Form 2.14

Signs—Office Building, Form 13.3(1)

Signs—Shopping Center, Form 13.4(1)

Signs—Single Tenant Building (Landlord's Form), Form 13.2(1)

Signs—Single Tenant Building (Tenant's Form), Form 13.2(2)

Single Tenant Building Lease, Form 1.3

Sole Proprietor Tenant—Termination of Lease after Death, Form 3.5(1)

Sublease (Another Form), Form 2.6

Sublease—Form, Form 2.5

Subordination and Attornment, Form 24.2(1)

Subordination—Nondisturbance, Attornment, Estoppel, and Subordination Agreement, Form 2.9

Taxes—Base Amount Tax Provision (Base Is Stated as a Dollar Amount), Form 7.5(1)
Taxes—Base Year Tax Provision (Base Is Stated as a Particular Year), Form 7.6(1)
Taxes—Base Year, Form 7.6(2)
Taxes—Definition, Form 7.2(1)
Taxes—Net Tax Provision in a Multitenant Development, Form 7.4(1)
Taxes—Single Tenant Building, Form 7.3(1)
Tenant Estoppel Certificate, Form 2.12
Term—Early Occupancy, Form 5.10(1)
Term—Existing Premises, Form 5.3(1)
Term—Failure to Deliver Premises, Form 5.2(1)
Term—Force Majeure, Form 5.4(2)
Term—Late Opening, Form 5.8(2)
Term—Office Building, Form 5.4(1)
Term—Option to Extend at Market Rent, Form 5.15(1)
Term—Option to Extend at New Base Monthly Rent, Form 5.13(1)
Term—Shopping Center, Form 5.8(1)
Term—Tenant's Option to Cancel the Lease, Form 5.16(1)

Use—Express Covenant of Continuous Operation, Form 10.10(1)
Use—Landlord's Warranty of Legality of Tenant's Use, Form 10.1(1)
Use—Liberal Single Tenant Building, Form 10.2(1)
Use—Office Building, Form 10.2(2)
Use—Radius Restriction, Form 10.13(1)
Use—Supermarket (True Exclusive), Form 10.4(2)
Use—Tenant's Limitation on the Covenant of Continuous Operation, Form 10.10(2)
Utilities—Office Building Energy Escalation, Form 8.3(1)
Utilities—Shopping Center Lease (Tenant's Form), Form 8.2(2)
Utilities—Shopping Center Lease, Form 8.2(1)
Utilities—Single Tenant Building, Form 8.1(1)
Utilities—Tenant's Assurance of Utilities, Form 8.1(2)

Waiver and Release—By Tenant Only, Form 26.3(1)
Workletter, Form 2.3